LIVIN

gill

Living in Rural Wales

Noragh Jones

GOMER

First Impression—July 1993

© Noragh Jones

ISBN 0 86383 971 1

This volume is published with the support of the Welsh Arts Council.

Printed by J D Lewis & Sons Ltd.
Gomer Press, Llandysul, Dyfed, Wales

CONTENTS

ACKNOWLEDGEMENTS

I would like to thank Meredydd Evans, Irena Paxton and Nia Rhosier for permission to quote letters published in the *Cambrian News* and *Wales on Sunday*.

Chapter 7 'Blod and the Brush Salesman' is a revised version of an article which appeared in *Planet* 76, August/September 1989, and I am grateful to the Editor John Barnie for permission to use it here.

I am indebted to Cynog Dafis MP and to Rev Patrick Thomas for sending me material to include in the final chapter 'Bridges between Them and Us'.

Bobby Freeman lent me a transcript of Mattie Thomas's essay on traditional cookery in rural Wales, and helped me towards an understanding of women's domestic work, which is included in the chapter on 'Women's Lives'.

This book would never have been written without the help of all those friends and neighbours, residents of Cwmrheidol and further afield, and visitors, who have talked to me about their own personal experiences of rural Wales. I am deeply grateful to one and all, whether willing to be named or preferring to remain anonymous. When I began keeping a diary to increase my own understanding of rural Wales, I did not know it would grow into a book. Even when I realised the material might be of interest to a wider audience, I soon found that many people are put off by tape recorders and prefer to talk informally, rather than be asked for interviews. In the case of visitors and New Age travellers especially, I found that casual conversation was the only way of getting to the heart of their ways of seeing this countryside. Throughout the years of collecting the material, I have been observer and participant, living and working in the place I am writing about, so I make no claims for an objective, impartial stance—my version of life in rural Wales has been shaped by my own experiences and by the people I have met and talked to, and come to know as friends in many cases.

Introduction

Since I came to live in Cwmrheidol seven years ago countless people have said to me, 'You are lucky to live in such a beautiful place'. If they are visitors they usually add, 'But don't you feel cut off—it's so remote?' If they are incomers like myself they want to know how I have settled down in a local community which is increasingly a mix of Welsh speaking local people and English speaking incomers. If they are locals they may express gladness that another empty old house has once again a light in the window and smoke rising from the chimney. Or they may see me as a statistic in the flow of incomers (60,000 have moved into Dyfed during the 1980s) whose arrival changes the character of entire villages and hastens the demise of a fragile Welsh rural culture.

Living here is a constant reminder that, as John Berger says, 'life is not a walk across an open field'. We are hedged about by our own and other people's expectations, and these are very visible in a rural society where every house and caravan, every inhabitant and transient, is known because they are in the community, even if these days they are not always part of it. What then does it mean to have a sense of belonging to the place where you live? Is it still possible in a fragmented world where people no longer share a common past or work together as neighbours on present tasks?

Living in rural Wales is based on my own explorations as an incomer in rural Ceredigion. The valley where I live is in many ways a microcosm of rural Wales. A hundred years ago it was a Welsh-speaking lead-mining community in decline, suffering depopulation as whole families left to find work in the coal mines of the Rhondda. In the first half of this century it was a quiet place, a close community of farming families who attended the local school and the Calvinist or Wesleyan Methodist chapels in the valley. There were summer visitors to the famous Rheidol Falls, who arrived by charabanc or on the narrow gauge Vale of Rheidol Railway on day trips from Aberystwyth.

9

With the coming of the hydro-electric scheme in the 1960s the one track road was widened and a Visitors' Centre was provided by the Central Electricity Generating Board, with landscaped walks and indoor exhibitions on the Nant-y-Moch reservoirs. The flow of visitors increased, and some of the old lead miners' cottages were bought for a song as holiday houses. In the upper valley the single track road remains to this day, and during the sixties and seventies most of the houses quietly decayed, though a handful were in occasional use as holiday homes. But in the 1980s the ripples of the English property boom reached as far as the upper valley, and semi-derelict cottages or even roofless ruins were bought and renovated for permanent occupation by incomers. The problem of rural depopulation gave way to the problem of creating a new kind of community, where incomers respect and contribute to the local culture, and locals can have a continuing sense of identity, robust enough to be open to new influences without feeling overwhelmed.

There are larger questions at issue here than what is happening in one small corner of Ceredigion. In Europe, east and west, in the 1990s, the voices of minority cultures and languages are being heard again. Some of them speak in fascist tones of 'ethnic cleansing', but others are the genuine voices of European liberals proposing a new way forward out of their disillusionment with a consumerist multinational way of life that threatens finally to submerge our sense of community and locality. The European Parliament has proposed strategies to support minority cultures, arguing that more is needed than a superficial tolerance by the dominant culture. These strategies include bilingual education policies, economic aid to encourage more business enterprise, and cultural policies to subsidise the arts and literature and media. Community adult education and public awareness programmes are proposed too, so that dominant cultures gain a greater understanding of their cultural minorities, since fragile cultures cannot be maintained without the sympathy if not the active participation of incomers.

In the end, though, official strategies are never enough. Everything depends on how individuals respond to each other in the daily interchanges. Since I came to live in rural Ceredigion I have talked to a whole range of local people and incomers about what it means to them as individuals to live in rural Wales, and how their lives are changing with the changes in their communities. These conversations are woven into the chapters of *Living in rural Wales*, and I am profoundly indebted to neighbours and friends from further afield for the insights they have provided. Along the way, too, I met up with many passersby—tourists and travellers and hippies—whose talk helped me to put together alternative ways of seeing rural Wales.

The past in Wales is very much part of the present, in the landscape and in people's minds and hearts. Everyone who has lived his or her whole life here has a story to tell which links up the little tradition with the great tradition, and so makes history come alive. Every old miner's cottage has its story to tell, too, whether it lies in ruins or is sympathetically restored, or modernised beyond the recall of its own past. I have tried to pass on these stories in the spirit in which they were offered to me, though I am aware that this is a tall order, especially for an incomer from Ireland. There are beguiling and comfortable parallels between the Celtic lands which conceal a multitude of ancient antagonisms. I remember the story of the Welsh princess Branwen, who, suffering from mistreatment at the hands of her Irish husband, King Matholwch, summoned her warrior brothers from Harlech to rescue her. They laid waste the whole island of Ireland till 'none were left save only five pregnant women in a cave', and of the invading Welsh warriors there were but seven men left alive to tell the tale.

I would like to think that the different ways of seeing rural Wales which I have recorded here are not in opposition to each other, provided there are enough bridge-builders in the communities—those who are ready to reach out to the Other, rather than pull up the old drawbridges. To borrow a bit of Irish mythology, we need to look for the Fifth Province, which the first woman President of Ireland referred to in her inaugural speech in December 1990:

> The fifth province is not anywhere here or there, north or south, east or west. It is a place within each of us—that place that is open to the other, that

11

swinging door which allows us to venture out and others to venture in . . . tradition has it that the fifth province acted as a second centre, a necessary balance. If I am a symbol of anything I would like to be a symbol of this healing and reconciling fifth province.

Collecting the material for *Living in rural Wales* has been for me personally the opening of a door on my part of Wales, and has made me far more aware of a sense of place as an important part of self-identity. Now when people say to me, 'You live in a very beautiful but very remote part of the world', I remember the old Celtic retort: 'The centre of the world is wherever you stand'.

Noragh Jones
Cwmrheidol, 1993

CHAPTER 1

Paradise lost or paradise regained?
The search for community

When you talk to people who live in rural Wales, whether locals or incomers, about their sense of place and why they live here, sooner or later the idea of community is mentioned. It is used to express strongly held beliefs (or unrealised dreams) about a way of living that is small scale, where you have a personal identity based on the place you inhabit, friendly relations with your neighbours, and a sharing of common interests and values.

But as the twentieth century nears its end community increasingly becomes a weasel word, even though it represents important human needs to belong, to have a part to play in your own locality. It has been taken over by government and public bodies, who use it to describe their strategies for 'community care', 'community schools' and 'community service', which have only become necessary because the old organic communities are disappearing. Then in the Thatcher years there were cuts and economies in these community services, and it was assumed that there are still old-style communities out there somewhere, which should again be made responsible for caring for their own mentally ill, their sick and their elderly. But the unemployment, the homelessness, the crime go on increasing, especially in the cities. And a growing minority of urban people began to realise their dream of escaping to the country, in retreat from 'the rat race', the failure of community, and a personal feeling of powerlessness.

The great influx of incomers into rural Wales in the 1970s and 1980s is part of this Europe-wide yearning for some rural idyll, a world we have lost in our high-tech city life styles. But when tens of thousands move from the cities into small country villages in search of community, they are in danger of destroying the very thing they want to find. For how can we relate to each other when fewer and fewer people living in the same place are likely to understand and share each others' ideas and values? What does it mean now to inhabit a place, when we live in a fragmented world, and can share thoughts and interests with people in the 'global village', but not necessarily with people in the village down the road?

The other half of the equation is the exodus of young Welsh people to the cities, in search of work and the big world beyond their rural upbringing. A close-knit community can be as uncomfortable as old slippers, prompting escape from the dubious security of rigid conventions. Your original community makes you what you are, but how do you get to be what you are fully capable of being? Many feel that you can only achieve that by going away and (perhaps) coming back again.

> In Wales you are just old Mrs Morgan's son, a prophet without honour in his own land; outside the ghetto, you are evaluated on an achievement rather than an ascriptive basis—it's what you have done, not who you are, that counts.[1]

Raymond Williams left rural Wales for Cambridge and spent much energy on the hopeless quest of reconciling the sense of community he carried inside (from his upbringing in the Black Mountains) with radical left-wing theories about community. At a lecture on Shakespeare's use of the word 'neighbour', he shocked the roomful of dons by standing up and arguing that Shakespeare's 'obsolete' concept of neighbourliness was still perfectly understood in his own Welsh border village. People there continued to practise mutual obligations and mutual recognition of each others' needs and skills at times of celebration or hardship, even if they also, being human, played the occasional dirty trick on each other and carried on petty feuding from one generation to another. But how far does that kind of neighbourliness survive when such rural communities are eroded by depopulation and later repopulation by incomers?

A hundred years ago in Cwmrheidol there were no doubts about the meaning of community, and in particular the Wesleyan Methodist community of the upper valley, which was focussed on the Ystumtuen Chapel:

Yr achos Wesleaidd, gyda'r capel cyntaf, a'i gwnaeth yn gymdogaeth ar wahân. Daeth y capel yn ganolbwynt nid yn unig i'w bywyd crefyddol ond hefyd i fywyd diwylliannol ac addysgol yr ardal. Clymwyd y teuluoedd yn gymdeithas glòs a gweithgar, ac yn wyneb anghyfleusterau a thrafferthion bro ddiarffordd, llwyddwyd i greu cymuned war a deallus heb geisio arweiniad na chefnogaeth gan odid neb o'r tu allan. [2]

(It was the Wesleyan Methodist movement, with the first chapel, that made a separate neighbourhood/community. The chapel became the focus not only for their religious life but also for the cultural and educational life of the area. The families stuck together in a close and hardworking society, and in spite of the inconveniences and difficulties of a remote district, there was success in creating a civilised and intelligent community without seeking any leadership or support from anyone from outside.)

Until the mid twentieth century the seasonal work of the smallholders continued to depend upon a very practical form of neighbourliness. Hay making and lifting the potatoes and shearing and threshing were all highly sociable activities before mechanisation, and the hard slog was shared by the local community moving round each farm in turn till all was done. Restricted transport limited social contacts to neighbours within walking distance and members of the same chapel, who met together not only on Sundays, but for weeknight meetings and singing festivals and enjoyable concerts and excursions.

There was a strong element of competitiveness running through all these community activities, religious or secular, which survives today in the local *eisteddfodau* and *cymanfaoedd canu*, the local shows and the sheep-shearing competitions. Personal rivalries added a spice to the often monotonous work of farming, and neighbours could take sides as to the quality of work of their favourite contestants. Stories of individual prowess (or equally of disasters and cockups) were relished around the fire of a long evening. There were Homeric tales of sheepshearing odysseys, of a hero tailor caught by rising floods, who finished stitching

15

a Sunday suit for a customer as he floated down the Rheidol on a bale of fleeces. This kind of competitiveness arose out of the community's consuming interest in their neighbours' doings. News was not something you heard on the radio or saw on the telly about the world outside your own locality. 'News' meant the latest stories about what the neighbours had been up to, and it was important (still is in rural parts) to be able to cap one story with another. The competitive spirit was an element in gossiping, too.

There was competition in the Sunday Schools and in the singing, and, behind the scenes, in the teamaking activities of the ladies. Competition had a function in uniting congregations, drawing them together in religious solidarity against other chapels, other denominations, especially during the theological splits of the second half of the nineteenth century in Nonconformism. It also encouraged a 'live and let live' spirit among members of the same small Calvinist or Wesleyan community, even when certain individuals were at daggers drawn with each other over a boundary dispute or a bad word by providing socially acceptable outlets for rivalry and aggression.

Competition was also connected with self-respect and pride in carrying out the essential tasks of life and religion as well as, or better than your neighbours, in spite of limitations of poverty and the blows of fortune (a wet summer, no work in the lead mines, the death of children from tuberculosis). The positive side of competition was to be 'well-doing' however badly off you were; to make sure your children got as good food as your better off neighbours, and were neatly turned out for chapel, even if their clothes were old and handed down. In the old style communities too, everyone needed to know the exact extent of their neighbours' skills because neighbours relied on each other for the whole range of expertise they needed in their everyday life. If the well dried up you needed to know who was the best at water divining; if you needed the roof rethatching, who was the best man for the job? If the cow went sick, who should you go to for help? So competitiveness had a practical function in the community.

But there are certain problems when the element of competition is divorced from the mutual supportiveness of the old style community, as is happening today. There is a danger of competition for competition's sake, with criteria for success laid down by outside experts, and of putting people in some pecking order which does not take account of their whole selves, but only of their skill in scoring the right number of points on the great occasion. What happens to creative subversion and 'losers' who in traditional close-knit communities were teased but given a place—even those who were 'not right in the head' or flouted the conventional morality by womanising or being overfond of the bottle?

There is a temptation to try and revive the old style community by clinging to a way of life that can no longer be sustained. Enthusiastic getting-away-from-it-all young incomers often have a go at self-sufficiency on a smallholding—and bake their own bread and make their own cheese or yoghurt, as well as growing organic vegetables and having free range hens. But most move on to other activities after a year or two, for such practical ingenuity is not essential as it was in the old days, when people had no choice but to subsist on what they produced, and live in houses which they had built for themselves, and make their family's clothes.

Romantic nostalgia for a folk past is indeed an obstacle in the way of creating new viable communities, which have to include the people who live there now but who have come from different backgrounds and traditions. Yet it is important to draw on traditional community ways of life where they are relevant. The 'peasant' intelligence, for example, based on practical skills and instinctual judgment (to plough a straight furrow, to build a pig sty, to take down a tree or layer a hedge) largely lost out to the 'educated' intelligence after the 1870 Education Act. Popular ingenuity remains officially invisible in our education system, though you can see evidence for it at every country show and on every well-run farm. We need to give a higher status to this kind of 'folk' intelligence, rather than indulging in romantic revivals of folk culture, because it is a bond between country people, whatever their origins, and a continuing focus of respect in a rural community.

There is little enough in common, it sometimes seems, between incomers and locals, if we are to judge by the situation in Cwmystwyth as described in the following two letters from opposing sides, which appeared in the *Cambrian News* in the summer of 1988. An English incomer wrote:

Sir,

I feel I cannot let the assertion made by the Country Landowners Association in last week's *Cambrian News* go unchallenged. Village communities are not being destroyed by the invasion of townspeople, but are being built up and reinforced. Far too many generalisations are made on this subject without supporting facts.

The facts for this village are as follows. When I came to the village 20 years ago to re-establish the village shop, which had been closed for several years, the village was dying, with a population of 73, 47 houses occupied, and only 14 children of school age or under. There were no meetings or activities except the church and chapel services on Sundays. We now have a population of 124, 70 houses occupied (only 3 or 4 are new, others are restorations of ruins), and 29 children.

There is a thriving village shop, two active societies with regular meetings, one operating in English and one in Welsh, and other regular activities, which are supported mainly by newcomers to the village.

The reason some young people have left the village is that their chosen careers demand that they live in a more populated area, not high house prices; in fact in most cases they move to areas where prices are higher—it would be difficult to find anywhere where they are lower.

Far from destroying this village community, the newcomers have contributed greatly to its revitalisation and well-being . . .

Since this letter was written, the correspondent informs me that the village shop closed down in 1991, as so many have in rural Wales of recent years, and that the proportion of incomers to locals is now 80/20, compared with 50/50 in the early 1970s. The next letter gives a local view on this.

Sir,

Last week's letter concerning the effects of migration from England into Dyfed village communities misses the central point—namely, the effect upon the linguistic character of those communities. Crucially, what is happening is that the population increase which he sees as a regenerating factor is destroying Welsh communities.

I have no wish to challenge the statistics which he presents in connection with Cwmystwyth. They may well be sound. But neither can he challenge the fact that the newcomers, with very few exceptions, live their lives completely through the medium of English.

Cwmystwyth was not dying when your correspondent moved here. It was certainly contracting due to serious political neglect, but preserving its identity in spite of that. That struggle for identity is the vital struggle and no amount of new building, or renovating old properties for residential purposes, by itself will serve to maintain that identity. Neither will economic development by itself further that struggle. Indeed it could run counter to it.

Such development, if it is to be relevant to the present crisis, will have to be vitally connected, at various key points, with using the Welsh language. To talk of 'revitalising' the historical entity called Cwmystwyth, without giving a central place to the Welsh language, is to misuse language badly.

One other point. The housing market in these areas is completely artificial in the sense that it is not related to the earning power of the majority of local wage-earners. House prices are dictated by external economic factors.

There is scarcely a working family in this village which is in a position to secure a mortgage that would enable it to buy any house that is occupied at the present time. Indeed what is virtually an old ruin in this village has just been purchased for £25,000. Most working families in the area would find it difficult to buy even that.

Yours sincerely
Meredydd Evans

It is clear from these letters that the small village of Cwmystwyth is no longer an organic community, but forms at least two communities occupying the same square mile, and no doubt friendly on the surface, but, as a Welsh speaker said to me, 'simmering away with buried discontents just below the surface'. The English incomers tend to develop their own kind of culture, which, if it could only be assimilated into the indigenous Welsh culture might well prove enriching. Many are environmentalists and anxious for rural Ceredigion to stay small scale, community focussed and pollution free. They are alert to any developments which threaten the peace and beauty of the place where they have chosen to live, but that can bring them into conflict with locals who are more concerned with getting work near to home. That often means felling forestry or driving gravel pit lorries or other jobs connected with 'spoiling' a landscape.

Both locals and incomers can take an interest in a place and its history, but they cannot share this interest on equal terms, because although many incomers try to learn the Welsh language at some point, very few reach a level of competence which would enable them to listen to a lecture or go to an evening class in Welsh. This cuts them off even from the community newspapers, the *papurau bro*, so the two communities tend to develop their own news networks and entertainments, which of course do overlap from time to time, but to the detriment of the Welsh language. So in Cwmystwyth the evening social activities in English are well-attended, mainly by incomers. The village shop had an excellent range of high quality produce, but could be seen as another loss for the local culture, since business was through the medium of English only. There were cultural links, for one of the proprietors, Marjorie Budd, wrote a successful children's book about the local estate Hafod. All these activities are admirable in themselves, but the more successful they are the more the remnants of the Welsh-speaking community may come to feel that their culture is slowly sinking, if not already drowning, under the incoming wave. Change may be a way of growing, but holds the threat of a takeover by dominant forces. How then do you 'save' a culture, without either pickling it in its past or letting it drift towards mid-Atlantic consumer life styles until everyone finally meets because they've reached the lowest common denominator?

Here are the voices of residents in rural Ceredigion talking about what community means to them, beginning with Miss Jenkins of Cwmrheidol talking about the old-style community in which she was brought up.

Miss Elinor Jenkins, 1908-1992

'I went to school at Aberffrwd—walked in all weathers of course, like the others from up on top at Pisgah, and from the lower valley. The ones

20

from the upper valley went to Ystumtuen School. That was around the time of the First World War. Miss Edwards took the seniors and Miss Thomas of Dolfawr the juniors. They were very strict in those days— you had to sit down and do what you were told. You wouldn't be allowed to run around the way they do now. There was an open fire with a fireguard. We took bread and butter sandwiches with a flask of tea at first, but eventually my grandmother came to live at Aberffrwd, and at midday we would go and eat our lunch in her house, and that was nice because it was family.

'I left school at fourteen and went to work in Aberystwyth straight away, because my father was ill and there were no social services in those days. My sister had gone on to [the big] school in Aberystwyth, but she had to come home and help Mother. My brother went out to work on a farm like all the boys, because the mines had closed by then. Girls as well as boys went to work on local farms, living in, or they went into service. That was what you did then. I didn't like animals, so I went into service. I only came home for holidays (a fortnight every twelve months), and I felt cut off from home, but there was no choice. I only got about five shillings a week for working from seven in the morning till ten at night. Eventually I gave up work because my sister fell ill and died, and my father too had died by then (when I was in my early thirties). I stayed home with Mother (she died in 1952) and we two kept the home going. We did the milking and made our own butter, and fed the skimmed milk to the pig. There was pig killing twice a year. There would be a new pig in the Spring and one in September, one to pay the rent and one to feed the family. We salted the sides and hams and hung them up from the beams. It was the same in every house in the valley then. We made our own brawn and used up every bit. There was nothing wasted. We made our own bread, too, in the bake oven, which was outside (where I keep the coal now). Once a week was baking day, and we roasted fresh meat sometimes as well as baking bread and cakes. You lit the fire inside the oven, then when it was roasting hot you scooped out all the hot ashes and it stayed hot for a long time. But roast meat was a rarity for us, and mostly it was bacon boiled over the fire. On a Monday Mother went to market in Aberystywth with butter and eggs to sell, and she might bring a bit of fresh meat back.

'In those days people used to call in when passing the house. They walked for miles on different messages around the countryside, and they would just knock at the door and drop in. Now you don't get that friendliness. Everybody has cars and telephones, so they drive past, or pick up the phone for a few words, but it's not the same. There used to be a very friendly atmosphere, and people calling in with the news. Of course you got the kettle on and gave them a cup of tea, and they really appreciated that because they had walked from Ystumtuen, say, or back from the shop at Goginan.

'Every house was occupied around here, and when we were growing up there were a lot of other children the same age as ourselves, and we all knew each other. We knew everybody in the valley then to talk to— always in Welsh. Then the mines closed down and there was no work and all the people went to south Wales to work in the coal mines. My father went down there as a miner, until his health broke down and he had to come back home. Many families moved there permanently, but he didn't want us to move down there to live. He needed to feel he still had his home back here in our own valley. He only came back Christmas and Easter and summer holidays. Before that he had worked in the Cwmrheidol lead mine, and that was very unhealthy. But everybody worked in the mines unless they had one of the bigger farms. Most of us only had a few acres, enough to keep a cow and a pig and chickens, but not enough to live on. There were no social services, so everybody had to work to get money. The mine was their living, even if they only got about £1.50 to £2 a week for long hours. It was around the first World War that a lot of families had to give up their cottages here (they were rented from owners who lived away) and go south for work.

'Although it was so unhealthy working in the lead mines there was a lot of good companionship. They all walked up the road together and worked together and ate their lunch together and walked home together at the end of a long day, in every kind of weather. After they all moved to the south there were fewer people left to go to the chapels and the concerts. But every family went to chapel every Sunday. I think it was Sunday School in the morning and a service in the afternoon at Llwyn y Groes, and then down to Aberffrwd for the evening service. I don't remember anybody complaining that it was too much. It was the mode of life. When you're a crowd together and you meet the other young ones and you know everybody, you don't mind it at all. We read parts of the Scripture and the Sunday School teachers explained it to us and then gave us something to learn off for the next Sunday, like a psalm or verses from the Bible. If you were told to do a thing, you didn't try to go against it, you did it. Life is very different now.

'The concerts were held at the School in Aberffrwd. People came from far away to provide the entertainment, as well as having the local talent. There were people from Ystumtuen and Ponterwyd and Goginan and Devil's Bridge. They all walked to the concerts and thought nothing of the distance. There was good singing and reciting and dramas in Aberffrwd and in Bethel. Now people go down to Capel Bangor for their entertainment, or into Aberystwyth. They no longer have it in the valley. Local talent used to find local outlets. Teaching music and singing is all part of the ordinary school programme now. But it used to be a labour of love, all voluntary work. Mr Morgan in the valley (Aneurin's father) walked for miles to work with different singers and choirs, to develop their talent. On a Sunday night after the service we used to stay behind and the older singers would have a singing school for the younger folk. We all knew each other, being at the same school and the same chapel. There were no strangers in those days, and there were larger families, which made things more sociable when you went into people's houses.

'You spoke Welsh to everybody you met. I didn't speak English when I left school, though we had been taught the English alphabet and to read English words—but I had no idea what they meant. I gradually picked up English when more and more people came to the valley who spoke English every day. I taught myself in a way. It's nice to be able to speak both languages and the younger you are the easier it is. If you understand Welsh it's nice because you can follow what goes on. But when people don't understand Welsh it comes quite naturally to you to change from Welsh into English for the sake of the English person. I speak Welsh with all the neighbours around here still, and in the Chapel. But in Aberystwyth it has changed. In the old days different people had little shops and you knew they spoke Welsh, but today you've no idea whether it's a Welsh person or an English person, so I tend to speak English. You change to the English language because you know that if they don't speak Welsh (or even if they do) they'll understand what you want in English. These things have been changing gradually since the last war—more English and less Welsh everywhere.

'But it's nice to see people coming to live in the valley again after the houses lay empty all those years. A lot of them went nearly derelict as a result of people having to go away and look for jobs. I like to see a light in the window and smoke coming out of the chimney again. Transport is no problem now that everybody has a car. But if you haven't a car there's only the Friday bus. There used to be a bus every day till everybody got cars. The buses were cut to three times a week and then once a week. You have no choice anymore when to go into town. There used to be the cheap Market Day tickets on the train every Monday, so a lot of people would go in together to sell and to buy. Now there's only me and Mrs Daniel on the Friday bus, because everybody else has their own car.

'There's a lot of tourist cars driving up and down the valley in the summer months. But even before the Power Station and the Visitors' Centre the valley was very popular with visitors. Sixty years ago they came on horse-drawn coaches before the days of motor buses. If anybody came to the door wanting tea we made tea for them, and gave them bread and butter and jam. There was the Stag Tea Room as well, run by Gwen's grandmother, and that attracted a lot of people who came to see the Falls. The road was very bad in those days, very rough, like the rutted farm track from Troedrhiwsebon to Pencnwch. But after the CEGB did the scheme we had a good new road.

'There was a lot of worry about the scheme [the hydro-electric Power Station] because nobody knew what effect it would have on our land and

24

our houses and our village life. I don't think it spoiled our life. It hasn't come to that, fortunately. We got electricity and mains water, where we used to have to use paraffin and carry water from the well on the far side of the river. There were jobs for valley people. There are some of the old customs left, like going to the local funerals to show respect—though the ministers used to know more about the lives of the people they were burying than they do now . . . No, the scheme didn't spoil our life. But there have been a lot of changes in my lifetime . . .'

In Miss Jenkins' house every possession confirms the story of her life. The family dresser, locally made, with its treasure of patterned plates and jugs, takes up nearly the whole of the back wall. The family Bible in Welsh has pride of place on it, and is protected from dust by a little white crocheted net. The grandfather clock which chimes the hours a little hoarsely now was made in Aberystwyth in 1861. The two tightly packed book shelves include the *Complete Works of Shakespeare* and Borrow's *Wild Wales*, but are mainly a Welsh language collection of commentaries on individual books of the Bible and other works which show the conscientious study of the Scriptures in Nonconformist homes. Miss Jenkins' own reading was the local papers (including the *papur bro, Y Tincer*) and mainly Welsh-language books from the mobile library. She liked both stories and interesting non-fiction about, for example, the Welsh in Patagonia.

Ros from the North of England

'When we first came we were ostracised—literally. Taboo. They wanted us out, full stop. They didn't tell us to our face. That's not their way. But Dewi told us, "They want you out", again and again in the first six months. Even now they've "accepted" us, well, they haven't really . . . they've just stopped positively trying to get rid of us.

'We're not going to change the valley. I don't want change, I want it to stay the way it is. It's Dewi who's always on about conversions and modern bungalows. When you talk about who's changing rural Wales it's the bloody Welsh themselves. If you go up to Cwmystwyth there's a load of travellers living there, but those kids don't want to change the

25

place either. They're there because they like it the way it is. Same with us—we've come here because we like the peace and quiet, so I'd be the biggest anti-change person there is. Like when Dewi talks about housing estates in the valley, I'd go mad. If the new owner of that ruin up the road tries to knock it down and build a new bungalow I'll do a Prince Charles. I'll go and sit down there and say, "You can't do it".

'If I'd ever had the chance to sit down and talk to the locals about how I feel about the valley and keeping it the way it is, they might have less animosity towards me. But I haven't had the chance. The way I was brought up it's natural when somebody passes to ask them in for a brew and a natter. But here you never get asked inside their houses. One day soon after we got here the two old ladies came walking along and it started to rain so they took shelter in the shed out there. I said to them, "Come in", but they wouldn't. They said, "We're going in a minute". It was quite a natural thing for me to say, "Come in for a brew —it's warmer and drier". You just don't know why they won't come in. They might be very shy people, or they might be turning down your friendship. That particular episode made me think. They don't even know what you are or who you are, so they keep out of your way. Later the old lady's brother wanted some hay taking down and we took it down for him, and they've been dead talkative ever since. But you shouldn't have to do them a favour to get to be trusted. Where I come from, if somebody moved into the street, you'd give them all the help you could, try to get them involved with local things. Here they look at you at first as if you were an enemy—especially if you look different. As if to say, "What are you doing here, in a nice respectable place like this?" You're suspect till you're proven innocent, instead of the other way round . . .

'In the end, after the first round of disappointments, what we found was that the old locals talked to us, because we were in with Dewi, and he told them we were helping him out a bit around the farm. He was in hospital for a while last winter and we fed the cattle, because it seemed the natural thing to do. I mean if you live in any sort of community, you do that sort of thing by instinct when anybody needs help. But the old locals, they're a community on their own, aren't they? Whereas, like, the rest of the people in the valley are foreigners like us, only they've been here a bit longer. The people who don't acknowledge you, or the ones you don't know, are probably the foreigners anyway. They might wave from the car occasionally, but you won't catch them stopping to offer you a lift. They don't want to know you.

'You would think as a normal thing your allegiance would be with the younger ones in the valley, not the older ones, but it isn't . . . People are people whatever age they are, and we all have to live in the same community. But I think Dewi is so old now, he's given up bothering what people think, or what's the approved thing to do, or how you should look or dress or behave. Whereas some of the younger ones who are still on the up and up are maybe thinking, ''Oh, here's someone moving in on me, and I don't know how to take them''. So they want you out. Mind you we did have a bit of a hassle over the dogs. One of them claimed the dogs had been down one night and killed his kid's pet rabbit . . . If I had a complaint I'd go straight to the person and complain, I wouldn't do it through the man next door. But anyway, what he did was complain through Dewi instead of coming here straight. Anyway we went and bought the kid two more rabbits and took them down to the house in a nice little cage. That gave Dewi a good giggle. ''It's the best thing you ever did'', he said, ''You've stumped him'' . . .

'What I think is, we all live in the same society here . . . I'm not saying we should get together every Saturday night, because I agree with having your own privacy as well. The trouble here is that they're out there looking at you through the window, watching what you're doing, but they won't come up and talk to you straight. Instead there's a gossipy thing, speculating about you. They'd like you to carry around a sticker saying ''I am that old, I have so many kids, I have done this and that'', so that they could find out about you without getting to know you as a person. Dewi wins out because he came here and talked to us from the beginning—even if he only did it initially so he could tell other people about us! Anyway he gets a bit fuddled after a glass or two, so he wouldn't get it right. In this community they all want to know what's going on, and what everybody is about, but they haven't the gumption to come and say to your face, "Look, what are you doing here?" There was a really solid barrier up against us for the first few months. It was horrible, really, walking past a house and feeling that they disliked you and were watching out for you . . . Maybe they weren't but you just didn't know . . .

'I think the basic problem is that people feel you're in this to get what you can, and that's just not true. They're always trying to work out why you are here, what you have come for. They can't understand that you haven't come for anything except just to live here. I'd be quite happy to sit in the middle of a room and tell them all about me, because I've got nothing to hide and nothing to be ashamed of, but would they do it, ha ha . . . If people had come up and talked to us when we first moved in, they would probably have found out that we were stronger on nationalism than they are—on the Welsh language, and keeping the countryside safe from development, and saving the close-knit community. Because where I come from in the North of England the village became a commuter town after the M6 came through. You got salesmen and fly by nights moving in, and housing estates going up. I've moved here to get away from all that, because what I want is to get out of the rat race and back to the community sort of thing . . . But try telling that to locals around here!'

One community or many communities?

'You can't say there's one community here, can you? It's a lot of different groups like anywhere else. It would be ideal if everyone was great friends with everyone else who lives in the same locality—but it would never be true. It's human nature for people to split off into their own little cliques.

'There are some events in the village like the Christmas Party which imply the togetherness of One Community, but even there you can see everyone sitting at their own table with their friends and hardly speaking to the rest. Last Christmas all the Welsh speakers (with a few exceptions) were gathered together, and the farming community usually sticks together, except that they have their own feuds going on. No, it's hard to see what community means here now. Even farming, which in the old days brought everybody into contact with everybody else, because you went round all the farms in turn to get the hay in, or the potatoes lifted—that's all changed now. With subsidies and farm machinery there isn't the same need for cooperation in the farming community. You bring in your own paid help as needed, rather than depend on neighbours. Look at old Dewi—the locals didn't like it at all when he let that tumbledown cottage to those hippy-looking people, but he had his head well-screwed on alright, because they did a lot of work around the farm which he's not up to now that he's getting on in years. Mind you, there's kin in the neighbourhood to come and help him occasionally—no doubt with some hope of inheriting the farm when he goes to his last rest! That's part of the community idea—that your own kith and kin see you're alright in your declining years, and then you see them all right in your will.' Another resident chipped in at this point:

'The problems arise these days when the old idea of community clashes with the new ways of doing things—not relying much on family and neighbours but paying wages to outsiders to work for you. Outsiders can be anybody from a dozen miles away, or English-speaking incomers, or of course Dewi's hippies. I think the relatives are a bit jealous of the hippies working on the farm, driving the tractor and feeding the animals and building up the woodstack for winter. There's always a bit of suspicion about motives in a rural community, so even when it's hippies (who aren't supposed to want material possessions are they?) the family might think they must be after something for themselves.' Some time later there was further speculation:

'The hippies get on with Dewi and like to do odd jobs for him because he's the only local farmer who really accepted them and treated them like fully human people. Others at first stuck a label on them—Hippies—and didn't really give them a chance to show what kind of people they are or what kind of work they can do. Mind you things have changed now, because people around here are basically accepting, even if they're a bit shy and suspicious at first of people who look a bit outlandish and don't seem to have any way of making a living. Now the new arrivals odd-job, and have their place here, like everybody else—people see they have their own skills to offer, and that's respected. Overall the community here is very elastic. As for Dewi—his own community keeps an eye on him—calls occasionally to make sure he's alright, and bakes him a cake from time to time. There's still enough of the old community spirit left for that. Oh, there's a certain amount of tut-tutting about the way he lives. He likes his tipple every night, but traditional communities are more tolerant than you might think—they do care . . . The hippies, I think, genuinely respect him because they don't care either about surface respectability. Anyway, they like his capacity for enjoyment and the fact that he's more open with them than the others can bring themselves to be . . . That's my guess, anyway!'

Peter Lord, Welshman by choice

'The arts community that I live in draws on people like myself, from a very narrow social band. That is unhealthy compared with place-based community where different kinds of people contribute a wide range of skills that the community needs and uses. That's integrating, whereas the kind of community I live in is divisive. One should aim to integrate and interact, but I find it quite difficult to communicate with some of the people in the valley. We don't seem to find common ground, so it remains uneasy, not because of dislike or mistrust, just unfamiliarity and not enough common vocabulary. It might have been different because when I first came to Cwmrheidol and was working on the house, I was invited to Sunday dinners by the Davieses, and Dan asked me if I would like to go to the Chapel with them. I wanted to join in, to say yes, but I just couldn't do it. I explained that I was used to Church (though I didn't go to services). It was a question of changing cultures in a very fundamental way. I've realised recently (while looking at chapels for an Art in Schools project with *Gweled*) that the relationship between people in chapels is very different from the formal rows in church, where you don't have to face anybody in close proximity. I'm attracted to the mysteries, but I can also see great attraction in the closeness of a chapel congregation, especially in tiny chapels like the ones here in the valley. But I would find that very difficult personally, so sadly I did not take up the Davies invitation to be more a part of the traditional Welsh-speaking valley community.

'The sense of place is enormously important to me, but it is to do with Wales as a nation rather than with particular small communities like this valley. I believe that's true of a lot of people like me working in the arts and on television, though some of them are different because they are lucky enough to have been born in Welsh communities so they have an extra layer of local interactions which I don't have.

'Being a Welshman by choice rather than by birth, I express my identity through interrelating with other people and their ideas—past and present. I had a terrible experience once—I was invited to share a seminar with the man who did the book on stereotype images of the Scots (*Celtic vision*), and there was this drunken bloke at the back who kept shouting ''Ask him where he was born—will you tell me where you were born?'' The right answer (which I didn't give at the time) was that I was born in England and I didn't have any choice in the matter. In a strange way a decision to identify with a country is a much more remarkable thing than identifying with it because you were born in it.

'I certainly have a bad reaction to any suggestion that I am English or to situations which bring out the Englishness in me. That's one of the reasons I avoid being with English people, not because I dislike English culture or English people, but because it's a question of who you want to be. There are many attractive things about English culture. It plainly is a very wonderful culture, very rich and beautiful in many ways, and it has great ideals as well as terrible ideals . . . But the English perceptions of minority cultures and cultures that have been colonised, cause them to come out with infuriatingly ignorant remarks, because English people on the whole have no reason to think about what it might be like to live in a colonised culture. The experience of most English people in Wales is so different from my own that I find it impossible to talk to them about Wales. I have nothing to say to them because what I have to say springs from a set of values growing out of the Welsh experience of community and nation and language—there is no common ground.

'For me, as well, there is the tension between nationalism and internationalism. To me internationalism is very desirable and necessary for all those reasons to do with creative cross-fertilisation. And the only philosophy I know which is truly internationalist is nationalism, based on the idea of respect for difference. Mrs Thatcher's idea of nationalism seems to be based on the idea that *We* are better and *Our* ideas need to prevail. It does not include respect for the minorities of the countries she rules. Internationalism is the idea that difference is creative and you must struggle to assert your difference and help others to assert their difference. So the importance of the Finns being Finnish is just as great as the idea of the Welsh being Welsh. In practical terms you start at home, but it's very different from nineteenth century nationalism and national socialism, which assert that one race is superior to another and has rights over it. One of the arguments I have in favour of nationalism is that unless people have some control over their own destiny in things like economics and planning, they are done for, because the so-called free market isn't free at all. I'll give you an example in Wales where intervention by local government has had a very desirable effect. In Gwynedd you cannot use anything but slate on a roof, and they enforce the use of slates rigorously. This maintains employment in the slate industry there. It also keeps consistency about how the buildings look, because slate was always the traditional roofing material.

'Unfortunately the planning rules in most of Wales knock the heart out of communities—visually speaking. You can see it here in the valley —the noddy bungalows which bear no relation to the traditional housing. I'm not against change, but change has to grow out of a tradition that belongs to a place, not out of the bad side of internationalism. I'm talking about the creeping tide of consumerism where people are offered what seems to be an ever expanding range of goods, but all it is really is a limited range of bland anonymous materials which takes away local community choices, and eventually makes everywhere look like everywhere else, so that you've lost the visual aspects of community.

'I have to add, however, that I would rather have six noddy bungalows in the valley, with local Welsh-speaking people living in them, than six beautifully restored traditional houses occupied by English incomers. Because in the end a community is to do with people, not things, and there isn't a community any more unless the people who live in a place have some appreciation of what that place means. Rural Wales is full of fragile small communities threatened with the destruction of their meaning by the influx of outsiders who do not, many of them, try to find out about the existing culture, or even appreciate that there is a different culture that is neither English nor British but Welsh.

'What I find particularly offensive is the way that some English incomers go on about the locals having no sense of tradition and destroying their own cultural heritage. When I was at university one of my teachers had a holiday cottage in Wales which she had restored from a ruin. It was an extraordinarily beautiful place, full of beautiful old things (like St Fagans), but always, after dinner, there would be at some point in the evening a tirade about the ignorance of the locals, and their ugly dwellings and the horrible contents they furnished them with. Looking back on it, now that I know rural Wales better, it was really amazing that she could sit there and say such things, when she was surrounded by wonderful things all made by fathers and grandfathers of those same local people.

'In the end culture isn't a museum. It is living interaction between people and their things. When people's sense of identity, and the identity of their communities (for sense of identity was traditionally bound up with the place you lived in), is invaded by internationalist culture from outside, you can't expect them to stay true to their own local and national traditions. So of course you get the noddy bungalows. But this house I live in is the traditional Cwmrheidol house, and when I first saw it I knew that it was right. It is humble and honest, well made in its own simple way. It says a lot about the local people who built it, and it belongs properly to the valley. It is part of the community's history.'

Margaret Davies, first Chairman of the Cwmrheidol Ladies Guild

'The Ladies Guild was set up in the early seventies—grew out of a Tupper Ware party in somebody's house! The idea was to bring people together, because people lived in the valley but never met. We all belonged to the same place—and Cwmrheidol is a unique place—so we developed our own little connecting group, though some women might still go down to the W.I. or *Merched y Wawr* in Capel Bangor as well. Our little group puts no pressure on anybody and is mainly sociable, and that is a relief for women who are very busy. There are more going out to work now, part-time or full-time, and many are busy on the farms (there are seasonable variations in attendance because of lambing etc). Also it's not just for the women in the valley, it's for everybody. The Ladies Guild runs the Christmas Party and the Carol Singing round the houses and the *Cawl Cennin* for St David's Day. On Bonfire Night the Power Station at first organised a party for the children of its own staff, but then the Ladies Guild came in on that too and everybody can enjoy the fireworks and the food.

'When you have a group like this based on place it draws together people from all walks of life and cultural backgrounds. You realise there is respect for people who have a position in the community, and not just respect for class or money and position. It is the same with the speakers we invite to the Ladies Guild. They are drawn from the locality and often the subjects are of local interest. I remember we had Erwyd Howells from Ponterwyd on the Nant-y-Moch community before the reservoirs came. We started in the 1970s with a talk and questions followed by a cup of tea. But we also had classes—dressmaking classes, because that was what women here wanted—we got together a group of a dozen and asked for a WEA tutor, and got one. Then the idea of making money came in, so now we have raffles and give the money to charity—local charities.

'Always the aim has been to have something for the children, because there is a very real problem for children in the valley after school. They cannot easily visit their friends, so it is important to provide events which include them. That is a good thing about our activities—they are for all the people of all ages. Last Christmas it was the teenage girls who were keen to keep the carol singing going, so they continued to go round the houses, because the mothers like to provide something good for the children to enjoy.

'An outsider might look at our programme and think "Oh, there's not much there of great interest". But for people who live here the important thing is that it brings people together (even if only once a year at the Christmas Party), and so it does its bit in bridging gaps in the community. It's *sociable*.'

'Alison' and 'Phil', English incomers

'Either you love it or you hate it when you're a student in Aberystwyth. We thought it was paradise and we couldn't leave, even though you couldn't get the "right" kind of professional jobs graduates are supposed to want. So we struggled on with a bit of this and a bit of that, to make ends meet while we did up the old cottage (which we got dirt cheap compared with the prices now). We did bed and breakfast for a while, before we had the children and needed the extra rooms for them. By that time Phil was a real expert at doing up old cottages, because we practically had to rebuild this one, so he got work rebuilding other people's, to bring in some money ... I had a go at goatkeeping and selling the milk and making the yoghurt, but the goats turned out to be quite a handful ... Now we're more experienced and have a steadier income from this small business which we started with all the help we could get from enterprise training and grants and allowances. We can just about manage, so long as the recession doesn't bite any deeper.

'Neither of us would want to go back to England now, or live in a city again, after being here. It's a different sort of community, even though you realise it's much more complex than your naive youthful dreams of rural utopia. The Welsh neighbours were friendly enough always, but we didn't get to know them as well as we did other English incomers like ourselves. We didn't go to the village chapel or to the social events that go with that, so it wasn't till the children went to school that I got to know Welsh-speaking parents better. That was when I started to learn Welsh, because the children were learning it and I wanted not to be shut out from their experiences. But like a lot of other incomers I got stuck because there just aren't enough people I can use it with. I realise it's quite an ironic situation, that as more and more incomers have arrived there's less need for me to speak Welsh—except at the school's activities, because the teachers don't make a lot of concessions to English monoglots. I understand, I think, how some of the Welsh must feel about hearing less and less of their own language around the place—in the shop and the post office and the pub, all of which are now run by English incomers who haven't managed to learn the language. Still, most of us have come to live here by positive choice, because we really appreciate a community small enough for you to know who everybody is, with a two teacher school on the doorstep, and beautiful country stretching in every direction. We have something to offer too, because this is where we've chosen to make our homes and bring up our children, so we're ready to fight to keep it like this. We've joined in protests against more housing on the edge of the village, and the threat of a rubbish tip down the road, and the low-flying planes from RAF Brawdy and so on ... Rural Wales is worth preserving. It's a very special place—even if it's not quite the same place for locals and incomers.

'I suppose you could call us Greens (though not too fanatical veggiburger). It's good here if you're green minded. We grow a lot of our own stuff, but you can also get organic vegetables just for ordinary in the market in Aber, not costing the earth like they would in your urban Sainsbury's. We've planted a lot of trees around the place, made our own birdboxes to nail up ... The kids love it all now, but I suppose when they're older they'll make a beeline for the nearest English city, just to be healthy rebels against us. I hope they don't, especially as they're completely bilingual, and into Welsh rock groups like *Sobin a'r Smaeliaid*, and adore that DJ, Bobs—the one whose signature tune is a pop parody of *Hen Wlad fy nhadau*, Land of our Fathers ... But it's rural Wales's tragicomedy that so many brought up here want to get out and so many not brought up here want to come in. They say young people have to go to find work, but I'd say it's much more complicated than that, because look at all the incomers around here who have set up their own businesses and made a go of it—including us, I suppose (keeping my fingers crossed against the recession).

'Well, you don't know you're in Paradise till you've been outside—and for some people even Paradise is not enough.'

[1] Ray Woolfe, 'Living in Wales', *Planet* 24/25, 1974, p. 89.
[2] J. Henry Griffiths, *Bro annwyl y bryniau*, Aberystwyth, Cymdeithas Lyfrau Ceredigion, 1988, p.7.

CHAPTER 2

Whose wilderness?
Reactionary peasants or virtuous folk?

The Ceredigion countryside meant very different things to different groups as far back as the eighteenth century. To landowners like Thomas Johnes of Hafod it was primarily a wilderness to be tamed, but to the *gwerin*, the indigenous folk, it was a known and loved locality, where every path and stile, every river and bog, bush and tree, house or ruin was thick with community memory and individual associations.

On the Hafod estate Thomas Johnes erected a magnificent mansion in the latest fashion, planted four million trees, and laid out a network of picturesque walks around the grounds, so that the steady stream of guests would be suitably entertained by cunningly contrived views of Nature. In order to create the Robber's Cave he had a tunnel blasted through the rockface for several yards, so that the visitor could be surprised and delighted by the sudden view of a plunging waterfall catching the light from above. He constructed a pagoda teahouse for his invalid daughter Mariamne on a high balcony overlooking the river, with distant vistas of the encircling hills, and an immediate view of the fairytale gothic mansion across the river. The views are now cut off by encroaching conifers, which is just as well since there is no longer a gothic mansion to behold on the far bank. Having fallen into disrepair it was blown up by the Forestry Commission in the 1950s, and all that remains of past glories is a heap of rubble which at certain times of the year is mercifully hazed over by the purple-pink splurge of rosebay willowherb.

But accounts survive of what it was like to arrive at Hafod in its hey-day, if you were one of the privileged gentlemen to whom Johnes delighted in displaying his improvements. This is how one guest saw the Ceredigion peasantry and their countryside:

> . . . there wasn't much traffic—all I met was a farm cart and a few labouring chaps with bits of sacking thrown over their heads and shoulders to keep the rain off, poor devils. The cottages I saw looked wretched too—altogether it struck me as the most poverty-stricken and unprepossessing area . . . then Hafod. I found myself standing on top of the world, so it seemed, and facing me for miles and miles were mountains covered with the most splendid woods I ever saw in my life, fairly glittering with the sunshine on the wet leaves. To find trees like those in the middle of that barren wilderness struck me at once as most extraordinary, all the more since it was obvious that they had been planted by a master hand. [1]

Thomas Johnes' energetic initiatives were directed towards transforming the 'natives' as well as the landscape, even though he complained that some of them went on working 'as slowly and indifferently as ever'. He was convinced that good food and decent accommodation would soon cause the surly scowls to give way to friendly smiles. He set up a school on the estate for the girls and little boys, and provided free medical attention for one and all. In fact, 'nothing that could improve the lot of the poor people was neglected'.

It was a great disappointment to Johnes that the peasantry proved so reluctant and obstructive in carrying out his agricultural improvements. For many years he preached economy and thrift to them, for their own sakes as well as for his profit, for he:

> could not endure to see the scarecrow figures crawling about in their vile surroundings, among the crops of thistles and molehills . . . he never paused to consider what might be going on in the primitive minds of these farmers: stubborn and secret to a man as their own hills, and as ready to resist every suspected threat of encroachment or interference. [2]

In desperation he even imported Scots farmers to set a good example of thrift and industry to the Cardis, who were however antipathetic to any kind of foreigners, as he found to his further cost.

The conservatism of the peasantry has always enraged landlords, although it is perfectly logical, since the only way they can survive is by slowing down Progress, which invariably sweeps away peasants. But there is another way of seeing the peasantry of Ceredigion, which sheds a quite different light on the lives of ordinary country people. In Wales, as in England, there were folk poets and writers of memoirs and diaries and letters, who express in their own language the missing meanings, the buried lives, seen from inside and not outside their own culture. Just as John Clare's poems give us a landscape where real cottagers work and relax and explore their familiar surroundings (the poet was even distrusted by some fellow villagers because he knew the unvarnished truths of the place), the memoirs and folk poetry of Wales give a new way of seeing the Welsh countryside, new heroes and different villains than those identified by the gentry:

> The new hero is a simple countryman . . . with sterling qualities capable of sustaining a cherished way of life. He is loyal, wise, pious, hard-working, and sufficiently sensitive both to enhance a traditional way of life and to sustain it . . . he is deeply rooted in his locality. His nature is not only in tune with Nature; it is capable of infinite expansion . . . binding generations still unborn to the landscape which will become the place of their birth. [3]

While Johnes and his friends from the wider world were discussing agricultural improvements and the Chronicles of Froissart, there coexisted alongside them the hidden world of the *gwerin*, interpreting in their own fashion the everlasting human condition of toil and love, happiness and sorrow, birth and death. This is the world celebrated by D. J. Williams in *The old farmhouse* and still celebrated in the Welsh speaking Wales of local *eisteddfodau* and *papurau bro* and local history publications. Here the *gwerin gyffredin ffraeth*, the wise and witty common people, are restored to life size, rather than reduced to miserable dots on the landscape or names on a rent roll or wages tally. *Y werin* have an organic and personal sense of history. 'My father', says D. J. Williams, 'knew nothing of history beyond what he knew of it as local lore or legend'. History was all around them in home and landscape, for he remembers how every piece of furniture in their house —the dressers and linen chests and tallboys and chairs—bore the chisel marks of eighteenth-century craftsmen along its oak selvedge. In such homes the Welsh Bible translated by Bishop Morgan in the seventeenth century was to be found since the Great Awakening of Welsh Methodism in the eighteenth century:

> . . . their knowlege of the Bible was marvellous. They read nothing else, of course, and they read it very closely; for was not every word of it 'the word of God'? My grandfather, on my mother's side, could turn at once to any verse you might want, and tell you beforehand on what page of his own big Bible it was to be found, and whether at the top, middle or bottom. [4]

While the gentry do landscaping and exert power over Dame Nature at some distance from the daily round of manual toil, the smallholders live their lives from cradle to grave in close contact with every aspect of nature, human and brute creation, wilderness and enclosures and common, sowing and harvesting, blight and plenty. There is a strong contrast between Jane Johnes' opinion that farming was 'one of the best amusements a country gentleman can take to', and D. J. Williams' insistence that a truly cultured man is the man who touches life in the greatest number of places. And that, he reminds us, is the requirement of those who dwell on the land and have to turn their hands to every kind of work, from midwifery to carpentry, planting and coppicing and dry stone walling, drudgery and delight, whatever the onslaught of the weather or of the seasons.

The *gwerin* and the gentry differed too in their approach to tree-planting. Thomas Johnes' dream was to draw such a cloak of green woodland across his estate that no mountain top should be left uncovered save where 'some jagged peak might be permitted to transcend the verdant mists of larch trees, or a spur of rock break forth from among the hanging woods; otherwise nothing naked should be allowed to offend the eye'. But what is nakedness? The hillslopes won from wilderness to cornland and grassland by D. J. Williams' ancestors, which a century and a half later were 'clothed' again when the Forestry

41

Commission planted its Brechfa conifers? From the locals' viewpoint this wiped out the painstaking struggle of their ancestors to make the earth fruitful. These new conifers were the wilderness returned.

Enterprising smallholders had their own tree growing cycle which kept them supplied with the various thicknesses of timber they needed about their farms for fencing and building and even furniture making. They grew seedling oaks and larch in places too steep for cultivating, and also along the tops of banks to give shelter to animals and crops. Thinning provided fencing and fuel, and the mature trees were turned into planks for every kind of carpentry around the farm. They used horses for hauling timber, and so were able to reach remote spots without gouging out great forest roads, as has to be done today even by bodies whose aim is to protect the landscape, because their operations are focussed on heavy machinery, rather than men and horses as in a previous era. It is easier and more profitable to clear fell and replant with grants than to manage a wood patiently over decades by thinning and natural regeneration and selective felling. You have to go now to the Centre for Alternative Technology near Machynlleth, not to the commercial forestry growers, to find out about traditional woodland management —planting and layering hedges, coppicing and pollarding, using the products and the byeproducts. Ironically, however, there is official encouragement again for farmers to return to what many of their forebears did as a matter of course—to plant hardwood coppices and put back hedges of thorn or beech. The crisis in stock rearing has meant 'setaside' and 'diversify'. The problem is that today's farmers no longer know how to use the products of woodland management, and are in urgent need of practical advice and help with finding markets— craftspeople, woodchip generators, saw mills in their own locality.

The economics of agriculture has always been a mystery, even in the eighteenth century. Thomas Johnes of Hafod brought many improvements to Ceredigion agriculture, by introducing the turnip, crop rotation and lighter ploughs. To his visitors (who came from great distances to view his exemplary treeplanting and productive estate) he was a successful example of the progressive agriculturalist and landowner. Yet his finances were in total disarray. He had a curious way of preaching thrift and economy to his tenants while failing to apply the same principles to his own business dealings. His record of timber trading lies more in the number of bad bargains he made selling his trees than in the millions he planted. Never short of new ideas, he at one time produced five tons of good cheeses which he then failed to get to market, and had to sell to his own workers at a few pence a pound. As an old local farmer said to a guest en route to Hafod 'Mr Johnes was a worthy man but was ruining himself with schemes'.

In the latter half of the twentieth century too, there has been no shortage of experts to give the benefit of their advice to the small farmers of mid Wales. After the 1939-45 War a horde of agricultural advisers were released upon the farming community of Ceredigion. It seemed that hardly any smallholder should continue in farming at all, for scarcely any could be seen to be making a profit, and it was logical therefore to give up and find some other way of living. But as always the situation looked very different from the smallholders' point of view. I was told this real-life story by local people:

'They brought out a report on agricultural economics (about 1948), and they found that only one farm around here was economically viable. But of course *they* assessed viability on things like farmers' salaries and wages for helpers and a standard of living that didn't take account of what you got out of the farm's self-sufficiency. Well, that wasn't the sort of life it was at all, really. There was one old woman around here who used to keep a pig and feed it on whatever household swill she could get hold of. The Inspector pointed out to her that keeping her pig was completely uneconomic, when you counted up the time and the effort she spent on that one pig. But you see she used to have her own pork and bacon and she would sell bits of this and that to neighbours, or give them bits of the liver and so on when the pig was killed, and then they would give her other things she needed in exchange. She just managed to get by—she scraped enough food to live well enough through the whole year. But anyway, the experts persuaded her to get rid of the pig, since it made no sense in their analysis of her time and money ... She took their advice, for after all they were the experts—and from then on she had no living left. She had nothing coming in. She didn't have her bacon or her pork. She didn't have her faggots or her brawn. She had far too much time on her hands, and nothing useful to do during the long hours of the day, once the pig had gone. She had nothing to exchange with the neighbours. She had in fact lost her livelihood, thanks to the experts . . .'

Now that so much farming has become agribusiness; and form-filling bears heavily on the smallholdings; and hill farm subsidies are determined at European Community level, is there anything left of the traditional ways and survival strategies of the 'Iago Prytherch' of R. S. Thomas's poem 'A Peasant'?

> Just an ordinary man of the bald Welsh hills,
> Who pens a few sheep in a gap of cloud
> Docking mangels, chipping the green skin
> From the yellow bones with a half-witted grin
> Of satisfaction, or churning the crude earth
> To a stiff sea of clods that glint in the wind . . .
> And then at night see him fixed in his chair
> Motionless, except when he leans to gob in the fire.
> There is something frightening in the vacancy of his mind . . .
>
> Yet this is your prototype, who, season by season
> Against siege of rain and the wind's attrition,
> Preserves his stock, an impregnable fortress
> Not to be stormed even in death's confusion.
> Remember him, then, for he, too, is a winner of wars,
> Enduring like a tree under the curious stars.

In the hill farms of mid Wales there are signs that the old hunger for land, the survival instincts, the obstructive tactics against officials of any kind, are by no means extinct. Many traditional hill farmers deeply resent the highhanded changes wrought in their familiar hills by public authorities like the Forestry Commission, the Nature Conservancy, and also by big business. There is anger and distress at the mishandling or miscalculation, as some see it, of agricultural grants and subsidies ever since we joined the EC. There is bitterness in facing the possibility that they may have to diversify from familiar sheep into unknown forestry, or even have to provide leisure facilities for urban visitors, who they regard as summer invaders with dangerous instincts for breaking down fences and chasing sheep with their 'pet' dogs (to a farmer a dog is a working animal). Here is one such resentful voice of a hill farmer.

'Ieuan Davies', sheep farmer

Ieuan Davies is a bachelor farming the same land as his ancestors in the hills of Ceredigion, with dog and stick, as they say. He is in his forties now, and lives alone since his mother died seven years ago. The farmhouse stands high on a south facing slope, with little protection from the prevailing westerlies except a few bent trees and a low drystone wall around the 'garden', a now neglected scrap of rough grass with a few straggling rose bushes and clumps of rhubarb under blue and white enamel buckets with big holes in them. He lives simply among the old things that have accumulated through the generations. The farmhouse kitchen has a floor of worn slate slabs and a big stone inglenook fireplace with a bread oven built into one side, and a niche for the salt box in the other side. There used to be an open fire and a wide chimney up which you could see the stars shining on a clear night. Now he has installed a glass-fronted Hunter stove with a stainless steel flue, that spreads a steadier warmth through the kitchen and even up through the open beam ceiling to take the worst of the chill off the upstairs rooms.

The old fashioned heavy table with bulbous legs often holds the remains of his last meal, which is also the beginning of his next—a half loaf, a chunk of cold meat on the bone, the sugar bowl and a drum of Saxa salt. A traditional Welsh dresser takes up the back wall, and is stacked to capacity with toby jugs and china dogs and old coloured plates, all greying with years of accumulating dust. A man doesn't dust, apparently, though the rest of the house is clean enough. On the side wall is a big book case with glass doors, that reaches up to the ceiling. It is stuffed to overflowing with farmhouse reading of the last hundred years, but you can see how books have gone out of fashion in the recent generation, for the vast majority are the old dark red and black tomes of

Methodist catechisms and Scripture commentaries in Welsh, and stories of missionaries and explorers, and Edwardian fiction in English. Pinned along the front of the bookcase are bright rosettes with Ieuan has recently won for his Speckled Face rams at shows. The big telly that provides the evening relaxation now instead of the book, stands in one corner, on the way out to the back kitchen. Ieuan tells me:

'Since the educated men got hold of farming it has gone from bad to worse. First they persuaded us to build up our dairy cows and gave us subsidies for that. Then they announced there was too much success in that and they were going to stop it. So many a family that had held the same farm for generations were forced to sell out to pay their debt to the banks. They were out of a living, but you never see those educated boys out of a living, do you? They never lose their jobs as a result of what they think up, sitting there at their warm desks making their decisions about things they know nothing about. Now it's happening again with the sheep subsidies. The educated men think there are too many sheep in Wales, so they're trying to stop us doing what we have done for hundreds of years. And what else can you do on land like this? Oh yes, they talk about the setaside money, but do you really believe they're going to give us money now for doing nothing at all, and watching the fields we've drained and cleared of bracken go back to a wilderness? Or grants to cover the land with trees, that we've broken our backs turning into good pasture?

'Trees! Look at what the Forestry Commission have done to the Welsh hills with their blankets of conifers. They've killed whole areas— now the plan is for us to join in the killing. I'll tell you, when the Forestry Commission came here in the 1950s they made compulsory purchase orders on family farms and they drove the people out. Now they're selling it all off to private companies and pop stars, and what do they care about those families that were driven out? Do you think those families have forgotten, though? It was our tax money that bought the land, but none of it is coming back to us, is it? It's always profits for the big boys who've already got the money. There's no help for the small people. We are told to do something, and then a few years later we are

46

told to stop doing what they told us to do, and to start doing something different. How can you "diversify", as they call it (and that's a word the educated are very fond of, especially when they realise they've made a mistake and don't want to admit it)? Look at this land around here. What else can you do but rear sheep on it?'

Ieuan Davies' first language is Welsh, but he is resolute in not speaking it to strangers. It is one of the few things he holds dear that is left to him, and he does not like to have it toyed with by outsiders. So if you try to speak to him in Welsh he courteously but firmly answers in English till you go back to English yourself. He has lost enough of the traditional things already, so he is for keeping the language to himself and the people it really belongs to, and that doesn't include me, an incomer.

'When the shop closed in the village the life went out of the place. There's no need for anybody to stop there any more. We drive through to get to the next village for our messages. There's still the Youth Hostel there in the old Schoolhouse, and that brings a lot of visitors in the summer. I often see them walking past here and I wonder what it is they get out of walking, for they don't seem to see the country they're walking through, the most of them. They just keep going, a big line of them, often, like it was an endurance test. I don't understand their mentality at all. A few of them come for the red kites, it's true. But the bird-watching brigade see as little of the real country as the rest of them. Their eyes are glued to their binoculars the whole time and they fail to see what is going on around them—unless it's to find a fence in their way, then over they go without a thought for the work that's gone into making it and keeping it stock proof.'

He made a pot of strong tea and set down on the table a big tin of assorted biscuits that people around here exchange as neighbourly Christmas presents—a variety of chocolate bourbons and pink sandwich wafers, shortcake and plain ones with hard coffee icing on them. He politely moved a couple of shirts which had been hanging from one of the ceiling beams to dry, as if it had suddenly struck him that you don't display your personal things when there are guests in the house. Then he sat down again to complete his litany of the outrage done to farming by the bureaucrats.

'If you came up by the riverside, you'll have seen the numbered bird boxes nailed up on the oaks by the Nature Conservancy. But there's not a bird nests in them. They put the blame on the farmers for that. They say it's us spraying the fields that keeps the birds away. But there were enough birds here before they put the land down to conifers. Now they want to put more trees everywhere, when trees are the bane of the place. Cut them all down and clear the bracken and you'd have plenty of good land after a few years. But you're not allowed to do it. You're not free anymore to do what you want with your own land. It's control, control, control wherever you turn. And paperwork all the time, no matter how small your place is.

'The worst thing of all is that they say we're overproducing food and that we have to cut back and let the land lie idle. But half the world is starving. How can you have it both ways? Is there nothing the educated boys in their offices can do to get the food we can grow to where it's needed in the world? That would be good work they could be getting on with, instead of tormenting the life out of the farmers with their chopping and changing the rules and regulations every few years. We're supposed to be diversifying into tourism next, no matter if you have a remote place like this, and the weather coming over it in waves that would keep the townees shivering in their beds at night and longing to get back to their pubs and discos.'

The Ceredigion 'Iago Prytherch'—portrait of a peasant survivor

The time-honoured peasant way of doing things is to stick to well-tried methods which have been handed down by generations of subsistence survivors, often in the teeth of attempts by Officials to impose progressive farming from above. There is no formal training as such, but rather personal instruction and demonstration in the everyday setting, well larded with warning anecdotes about how not to do it, and jokes to spur on the flagging apprentice. But the more that outside controls are imposed on the small farmer, the more formal agricultural education becomes, the more is this peasant mentality forced into defensive positions which may this time prove to be the final retreat, as far as Welsh hill farms are concerned. For many of the smaller farms have seen their incomes halved in recent years, as sheep prices fall and the Common Agricultural Policy (CAP) reverses the great subsidy bonanza of the seventies and early eighties. It is no longer a good prospect for children to help on the farm with the hope of inheriting it, for the income will not ensure them a living wage in the meantime, and they cannot afford to buy a place of their own, for capital prices are still high in spite of the agricultural recession, at least for local people whose main capital is an interest in a family farm where the older generation is still resident. Now the estate agents advertise farming units of twenty to seventy acres as 'having potential', or as 'ideal for a beef/sheep fattening unit, plus pony stud or farm guest house with trekking etc.'

Yet, here and there, there are small pockets of resistance, where the peasant survivor sticks to the old ways of doing things, or indeed applies his native cunning to the new opportunities that have arisen for selling derelict ruins or redundant farm buildings to the people who still have money—often incomers who have brought in capital from urban enterprise. One such is the Ceredigion 'Iago Prytherch'. This old farmer holds much the same convictions about landholding as his twelfth century counterparts, described by Giraldus Cambrensis:

> The Welsh people are more keen to own land and to extend their holdings than any other I know. To achieve this they are prepared to dig up boundary ditches, to move stones showing the edges of fields, and to overrun clearly marked limits. So prone are they to this lust for possession that they are prepared to swear that the land which they occupy on some temporary or longer established tenancy agreement of lease, hire, renting . . . is their own freehold and has always belonged to their family, even when they and the rightful owner have publicly sworn an affidavit about his security of tenure. Quarrels and lawsuits result, murders and arson . . . not to mention frequent fratricides. [6]

Iago views with a baleful eye any fencing by new owners of adjoining properties, for fear it means a diminution in open land which he likes to think of as 'common', that is, for his own use. He has a fine memory for the old days, especially for activities which might justify his claims about 'common land'. But he jealously guards his own land rights. 'You can't touch that stuff—that's us', he says when some newcomer hopes to get a few old stones or mine waste from the dumps on his land. But he might accept a 'sweetener' for it.

Yet the lust for money vies with the lust for land in the heart of the Cardi, and when the domino effect of the south east England property boom reached Ceredigion in the late eighties, Iago was one to make a killing, by selling off the roofless stone shells that had lain empty in his fields since rural depopulation after the war. Then his problem was what to do with the fortune these transactions brought him. For he has not the faintest idea how to spend money, coming as he does from a long line of subsistence farmers whose lives never yielded much in the way of spare cash at all. It is unimaginable (to him and to the neighbours) that he could ever change his life style, though he occasionally dreams of moving to a smart new bungalow with hot and cold water and a radiator in every room. But he would be uneasy in such comfort and would never be able to accept a standard of living which keeps rooms warm even when there is nobody in them. He will be in Tyddyn Isaf till the day he dies, for it is his own place and that is what keeps him going. He will go on wearing his shiny old suits, which are hung on the apple tree for an airing from time to time, and his flannel combs which he spreads to dry on the thorn hedge. And what will happen to the money? He will hoard it in the time-honoured way of Iago Prytherchs when they receive an unexpected windfall—not they, but their kith and kin will be the spenders, and that is the heirs' reward for looking after elderly kin.

In the meantime he may not reach acceptable standards of farming by comparison with successful neighbours, but he is always on the go, at his own selected occupations—carrying fodder out to the wintry fields for his stock, mending the collapsing fences with orange bailer twine, letting out the hens from their not quite fox-proof, rat-gnawed henhouse, cooking the dinner for twelve noon, looking out for passersby. Because he is part of a rural community he gets looked after by family and neighbours, where his urban counterpart might be another statistic on the social services' register. He gets mince pies at Christmas and the occasional home made cake, and a bottle of whisky now and again, and people dropping in, not just out of duty. For he is a 'likeable and dear old man' after all, with a witty way of using his Welsh to baffle English speaking authorities, and his English (which is poor) to baffle other unwanted callers.

His attitude to the changes brought to the Welsh countryside in recent years is the accepting fatalism of the peasant survivor through the ages. No political stance for him, though he is a Welsh-speaking *gwerinwr* through and through. In his eyes, redundant Methodist chapels might as well be 'nice bungalows for someone', and he is delighted though amazed that there was no shortage of potential purchasers for his derelict cottages when they went on the market. The amazement, I think, stems from his incredulity that so many people want to live in 'this beautiful place' and enjoy 'this super scenery', because he has worked here all his life on the land and has never once thought of it as 'scenery' or 'beautiful'. It is the place of familiar toil and known faces, that is all, and that is enough for him. His heavy sense of fatalism makes him unexpectedly open to change and to strangers. He goes with whatever happens, for to do otherwise would be *traha*, what the ancient Greeks called *hubris*, the arrogance that can lead to a man's downfall in the scheme of things. And anyway, does it not say in Leviticus 10, 33-34 that 'If a stranger sojourn with thee in thy land, ye shall not vex him. But the stranger that dwelleth with you shall be as one born among you, and thou shalt love him as thyself; for ye were strangers in the land of Egypt: I am the Lord your God'?

[1] Elisabeth Inglis-Jones, *Peacocks in Paradise: the story of a house,* Carmarthen, Golden Grove, 1988, p. 15.

[2] Elisabeth Inglis-Jones (as above), p. 162.

[3] Emyr Humphreys, *The Taliesin tradition,* London, Black Raven, 1983, p. 63.

[4] Sir Henry Jones, *Old memories: autobiography,* London, Hodder & Stoughton, 1922.

[5] R. S. Thomas, *Song at the year's turning,* London, Hart-Davis, 1965, p. 21.

[6] Giraldus Cambrensis, *The itinerary through Wales,* London, Dent Dutton, 1912, Book 2, Chapter 4.

CHAPTER 3

Earning a living in rural Wales

Although many people still think of farming as the backbone of the rural economy, the number of people in full-time farming on family farms has been falling steadily for decades, and 'changes in agriculture are likely to cause the loss of around 300 jobs per year in mid Wales alone'.[1] Yet farming remains a far more significant occupation in mid Wales than the bare statistics might indicate (in some rural areas there are still 20% engaged in farming, compared with 6% in Wales as a whole, and only 2% in Britain). This is because it represents a traditional way of life in the Welsh-speaking rural heartlands, and every loss and drift of young people to the cities is a threat to language and culture as well as to the rural economy. The future of farming is at the mercy of the Common Agricultural Policy, the GATT negotiations, and the EC Single Market legislation, and the news is not encouraging. The main thrust of the Brussels policy is to control surpluses and cut costs of subsidies, and since subsidies account for about 70% of net farm incomes, which have been falling steadily during the 1980s, the future is bleak. However, a large proportion of mid Wales land falls into the category of Less Favoured Areas in the EC and therefore is likely to attract help towards conservation and environmental uses like hardwood planting and amenity set aside. But that requires a fundamental change of attitude and practical strategy which many farmers find uncongenial after their own and their forebears' struggles to turn unpromising hill land into good pasture.

Tourism is one of the means of diversification proposed to the farming community, and already in rural Wales around 13% of agricultural holdings do some tourism. Indeed it has been estimated that visitors spend in one year something like £1,000 million, which is more than the annual value of farm output, for Wales is one of the most dependent EC

52

countries on income from visitors.[2] But this can lead to cultural stress, too, since high tourist pressure on an area dilutes and diminishes the indigenous culture, unless ways can be found of using tourism as an economic base for the language and culture, and maintaining the original families in the countryside by supplementing but not replacing their farming activities with this diversification. Few people, either residents or visitors, want wall-to-wall heritage countryside where there are few traces left of authentic rural life, but only a reproduction version for tourist consumption.

Another striking feature in mid Wales is the number of small enterprises and self-employed people, many of whom are incomers who want to live in the countryside and have to devise a way of earning a living from home. Here are some of the individual stories of people who live and work in and around Cwmrheidol.

Nancy and Dai Charles Evans, sheepfarmers

'Dai's family have been here for three generations, and I come from the Ponterwyd area. Originally the family moved out from Aberystwyth (where the three brothers were carpenters) to the smallholding here, because one of the children was a sickly child, and they decided to move to the country and run both the smallholding and the Stag Cafe by the Falls. In those days there were about 25 acres of woodland and 11 acres of pasture here. Before the Forestry Commission bought the woods, smallholdings went right up to the top of the hill at the back, and they used the woods for their fuel and for making fences and other farm needs. They talk about self-sufficiency again now, and that was what it was in those days—your own fuel and food—a cow, a pig, chickens and a garden that took up half the field out there, to grow potatoes and all the other vegetables for the family.

'When Dai and I set up here thirty years ago, we still kept a cow and chickens, but no pig. I made butter not in one of those old wooden churns but in a small glass churn. All the smallholdings were the same— they grew their own hay and corn and had time to harvest it. I don't know what's happened to us at all. There used to be less travelling about and more time to help and to do things. But during the thirty years we've been here a lot of changes have come about. When the Power Station opened in the early 1960s I got a job as a guide (for 17 years I did that) and had no time to work on the smallholding. Dai too got work there, running the fish farm. The cow was a bind, so eventually for the last twenty years we have been keeping sheep only. But in 1982 my brother died in Ponterwyd and that holding was willed to our daughter Amanda, so we have run that holding as well—it's a mountain sheep-walk. Amanda was looking forward to making this her career as well, but sheepfarming has gone down so badly these last years that that is not possible and she has had to get an outside job (with the Royal Welsh in Builth, as an organiser). She is sad about not taking over here.

'The fall in market prices has been so bad that in the last few years we're only just turning over and making next to nothing. Without the subsidy I don't know what the future will be. Looking at it in a long-sighted way, a lot of farmers will have to go out of farming because of the recession, and eventually, I suppose, things will get better. The people in the worst trouble are some of the big farms, in debt to the banks and with falling incomes. We were brought up not to spend money till you had saved it, so it is not so bad for us, though the costs of farming are always going up. Years ago it was different. You did not use the big amounts of fertiliser, you didn't have to give them all these injections and doses. Now it is very intensified and the costs are high.

'We used to have 60 ewes, now with the Ponterwyd sheepwalk we have about 400. We put the rams to the ewes (but not the first year ewe lambs) at the end of October. We bring 85 ewe lambs down to tack in Capel Bangor—they'll be going back into the flock for next year, to keep renewing it with young ones. In the Autumn we have to dose the whole flock—for worming—and you're talking about £100 a time. Again you have to inject the ewe lambs for several different diseases like pneumonia and other things. Then the work slows down till the second week in December when we start feeding with hay, and then in a fortnight we put out multi-vitamin Rumavite block for them. We use 6 tons of that in a year, and that comes to about £1200. The hay we need is bought in because it is cheaper grown in bulk though in the old days everybody grew their own. We get in 14 tons in November and another 5 tons in March. Last year's price was £86 the ton.

'We feed regularly from the second week in December till the end of May. For the past ten years we've had good winters, but before then we used to have to dig them out of the snow. Back in the really bad winter of 1947 most of our sheep suffered and we only had 7 lambs in the end. But they weren't fed specially then, because the farming wasn't intensive. We had the same breed of sheep (the Hardy Welsh) but the lambs were smaller compared with now. You have to spend a lot of money on them now, but up till the last 3 years it was paying. What you get from the government you have to spend to keep them going. In New Zealand they lost their subsidies overnight, but sheep farming survived because it has levelled out. But a lot of farmers had to go out of farming. Here this year things seem to be not as bad as we feared, but it's no use saying, "Oh, this is lovely, we are alright now", because it is only a temporary relief.

'This morning I was listening to the radio, and (its the Glorious Twelfth today, when grouse shooting begins) they were saying, "Why not give grants to farmers to have heather moors?" But the farmers won't want to put the land back to what it was before they cleared it of heather, will they? *Yr hen whîl fawr yn troi*, it's the old wheel turning full circle, as they say. They have these ESAs too, environmentally sensitive areas in the Cambrian Mountains, and that affects us. We have 70 less sheep on the Ponterwyd sheepwalk because it is an ESA and they are paying us to have less, on condition that we keep it just in the old-fashioned way—no fertilisers, and we have to ask permission even to dig drainage ditches. We're going back to what I can still remember from the old days.

'Anyway, to get back to the farming year—as well as feeding them through the winter we inject all the ewes six weeks before lambing with the 8 in 1 stuff for dysentery and a whole lot of other things. Our lambing starts in the beginning of April and for a whole month it is a full time job for the family. When things go right it is fine, but it doesn't always. The lamb should come with the head and two front feet coming out first, but if you get the back feet coming first you have to push it back. Occasionally the back of the lamb comes first and it's alright if you can get it out quickly. Sometimes a ewe can't lamb and the head is sticking out and if you don't help the ewe will suffer, so you have to keep an eye on them all, even on a bad night. Today if you call the vet it's £10-£12 so you try to do everything yourself. If the ewes won't suckle their lambs you keep them in and put the lamb to suck three or four times a day and in the end they take to them, though it takes patience beyond with some of them. With all the intensive feeding they are in good condition, but we still get 16-18 ewes out of about 360 who don't lamb. The lambs these days are healthier too, and there's a very low death rate. Not more than 20% of hill ewes have twins, though as the sheep get better and stronger the proportion of twins keeps going up.

'We keep the lambs for four months and then the first lot go to market, and another lot each of the 4 or 5 following months as well. There are weekly markets in Devil's Bridge and in Aberystwyth. The recession affects even the middle men, for recently one of the Auctioneers and Estate Agents firms went into liquidation, though they were a longstanding firm. And that left a number of farmers in a bad way, if they had sent a good proportion of their stock to the last auction, for they failed to get the money due to them from the sale.

'We don't keep our ewes beyond four years old, but sell them on to lowlands farmers who keep them for another two years, because our sheep walk is hill land and we keep our flock young, with a quarter of the ewe lambs having a winter on tack and then returning to their own flock in the spring.

'Shearing takes place at the end of June or the beginning of July. Years ago, with manual shearing, we needed 12 to 15 people, but today all we need is three or four shearers. They are my sister's children, but they also are a group who go around a lot of farms within a radius of 20 or 30 miles and specialise in shearing. I haven't done a lot of machine shearing but I used to do a lot of hand shearing, and my daughter Amanda will use the machine shears. Not a lot of women used to shear (the women used

56

to have the job of tying the feet and preparing them for the men to shear), but nowadays the girls shear with the machine just like the boys.

'The price of wool has fallen something terrible these days, the wool business is a terrible business, because there is a glut of wool on the world market. And yet if you go to look for wool (or meat for that matter) in the shops the prices stay high. It's a world-wide problem but what can you do when there's nothing else to replace sheep on the farms?

'A lot of people have turned outbuildings into holiday homes, but if everybody did that where would you get enough visitors to fill them? Three months at the most in the summer they are used, because we don't get the weather people are looking for on holiday.

'Farming has always been a way of life as well as an income, so a lot of communities will change in the present crisis, with the prices tumbling down from £30-£34 a ewe in 1981-83, to last year's price of £14! I wonder sometimes will it go back to what it was like years ago, when the big families like Nanteos owned it all? Where there were two youngsters at home once to help, they now both go away instead of joining the family farm. There's no longer the number of smallholdings because you can't make a living. So it's the passing of a way of life when the places go and the young people go.

'Mind you, there is still a lot of life about in the countryside. When Amanda was at home she belonged to the Young Farmers' Club at Trisant and they have a lot of people taking part in their meetings. They have drama competitions (in English and in Welsh because there are so many English-speaking children now), and public speaking contests, and the Young Farmers' Eisteddfod. At their weekly meetings they have speakers like the vet, or someone talking about first aid. But the big event of the year is the Rally/Rali, with competitions in sheep shearing and fat stock judging, cooking and flower arranging. And the big thing is the tableau on a theme, with other YFCs competing from around the country. The Young Farmers' Queen for the year is chosen as well and crowned at the Rali. She would be someone who had been a leader/ chairman in her own club, and had been outstanding in the acting or the public speaking or other competitions during the year . . .'

Phil and Heather Smith

The Smiths earn their living by running two small businesses—a TV sales and repairs service and Heather's Studio Workshop, which sells photographic studies of scenery and wildlife. They run both from their home in Capel Seion, and do all the work themselves. This is their story.

'Knowledge of redundancy came quite suddenly, on 1 May 1977, when the industrial electronics company I was working for went down the can. The power generation business was sinking because British industry was shrinking at that time, and after twenty years, when the prospects seemed to be good, I was out . . . it was finished. I just wanted to go away and be on my own for a while, so we bought a caravan (to have a home) and I came (on my own at first) to Wales, where my brother George was living in Cwmrheidol.

'I fell in love with Wales. I was suddenly immersed in lots of wildlife and beautiful country, and lost all the strife and tension that had been building up. Of course I sat down and wrote lots of letters for jobs, but the trouble was I had gradually climbed up the ladder on my personal skills on the job, and when the ladder was suddenly whipped from under me, I was left not just jobless but without formal qualifications . . .

'I spent six months or so photographing birds—unskilfully—in between applying for odd jobs (without much enthusiasm or success). I got hooked on the wildlife and took really bad photographs of birds with great hunks of bread showing that I used to attract the birds. You need to shoot within six feet of them, and you could feel the wing beats on your face . . .

'I stayed with brother George for fifteen months, looking out for a place we could afford. We knew Brynllwyd was coming up for sale, because it belonged to Uncle Edwin who was uncle to George's neighbour at Tanyrallt. It felt right because it needed a lot of work done, and we had already done up two boats for living in, so we thought we could improve it and sell it if things didn't work out. We had no clear idea of the future at that point, but we wanted something with work-shops, and in the Aberystwyth area where there was an English school, because Gary was ten when we came and had only had one term at the

Welsh primary school in Penllwyn (where at that time there was only him and two other English speakers, and the teachers translated everything for them, and he still has good memories of that term).

'When we moved into the house first there was a lot of woodwork and re-decorating to do. The idea of the TV workshop came in January 1979 . . .' Heather took over the story. 'Phil had been in the TV industry before, so I said to him, ''You've mended TVs before, you can mend them again''. I had gone out and got a job for 15 hours a week in Bronglais Hospital, as secretary to the Senior Nursing Officer. Phil was drifting along (he was still on Valium) and dreaming about making a living out of photographing birds and grasses. But he started doing the TVs, using the old parlour as a workshop, and in about a year and a half we were able to keep ourselves—off the state and off the pills . . . It felt like coming home at last, and we didn't want to go anywhere else.'

Phil added, 'At that time we had little contact with local people, so we weren't aware of the Welsh thing, the language and so on, but we did notice the way of life and liked it. It seemed like a far better way of living, where people stopped cars in the middle of a country road for a chat, and there was everywhere a lovely pace of life. Like coming into a haven. And there was the seaside there too, which Heather specially liked, having been brought up in Eastbourne. So we both wanted to stay, and things just very gradually grew on the business front, through continuous advertising. At the same time we were doing the house—it needed a hell of a lot doing. There had been a single storey kitchen and downstairs bathroom leanto at the back, which was freezing all the year round. We built a two storey extension in its place, to give us a proper upstairs bathroom and extra bedroom (because the latest idea was to do B & B).'

Heather took up the story. 'I did B & B for three or four years, but there were too many people doing it all down the road here, then, so none of us made a decent living out of it. Eventually the three big ones retired, and then it would have been better, but Phil persuaded me to stop, because he hated visitors in the house. The TV business though still needed topping up with the B & B, unless we could find another way.

59

Strangely enough it was some of the visitors who gave us the idea of selling the bird photos. We had some of the latest hanging on the wall, and people noticed them and said, ''You should sell those—you should print postcards of them''. But you need to print 5,000-10,000 postcards at a time to keep the cost down, and you only retail them in batches of fifty, so that didn't seem on. But we did start the picture business in 1985, and the pictures were local because we hadn't the money to go out for long trips in the car (or for meals, or coffee even!), so we went walking locally and Phil took the photographs. We started off with premade frames from the big stores, and it was a while before we met an agent for our framer (by a lucky chance, at some show), and got a trial run. We started with 10″ × 8″ frames, with 5″ × 7″ prints, but people found the pictures a bit small, so we improved the size. It was marketing that was the terrible problem . . .'

Phil broke in at this point. 'Heather was too nervous at the start to go into a shop on her own and start the talking (like she does now), so at first we both went in. We started with the garage shop at Ponterwyd, and then a shop in Aberystwyth (now no longer there—that's one of the hazards, shops folding). Anyway now Heather knows she's got a good product and she even pulls the stuff out of shops if she doesn't like their attitude—some shopkeepers can be a pain in the neck—''it's not worth putting them on the wall'', ''they're not selling well, you know'', moan, moan . . . At first we were grateful for any interest, now we suss out shops very carefully before we decide whether they're a good outlet or not. We walk around a town and look at what else they're selling and try to decide on the best place in regard to both the goods they sell and the kind of people that are running a shop. We've gradually learnt a lot. Like we have to price the pictures very carefully because people on holiday going into craft shops want presents and souvenirs to take back, but only have so much money and there's a barrier—probably around the £10 mark at the moment. So in order to sell a decent number we have to mark them down at present to about a pound less than we should, considering the actual cost to us. It's the recession too. People just have less money to spend on extras, and on holiday, so last year we were down about 16% compared with before, but this year it may even out again, we don't know yet, because there is the Eisteddfod in Aberystwyth and we will be selling the pictures there, and that should help.'

Heather said, 'I've been going to one of the pre-Eisteddfod groups—meeting with local people to learn some Welsh, and I'm getting help from *Siop y Pethe* in displaying the pictures in the Eisteddfod. We had to translate the names of the photos into Welsh and that sometimes gave us some problems—words like waterfall and estuary—is it *rhaeadr* or *pistyll*, and do you use *aber* or *moryd*? The whole business of marketing is a tough one to crack. I offer sale or return in new outlets, but after a year they go onto buying them when we deliver them to the shop. The sooner the better, because sale or return means you can have £1,000 worth of goods out in the shops and nothing coming back to you direct. We are always trying to extend the outlets, you have to keep on building a business. But the problem with pictures of scenery is that they sell better of course in the area you take them in, so if you want to extend your outlets you also have to go further afield to do the photography, and weather conditions are unreliable so you can have wasted trips. But it's something we both like doing and it has paid for better and better cameras, and also subsidises our outings in the car, which we would want to have anyway. When eventually we retire from the TV business the Picture Workshop will carry on and allow us to travel about in Wales which is what we want to do. We are contemplating buying a little caravan as a dormitory for photography trips. It's the jam on the business bread . . . '

Phil talked about the problems facing the TV business. 'Sets are becoming more reliable all the time, so there are fewer repairs needed. Also it's becoming a pain, because till recently TVs tended to have standard faults, and that was easy. But modern equipment requires a different approach—it goes wrong more rarely but when it does it's difficult and costly to put right, because it's so complex. You get TVs with built-in video recorder and satellite receiver as part of the set, which makes no sense since a TV lasts 15 years but a video recorder only 10. As companies cut costs, too, the service manuals are getting worse—no longer giving you a circuit description although the circuits are more and more complicated.

'Marketing the TV business is important, because I want consciously to produce an image different from the big TV guys, who don't really care a damn, once they've made their sales. I want to be a *concerned* dealer. I sat down once and doodled with a lot of words that described what I was after—like friendly, reliable, expert, personal, specialist . . . It's important in the country because so many customers come by word of mouth, and it's great when someone comes in through the door and says "You've been highly recommended by so-and-so". Country people get confidence as well if they read your ad in their own *papur bro*, community paper, because they are very attached to the known and familiar. So I use ads in every number of *Y Tincer, Y Ddolen, Yr Angor,* and also *The Cambrian News.* I reckon I get at least two customers a week from advertising. And people get to trust you, if you're known, so farmers ring up from remote hill farms and say, "Just bring me a TV and a video—I'm leaving it to you to bring the best value". And I do . . .

'Course it's not all a bed of roses. There are money problems, like the big companies not settling up with you for ages, and the small fellows of pathetic inadequate lives who try to steal hire TVs and videos, but do it so incompetently they get caught by the police and then I have to go to the Small Claims Court, and some people think I'm some sort of capitalist bully because I need to get my money back!'

Norma and Paul Stephens

The Stephenses run the Cwmrheidol Teagardens near the Power Station, and like so many people with small businesses in rural Wales, live and work in the same place. That is part of the attraction of this way of life, but it also brings its problems, as this story shows.

'We came from Kidderminster, and have been eleven years in the valley now. We first found the valley on holiday and fell in love with the place. The valley was something else—there was a tranquil atmosphere and the local people were nice—Dan Davies was the mainstay of everyday life around here. [Dan died on May 19, 1992, at the age of seventy, and was buried at Aberffrwd Chapel after a funeral service to which hundreds of people came and where a tribute was paid to his ever generous hospitality to all the people he encountered, whether locals or incomers.] Dan started chatting to us and we got to know more about the valley. I had a perfectly good job with British Leyland at that time, it was well paid—but redundancies were coming in 1979 because of changes in the motor industry. A lot of staff were going, and I began to think about a change. We were looking for a good place to bring up the children (Darren was 11 and Debbie 8) away from the rat race. We wanted them to grow up to appreciate the country, and we wanted them to get a better education—more personal, individual treatment in the schools.

'It was a big decision, because I had been twelve years with British Leyland, and they weren't giving redundancy to tradesmen at that time, only to the professional staff. All we had to set up with was the money from the house and three weeks' wages and a bit of savings. When I took the factory on the Aberystwyth Industrial Estate the Development Board for Rural Wales offered a flat with the factory, but we turned it down because it was so cramped and there was no ground. We stored the furniture in the factory and lived in a caravan at Abernant for a fortnight and then the Council gave us a house in Penparcau, after a bit of pressure—because of me starting the factory and the hope of employing people.

'Then this cottage came on the market. It had been a holiday home and was in an appalling state, but we came to live here. As the business got off the ground we decided to live in the caravan on the bit of ground that went with the house. We applied for a grant to do up the house and so I had to do double the work. I plodded on but it was sheer hard slog— working in the factory during the day and thinking about the next job on the house, then working on the house every evening. I had to get a six months' extension on the house, because we had sickness in the family. I was really pushed to the limit, and two and a half years passed before the house was finished. We were crowded together in the caravan with the two children, and Darren had no place to study—he used to go and sit in the car to get his homework done.' Norma took up the story at this point.

'Both the children went to Penparcau, a bilingual school, but Darren only had six months to get Welsh, and he put up a barrier and went on to Penglais [the English-medium secondary school]. Debbie had three years to get Welsh and she went on to Penweddig [the Welsh-medium secondary school]. She had her problems still, but the teachers in Penweddig were very good at helping her. She did nine GCSE subjects and got them all. They both joined the sea cadets, and Darren played for the local football team—he was really into local sport and made a lot of friends. The one big worry we had moving from Kidderminster was the effect of the upheaval on them, but they settled down here and made friends. Kids are very adaptable. We are full of pride now because they saw what they wanted and went for it, and are both doing well in the Navy. I've always said to them that nothing would be handed to them on a plate and they'll have to work hard to get where they want.'

'We thought it was vital for a girl more than a boy to learn the language well, because the kind of job she might get—service jobs in a local solicitor's office, or as a receptionist—needed people to be bilingual. As it turned out both of them went away to the Navy, but they never come home without seeing their friends. They got to be well liked and accepted by the local community, and it still goes on when they come home . . . '

'But we were talking about the business side of things—well, the joinery business was doing well, though it was a job to break into the local community. I went to Welsh-speaking classes to be able to speak to Welsh-speaking customers—that breaks down barriers, I know, but it's a job learning the language . . . The Tearoom was Norma's baby and the joinery business was mine. A lot of visitors to the valley kept asking, "Is there anywhere to get a cup of tea or a bite to eat?", and I said to my wife, "Would you be able to cope if we did a teashop?" She said yes, she'd like it, and the Tearoom took off. We'd spotted an opening and it was fine at first . . .

'Then the unimaginable happened. I had a heart attack and the doctor said not to do the heavy lifting and I thought the stress of the business was too much for me and I sold it. It was a good going concern and that was alright. But then I was hanging around for a year, till on my daughter's advice I found out that there were twelve months catering courses available on employment training at the Catering College in Tanybwlch. I got the certificate and then went on to vegetarian and cake decorating. I really took to it, so signed on for another year. The intention was to get the experience and put it to use in the Tearoom with Norma. I went on into the second and third year and it would have been alright until the recession struck . . .' Norma continued the saga of the cafe's ups and downs.

'We went for a restaurant licence (a drink with your meal) but too many people just wanted cans of beer to take away. I had to take a lot of abuse from customers who just wanted to drink, and we didn't want to bring the wrong sort into the valley—throwing cans down and making a nuisance of themselves to locals. We wanted evening trade to build up the business—people driving up the valley for a meal and a quiet evening. We don't have the evening trade any more. We had to give up the licence. It was like from the time of the heart attack we got a series of little setbacks which set everything we had built up tumbling down again. Since we've had the recession people bring their own sandwiches and only buy a kitkat or a piece of cake. The homebaking was a waste because we had to throw a lot away—the chickens were getting apple pie and cream! We try to do traditional things like home-made faggots and peas, bread and butter pudding, treacle tart—we thought it would be a new niche in the market, but even that has gone down with the recession. We do traditional Welsh cakes as well, like bara brith and shearing cake and honey cake, to bring back the old cooking. But this year the recession is biting so hard we are wondering whether we can last another year, what with the business rate, the twelve months' public liability insurance and all the overheads which you have to pay for the whole year, when you are only doing business for about one month in the summer. The nitty gritty is that not enough people come down the valley and those who do get refreshments in the Power Station Visitor

Centre. We've really had a go and even considered moving away. But the Catch 22 situation is that this property has dropped so much in value since 1989 that no way could we afford to move away. It's no good trading through the winter, and there seems nothing left for us but to live on benefits. I'm no employment prospect at 50 with a history of heart attack. And Norma's health has been bad this year, too . . .

'If they want to promote these beautiful valleys in Wales, the only way is to signpost the facilities properly. I am convinced there is an opening for a venture like the Valley Tearooms—a personal touch to promote the beauty of these little secluded valleys. But when you go for help you cannot get it. I went to Dyfed Highways, the Tourist Board etc about putting up a notice at the A44 turnoff, indicating in symbols the facilities available in the valley. The Nature Conservancy and Dyfed Wildlife Trust have encouraged nature trails, and there are camping and caravanning, fishing and fish breeding, so there is plenty going on to draw the visitors in. The answer was, ''all that information is in the Tourist Office'', and I said, ''Yes, but the Tourist Office is shut in the evenings and on Sundays and it doesn't cater for motorists who want to turn off somewhere interesting on the spur of the moment''. Then they said that not enough thousands of vehicles come up the valley to justify the sign. Well, they wouldn't, would they, if they don't know about what's there?

'I had another go at publicity to try and get the Tearooms known to all the people who come in the evenings to see the lights on the dam. There is nowhere for them to go but sit at the picnic tables, and some of them make their own tea. I proposed to Powergen that during the hours when their Visitor's Centre was shut we could attract people up to the Tearooms by putting a notice down by the bridge at the dam. In return I offered to give out pamphlets and promote the Power Station, but the manager gave a categorical no. We felt that Powergen could have done a lot more to help us . . . It's like everybody thinks that people starting up in business get all sorts of grants, and that caused envy and resentment among local businessmen of people starting up on the

Industrial Estate—at that time we got nothing but they wouldn't believe it.

'Since then we've been up against the EC regulations, which get worse all the time. They treat a struggling concern like ours the same way as if it were a 5 star Hilton hotel. They want you to replace your wooden kitchen fittings with stainless steel if you're doing food—even if you're only operating over a short summer season. And at the same time they're talking about promoting tourism in the countryside to help people diversify and go on living in places like this. It just doesn't make sense . . .'

Susannah Kenyon Jones

'After finishing university I went to stay with a friend near Lampeter, and I decided I had to leave suburbia (in Essex) for Wales, being sick of the rat race and the emphasis on materialism. At first I thought of having a rural base in Wales and somehow commuting to work in the city, but it didn't come off. It became more important for me to live in the countryside, because Wales doesn't concentrate so much on the material things that seem to preoccupy so many people in England . . . At first we did up a derelict cottage in Gwynedd, but then John was doing a degree in Aberystwyth and we lived in a village near Lampeter where our friend Paul was farming. I was not really occupied enough at that time and we talked of lots of ways of making money from the land, and eventually thought of trying to grow Christmas trees (Paul had already tried selling Welsh Christmas trees in London). There is quite a bit of marketing Christmas trees in the Lampeter area.

'When I first started I was greatly helped by the Forestry Commission, and I was grateful, because my only previous experience of growing things had been a crop of cabbages which failed due to the ravages of cabbage white butterflies that year, but there was an unexpected crop of mushrooms as a result of using horse manure, so it wasn't a complete disaster! In early 1984 I planted 10,000 trees (you get about 3,000 to an acre) which should have been a commercial proposition. But because of the recession there have been a lot of bad debts (probably about £3,500) and it's a difficult site, my Lampeter land. The trees do well because it's boggy ground, but it's hard to harvest. I found it is better to sell the trees when they're small, because bigger trees need extra labour to harvest and it's difficult to get good casual labour. If you do without extra labour you have to stay small scale (about 400 trees every Christmas) but that isn't enough to give you a main income, so you have to do other things, or else expand till you can employ help the whole year round. Even then the trouble with marketing Christmas trees is that it all comes in one week in December, and you need a lot of help . . .

'The Christmas tree experience has been good because when I came to Cwmrheidol and had to get planning permission to rebuild the old roofless house, it was necessary to satisfy the Planners that you have to live there for agricultural purposes. We have been there for one year now, living in the caravan and hoping eventually they will give us planning permission to rebuild the house, if our business plan is considered viable. You could earn £7,000 a year (that's their minimum agricultural income you're supposed to make to justify living there), but I might not be able to do it, out of the Christmas trees. I would prefer to diversify and do B & B and poultry and free range eggs . . .

'The first problem was getting the road made through to the place, and then getting electricity to the caravan. We use Calor gas for cooking and the new shower. With two small children it's wonderful to have a shower and a washing machine now at the end of our first year. The children love it here, as I do. There's such a peaceful feeling and you feel you don't have to hurry to get the house done up—which is just as well. What were the first things I did? Well, I tried to get rid of the bracken because two or three acres out of the twelve were covered in bracken. At the moment Dai has his sheep on about eight acres for eight months. That leaves me with about two acres where I have already planted 5,500 Christmas trees. I'm going to plant more this September and next September if the weather's OK. I planted the first lot in March and April this year (they bud twice a year and you have to plant them when they're dormant).

'It is jolly hard work because you have to do a lot of digging and bending over. The field is quite steep and it would be difficult to use a tractor so it's all done manually. You're supposed to put them into a weed-free environment and most people spray with chemicals before and after planting (to stop grass and perennials). You spray quite a bit for the first three years to keep the weeds down, and you might have to spray against aphids too, because they can completely destroy your trees from three years on. I'm trying to do it organically (I hope to get the Soil Association logo to sell them as organic produce), so no chemical fertiliser and no chemical spraying. I got the geese because they are close grazers and keep the weeds down and the grass, and they also command a high price on the Christmas market—but I'll have to get somebody to help me kill them because I'm squeamish and they are quite big. I'm using an organic fertiliser (blood, fish and bone) and might use mulching —dead bracken or maybe old carpet squares to stop the weeds.

'The worst thing to happen this year was the drought in May and June after I'd planted them, which killed off some. The problem is the field is south facing and well-drained. Anyway you expect to lose a proportion. In two or three years the first ones will be ready to dig up and pot, and I shall leave the roots on (more people like that) and maybe decorate them myself. I think John's China connection will prove useful, for I could import decorative pots and fairy tree lights and so on—they're so cheap in China it would be a great help to profits.

'The whole point of being self-employed is that you have your own ideas and you have to develop them and put them into practice. But you have also to face up to the fact that if it wasn't for the government supplying family credit, or having some other source of income besides your small holding, it is almost impossible to make a family living from it. It's physically very hard work for a woman (I can carry ½ cwt of grain, but a male farmer can carry two bags of cement). Time is always a problem, because I am trying to have a relaxed attitude and make the children contented rather than rushing around and getting neurotic.

'You have to be canny to survive in farming work, because you have to stay up to date with all the rules and regulations and grants. The best way is by talking to people. Self-employed people help each other tremendously—there's quite a feeling among them. You can go and consult the Farmers' Union or ADAS or the Forestry Commission if you have specific problems, but they seem to end up suggesting I try someone else—perhaps I'm not a big enough enterprise for them? The Soil Association inspector is very helpful, and there's an Organic Advisory Service—but not in Wales. I've been to the Centre for Alternative Technology quite often, and they've been useful on giving advice about supplementing my basic electricity supply by generating electricity from the stream, and how to dispose of human excrement organically while conforming to the septic tank regulations . . .

'The good thing about it all is that it feels like home, a benevolent place for me and the children to be in. The bad thing is that it is physically very demanding—it is such a steep holding, and easily affected by drought. But I really enjoy having the ducks. Starting with four ducks and three drakes (muscovies), we've expanded now to forty after six hatchings, and I've been on the phone to local butchers this week to see if there's a market for some of them. But they say demand is low at this time of the year so I'll probably have to keep them till Christmas. I'd like to go into soft fruit production, because I'm sure they would do well. But you get 50p a lb through Frosts and it takes an hour to pick four pounds, so you can see why a lot of people sell them self-pick. I've got ideas for trout ponds, too, but again you pay a lot for trout feed, so the problem is having sufficient quantity to make a decent turnover, without it taking too much of your time.

'It's a great headache expanding to make a scheme economic, because there's machinery to buy and more people around, and disasters can happen and it can all get very expensive. So I tend to work on a number of projects, all rather small-scale (perhaps in future trout, free-range eggs, a bit of tourism), and linked with the aim of self-sufficiency. What I'd really like one day is to make the place into some kind of retreat or meditation centre, a refuge for people whom life has put under strain, where they could enjoy the tranquillity here and recuperate. A while back I wrote to Amnesty and asked if political refugees would like to come and camp here for a therapeutic holiday, but I got no reply. I do some meditation myself sometimes and I'm quite sure we have to find alternative ways of approaching the world's problems and using the world's resources, and we need to start wherever we are . . . '

Janet and Tom Williams (Institute of Grassland and Environmental Research)

Janet works as a Scientific Officer, and Tom as Station Engineer in the old Plant Breeding Station (PBS), now IGER, at Plas Gogerddan on the fringes of Aberystwyth. They live in the last occupied house at the head of Cwmrheidol, where they have land of their own, as well as commuting the eight miles to work every day.

Tom: 'I was born in north Wales, so I'm a stranger here still! My parents came to live in Machynlleth in 1947, and I went to local schools before going off to Liverpool Docks as an apprentice in the power station. That was a shock for me after life in rural Wales, alright. Anyway after National Service, I came out of the army in 1960 feeling very relaxed about life but with no idea what to do. I got a job in the PBS, and during my thirty years there I have moved from science to the technical side and for the last five years I've been Station Engineer—electronic engineering is my field. There have been a lot of changes in that time. We used to have a tearoom for all fifty or so of us, now there are getting on for 300 staff and it's got more impersonal and more specialised—less friendly I suppose.'

Janet: 'I'm in Acclimatory Physiology, which means plant responses to climatic changes and their ways of adapting. Some of us do third world projects on drought resistance and heat tolerance in maize or sorghum, say. We have a lot of foreign students learning techniques to take back to the third world . . . The changes recently have been away from government funding and towards private funding from the big firms like ICI. There's also EC money for environmental research. My boss is currently looking for funds to research global warming or fluctuating temperatures, where our cold response work could be important. I am freezing seedlings (mainly grasses and cereals) down to − 20 degrees, to find the temperature at which 50% of them will not survive. It's Norwegian Timothy at the moment which is as hardy as anything we've ever tested. The object is to breed cold tolerant varieties, but also to understand the biochemistry of cold tolerance ... We've always regarded ourselves as links between the fieldwork and the systems people who look at the internal plant mechanisms. Traditionally we had the breeding of varieties for the farmers, but recently we're more involved with the private seed breeding people than with the government—it is the companies now who fund us and put the seeds on the market, though the government still fund our pure research. Flavour of the month at present is molecular biology, and it's not good to be in green wellies. It's more about breaking down DNA and that involves breaking down organic solvents and enzymes, so we have to have safety cabinets for manipulating dangerous substances without getting contaminated by carcinogens, for example. It means Health and Safety has tightened up considerably compared with the days when you hear of colleagues who used to wash their hands in organic solvents to get paint off!'

Tom: 'Yes, Health and Safety is so tight that even the electric kettles have to be tested once every 12 months! It's becoming quite difficult just keeping up with the legislation, and the scientists get annoyed if you stop them using their 'fume cupboards', say, because you have to test them. It gets more difficult with the shift from 'nearmarket research' (field plots and animal responses to different grazing crops) to molecular biology which involves gene manipulation. When we took the cuts 5 or 6 years ago the barley breeding department was cut completely, now our only cereals left are oats, because our wet westerly climate makes them of relevance. The agronomy department used to be the biggest, now it's the smallest, but we still do work directly concerned with finding alternative resources for the farmers of rural Wales. That was how we went into llamas—we had a short-term grant for three years to check out the meat and wool production from llamas as alternative to sheep. There was a lot of interest from the public, which was quite a security headache

72

at first. A lot of locals wanted a Sunday afternoon outing to see the llamas.

'Our scientists also test additive systems for silage—to counterbalance acidity, say, or increase sugar content, to improve weight gain in the animals. The problem is, how do you reconcile that with the surpluses? Well, it means you can use less nitrogen in the ground to grow beef, and that helps environmentally. And you can use less ground per animal to produce the beef. But it still doesn't quite convince—to go on intensifying in the present situation.'

Janet: 'There are other problems, too. We do have an environmental remit, but at the same time as we are trying to produce disease resisting plants, private industry do more of their own R & D, and they might look on it as more important to keep on using pesticides because there's more profit in that. There is more emphasis among ordinary people now on the dangers to the environment, so there's no use us getting into an ivory tower. But pure research in molecular biology can produce results. Carbon dioxide enhancement is our buzz word now, because increased efficiency of CO_2 utilisation in plants would counter environmental pollution. And it's important to work out how plants will cope with possible future conditions caused by global warming plus increased levels of carbon dioxide.'

Tom: 'At the same time we are doing "new" research which takes us right back to the old farming methods in rural Wales. Agroforestry is back in, so our colleague Bonsai Bill grows trees in test tubes to look at the competition between different species, with a view to bringing back pigs feeding on acorns under the trees. That's no longer one of the old ways—that's diversification! But the real problem with any form of diversification is that the average Welsh farmer is very resistant to change—not like the keen business farmer of southern England, who will pour money into a new crop and take the profit (if it works), or change to another idea (if it doesn't work). The problem here is that since about 1970 the small farmer has been creaming off the money (till the bad recent years) but doing nothing with it but put it in the Building Society. They're the product of a long line of survivors through the

73

ages—efficient in the known ways, and frugal, but never risk-taking. The Welsh farmer will take out the hedges for one subsidy, and put them back again if there's another subsidy, but he won't risk his own money—he'd rather keep it stashed away safe (or not so safe, stuffed under the mattress). But at the same time there are people around who took risks in the 1970s and got into debt with the banks to develop farms, and now they're stuck with fallen incomes and the debts still to pay off. So not many are winning in farming at the present time.

'The PBS has had its good times and you could have a permanent career there. Now it's more likely to be three-year contracts and not permanent posts. There have been exciting breakthroughs in research, like the first tetraploid grasses (with four times the number of chromosomes—big leaves and increased photosynthesis) which reached the commercial market around 1980 and won the Queen's Award for Industry, because you got a better leafy crop of silage. I've been reading recently George Waller's book *Prophet of a new age*, about Sir George Stapledon's work in the PBS before World War 2. He was the father of grass research in the world of that time, and PBS was the mother. The new varieties went all over the world, as well as increasing Britain's agricultural efficiency at a time when imports were getting tricky. There *are* exciting breakthroughs every so often—that's what makes research worthwhile. Although I'm an engineer, I have an inherent confidence in living systems' ability to compensate for whatever you do to them, to adapt to their environment—like global warming.'

Janet: 'Provided it happens over a long enough time. Plants are such complex systems that they can adapt, but you have to help them to speed up evolution. On our own land here in the valley we are introducing enough plant variability to ensure survival in case of global warming. We have brought various species into the valley, including Mexican fire trees and New Zealand hohirias, in an effort to get a mix of native and exotic and flamboyant jobs. It's very satisfying, trying to get a mix of forms and flowers and scents that will keep going through all the year, with their different timing. It's a challenge to try and grow these things

74

in the valley. We brought back some paulonia seeds from a Barcelona park and because it has to withstand frost here we have planted in three different places to see what is the best. It is doing well in Cwmrheidol, so that is rewarding.'

Tom: 'One of the challenges we have now is the extra 50 or 60 acres of woodland we have recently bought. It will be cleared of its conifers by the present owner before we take it over, but then I think the only practical thing will be to plant acorns. We have a prolific oak tree by the house which will provide bucketfuls of acorns. I've talked to the Forestry Commission people and they say that's acceptable, so I'm looking forward to sowing them either direct into the cleared ground, or maybe rooting them first in a little nursery. All we'd expect from grants would be for the fencing. It was all oakwoods in the valley till the end of the eighteenth century, so we are trying to put it back at our end. It's fanciful but nice to think of a new oak wood flourishing where there were only conifers before—even if it won't grow to maturity in our own lifetimes.'

Janet: 'Yes, it's putting something back into the earth, after so much has been taken out of it in the valley for so long.'

Ian Jones (A. J. Plant and Property Investment Wales)

'I was born and brought up in Clarach till I was four or five years old. My father was a farmer and his father was a professor of agriculture in the college. His mother was a Scotswoman who lectured in the Dairy Department and also ran a number of farms—she was a woman of unlimited enterprise and farmed organically. I was free to make up my own mind about my future, but school influence (I'm an ex-Ardwynian) meant I went to university to do physics. After a year I took a year away and spent it travelling around North America, and getting work on various construction sites. I came back and studied Civil Engineering, graduating in 1974. I worked for a consultant in Cardiff, then was six years in London with BP and was transferred to Aberdeen for three or four years. I came back here with a view to doing some consulting work as a civil engineer and to develop a small business on the gravel pit site (which my brother was running) in Cwmrheidol. It was a time of business expansion so I ended up doing a lot for A. J. Plant, and less and less as a civil engineer. At that time we needed to put a lot into developing management systems and business plans. That was seven years ago, when the turnover of A. J. Plant was a tenth of what it is now.

'At that time there was no large scale contractor in the area—all the major contracts went to outside contractors. What happened was they brought in their own agents and managers and foremen, and fleeced the local sub-contractors and the clients, and took the profits away with them. So we identified the need for import replacement. It was argued that local firms didn't have the expertise, but I was a civil engineer so we had our internal expertise. There was a Catch 22 at first: you don't get a contract until you're on a tender list, and you don't get on a tender list till you've been awarded a contract. But we got through that barrier . . .

'In 1987 we looked at the building side a lot more, because a number of local companies had ceased trading (mainly through deaths), so we thought we could fit in that notch. Also development opportunity came, so Alan and myself and another formed Property Investment Wales. At present we're finishing off the halls of residence for the University, and trying to get the harbour scheme off the ground. Now 80% of our time is on Property Investment Wales, and 20% on A. J. Plant (which employs 215-220 people)—the Cwmrheidol gravel pit is only 5% of the turnover. We were looking to replace the outside developers coming in and exploiting the local situation. Our strategy is to offer a good deal with no strings attached and no question of extras added onto the original package. We have two full-time quantity surveyors and one architect (part-time), and employ local architects and all local contractors. We offer a turnkey package right through all the stages from design to managing the construction, and do our best endeavours to give the client value for money. We have gone into housing as well as public contracts like the University village.

'The contracting side is very difficult in the recession because outside contractors are looking further afield to find diminishing opportunities, and that makes the situation very competitive. There's no real need for this area to have a recession, because we didn't have the extremes of boom in the late 80s and shouldn't have to suffer the extremes of bust now. There are higher real interest rates now than at the beginning of the recession, and a balance of payment deficit. If we can't export more than we import in a desperate recession like this, how do we get out of it? Only by adjusting the currency—the pound is too high. As far as we are concerned here, we still sell houses because we are keeping to value for money, and the student village will be a big chunk of our work for the next two years., But yes, we have to think hard about continued expansion.

'I'd have to say no on continued expansion, because the recession wouldn't allow it and the parties involved don't want it. Many businesses end up expanding despite themselves—you end up having obligations to your work force and so you have to expand, and you are building up your overheads all the time, so at some point you need to call a halt. We're looking to making strategic decisions at the present time about our future. Alan's been in the construction business for over thirty years and that is one of the most demanding cut-throat businesses there is, so he's entitled to take stock ... It's policy now to trim our work load, pick and choose more and remove the bits that give you less pleasure than others.

'My original intention when I returned to Wales was to develop a business on the Cwmrheidol gravel pit and do consulting work in engineering, but life hasn't turned out like that. No change means you die, so there is continuing development. The latest plan is the Coarse Fishing which we began this July for visitors to Cwmrheidol. We have three lakes and a mile of the Rheidol, so hopefully next year we will extend the season by offering game fishing as well, and then rowing and canoeing and wind-surfing. We already get people coming up from Borth on stormy days to our sheltered lake. The gravel pit is coming to an end now, so these new opportunities open up. There again, there are always objections to anything like the gravel pit, but when you look at the finished article, as it is now, it provides a more varied habitat for wildlife than anywhere else in the valley. We have more species of birds attracted there, so the end result is not a bad one. To get an omelette you have to break eggs. We're back to the problem of people being against any kind of change even though the present situation isn't helping rural Wales to keep its young people or create work.'

[1] Channel 4 on TV, *Gazetteer to accompany the series The land of Europe*, London, Channel 4 Television, 1990.

[2] European Centre for Traditional and Regional Cultures, *A study of the cultural and linguistic impact of tourism*, Cardiff, ECTARC, 1988.

Chapter 4

The Cwmrheidol lead miners

Before the days of commuting you lived and worked in your own locality, which was your special place, your *bro*, a source of identity based on belonging to a community where home and work were interconnected. For most of the last century Cwmrheidol was a close-knit community of inter-related families who were smallholders and leadminers. The lead mines reached their boom period between the 1850s and 1870s, when the dressed ore fetched prices of £12 to £15 the ton. But as early as the 1830s the township of Cwmrheidol was noted for its industrial development as well as its picturesque scenery. Samuel Lewis in his *Topographical Dictionary*[1] of 1833 says that 'the greater part of the 649 inhabitants had employment in the extensive lead mines', but guidebooks continue to speak of the scenic beauties of the valley throughout the opening up of the fifteen mines.

There were no large scale mines in Cwmrheidol consistently making a profit for the owners or giving secure and steady work to the inhabitants. Their operations were irregular and intermittent, subject to whims of local or distant investors. They frequently went into liquidation, and changed hands from one group of speculators to another, all hoping in vain for lucky strikes and rich returns. The men, women and children who worked for the mining companies needed to keep their smallholdings of a few acres going, to provide the basics and supplement their meagre and unreliable wages from mining.

In Cwmrheidol many of the children started working as ore-dressers between the ages of eleven and twelve, and this was the beginning of grinding toil which was reckoned to take at least ten years off a man's life expectancy. The Royal Commission on Mines[2] in 1864 collected a mass of first hand evidence which showed that men who grew up in agricultural work and did not go into mining till they were in their twenties, were not so badly affected by bronchial disease as the ones who started as children. 'Miners' asthma' was the killer, and led to many dying between forty and fifty. It was brought on by the dust from drilling, so many miners preferred to work in wet conditions which kept down the dust, though that in turn brought on rheumatic problems. In the Llywernog Lead and Silver Mining Museum near Ponterwyd visitors today can walk along a mining tunnel or adit, which is not high enough to allow standing up straight, but has to be negotiated in an uncomfortable stooped posture. However visitors are not subjected to water dripping from the roof or accumulating under their feet, as the old miners were. The Museum has a fine display of drills, showing how the more efficient could be the more dangerous, until the miners' health was taken into consideration in the design of the drills. 'The widow-maker' was the nickname given by the lead miners to an 'improved' drill, till it was modified with water jets to keep the dust down.

When blasting operations were going on the smoke was a further hazard. Miners told the Royal Commission that 'in the case of men going into the powder smoke, in the end the spit would be quite black for the rest of the day afterwards, and the water which is thrown down upon the bottom of the shaft [to keep down the smoke] is very much discoloured and smells very bad'. Ventilation was poor in the smaller mines, because of cost-cutting, and only in big mines like Cwmystwyth was there a proper ventilation system. At Cwmystwyth air was driven through zinc pipes by a fan powered by a six-foot water wheel, and this was efficient enough, they said, to drive air for a mile, and to clear out powder smoke within two minutes after a blast. But in smaller operations the ventilation could be so poor that the miners' candles could scarcely be kept burning, and inevitably they inhaled particles into the lungs. They 'spit a black spit for weeks after leaving a mine, and the sputa of people is darker after only two years in the mines, from some affection of the lungs'. A local doctor reported to the Royal Commission that 'they are more pale and subject to coughs, and they decay sooner than agricultural labourers ... Bronchitis and consumption I have noticed to be the most frequent diseases of miners'.

Hard physical toil was the rule, as well as punishing working conditions. The shift was eight hours in mid Wales, and access often involved arduous ascents and descents of vertical iron ladders. There was a specially long run of vertical ladders connecting up the Ystumtuen mine workings with the Cwmrheidol mine at the head of the valley. The tools in the early days required a combination of brute strength and sound judgment—picks and sledge hammers, manually operated drills and borers, allied to the use of powder blasting. Each man collected his day's supply from the isolated powder house on the mine's periphery. A candle was usually fixed to the miner's hat with a lump of mud, and he carried with him a supply for the shift, as well as his tools. The ore was wheeled out along adits just wide enough to ensure the passage of, in the earliest days, wheelbarrows, and, later, bogeys running on metal rails. It was wet and dirty work, but changing sheds were rare and washing facilities even rarer. In most cases the workers walked home in the flannels they wore underground. Occasionally 'the clothes of the men are hung up to dry in the clothes house, unsweetened by fresh air', and only got laundered when taken home from time to time to have tears mended.

The miners' cottages were poor and damp, so likely to aggravate any tendencies to tuberculosis and rheumatism stemming from the mining work. As the mines developed there was overcrowding, because the children stayed at home and earned money on the ore-dressing floors, where previously they had gone off as live-in farm servants at the age of eleven or twelve. Many of the cottages also took in outside miners as lodgers, because it was an extra hand to help on the smallholding (in lieu of rent) or it brought in a bit of extra money. The general assumption is that in Ceredigion there was an influx of Cornish miners attracted by the lead mining boom in the middle of the nineteenth century, but in Cwmrheidol the incomers do not seem to have come from outside the parish. Ystumtuen Chapel has no Cornish names on the headstones, nor has the Bethel built in the valley in 1872, though these are the Wesleyan

81

denominations which are said to have attracted the Cornish mining families. The names in the Census Reports throughout the mining boom of mid century continue to be Davies and Jenkins and Morgan and Benjamin and Jones, so it looks as if only some of the mine captains came from Cornwall—Captain Ridge of the Cwmrheidol Mine for example.

The humblest cottages were one-room cabins sixteen feet by twelve, usually built by the occupants themselves from local stone and timber, or with mud walls often in the early days. But the agent of the Pryses of Gogerddan (who along with the Powells of Nanteos owned most of Cwmrheidol at that time) told the Royal Commissioners:

> I do not allow any mud cottages to be erected on the Gogerddan estate, so that in selecting ground for the miners' cottages, I get them as near to the mine as I possibly can, in order that they may have stones taken up from the mines.

The one-room cabins were sometimes divided by hanging sheets of blue and white checked linen from the roof beams, or by nailing together a plank partition, though often not going up to full ceiling height. The windows were small, usually only at the front of the cottage, and not made to open, because it was considered that there were enough draughts already from door and chimney. The floor was of earth and the roof likely to be thatched. An inspector of miners' dwellings further north noted that the usual breeder of disease was 'a cesspool in front of the house and a heap of rubbish to keep it company', so that more than half the houses had one or more of their inhabitants lying ill.

But there were changes for the better in the latter half of the century. The standard Cwmrheidol house erected or rebuilt in the 1870s to 1900 was constructed with thick stone walls, a roof of slate, and floors of slate slabs or wooden boards. It had two rooms downstairs and a loft above for sleeping and storage. But by then the mining boom was over and only the more prosperous were left to live in such houses (See Houses as the landscape of history, Chapter 12).

There was a brighter side to the material lives of the miners, however. A more optimistic Royal Commissioner in the 1860s noted that

Most of the families have allotments of ground as a garden or small farm, so that the miners have the advantage of short hours, country air, and agricultural pursuits for leisure time ... they have a better diet than their fellows in towns, having a good supply of vegetables, milk and bacon ...

They had, too, ancient rights over what was considered to be common land, though the big estates were not always in agreement with them over this. In the middle of the eighteenth century Lewis Morris observed that the Gogerddan estate 'have closed and impounded from the common; the poor neighbours being not able to dispute with them ... most of them being originally but cottages and encroachments upon the mountain'.[3] Traditionally the common rights were of grazing, cutting turf, collecting heath and wood for fuel and for constructing their cabins. Sometimes the estates would supply their tenants or leaseholders with stone and timber to rebuild the poorest kind of cottages, and add to the value of the estate.

Mining operations

Horizontal tunnels (adits) were cut into the hillsides to get access to the lead ore, especially before the industrial revolution brought machines which made it easier to sink vertical shafts for ventilation, drainage and taking out the ore. The adits were strengthened with wooden props, usually oak, since this was available locally, was durable and could withstand the bad air in the mines.

Gunpowder for blasting came into common use in the eighteenth century. Before that, says Lewis Morris, the Crown Surveyor of Mines in the 1740s, rock was split by lighting fires on the spot, and then throwing cold water onto the heated stone to crack it. After that the men would break it up using a series of borers and wedges. The wedges, he says, were 'sea stones, with one end nicked off to an edge, and there is an impression on the other end where they used to strike them'.

Drainage and ventilation were perpetual problems in the mines. In the early days the simple approach chosen was to raise the water in wooden buckets or 'kibbles'. A horse gin, or 'whimsey', was in use at the old Ystumtuen mine to haul buckets up the perpendicular shaft. Lewis

Morris drew a careful diagram of the arrangements (it is preserved in a manuscript in the National Library) in the 1740s, which shows the new whimsey and also the ventilating shaft with a hand operated fan at the top.

A century later it was usual to have a series of pumping engines powered by water wheels of twelve to fifteen feet in diameter. In the larger mines there would be a series of water wheels, worked by the same stream of water, which was carefully channelled to provide power for hauling and crushing ore as well as drainage and ventilation. Water power was dependent on a good water supply and some of the mines had problems during long dry summers. They had to channel water long distances from an unfailing source like the River Rheidol, or build reservoirs (like the Ponds on the Ystumtuen plateau). A mine leet can still be followed in places along the Rheidol near Ysbyty Cynfyn. These water channels or leets, says Bick, 'can be made quite feasibly with merely a rule: simply by cutting a preliminary ditch a length at a time, allowing it to fill with water, and excavating the necessary depth for the required gradient'.[4] When the terrain was rough and steep the water had to be channelled through stone or wooden (oak) aquaducts, traces of which may be seen still in the Rheidol valley.

Hauling the ore out of the mines was in the more primitive days done simply by shovelling it into wicker baskets which were strapped on the miners' backs and carried up ladders to the surface. Then they used wooden wheelbarrows to move the ore along the levels to a loading point, where it was emptied into stout buckets of wood or iron known as 'kibbles'. These were hauled to the surface originally by two men operating a windlass. By the mid eighteenth century horse power was widespread, and in the mid nineteenth century water wheels were a common sight in the Cwmrheidol district, turning in stately arcs against the sky at every mine in the valley. The early water wheels were made of wood by the mine carpenter, but iron wheels were later manufactured in the big cities like Leeds and Manchester for supplying to the mining trade.

Once the crude ore had been brought to the surface, the next process was 'dressing', which meant getting rid of the dross and preparing the ore for the smelting furnaces in Aberystwyth or further afield. Before the impact of the industrial revolution made itself felt in this area, large numbers of women and children were employed to break up the crude with hammers, on the mine banks. Water-powered crushers came into Ceredigion from the 1840s. At Caegynon in Cwmrheidol, for example, Absalom Francis installed a thirty-foot water wheel with a crushing mill and dressing apparatus, in the 1850s. This turned out to be doubly fortunate for him, because in the process of digging the wheel pits the men hit on a new ore-rich lode which gave Caegynon Mine a profitable twenty-year run, returning 371 tons of lead ore and 700 tons of blende between 1853 and 1875.

The crushing mills were rather like giant mangles, into which the crude ore was dropped to be broken up into more manageable pieces for the subsequent processes of 'jigging' in water to separate out the heavier lead deposits, and 'buddling' or further refining to pick up additional lead ore. Jigging was done in large iron sinks, and buddling on circular floors (the Temple Mine near Ysbyty Cynfyn still has an example). Both processes needed an unfailing water supply for washing the lead ore out of the crude.

Even when the dressing was getting more mechanised, there was plenty of work on the dressing floors for young women and boys and girls above the age of ten. Captain Ridge, manager at the Rheidol Mine (later the Rheidol United), described in 1863 how the ore was brought out along the adit levels, then drawn by horses along three-hundred fathoms to the dressing sheds, where twenty boys and girls did the dressing. He was proud of the fact that they were protected from the weather in covered-in sheds, whereas in the smaller mines they were exposed to the elements without any shelter, and suffered cruelly from cold and wet. The girls got wages of 8d, the boys 10d, and the young women 1 shilling for a shift. The miners earned 12/6 and 15/- a week, during eight hour shifts. While twenty children and young women were employed in this labour intensive surface work, there were only six miners working underground. But of course the proportions depended on the development phase a mine was going through. In the 1880s, when the Rheidol United Mine was less productive it needed more men underground to supply the dressing floors, and there were equal numbers of surface and underground workers. In 1891 there was only one man left working there, as the slump in world lead prices was felt locally:

Employment figures for Rheidol United Mine [5]

Year	Underground	Surface
1882	14	15
1883	14	18
1884	8	10
1885	11	9
1886	10	10
1887	12	9
1888	6	5
1889-90	6	3
1891	—	1

At the peak of the lead-mining boom in Ceredigion 10,000 tons of ore was produced. By 1890 this had slumped to 1,666 tons per annum. Even during the good times the smaller mines like those in Cwmrheidol were victims of distant stock market speculation in mining shares, and this affected local employment. Mining companies frequently went bankrupt either from under investment or as a result of reckless capital expenditure unjustifiable in terms of the actual returns from the mine. The Rheidol Mine, later the Rheidol United, about which Captain Ridge was so self-congratulatory in the 1860s, proved to be in fact a very insecure financial proposition. It went into liquidation in 1871 and then changed hands several times as different mining companies tried to make a go of it. Local people's jobs were at the mercy of market forces way beyond their control. And yet that is not the whole story, for throughout the history of mining in Ceredigion there are stories of individual initiative and hints of a way of life in the close-knit mining communities that suggest other ways of considering the meaning of work in the context of community.

The enveloping ambience of Welsh Nonconformism meant that people were expected to be sober, thrifty and industrious. An individual had a duty to develop his or her talents to the full, rather than burying them uselessly in the ground. So there were always some mining families who interpreted these injunctions literally. They were the men who preferred to avoid whatever paid shift work was on offer, and instead became 'tributors'. A pitch, or the whole of a small mine, would be contracted out to a local work gang of buddies, who would use their own ingenuity to extract and raise the ore, for which they would be paid £4-£6 a ton. Resourceful hardworking women too could earn according to their will to work. In the Esgair y Mwyn workings in the 1750s one Jane Evans was paid 5/6 the ton for washing ore, and Jane Thomas got £3 the ton for picking lead ore from the waste heaps. But such initiatives brought high risk, and workers striking out on their own often ended worse off. They did not have the capital to exploit even the smallest mines and they were equally at the mercy of outside forces. After the Napoleonic Wars, for example, from about 1815-1830, the price of lead ore tumbled and the tributors were offered only £3 the ton, half of what they had been given when demand was artificially high as a result of the war.

Yet the Cwmrheidol miners were sustained in good times and in bad by their religious beliefs and by the spirit of community which grew up around the early Methodist congregations. Methodism first came to Cwmrheidol through the enthusiasm of an overseer in Rhiwrugos Mine (later part of the Rheidol United, but at that time in the mid-eighteenth century owned by Champion's of Liverpool). The early prayer meetings were held in farmhouses in the valley, and endured a good deal of derision and persecution from rough fellows in the locality. On one occasion the Methodists were in the middle of a meeting in Dolfawr, when they were attacked viciously about the heads and backs with stout sticks, and one of their number was almost killed. The building of the first Calvinist Methodist Chapel in Aberffrwd led to much 'suffering for the Lord', since local persecutors pulled the work down overnight and tried to stop them bringing in building stone. It then proved extremely useful that there were miners in the valley, for

> As they were both masculine and in the spirit (which was to be perceived in their ability to split the stones), their persecutors were afraid and no longer persisted in their opposition.[5]

There is an account of the community spirit generated by Methodism in eighteenth-century Cwmrheidol which throws a very different light on the farming and mining families from the gloomy material facts in the histories and Royal Commission evidence. In the *Coffadwriaeth David Jones*[6] is described the spiritual zeal of the people, so that, in spite of persecution, 'brotherly love and the gospel filled the breasts of the brothers'. On Sundays they crossed the hills to Llangeitho to hear the inspired preaching of Daniel Rowland, one of the great founding fathers of Welsh Methodism. They would set out at dawn and return late in the day, singing hymns and praising the Lord to shorten the long miles of the return journey, 'the world and its things far from their minds'.

While Absalom Francis, the Cornish entrepreneur, looked on Cwmrheidol as ripe for economic exploitation if only he could hit on the right combination of good management, secure tenure of leases and effective technology, the Members of the Methodist community who were born and brought up there looked upon it as their own place, the source of their sense of identity which grew out of interlocking influences of family, work mates and religion. There was, after all, in the early nineteenth century, enough local talent for the Messiah to be performed in Ystumtuen Chapel, though now you would have to go into Aberystwyth to hear it live. And John Morgan, a worker in the Bwa Drain Mine, was a respected figure among the local Methodists because of his role as Methodist circuit steward, Sunday School teacher, exhorter, and because of 'the beauty and usefulness of his Christian life'. It did not matter that he was, as outsiders might see it, 'only a lead miner'.

When the first purpose-built Wesleyan Chapel went up in 1822 in Ystumtuen (which served upper Cwmrheidol till the Bethel was built in 1872 down in the valley), it was entirely the result of community effort. Lewis Williams of Penrhiw gave the land, and local masons and carpenters gave their services free. The outsider who came to conduct the opening service at first saw only the poverty-stricken material circumstances of the mining area, and was shocked that a big new chapel should be wasted on such a poor-looking isolated district. But when he met the congregation, he came to realise that

> The Sabbath at Ystumtuen was a high day; whole families coming together brought with them their food, and devoted the whole of their day to the service of God. Winter and summer, many came two, three and four miles to the early morning prayer-meeting, and the Sabbath was a day of gladness and great grace. [7]

The very isolation of the area became an incentive to develop their own resources. Because it was so hard to get visiting preachers, they became famous in Methodist circles for producing their own. The Reverends Isaac Jenkins, Ebenezer Morgan, Isaac Jones and William Morgan were all well-known figures in the middle of the century. When later it came to expanding and building Bethel in upper Cwmrheidol, a local man, John Benjamin took the initiatives necessary. A Victorian historian of Methodism in Wales was moved to remark that 'there is no locality in Wales, thinly populated, isolated, and labouring amid many disadvantages, which has been more productive in good works than has Ystumtuen'. [8]

Learning and literacy among the lead miners

By 1850, when the mining boom was at its height, there were scores of Welsh-language magazines pouring from the presses bi-weekly, monthly and quarterly. They were imbued with the Nonconformist spirit and aimed at popular readership. But where was the audience for all this reading material in the days before state schools were universally introduced in the 1870? The famous circulating schools of Griffith Jones

89

of Llanddowror (1683-1761) saw to it that people of all ages were taught to read in their own language, so that they could read the Scriptures. The movement was part of the Great Awakening of the 1730s onwards which brought Welsh Methodism to birth. Thomas Charles of Bala revived many of the Griffith Jones strategies between 1788 and 1846 with his Sunday Schools movement for people of all ages to become literate Christians.

The aim of these early movements was to bring the people nearer to God rather than to impart secular information, but the strategies were from an educational viewpoint very sound. People of all ages were helped towards literacy, their schooling was fitted in to the rest of their lives so as not to interfere with their getting a living, and the whole was given an ethical base. The language of their own culture was used rather than English which was the medium of the 1870s schools. In Thomas Charles' schools the people learned to read the Welsh Bible in six months on average. English, he considered, was connected only with temporal concerns, and they could take two or three years just to learn 'dry terms' without receiving one idea for their improvement. He sadly observed, too, that as the majority of children died young, 'the things pertaining to their eternal felicity are of infinitely greater importance to them than the little concerns that belong to our short existence' here on earth.

The Sunday Schools in this indigenous cultural tradition even wrung respect from the notoriously critical Education Commissioners of the 1847 Blue Books:

It is impossible not to admire the vast number of schools which have been established . . . and the striking and permanent effect they have produced on society.[9]

These were the schools where the lead mining communities won an element of literacy—if they won it at all, for there are indications that many of them signed their names with a cross (in baptismal and wedding registers in the chapels), though that only indicates that they could not write, but they might still be able to read, for reading the Scriptures was the educational priority. The practice in the Sunday Schools was to read and memorise Scriptural passages, and they were questioned on these the following Sunday. There was singing as well, and in some of these schools, the Commissioners acknowledge, 'the vocal music is exceedingly well taught and practised'. Both children and adults often got their only chance of learning from these schools, for few families could afford the time or the pennies to give each of many children more than a term or so of 'book learning' at a day school, even if there was one within walking distance. Children were expected to work like everybody else. They did ore dressing at the lead mines from the age of ten or eleven, or looked after the younger children, or milked the cow and fed the chickens and collected the eggs and fetched the water.

In the heyday of mining in the mid century mining companies set up their own schools at the bigger mines, like Goginan and Ysbyty Ystwyth, just to the north and south of Cwmrheidol, though there was no mine school in the valley itself. Messrs Taylors' Mining Company set up the Goginan school for their employees' children and for others in the district, at the cost of one penny a week. The teacher there at one time was Owen Owen, a Baptist minister who later opened his own school at Taliesin. He observed that although there was a desire for education among the poor mining families, their hopeless poverty made it impossible to get. But he was impressed nonetheless by their Scriptural knowledge and their ability to quote verses from memory, although 'the poor are very ignorant of secular knowledge, and of history and the elements of geography and stronomy they know nothing'. While he was teacher at Goginan he preached as well and concerned himself with the moral as well as mental improvement of the mining families. He seems to have been one of the more balanced persons to give evidence to the Education Commissioners:

As to Scripture knowledge the people are better informed in Wales than in some parts of England ... The morals of the people are improving. It is common still for women to be in the family way before their marriage, but ... this intercourse is only with the man to whom they are attached, and a common woman would be scouted in any of the villages.

By contrast, the Royal Commission's Inspector who visited the school at Goginan spent his time on strangely desiccated and arid questioning:

Who were the apostles?—Dead silence; nobody knew. What were they to do?—Same result. Who appointed them?—Christ. How many were there? —Long pause. First boy.—Two, Sir. Another boy.—Twelve, Sir. Who was the apostle who wrote the greatest number of the Epistles?—Nobody could tell. A penny was here promised to the first who could tell who it was . . .

Will Christ come again? First boy—No. Second boy—Yes. What will he come for?—To burn the world. The mission of the prophets was explained by one girl only; and they were said by another to be Moses and John; and this was corrected by a sharp boy, who said they told of John he thought, but what John he did not know . . .

Judea was in this country; Scotland joined Wales; Ireland was a town and one thought it was a country; France a Parish . . .

The children had not, in any case, been taught geography, it emerged later in the Inspector's report. Nor did the inspector see fit to question the children of the miners about the practical skills they learnt in their everyday lives, from parents and mentors in the community.

The miners may have been in formal terms uneducated, but they possessed above average skills in measuring and assessment when it came to driving levels, or carrying out blasting operations, or hauling ore to the surface. The mines could be dangerous places without the cooperation of work mates and the skills and judgment that come of practical experience and everyday problem solving. They were not afraid to acknowledge the value of intuitive knowledge, either, which no doubt the Education Inspectors would have dismissed as rank superstition if they had been told about, say, 'the Knockers', who made a hammering noise underground to lead the men to good veins of ore. Whatever the rational explanation—perhaps the movement of underground streams through fissures in the levels—the intuitions of experienced miners were essential in locating and following up ore-bearing lodes, and even the great Royal Surveyer of Mines, Lewis Morris, did not scorn the kindly guidance of 'the Knockers', who he said had been particularly helpful to him in opening up the profitable Esgair y Mwyn mine.

The decline of the Cwmrheidol lead mines

The problem had always been in Cwmrheidol that the cost of getting the ore out was too high. There were lots of promising veins of ore, but it was difficult to hit on the right combination of imaginative managers, capital investment and effective technology. In order to attract the necessary capital to keep the mines operating, the mining companies naturally exaggerated the profitability of their concerns, so it is hard to get at the stark financial truths. While, for example, the Companies were assuring readers of the *Mining Journal* (1848) that the area was one of the best mining districts in the United Kingdom, and success was certain if investment money was forthcoming, a local miner wrote in revealing that £6,000 had been sunk in the Rheidol Mine since 1830, and there was no hope of recovering the money. Such miscalculations helped to keep wages depressed and jobs unstable.

A survey of the rises and falls in the fortunes of the Rheidol United Mining Company is enough to illustrate the endemic problems. The company was launched in 1841 by raising (with difficulty) a working capital of £2,500 in £25 shares on the financial markets. Work began at the Rhiwrugos and Nantglas mines (on the south side of the river a little way past the Power Station, you can see the old workings and the foundations of the ore-dressing floors, at the bottom of the Nant Rhiwrugos ravine). These had been worked intermittently by local farmers, bringing in a bit of profit from time to time. Now they were merged with the Llywernog Lead and Silver Mines near Ponterwyd (the present Mining Museum), but the manager J. H. Shears had no success, and got rid of the Cwmrheidol sections to Abel Gower, an experienced man who had worked the mines on the Nanteos Estate. He failed as a result of market forces, which drove the price of lead ore down in the late forties. A new company was launched in 1853, the Rheidol United Mines Company. They acquired the adjoining mines of Allt Ddu, Gwaithgoch and Llwybrllwynog (known as the Fox's Path) from the

93

Nanteos Estate, and employed Captain Grieves to survey the prospects and put the mines on a profitable basis. There were indeed returns of ore in the official statistics for 1853, 1854 and 1855, and reports of promising lodes being opened up, yielding a ton to every fathom. Optimism recurs in all the surveys from then till the company went into liquidation in 1871, and the leases, plant and machinery all went up for auction. But then surveys were usually occasioned by the need to sell more shares and raise more money. By the end of the 1860s the best that could be said was that 'the Rheidol United have been selling blende and ore enough to pay costs'.

Even at this point, a low ebb in the history of the mines, the Cornish mining expert Absalom Francis carried out a new optimistic survey (to ensure a sale following the bankruptcy of 1871).[10] The new company, the Silver Hill Consols Mining Company, advertised itself as having a profit potential here of £2,000 of ore a month, which would leave a clear profit over costs of £700 for the lucky speculators. In fact developments were on a much more modest scale, with an energetic Captain Ridge driving new levels at the Foxpath and Pantmawr workings. They did not produce enough ore to pay for the costs of driving shafts and pumping and extracting. By 1877 they once again gave up working underground because the returns of ore were tailing off so badly and conditions were increasingly difficult due to flooding.

When the leases came up for renewal in the early 1880s, a Mr Powys, whose main mining interests were in Devon, took over the Rheidol United, but after some years of trial and error he too failed to make any profit, lost the capital he had sunk in it, and gave up. It was always a case of having to sink a further fifty fathoms of shaft in the hope of striking a richer vein of ore, but the cost of doing so somehow was never repaid. By 1890 Mr Powys' company owed back pay to the workers, rent to the Nanteos estate, and had lost another £1,400 extending the Gwaithgoch levels without return. He left the area for greener fields.

Lead prices were falling steadily from the 1870s, as a result of cheap imports, and this brought the era of the lead miners to an end. Rural depopulation followed, as work tailed off and people left for the south, where there was plenty of work in the coal mines, or for Colorado, Idaho and Montana, where new mines were opening up at the turn of the century. The 'Cardis', one old miner remembered, had a monopoly as '*sincwyr*', the men who sank new pits, in places like the Rhondda, for they had had so much practice in their own lead mines. The few who stayed behind struggled to make a subsistence living, with a bit of work on the roads, a bit of labouring on building or farm, and using their own acre plots for home produce. But '*ar y cyfan gwael iawn oedd eu rhan*', 'on the whole their lot was a miserable one'.[11]

There were spasmodic attempts to start new mine ventures this century. A London entrepreneur called Hodgkinson-Carrington put together in the 1930s an ambitious scheme for a vast consortium of all the mines in Cwmrheidol, which would lead to a huge hydro-electric smelting works and sheet rolling mills on the site of the Gwaithgoch dressing floors. The aims were to produce 100 tons of lead sheet and 100 tons of zinc sheet per week, plus 50 tons of zinc sulphide. The cost was estimated to be working capital of £160,000 initially, and the profits were guesstimated to be £290,000 per annum. But Consolidated Gold Fields, from whom it was hoped to get the necessary startup capital, were not convinced. The great scheme came to nothing and the mine machinery was sold off around 1933.[12]

Caegynon and Cwmrheidol mines were the last ones to give any work, in local memory. The fathers of several valley families worked in Caegynon in the late 1930s, and Captain Greenall lived in Hafod y Glyn during the time he was running the mine. But the last of the mining captains to carve an undying image in local memories was undoubtedly Joseph Dandrick of the Cwmrheidol Mine at the head of the Valley. This mine had continued to work on and off at the beginning of the century. There were dressing floors to process the ores from the Ystumtuen lodes (via Tynyfron levels and a tramway slanting half a mile down to the Cwmrheidol Mine) and from Alderson's level high up on the Cwmrheidol Mine complex. And when the narrow gauge Rheidol Line opened in 1902, the dressed ore was conveyed across the river and up to Rhiwfron Station on an aerial ropeway. Ironically the railway came too late, for the

95

mining industry was in serious decline. But that did not deter the imaginative Captain Dandrick, who arrived in 1930s, a Polish Jew fleeing from fascist anti-semitism.

His schemes for resurrecting the Cwmrheidol Mines were alas in the continuing tradition. 'Dandrick didn't get a shovelfull of lead out of the mine, but he had a company going to make a big splash. He had three or four new lorries, and took on boys back from the war. They moved a bit of ore about whenever it was needed to impress the investers. They would come down on occasional trips in their big cars—they didn't have a clue about what was going on, which was not a lot . . . Still Dandrick did give jobs to locals. He even built a canteen on the mine and did a lot of repairing. Price the postman used to time his daily trips (on bike) to end up there for dinner every day . . . Dandrick had plenty of schemes, though none of them came to much in the end. He was going to sell yellow ochre extracted from the mine, for using in paint manu-facture . . .'

But the prospectors from Canada who installed drilling machinery to take ochrous samples from the mine soon got into trouble for allowing poisonous effluent into the River Rheidol, with disastrous effects on the fish population (the river is a favourite with the Aberystwyth Anglers' Association). The last scheme was short-lived, a brief flurry of activity in 1969, and Dandrick died a few years later. Since then, with every passing winter, gales obliterate a little bit more of the mine buildings, and the usable materials—of slate and roof timbers—disappear in the twinkling of an eye after every gale. There is a long tradition in rural parts of waste not-want not, and what good are old ruins to anyone?

The last say about lead mining in mid Wales should go to one of the local miners. Dan Jones of Goginan, before he died in the 1950s, put down his memories and thoughts in *Atgofion llafurwr i ieuenctid Cymru*,[13] which he printed himself on a hand press and struggled to complete during failing health. And unexpectedly it turns out that here is a Cardi miner who is a Marxist, and his analysis of worker exploitation pulls no punches. He asks, Where did the profits go? The cream went to the capitalist and the skim milk to the workers. The life of a miner was held cheaper than machinery in the old days, and there was no concern about the safety of working conditions. The smoke and dust from the previous shift hung about the levels to choke the next shift, and all they could do was shake their coats to try and dispel it. When the drilling machines first came in there was so much dust that the men could not see each other, and could not help breathing it in till they were choking and caught often fatal chest diseases. Afterwards they improved the drills and used pressure water jets to keep down the dust. But on the whole the capitalists did not care what the working conditions were like in the mines or about the workers' standard of living. They were conveniently blind to the:

lack of fresh air, working in the smoke, getting soaked through crossing the hills to work, and walking home in wet clothes, and the mothers' struggling endlessly to dry their men's clothes, or have them beginning to dry out by the next morning.

The wages were so low that the miners lived in perpetual poverty-stricken conditions, no matter how careful they were at managing and growing their own vegetables and having their own hens. In the 1880s a miner got fourteen shillings a week, and by 1914 three shillings and fourpence a day. At the turn of the century Dan Jones was taken on as a surface worker at Level Fawr in Cwmrheidol, when he was fourteen years old, and he got one shilling a day. He and other boys set out to walk over the hills from Goginan into Cwmrheidol every Monday morning before 4 a.m., with a loaf of bread and a pack of food for the working week on their backs. They had lodgings from Monday to Saturday afternoon, which cost them one shilling and threepence (potatoes and soap were included in the price). It was, says Dan Jones 'no heaven for the landladies either', at that price, but nobody could afford more.

The masters were often religious leaders in the Chapel, but for an ordinary miner the preacher's talk of a paradise after death was no comfort to men who 'at that time were in a little hell of our own as workers from morning to night, from cradle to grave'. In the Sunday School, he says, 'we heard about Jonah in the belly of the whale, and

97

Daniel in the lions' den, and the old teacher would remind us that half a loaf is better than no bread, and that up above would our Paradise begin'. But the kingdom of heaven was always up in the clouds and the ministers were not interested in working for it on this earth. Indeed they squeezed the poor miners more by demanding money for church funds, yet they would not support the workers when they tried to set up trade unions—'The Methodists threw out the members who dared join a union'.

Religion and superstition, Dan Jones concludes, are twin evils in the way of improving the working man's lot in life. Both stand between him and the use of his reason, preventing him from thinking for himself. This puts a weapon in the hands of the capitalist which they do not hesitate to use in every part of their far-flung empires, to keep the poor in low-paid work slavery. And his peroration is Marx's ringing call to the workers, given in resounding Welsh: '*Gweithwyr y byd, ymunwch, does gennych ddim i'w golli ond eich cadwynau, a byd i'w ennill*', 'Workers of the world unite, you have nothing to lose but your chains, and a world to win'.

But even the poorest workers have their own ways of surviving and getting their own back on the employers, so it is fitting to pass on one or two anecdotes which Dan Jones tells of the strategies used by the local lead miners. When his grandfather John Morris Jones was cheated by an old mining captain (who took advantage of his discovery of lead ore to take a lease on the land and work the discovery himself) the miner got his own back in an appropriate way. He spread the news in the pub that he had made another discovery, and he scattered a few hunks of lead ore to lend credibility to his claims. The Captain fell for the temptation and wasted good time and effort having the rock opened up, and could not understand why there was nothing there but the few chunks of ore planted by John Morris.

But the trickery could rebound on the tricker. John Morris Jones was in turn tricked by the local doctor who gave him five sovereigns for revealing yet another rich vein of lead ore on the slopes of Plynlumon. The doctor sold it on for £2,000 to a mining company, while persuading

John Morris he was lucky to have even the five sovereigns, since the mine was far too high and remote to be exploited. In the event, John Morris later found himself short of a job and the only opportunity was this very same remote mine. So he ended up working for six shillings a week, taking out the lead he himself had discovered. *'Wel, peth mawr oedd bod yn sgoler yr adeg honno'*, 'a big thing it was to be an educated man like the doctor at that time', was John Morris's fatalistic conclusion.

[1] Samuel Lewis, *Topographical dictionary of Wales.* London, S. Lewis, 1833.

[2] Royal Commission on the condition of all the mines in Great Britain to which the provision of the Act 22 & 24 Vict. Cap 151 do not apply, *Report*, London, 1864.

[3] Lewis Morris, *An account of the lead and silver mines in the King's Manor of Perverth in the County of Cardigan*, 1744. (Ms in the National Library).

[4] D. E. Bick, *The old metal mines of mid Wales, Part 3, Cardiganshire*, Gloucester, Pound House, 1976, p. 70.

[5] David Jones, *Coffadwriaeth David Jones*, Aberystwyth, Jenkins, 1841.

[6] David Jones (as above).

[7] David Young, *History of Methodism in Wales*, London, Kelly, 1893, p. 345.

[8] David Young (as above), p. 347.

[9] Royal Commission on Education in Wales, *Report*, London, 1847. (Known as the infamous Blue Books).

[10] Absalom Francis, *History of the Cardiganshire mines*, 1874, Sheffield, Mining Facsimiles, 1987.

[11] Dan Jones, *Atgofion llafurwr i ieuenctid Cymru*, Goginan, [privately printed, c. 1950].

[12] R. J. Pritchard, *The Rheidol United Mines*, Sheffield, Northern Mine Research Society, 1985, p. 31.

[13] Dan Jones (as above).

Chapter 5

Womens' lives in rural Wales

A newcomer to rural Wales cannot help being aware of the strong division of interests between women and men, for at many meetings in country halls the women still sit on one side of the room and the men on the other. They talk in their own groups mainly about their own separate interests, though there are perfectly courteous greetings between the sexes at beginning and end. This situation, it is argued, does not arise from any sexist discrimination, but is a natural consequence of the strongly differentiated male and female roles—in the home, in farming and lead mining, and in the churches and chapels. It certainly makes it difficult to find out what women felt about their lives, because theirs has traditionally been the private sphere of hearth and home. They were not, and to some extent are still not expected to raise their voices in the 'male' arenas of religion and politics, nor to record their own versions of history for posterity. Images of women in the past are therefore massively reflected through men's eyes, as mothers, pious women and moral custodians of the family, helpmeets of their males, and, occasionally, lustful 'bad women' at the service of men's physical needs. It is rare to come across women's own voices reflecting on their lives, or to read history texts which give a women's perspective of a place or period. The first volume devoted to Welsh women's history only appeared in 1991, with the avowed aim of rescuing the submerged lives of women over the last two centuries, and redefining Wales as not merely 'the land of our fathers', but our mothers' land as well.[1] Yet Rosemary Jones makes the point that though women exercised little formal public or political power, 'they played a central role in structuring popular values at a neighbourhood level', through for example the *ceffyl pren*, the 'wooden horse', a ritual used in close-knit communities for shaming those who deviated from the sexual or marital norms. Gossip networks too enabled women to monitor unapproved behaviour, and was rarely 'idle', for it 'served to define the accepted boundaries between "respectable" and "deviant" conduct, and could exert a devastating influence over the personal and professional lives of its victims'.[2] This situation is changing fast, but has by no means died out completely in rural communities.

Because it is so rare to come across women's own voices reflecting on their lives, the first part of this chapter tries to imaginatively reconstruct what it was like for women in the past. In the present day women can speak for themselves, and their voices are heard in the second part, speaking of their everyday lives.

Women in the chapel culture

'Look you at God of the Bible', says a character in Caradog Evans' *My people*. 'He commanded and threatened and dictated. And is He not a Welshman? So we lift our voices to Him and tell Him what we want and what to withhold from our neighbours'. The women in *My people* suffer abominably. There is the poverty-stricken old woman who saved her pennies to give the preacher a Bible, and having died alone of hunger is gnawed by rats. There is the deranged wife and mother who is exiled to the hayloft, and exercised by her husband in the fields at night confined in a halter. Cruel satire, yes, but with a bitter kernel of truth. One reason why the women suffer so is because of their unlikeness to the Big Man, the divine image, and the patriarchal downgrading that results from being born a woman rather than a man, and therefore not directly in the image of God, in patriarchal interpretations of the Scriptures.

Methodism in Wales expected women to be as devout (or more devout, for they had greater moral influence on their families) than men, but permitted them no individual part in chapel meetings, where it was the men who did the praying and the preaching and the public leadership. The exception was during revivals, when role reversal meant that those who were normally silent (the humbler cottagers, the young and the female) became active and eloquent in prayer meetings, bearing witness and encouraging converts and travelling the countryside with

101

the leading evangelists. Relaxation of the usual patriarchal controls enabled women young and old to express themselves in public directly to God instead of through the medium of male ministers and prayer leaders. They were able to give voice to their spontaneous inspiration, without the usual inhibitions ('Is this the right thing to do?' 'Will people disapprove of me if I do this?'). In some chapels they held their own revival prayer meetings, but even in mixed meetings it was sometimes the young women who were the first to break out into praise and prayer.

Such behaviour was bound to attract criticism from the traditionalists in the chapel culture, who quoted Paul against women unwilling to be silent in church or subject to male leadership. They should keep to their proper feminine role in the chapels, which was tending to the teas and doing the washing up, and entertaining the ministers to Sunday dinner. A description of a Ceredigion community at the turn of the century says:

> Though women were the most numerous attenders at prayer meetings . . . the public work of reading, praying, contributing testimonies of one's experience, and addressing the meetings on relevant topics was exclusively the work of the men present. Apart from Sunday School work and 'young people's' activities the contribution of the women was virtually limited to reciting a few verses when asked to do so. Women who did become prominent were extremely few in number and were regarded as oddities. [3]

Yet many women were as well read in the Welsh Bible as their men. They are pictured sitting sewing or knitting in the cottage kitchens, with the Bible open on a little round table at their side, or teaching the children the words of their favourite hymns so that they could sing together in the family. But in farmhouse Sunday Schools the women took the younger children's classes while the men tackled the more abstruse discussions of difficult texts:

> We had one class of women in the parlour, presided over by my grandfather; another occupied one of the bedrooms. Young and old were there, from my great grandmother in my grandfather's class down to the young children of five or six who sat on the hob by my mother's side. [4]

102

The writer goes on to describe the roles of women and men in the chapel culture of the mid-nineteenth century. The father had the honoured position in the house, sitting at the head of the big kitchen table with the folio Bible open in front of him, discoursing with the 'grown-up men'. The mother's role is to welcome the visiting folks with 'her beaming face, kind words, and efforts to make everyone about her feel comfortable'. The ideal woman was gentle and mild, full of care and sympathy for one and all, her family and callers. She was above all the Mother who knew much suffering but enjoyed the true happiness of Christian riches, whatever her material poverty. 'Don't take offence, now', says a character in Daniel Owen's novel *Rhys Lewis*, 'but the fact is that whenever I heard that your mother was in trouble I would laugh and say, "Well, this is another feast for Mary Lewis".' She had the resources of her religion to fall back on, after all.

The problem was that these Christian riches of women were given no public outlet, so their stories are lost, or told through men's eyes. In *The old farmhouse* D. J. Williams is conscious of his mother's abiding religious sense, but equally aware of her inability to give it public expression. 'It is my belief that her life, every minute of it as it came, was one secret prayer', but, 'I never saw my mother do anything in public beyond questioning Sunday School occasionally when it was the turn of her class. She did it simply and suitably'. He concludes that his mother had all the attributes of a great character, but never had the chance to bring them to fruition.

The notable exception to women's hidden spirituality in Methodist rural Wales was Ann Griffiths (1776-1805), who lived the life of an ordinary woman in a farming family. When her mother died she took over as her father's helpmeet at Dolwar Fach, and later she married and became her husband's helpmeet, till she died in childbirth a year after their marriage. But as she went about her daily work in house and farmyard, Ann composed a collection of hymns which have since been recognised as some of the finest in Methodist hymnology, and are still sung today. Sometimes she dictated the words to her maid Ruth, and sometimes she scribbled them on scraps of paper, so that Ruth could fit

103

tunes to them in her spare time. Fortunately Ruth had the superb memory of a pre-literate oral culture, and after Ann's death she was able to recite them to the Methodist preacher John Hughes (whom she had married). They were thus accidentally preserved for posterity.

Ann Griffiths' story is in poignant contrast to her male counterpart, the great hymn writer Williams Pantycelyn. He was free to travel extensively, to arrange for the publication of three editions of his hymns during his own lifetime, and to leave detailed instructions about the continuing sale of his books when he died. In *her* lifetime Ann's only means of giving her hymns to an audience was to sing them around the house when there were visiting preachers present, who indeed listened and asked for them. Ann worked from morning to night around the farm, and, as a Religious Tract Society writer put it in the 1880s, 'her prayers accompanied the work of her hands; her hymns were often composed in the midst of her household tasks'. The writer duly acknowledged her talents in a Biblical metaphor: 'As the song of Moses was seconded by the song of Miriam, so the song of Williams Pantycelyn was seconded by a young prophetess of Christ, Ann Griffiths'; but remained oblivious to what many women today would see as the double burden that Ann Griffiths had to bear in a patriarchal society. Women could express their talents but only after they had fulfilled their traditional domestic roles adequately, and they need not expect public recognition even then, for a true woman always remained in the private domestic sphere.

In the case of Ann Griffiths, fortunately, we have some of her letters to spiritual friends, which shed a rather different light on women's ambitions and frustrations. It is clear that from time to time she longed for relief from woman's daily round, in order to develop the things of the spirit. 'I was willing to give all I possess, the good and the bad, for the Son, in a mystical marriage', she writes. And again:

Dear Sister,
    I am sometimes absorbed so far into these things that I completely fail to perform my duty with regard to temporal things ... although it is very

good here through a lattice, and the Lord sometimes reveals through a glass darkly as much of his glory as my weak faculties can bear.[5]

She experienced 'raptures' which when they came over her caused her to break out into joyful cries, but she had to take care to be in the privacy of her room when they happened, so as not to disturb the ordinary life of the farm. Her mystical experiences also occurred out of doors, in the inspiration of her mid Wales landscape, and led to the composition of lines like this:

> O happy hour of rest eternal
> From all the labours that I bore
> Steeped in a sea of glorious wonders
> Endless without bound or shore.

John Hughes assumed that one of her great joys was preparing meals for visiting preachers and knitting stockings for them, but her own words sometimes reveal an occasional clash between household demands and spiritual expression, though based as usual on biblical texts:

> Weary is my life, by foemen
> Thick assailed on every side
> How like bees they swarm around me
> From morning light to eventide—
> And some there are from my own household
> Leaders of the hellish troop . . .

She might just have agreed with the sentiments expressed in Menna Elfyn's recent poem '*Wnaiff y gwragedd aros ar ôl?*' (Will the women please stay behind?): 'Listen, little masters, if Christ came back today, He'd certainly be making his own tea'.[6]

Women's work in rural Wales

A woman who did not 'find solace easily, as women and girls usually do, in the work and warmth of the house and hearth', would seem to have some puzzling 'complication in her nature', says D.J. Williams in his great classic about his own farming family in mid Wales, *The old farmhouse*. He tells the story of Pegi, who, though 'light and feminine in her body', chose to put on clogs, take up mattock or billhook or hatchet and do 'men's work' around the farm. She was happiest cutting wood or hedging or fencing, with her long skirts tucked up around her waist out of the way, revealing her thick black stockings and brass buckle fastenings on her clogs. If Pegi stands at one end of the spectrum of women's responses to traditional female roles, then surely Margied stands at the other end, representing perfect acceptance in contrast to Pegi's perfect subversion:

> Margied could never get enough work to satisfy her, mending and knitting stockings for them all [8 children], and nothing pleased her more than to find a stocking with holes in it that would give her an opportunity of showing her skill in making it better than new. [7]

But this gentlest of women died of consumption while still young.

In contrast to women seen through men's eyes, Kate Roberts gives us an opportunity of seeing women's lives through a woman writer's eyes. One of her best-known novels is *Traed mewn cyffion, Feet in chains*, which tells the story of a marriage in the slate-quarrying, smallholding community near Caernarfon, which was Kate Roberts' own locality. It is made clear from the start that the wife Jane Griffiths is subject to her husband's wishes, and that social approval depends on her ability to perform the clear cut duties assigned to women. 'I don't think Ifan will like you going to Church' (rather than Chapel), says Jane's sister-in-law as she explains the community's expectations of a young bride. 'Ifan and I talked about that before we were married, and he doesn't mind where I go', replies Jane. 'Well,' retorts the sister-in-law, 'his father would have been surprised to hear Ifan say such a thing'. So if the younger generation of males show signs of violating community norms, some of the women themselves will invoke the older generation to persuade other women to conform.

Women's work lies exclusively in the domestic sphere, and it is up to the men in the novel to decide about religion and politics and other public sphere matters. But this is more complicated than a first reading of Kate Roberts' novel might indicate, for Kate Roberts is writing out of her own understanding of women's experiences in the slate villages, and shows that domestic rituals have their own sacramental quality, above and beyond the unending hard work they involve.

The week starts with washing day, and the new wife has to learn the right way of doing things, with the help of her sister-in-law:

> Jane was busy scouring the quarryman's clothes on an old table beside the spring. She was scrubbing the corduroy trousers after the first washing; the water squeezed out was thick and grey ... The working jacket was boiling on the fire in the house ... Taking the trousers from the table and rinsing them in a bucket of clean water from the spring, she carried them into the house. Placing the trousers in the big pan she pulled it to one side of the fire and put the kettle in its place. [8]

She makes tea and pancakes for herself and Geini, a symbol of friendly solidarity between the women, for throughout Kate Roberts' stories the making and serving of food has an emotional significance.

Jane's baking and cooking are offerings of love and support to her husband and children and sister-in-law Geini. A simple dinner of pickled herrings, new potatoes and oatmeal bread, with unstinted buttermilk to drink, is her offering to her son on leave from the army, before he has to go back to France (and death in the trenches). The boy too understands the meaning of food, for he says to his mother as a last farewell: 'If you ever have ten minutes to mix a cake, remember me'. When she hears that he has been killed, she continues her usual baking and cleaning and washing, but as if she were an automaton, for the meaning has gone. Her cooking now becomes a memorial ritual:

> She prepared the food as usual. She boiled a lamb's head with the liver and chopped it into small pieces in the broth. She pickled some herrings in August and they all had to admit that they enjoyed their food ...

But 'it was difficult to churn and the butter came out soft'. She also mourns for her dead son by frequently dusting his books in the best kitchen—another example of the emotional meanings of housework.

Slovenly housework on the part of Jane's daughter Sioned is the first sign the mother has that Sioned is in emotional trouble (her feckless townee husband has run away with another woman). Sioned's house is not exactly dirty, but not sparkling clean either. The air of neglect and untidiness around the house and on the little boy are signs of emotional apathy and a failure to go on caring. When all is well with a home, instinctive beings can always tell, whether male or female.

When the child Owen is waiting anxiously to hear whether he has won a scholarship to the grammar school, he takes comfort from the orderly house and home baking which demonstrate his mother's caring attentions:

> The tea was good, especially the bilberry tart. The house, too, was pleasant, the oak furniture shining, the loaves of bread set on the floor to cool, the traces of the smell of baking still lingering in the air.

It works the other way round as well. Lack of appreciation of the mother's meals are used as a sign of waywardness and rebellion. Sioned turns up her nose at the family breakfast of home-made bread and butter, muttering, 'An old place like this, cut off from the world, way behind the times, eating the same thing day after day'. Since the family do not express their feelings openly, but through the medium of food, most often, the mother chides Sioned's independence with: 'Perhaps you'll be glad to eat at this table one day.'

Food is used to soften the breaking of bad news. When the wayward (or independent?) daughter Sioned is abandoned by her husband, the mother goes home and lights the fire and fries a big plate of bacon and eggs for her husband. She leaves him to eat in peace and quiet, suppressing her own distress, before telling him the bad news. When he goes completely inert in inarticulate misery, she gently draws him out and helps him talk it through. They sit there as the sun goes down and the kitchen grows dark, and she succeeds in getting him to face up to the blow and accept her practical suggestions for bringing the child out to the farm to live with them. Although her words are heavy with fatalism: 'We'd better go to bed and wait to see what tomorrow will bring,' she is in fact the realist and decision-maker in this as in the rest of the family's emotional upheavals. The husband can cope with the terrible physical hardships of slate quarrying, but not with the psychological worries over the growing up children. He gladly leaves such things to her.

A similar situation arises over the sick and the dying. It is the women who have to combine their emotional expressiveness with an earthy practicality which upsets the cliché about women's emotions unfitting them for practical decision making. They are expected to nurse the sick, to comfort the dying, and at the same time do all the extra housework involved in offering hospitality to calling neighbours, and find some space for their own sorrow as well. Geini and Ifan, sister and brother, behave in very different ways at their mother's deathbed:

> Ifan would come there and sit by the kitchen fire, lost in thought. Now and again he would go into the bedroom, glance at his mother, and that was all.

Geini, on the other hand,

> had to prepare food for them all, there was more work to be done looking after them than tending their mother, and not one of them offered to help wash the bedclothes . . .

For the women there is no escape into contemplation when the great events of life and death are taking place. They are actively engaged, and, clearly, if they escape the diversion into fussy practicalities that bedevil some domesticated women, they can achieve an impressive wholeness which unifies physical, emotional and spiritual aspects of their humanity. Jane Griffiths and to a lesser extent Geini are notable examples of this wholeness.

Women's consciousness of politics in *Traed mewn cyffion* is worth considering in some detail, for again a first reading might suggest that the women leave politics to the men and stay in their cosy domestic sphere, but a second reading suggests a more complex understanding both of politics and of women's role in it. As Owen is growing up he discovers the delightful companionship of a male peer group, and is growing away from his mother's influence:

109

This was the best companionship that Owen had ever known. There was a kind of tacit understanding among them. Nobody discussed it, but it was there . . . [They discussed worldly matters] from South African War to the Disestablishment of the Church. United as they were—males in groups— this naturally involved looking down on other groups, especially females.

Another of the sons joins with his fellow workers in the slate quarry to set up a branch of the Independent Labour Party. They read socialist tracts in English and struggle to understand their local situation in terms of theoretical capital and labour conflict. But there is no overt political talk in the home, for it is seen as a thing between men, and it is women's role to go on nurturing their sons, no matter what one-sided intellectual nonsense their heads are stuffed with, as a result of alien influences.

The only time that the mother gives vent to her political consciousness is when a government official visits the farm to see whether she is entitled to a pension as the mother of an apprentice teacher killed in the war. Suddenly a dam bursts within her and out pours her rage at the war, at God, at the injustice in the world. She grabs a clothes brush and beats the official round the head till he flees. Her dear son has been killed, while 'something like you is allowed to live', she cries out in protest against the whole political establishment that ignores the personal consequences of official interventions and political decisions.

So here we have an instance of how women's consciousness of politics does not divorce the public and the private, the rational and the emotional. Jane considers the impact of political decisions on her home and family, and universalises from her own experiences to intuit wider injustices. The personal is indeed political, and the political is personal, as the much later feminist movement more emphatically asserted in the 1970s. The quarrymen sons by contrast engage in formal discussions based on socialist theories, and have a hard time persuading the chapel deacons and their older co-workers that these have any relevance to their own work situation. The male and female approaches never manage to converge in the novel to reach a higher synthesis, because that would subvert the traditional male and female roles. It is the same with economics. For the women economics is personal and practical. When times are hard the mother tries to rear more pigs, for the women were the family money managers, and it was the pigs that paid the loan on the house and the rates. She finds that the cost of pig meal and her own extra labour mean she is hardly any better off. While her socialist son talks with his mates about the social injustice of working in the slate quarries for only three or four pounds a month, the mother manages the practical effects of these miserable wages on her family, even if she does not understand the cause, for women are not brought into conversations about this kind of politics, or invited to join the Independent Labour Group.

She never saved on food, however poor they were, for we have seen how the family meals had a sacramental significance in keeping the family together. Instead she would cut down on clothes, by altering and passing on clothes from one child to another. She would never buy herself anything new, except when she had to, in order to be a credit to her children at a public event like a school prize-giving. She made their underclothes herself, darned their stockings, scraped and saved to see them off on a good start in life, even though it cut her to the heart to see them leaving home. Her sense of economics was as personal as her sense of politics—but both were a significant part of her consciousness, and point to the incompleteness of a politics or an economics that limits itself to abstract reasoning or public action, while ignoring personal responses and domestic action.

Women at the hearth

It could be argued that the invention of the cooking pot was rather more significant than the invention of the wheel, but kitchen things tend to get less attention in patriarchal anthropology than hunting and warrior gear. For women through the ages, however, the hearth fire and the cooking pot have been the means of sustaining their families in fat times and lean. If the men manage to bring home a deer occasionally from their hunting trips, well, venison stew is great, but success on hunting trips is intermittent and unpredictable, so country women have always had their own sources of food to rely on. In traditional societies

111

men might be the farmers (though women often were. and still are in most of the developing countries), but women grew the vegetables and medicinal herbs to keep the family in everyday health. While the men went hunting, the women and children also went gathering nuts and berries and wild mushrooms or whatever else their locality provided. In novels set in rural Wales there is a considerable amount of bilberry picking, blackberry gathering, the getting of mushrooms from unploughed pastures, and hazel nuts from the high hedgerows. Such activities continue in the countryside today, but more as a family outing (or rather a women and children outing) than a necessary element in the daily diet. Traditionally, too, women have the care of the poultry and dairying, and so keep a daily supply of eggs and milk and cheese coming into the house.

In rural Wales in the last century the farmhouse kitchen formed the heart of the house, where the family cooked and ate and worked and took their leisure, and often slept, too, in box beds along the back wall. The well-provided kitchen of D.J. Williams' family is described in *The old farmhouse*:

> The kitchen was large and the heavy oak beams under the cross rafters were low. To these hung an abundance of the usual farmhouse commodities, hams and thick sides of bacon, a few pieces of beef salted black, nets of shallots and ropes of French onions, baskets of varying sizes and shapes, a couple of pigs' bladders full of lard, and 2 guns . . . and not often was the ceiling seen without some game, long-eared or feathered, hanging from it. Usually these were sold to the local carrier . . . But fairly often a leg or a wing could be seen boiling up heartily to the surface of the fat-spangled broth beside a piece of bacon or ham or beef.[9]

The cookery of the Welsh countryside comes straight out of the everyday lives of the smallholding families, rather than being a watered-down version of what went on in the kitchens of the gentry, who were striving for a touch of London elegance or spa town cuisine. It was therefore slow to change over the centuries. In the Laws of Hywel Dda (tenth century) the two commonly used vegetables are named as cabbages and leeks. In 1188 Giraldus Cambrensis noted in his journey

112

round Wales that 'almost all the population lives on its flocks and on oats, milk, cheese and butter'. In the 1920s Mattie Thomas collected old recipies in common use in the early nineteenth century and says that every girl was taught by her mother to make oatmeal bread, various thicknesses of oatmeal porridge, and oatmeal dumplings which were used towards the end of spring as a substitute for scarce potatoes, in the *cawl*, the universal broth. Here is the recipe she gives for everyday *cawl*, made in the old way in a cauldron over the open fire in the inglenook:

> Put four gallons of water in a three legged cauldron and bring it to the boil. Put in a large piece of salted bacon or beef. Boil for an hour and a half. Lift out the meat and place on a large wooden dish. Put in the vegetables and herbs (peeled potatoes, cabbage, swedes, parsnips, carrots, leeks, parsley and savory). Mix 2 tablespoons of oatmeal to a paste with cold water and add. When well-cooked remove from the fire. Fill a bowl with cawl for each person, each then helping themselves to meat from the wooden dish on the table.[10]

There was another version of *cawl* for the poverty-stricken who had neither meat nor vegetables left in the house. This was *cawl llaeth* or milk broth, made by boiling up skim milk with oatmeal and salt, and served in wooden bowls with bits of barley bread broken into it and stirred. Another alternative for the poor was *cawl pen dafad*, sheep's head broth. Parsley and leeks were usually grown in the gardens of even the poorest houses, so these were used to add flavour, and oatmeal dumplings or potatoes provided the carbohydrates. At various beneficient times of the year the basic *cawl* was enriched with the addition of game. Wood-pigeons who flew in to feed on the green shoots of growing crops in the spring might end up in the pot, if they were unlucky. The height of luxury was considered to be *cawl coch ysgyfarnog*, hare broth, to which were added turnips, leeks and parsley, and potatoes or dumplings during the last stage of boiling.

The three-legged black iron cauldron used for boiling the *cawl* continued in use into the early twentieth century, though modified forms emerged in order to adapt to the closed castiron ranges that replaced the open inglenook fire with its pot crane for suspending pots at the right height over the heat for slow simmering or fast boiling. The Romans are said to have introduced the three-legged cauldron which remained the standard cooking pot for about seventeen hundred years, but that attribution is questionable. The cauldron is likely to go back much further than Roman times, for it is a symbol for rebirth in pagan Celtic mythology, and decorated bronze cauldrons have been found as part of the burial treasures of Celtic princes and princesses. The cauldron shape lived on in the mass manufactured soup pots of the early twentieth century, shiny black on the outside and with blue enamel linings, still with a semi-circular handle over the top, more suited to the open fire than the modern stove, where a side handle is more convenient. Examples of the old three-legged cauldrons can still be seen now in gardens, where they are much prized as plant pots for showing off geraniums. Indeed garden centres now supply black polythene reproduction cauldrons, the final death throes of a cooking tradition that goes back into prehistory.

The habit of cooking by the boiling method was the norm on an open fire—even the Michaelmas goose was often boiled rather than roasted. But bakestone cooking was also vital, for flatbreads and pancakes and 'Welsh cakes'. The *llithfaen*, baking stone or griddle, was originally an actual stone slab heated up on the fire till it retained enough heat to cook various thinbreads (like oatcakes). This method is of great antiquity, for in prehistoric Ireland they even heated water by putting hot stones into it, rather than putting the water over the heat. Stone cooking slabs retained heat long enough to cook bread and cakes without them getting scorched and blackened from being directly over the fire. But as the bakestone gave way to the iron griddle suspended over the fire by a semi-circular handle, the art of fire management became more important. The experienced cook could make accurate judgments on what effect the wind direction would have on the fire, and what was the best kind of fuel to use. Bunches of gorse were collected to give a bright hot flame, and for a slow sustained heat turves of peat from the moors were banked up on the fire.

Oatmeal bread was everyday fare in country dwellings, and was the

114

standard fare baked on the griddle. It would keep for six months if stored in a good dry place. A soft dough was made by stirring skim milk into oatmeal, and adding a pinch of salt. It was rolled out very thin into large circular pieces which were often divided into quarters and cooked on the griddle. Modern mass-produced oatcakes are often still made in triangular shape, though the functional reason of fitting them onto a round griddle is no longer relevant.

The variety of griddle cakes increased as the nineteenth century wore on and more country people bought refined flour and raising agents, cheaper sugar and imported raisins, from the grocer's. The traditional *pice maen*, Welsh cakes, eaten in all parts of Wales as a teatime treat, are still popular. Here is one Ceredigion recipe for them:

Mix together a pound of flour, a pinch of salt and a teaspoon of baking powder. Rub in 6 ounces of butter or margarine, then add 6 ounces of raisins (or raisings and currants), and 4 ounces of sugar. Stir in a beaten egg and a little milk, fresh or sour, until you have a firm dough. Roll out on a floured board to about half an inch thickness. Cut into circles with a floured drinking glass about three inches across. Cook on a lightly greased griddle (or thick iron fry pan) for about five minutes on each side.

They can be eaten hot or cold, plain as they are, or spread with butter or jam or honey. A sprinkling of cinnamon is often added to the mixture or sprinkled on the cakes after cooking.

Nothing was thrown out in cottages where the inhabitants were familiar with scarcity at some time in their lives. A favourite supper dish was toasted cheese on oat or barley bread. Stale cheese could be used up in this way, so it was economical. Once the big home-made circular cheeses (wrapped in muslin and stored in the loft) were cut into, the triangular wedges were kept in those flowery cheese dishes of the same triangular shape (now mainly seen in antique shops). After about a week the cheese would dull and harden, so it had to be toasted or fried to revive it.

Until the separate brick baking oven became popular in the second half of the nineteenth century, bread and cakes were baked in the iron

115

cooking pot over the fire too. The woman of the house built up a slow burning peat fire and piled up peat turves on the lid of the pot also, to give an allround even heat. Mattie Thomas gives a traditional recipe for brown bread cooked in this way:

> Place 5 pounds of wheat meal in a large bowl and put a tablespoon of brewer's barm in the middle. Wet with lukewarm water till a flexible dough consistency. Knead well and allow to rise in the warmth of the fire. When risen, heat the cooking pot and grease with pig lard . . . Put the loaf in the pot, put on the lid and bake for two hours over a peat or fern fire which is red hot, with fire on the lid as well as round the pot.[11]

Cakes could be cooked in the same way, and included *bara sinsir*, gingerbread, *bara brith*, a spicy fruit loaf like the Irish 'brack', and rich fruit cakes for Christmas. When the separate oven came into the farmhouse kitchen, it was built into one side of the inglenook, and could either be heated up by its own fire lit underneath, or by lighting a fire in the oven itself till the right temperature was achieved, and then raking out the ashes before putting in the bread or cakes. It still demanded great skill and judgment to get the right level of sustainable heat to ensure the bread or cakes would rise properly and be evenly cooked through to the centre.

Milk puddings were common, for every smallholding had its own cow and there was plenty of milk for most of the year. One test of a growing girl's cookery skills was her ability to make *sucan*, a pudding made of oatmeal and sugar and milk, which now seems to have disappeared from the recipe books. It had to be just the right consistency to thicken and set properly, without lump or blemish. If the smooth surface showed any sign of wrinkling, it was said the girl would marry a boy with an ugly face.

Crempogau, pancakes, are a treat not confined to Wales, but shared with Brittany, Scotland and Ireland. They are easily made of simple ingredients always available in the country:

> Put half a pound of flour and half a spoonful of baking powder into a bowl, and stir in two tablespoons of melted butter and two eggs well beaten.

Gradually beat in a pint of milk (or buttermilk) until the mixture is very smooth and light, with fine air bubbles showing on the surface. Lightly grease a griddle or heavy frying pan, and drop the mixture, a tablespoon at a time onto the hot surface. When the pancakes are the right colour, a yellowy gold, turn and cook the other side.

My mother in Ireland used to pile them up in towers, with butter, sugar and a squeeze of lemon between each layer, and we children would eat our way through a tower each on coming home from school. When they were cold they were leathery and unappetizing, but could be fried up for breakfast the next morning with bacon and eggs. Now the fashion is to have stuffed pancakes, sweet or savoury, whether in Breton or Welsh restaurants, or in Little Chefs, but that is, as far as I know, a modern development in the Celtic lands. Traditionally pancakes were a teatime treat made fresh for your children or for a friend calling. In Kate Roberts' stories set in rural Wales unpopular callers are given only bread and cheese, but real friends get pancakes. In *Traed mewn cyffion*, Jane rushes to make pancakes for her kindly sister-in-law Geini whom she likes. 'Take plenty', she urges Geini. 'I put some cream from the top of the milk on them'. The fresh golden pancakes 'steeped in butter, slipped from the fork on to Geini's plate'.

Drinking tea was a rarity for ordinary country people till the second half of the nineteenth century. Buttermilk was always plentiful and was the normal drink to go with meals. It could be poured over new potatoes for a popular summer dinner, too. A common drink which was thought to be refreshing was made by simply stirring a spoonful of oatmeal into water. Flummery was a thicker drink made by mixing three basins of oatmeal into three quarts of water and adding two cups of buttermilk. *Diod fain*, small beer, was said to be a fine remedy for pepping people up after a hard day's work. It was made by adding chopped nettles and agrimony to five gallons of boiling water, and letting it stand overnight. Then it was brought to the boil and a handful of hops thrown in. After boiling for ten minutes the brew was sweetened with brown sugar to taste and let cool to blood heat, when half a pint of brewer's yeast (*burum* or barm) was added. Another night of letting it stand, and it was ready for drinking the next day.

Mead was drunk in medieval times at the courts of the Welsh princes, and recipes for it continued to be handed down into modern times, though its consumption may have been frowned upon by nonconformist morality. The twelfth-century *Hirlas* poem of the Prince Owain Cyfeiliog sings its praises in no uncertain terms:

> Cup bearer, pour forth the sweet strained mead
> for those quick-speared and toil-worn in the fight,
> pour it from proud gold-handed drinking horns . . .
>
> Cup-bearer, bring the cordial to us all,
> by the great bright fire's light and torches' gleam;
> cup-bearer, thou sawest wrath at Llidwm field;
> the men I honour, honoured they shall be!

Mead was made in June when the honeycombs were ready. The honey was extracted from the comb and a gallon of water poured over it. After leaving it overnight, it was slowly brought to the boil and skimmed. A handful of hops was added and the mixture allowed to go on boiling for about a quarter of an hour. Yeast was added when it had cooled to blood heat, and it was left to ferment overnight, covered with a cloth. The next day it was skimmed and poured off into earthenware storage jars, which were tightly corked and buried up to their necks in boggy ground till the following spring, when the mead would be ready for drinking. Individuals had their own favourite additions to this basic recipe, such as a few cloves or a piece of root ginger, or lemons if they were to be had, or a bunch of herbs from the garden.

Mead is now back in favour and made on a commercial scale in Wales, but mainly as a tourist attraction at those heritage 'medieval feasts' where serving wenches in antique costume bring round the mead as an aperitif or liqueur, while harps tinkle in the background, and rich Americans are enchanted. Welshmen prefer to drink beer, and few Welsh women retain the old knowledge of how to make love potions from mead, as they did a hundred years ago, or more. They used to keep back from bread making tiny scraps of the dough from nine separate bakings, make these into a little cake, and add it to a loving cup of mead or cowslip wine. The indifferent lover or husband who swallowed this potion was expected to be restored to his first careless ardour towards the giver. Failing that, the Methodist Welshwoman tended to fall back on the poetry of housework. Kate Roberts is the expert in minutely describing such sublimations:

> An odour of cleanliness, a scent not unlike the scent of summer, or of apples beginning to dry, pervaded the cupboards and drawers where she stored her clothes and linen. The clothes lay in the cupboard like books piled one on the other, their back to view, in neat rows. Such a 'grain' was there on her clean linen, that you would almost imagine you still felt the heat of the iron, if you pressed it to your cheek weeks after it had been ironed. In short, one look at Meri Ifan's home was enough to convince that housework was akin to poetry and not a wearying and a drudgery. [12]

Medicinal remedies were part of women's cooking responsibilities, too, and early cookery books always include healing lotions and ointments and poultices as well as recipes for food and drink. Lady Llanover, while aiming at the gentry in her recipes, was an enthusiast for Welsh things, whether costume or the language or country remedies which she learnt from her own household servants. So her classic cookery book includes instructions on when to pick herbs for drying (thyme during June and July, basil from the middle of August, savory from the end of July, marjoram in July, parsley, fennel and chervil throughout May to July), and hands on possibly authentic but probably reinvented folk remedies

For St Vitus's Dance
Take as much mistletoe (that which grows on the whitethorn) and moss from the bark of the ash-tree as three quarts of water will cover, boil them till they are reduced to three pints; strain it, and, when cold, take a teacupful three times a day.
N.B. This prescription actually cured a Welsh boy when all other means had failed. [13]

Mistletoe and ash were sacred to the Druids, the medicine men of the pagan Celts, but who knows how much wishful thinking by the antiquarian-minded Lady Llanover (or jokes played on her by locals) preserved such 'remedies'?

Women talking about their lives in rural Wales, 1

'When I married and we came here to settle down (it was around 1950), we tried to make a go of farming. We started with two cows and worked up to six. I had lived in the country and had been on a farm up north, but I had never milked a cow in my life. Brave? No, it was foolhardy really. Nearly gave me a nervous breakdown. The way we lived was, I used to get up at six in the morning to get the milking done, and it was one long struggle all day through, keeping the farm going. My husband had to learn how to grow corn and root vegetables. He learned to plough just by doing it, because I don't think people can tell you things like that. Though it was a smaller community in those days, and neighbours went around the different farms to help at busy times. When we were getting the hay in people would come and give us a hand, and then we would go and help them in turn. There weren't the bailers in those days. It was all done by hand. Forking the hay onto the cart was a very perilous procedure with a horse, because the horse would sometimes jerk forward . . .

'It was a very hard living for us, because we only had twenty acres and that was too small really. To be comfortable you needed fifty or sixty acres at least. Most people on the smaller farms needed (and still do) a subsidiary job to keep going. They got work on the roads or as farm labourers. In the end we scraped the bottom of the barrel when some of the cows died. I had to go back to work myself. I got a job teaching in town in the end. But before that we did struggle to keep going. There was a pig sty here, so people said to us, "Oh, you must keep a pig". I asked our labourer would he like to feed a pig and he looked scornfully at me and said, "Cows and pigs are women's jobs". That was that. I had to feed the pig. When it was time to kill the pig, there was a man who went around all the farms just killing pigs. It was his profession. He did the killing alright, but then we had the corpse to deal with ourselves. I had all the back numbers of the *Farmer's Weekly* spread out around me on the floor, trying to find the best way of curing the pig. We sold half of it, thank God, but even then we had far too much. It's very dreary meat when you have it day in and day out, but we felt we had to use it up, and there were only the two of us. We salted it on the slab in the dairy and hung it up. We couldn't get through the hams fast enough and they went maggotty all the way round the bone. There were no fridges to put things in, in those days—we didn't have electricity till 1960. So the pig was not a big success! When the question came up, ''What's for supper tonight?'' the answer was always the same—''bacon''. Groans all round. But it was a life saver for people who couldn't afford to buy butcher's meat.

'As people became more prosperous they would go to the shops for variety. They didn't want bacon all the time. Self-sufficiency is being talked of again, with the green movement getting fashionable. But the first time round self-sufficiency meant poverty. You lived off the pig and the vegetable plot because you had no choice. So it was *cawl*, bacon broth, every day for dinner. It was certainly a healthy diet compared with all the over-refined shop foods. Home-made bread and butter, buttermilk to drink, oatmeal porridge, fresh eggs and vegetables—it was wholefood with nothing taken out and no chemicals added, as people would see it now. But then it just seemed dreary and people longed for all the unhealthy tinned foods and shop cakes and processed cheese, because they were treats, a break from the everyday monotony of home-produced fare.'

Women talking about their lives, 2

'I married a Welshman and came to live near Machynlleth in the 1970s, when everything was still quite traditional in the rural villages. I had my own career, but of course Gerallt wanted me to join in the local social life with him. I can't say I enjoyed sitting through long funeral ceremonies or entertainments and concerts in a language I couldn't understand. I did pick up a bit of the language, but I couldn't see why I should struggle to speak it badly when everyone around me could speak English so much better than I could speak Welsh. But I suppose I was accepted because Gerallt does so much for the community. Anyway he now goes to his own Welsh-speaking activities and I go to my English-speaking ones, though of course there are occasions when it is a social duty to appear together and I will do that when it's needed.

'Sometimes we fight over the television, because he switches it on to the Welsh channel and I switch it back for my favourite English programmes, and he sometimes missed that sacred soap opera, *Pobl y Cwm* . . .

'At work—I run a small business of my own—I've decided that as long as you get people's names and addresses right (in spelling and in pronunciation over the phone) you are alright. English is the language of business dealings with few exceptions. Because after all the Welsh do not take to business all that successfully. They were applying in such small numbers to take up Enterprise grants that now the Welsh Office has had to start a new scheme to encourage them—the *Menter a Busnes* project. It's surprising really, when you think that the virtues of Nonconformism are all about hard work and thrift and doing well by your family. Capitalism and protestantism are supposed to go together, but perhaps the most enterprising went to South Wales or emigrated to England or America, leaving the others to plod on from day to day. They're very fatalistic, I sometimes think, the rural Welsh around these parts. Maybe it's the special blend of Calvinism—that's about pre-destination, after all—and conservatism with a small c. Look at the farmers in crisis yet again with these latest cuts in subsidies. They can't think of any alternative to filling every inch of mid Wales with more sheep, even though they get less and less money out of them. I get tired of the sight and sound of them, I must admit. Why don't farmers take this setaside money and show some initiative? Planting woods and making farm trails and demonstration smallholdings or something? I'm all for the enterprise culture myself, and I think there's a lot of room here for developing rural enterprises. But you definitely need imagination and a lot of grit to market your scheme, whatever it is . . .

'It's the same story of conservatism again when it comes to women's roles in the Nonconformist ethos. It's always worse for a woman than for a man to go outside the conventions, whether it's business or sex or drink. So people are horrified if it's a woman on a drunken driving charge, like that woman down the way from us, because it got into the *Cambrian News*. The Welsh drink but are not supposed to be found out. A community like this is a patriarchal, so men may behave badly but women may not. Like, man is the sinner and woman is the stronger and purer, because it was the women who had to uphold the Nonconformist values in the home, where it really mattered, never mind what the male ministers thundered from the pulpits on a Sunday. But the women always had a difficult time, because if the atmosphere in the home got a bit too good and pure, the men would scarper to the pub or even clear out altogether. Anyway, many a Welsh mam just ruined her men, and now it's up to Welsh wives to undo that and try to get the men to take their fair share of the household chores . . .

'There were some good things about Nonconformism. The children were encouraged to do better than the parents and get on in the world, but to do that they needed English. Now they say it was a scandal that children had to wear the Welsh-not at school if they were caught speaking Welsh, but it was the Welsh teachers who did that in the hope of giving the children a better chance in life, materially speaking. If they did well they got out, because hearth and home was music and stories and dreams, not ruthless achievement and progress. It was a thin enough life, in spite of the community spirit. I often think—hard physical toil, respectability to be kept up all the time, Chapel the only focus of social life. Even when they did manage to make money without leaving their communities they had no joy in spending it, they would rather hoard it —though all that's changing now. You don't hear that old joke so often about "Why are there no Jews in Cardiganshire?—Because they couldn't make a living." The ones who showed enterprise went away and made fortunes in London and Manchester in drapery or whatever. The ones who stayed behind never developed an enterprise culture, and now they criticise the English incomers for taking over the village shops

123

and pubs and garages . . . If the women had had a freer hand outside the home, like they had inside the home, it might have been different, but they say the Cardi women drive from behind and don't like to be seen outfacing the men in public. Even in farming it's sometimes the women who are the best people with sheep. Some of the finest around here are women, who are turned to for help when there are lambing problems, say. But it doesn't change the way women's work is still seen by a lot of country people, as first and foremost the house and the children. It's hard for women no matter how skilled to break out of the conventional moulds and be properly credited for what they do. It puts a strain on the relationship between the man and his wife, quite often, and that is worse for the woman than for the husband. The men have their male preserves to slope off to for moral support. The women get their moral support from the atmosphere at home and if that goes sour they are the ones who suffer the most.'

Women talking about their lives, 3

The view from inside the chapel culture (which is declining steadily, but still a significant force in rural communities, an atmosphere sensed even by those who do not belong to it) is very different. Here is an older countrywoman talking about her life. The chapels are losing the younger generation and members are steadily getting on in years. She and her husband are among the two dozen or so who regularly attend the local chapel. They have a smallholding and are informal leaders in the community, collecting news for the *papur bro*, winning prizes for their produce at the local show, and always warm and welcoming to one and all, speaking to family and locals in their own language, which is Welsh, and to incomers in English. She is enthusiastic about local history and can bring out old records and photos and Welsh local history books, to back up her own fine memory of the community's story, past and present. Her life has been hard at times, but always sustained by a sense of place and community identity.

'In my young day we carried water from the spring the other side of the river, and we had no electricity till the 1960s. There was always plenty to do when I was a child, though it might seem a quiet place. I went to the local school which opened in 1900 and closed down in the 1960s when it was down to three pupils. While the school was going it kept the *eisteddfodau* and the concerts alive, for that was where they were held, but after the school closed there was nowhere, for the deacons did not want the concerts to be held in the chapel. In those days anyone who could recite or sing or do a sketch took part. There were great celebrations, like the welcome home for the boys on leave during the war. There was no shortage of people to stand up and do their piece, and the women did lovely suppers for everybody . . .'

A recent article in the *Western Mail* mourned the decline of the Chapel culture in nostalgic detail for such socials:

Yn ein sosials ni, fe fyddem yn cael te mewn cwpanau tsieni claerwyn ag ymylon glas iddyn nhw, a'r rheiny'n gorffwys ar saseri o'r un lliw ar lieiniau bwrdd fel carlwm o wyn. Rywsut roedd mwy o flas ar fara menyn a darn bach o gaws, a chacen fadeira i ddilyn mewn sosial capel.

(In our socials we would have tea in shining white china cups with blue rims on them, resting on saucers the same colour, on table cloths like white ermine. Somehow there was more taste to the bread and butter and little bit of cheese, and madeira cake to follow, in a chapel social)

'There would be special preaching services every Whitsun in the different chapels, and those would be big occasions. The visiting ministers would be entertained in people's home and the women would do spring cleaning and a special baking, and the men would whitewash the place to get it all in good order for the visits . . .

'What happened in the old days was that the eldest daughter stayed at home to help her mother with the younger ones, though she might do days out at busy times on the bigger farms and bring home a bit extra. The other girls would go into service to the bigger houses nearby, if they could, but often they had to go off to London to get work—a good many of them stayed in the Welsh community there and got jobs on the milk rounds . . .

125

'During the two world wars the women in the valley worked at tree barking, but work was scarce. More and more left when farm servants were no longer kept. There used to be a farm servant on every farm. There were a lot of houses lying empty till the valley got opened up to the outside world in the 1960s with the Power Station coming . . .

'The Power Station was seen differently by locals and incomers because of the different viewpoints among people who are born here and people who have come in. We locals couldn't get up and go somewhere else if the scheme spoiled things, because we have our ties to the place and we couldn't afford to move. The incomers had moved from somewhere else already, so they could always move again. Even if it might be very inconvenient, it would not be a complete break with your own place. Naturally they wanted it to stay the way it was when they were attracted to the valley in the first place. But we had seen many changes in the past in our own families and could put up with more, especially if it meant more jobs. My father like so many others here had gone to work in the coal mines in the South when the lead mines were coming to an end. We only saw him in the holidays and then he died when I was only ten. Many of the women kept things going on the smallholdings when they had to, with help from the neighbours when needed. It was always a hard life as well as a full one. One of the lead mines was called the White Man's Grave, but my husband's grandfather walked from Pontrhydygroes to work there, for it was a living. Sometimes the miners stayed in the barracks and only saw home at the weekends. Yes, it was hard . . .

'So when the Power Station came it meant work for some of the locals —full-time for the men, and part-time for the women, who got jobs doing cleaning or as guides during the season. It was a good proportion of jobs, considering that so many of the locals in the valley are self-employed farmers . . .

'There's an old lady in her eighties now, who remembers still how she went on a trip to Belgium when she was young, and she overheard strangers on the boat talking about Cwmrheidol, and they were saying that Cwmrheidol was the most beautiful place in Wales. So it's a famous place we live in, though you don't mind about that when it's your own

126

place, except that you're proud to hear it well spoken of. The hardships were part of the valley history. They meant that the school I went to was down to three children in 1961 and had to close. So many had gone and their houses were lying empty. The last house lived in was Gelli Fach and beyond that it was a valley of ghosts till people came to live at the head of the cwm again in the 1970s. So it's always been changes, one after another—that's the story of the schools and the chapels and the lead mines and the smallholdings. But we carry on as best we can.'

Women talking about their lives, 4

'I am not one of those recent immigrants you hear about who are deeply shocked to find they are not still living in a bit of England, who can't get over the fact that this is another country with a strange language clouding up the meanings they thought they knew ... I'm only moderately shaken when I hear my own children chattering away to each other in Welsh (which I cannot understand beyond a few banal phrases which I'm too self-conscious to use). Maybe at last it's time for me to learn it properly, but I might find it too ridiculous at forty to start a new life as a Welsh "convert", when I've been living and working here for nearly twenty years, and even my neighbouring Welsh farmer (across whose land my track goes) expects me to speak in English. I suppose you could say I belong to an incomer ghetto, when I think about it, because all the friends I see regularly seem to be English incomers like myself and our gossip rarely extends beyond our own exclusive circle.

'They say you only put roots down in a new culture by bringing your children up in it. Well, I've dutifully done that, but I'm not sure yet whether I'm glad or sorry. I mean, why should I sacrifice a kind of English closeness and familiarity between them and me for the sake of some dubious theoretical cause like helping a minority culture which I could never be part of myself? It's too soon to know how they will feel when they grow up able to speak Welsh, but still being part of this kind of incomer ghetto I was talking about. At the minute I suspect they use Welsh in the house only as a secret language so that I don't know what they're up to, rather than because they're falling for the culture. Well,

127

I can't say I will find it all that distressing if they continue to identify with English incomers here and not the full-blown indigenous culture. Because I do think incomers have had too bad a press recently. Pantomime demons in the ongoing soap Celts versus *Saeson*. In fact the incomers I know around here have a lot to offer as people, whatever their national origins—enterprising, fun to be with, ready to help you when you're down . . . There I go, singing my own trumpet—but I do get a bit bored when I hear about goody-goody converts trying to be more Welsh than the Welsh. They seem to lose their sense of humour in the process, as well as their sense of proportion. If the Welsh themselves can't save their language no amount of incomers are going to manage it for them.

'But don't run away with the wrong ideas about us old-style incomers. We have committed ourselves to mid Wales really and truly, in our own way. When we came in the early seventies the rural communities were really going down the nick. We rebuilt the old cottages, started our little businesses or crafts or what have you, sent our children to the declining schools and supported the bilingual education they got in them instead of clamouring for English-language only (like this recent lot of trouble-makers, Education First), though about three quarters of the kids were English. Of course quite a few of us mislaid our original spouses and so there are plenty of women and children living like I do, earning my own living, bringing them up without a partner to help. Sometimes it's quite tough, keeping going—money-wise, emotionally, everyway. There's not a lot of time or energy left over for extras—like, I'm afraid I have to say, this Welshness that needs saving . . . It's a bit too traditional nonconformist for me. Honestly I'm not quite sure what it means in the 1990s, when we're all meant to be fulfilling ourselves as great sensitives and Europeans as well. Oh, I know all about the background—I'm a great reader, as a result of not having babysitters and staying in a lot when the children were small . . . I'm not just emotionally grabbed by Welshness as opposed to individuals whom I care about, as I also care about this place where I will probably live out my life. Maybe what I need is a Welshman who is neither an MCP or an imitation Englishman or a brooding *gwerinwr* . . . Where are they?'

128

Women talking about their lives, 5

'I had been nursing my mother through her last illness—in the south east (I mean England) and when she died and the house was sold, I was simply footloose and keen to move to the country and start a new life. I had thought about various English country idylls, like the Cotswolds, but even though I had the money from the house, I hadn't enough for that part of the country, and I finally found myself looking further and further west, till I found this place in mid Wales. As you can see, it's on the outskirts of the village, and I wanted somewhere like that—like a lot of women living on our own, I feel very cut off, and not quite safe, living in an isolated house. I had to find a way of earning my living, but I had enough money left over to give myself a year working out how. That was seven years ago.

'It's all turned out very differently from what I had thought it would be like when I left the south east. As soon as I moved in, I found out what had never occurred to me—that this was a largely Welsh-speaking village and that I couldn't even join the local societies unless I spoke the language. Of course it's possible to live here without joining in—my neighbours are perfectly happy just living in the place and keeping themselves to themselves. But that was no good for me. I was on my own and needed to establish new networks of every kind—church and job and social life, if possible. So yes, I learnt the language, and got myself a job as a social worker in this area, where you have to be bilingual to get the job! Amazed responses from my old friends, who couldn't believe it. But I was simply determined to do whatever I had to do to make this new life of my own that I had dreamed about for so long, while nursing Mother . . .

'I could never have done it, in spite of going on the intensive Wlpan Welsh course at Lampeter that first summer, if I hadn't had really kind local support, especially from the *Merched y Wawr* [Welsh-speaking women's organisation in rural Wales]. They welcomed me to their meetings, even though for the first year I used to sit like a mouse, afraid to try out my Welsh among such experts. But I listened and finally I was able to understand what they were going on about, and then I did speak out, and they all turned round and looked at me, as if the cat had started to talk! This branch of the *Merched y Wawr* is on the elderly side, and some of the young women from the village think the one down the road is livelier and go off to that. But I'll always stay with this one, for without these women I would never have been able to do what I had to do—settle in the village, and improve my Welsh to the point where I could get a professional bilingual post, *and* make good friends . . . The other thing I found when I started working was that you learn more about rural Wales in three years as a social worker than you'd ever dreamt of, but that's another story . . .'

Women talking about their lives, 6

'I'm an incomer too, even though I'm a *Cymraes*, a Welsh-speaking Welsh woman, because in this village anybody from more than ten miles away is an outsider. For me my Welshness is so much a part of my identity that I probably wouldn't even think about it as an issue were it not for the changes I see going on around me in the rural communities. We have small children and we always speak Welsh here at home. But they go to the village school and there is a big shift happening as more English-speaking children enrol there. They may all be taught to speak Welsh as well as English, but you notice how hard it is for Welsh-speaking children like ours to spend their whole day in their own language—once you get a majority of English speakers, English dominates and Welsh goes to the wall. Sometimes I get the feeling that I might as well be living in some part of England, although this is Dyfed and it has its own history and culture that is all part of my identity. What do I want to happen? Well, I certainly don't want to draw up the drawbridge and keep the stranger out, because that is no answer in the long run. What I would like to see is the newcomers being ready to meet us halfway, so that we could all be part of a community that keeps what is valuable in the old traditions, but is also part of the modern world I want for my children.

'What kind of modern world? Well, I went to Greenham Common, and I'm one of many Welsh-speaking women working for peace. I'm all for women here moving outside their traditional domestic interests, though I wouldn't want to throw those out, or undermine their importance, for it's very important to me and other Welsh-speaking women to have a strong home base for venturing out into the "political" world, in our own communities or further afield. What worries some Welsh women about feminism is that it sometimes seems to be throwing out the baby with the bathwater, or getting rid of a very important reason for changing the world—that you want it to be a better place for your children, and that means keeping their own culture alive for them . . .

'If we could join with incoming women to work for a fairer place for women in every department of Welsh life, that would be something I would be happy to be part of. But both sides have to feel easy with each other and you only reach that position if you're prepared to really get to know each others' valued things, and find out what you have in common. You can't just become part of a community by turning up and living there, and wondering why the locals aren't more friendly and welcoming. And you can't turn up and want to work for peace or equal opportunities, without understanding about the community and the culture which these causes have to be rooted in, if they are to have any meaning for Welsh-speaking people . . .

'Sometimes the problem is that we Welsh—and especially we Welsh women—are so anxious to be friendly and keep things nice and pleasant, at least on a superficial level, that we bury a lot of our own strong feelings or suffer a sense of inferiority, and won't speak out about our language and culture and things like that when there are outsiders present. How on earth then can we get newcomers to appreciate that we have our own way of life as a nation that is worth finding out about and joining in, even if it takes a lot of effort? Not by sitting in silence at community meetings of whatever kind (parent teachers or governors or community council), disagreeing with everything a speaker is saying but not prepared to stand up and put in another point of view. It's better to be sincere than to be fluent, but a lot of Welshwomen are scared stiff to argue with confident fluent English incomers—even if they're women too ... who might even be glad to have their views broadened. After all, they have chosen to come and live here and have sometimes an angry sense, I think, that it is a different country that they can't understand ...

'Understanding each other, that's what it's about, not shutting yourself off and making little jokes about *Cymry* and *Saeson*. If we could only delight in our different culture, and be proud to show it off to incomers—that would be an antidote to this drab old sameness everywhere, which comes from losing your sense of identity and place ...

'I know a lot of incomers are looking for something different—small-scale, a place that has its own identity, a good place to bring up your children—and that is why they come to our country. I think Welshwomen have a part to play in explaining our communities and our culture to incomer women, and getting them to want to be a part of this culture of ours. Because women are better than men at connecting, aren't we?'

[1] Angela John (ed.), *Our mothers' land*, Cardiff, University of Wales Press, 1991.

[2] Rosemary Jones, 'Women, community and collective action', in Angela John (ed.) (as above), p. 23.

[3] David Jenkins, *The agricultural community in south-west Wales at the turn of the twentieth century*, Cardiff, University of Wales Press, 1971, p. 190.

[4] Robert Roberts, *The life and opinions of Robert Roberts, a wandering scholar*, Cardiff, Lewis, 1923, p. 205.

[5] Ann Griffiths, *The hymns of Ann Griffiths: critical Welsh edition* edited ... by John Ryan. Tŷ ar y Graig, 1980.

[6] Menna Elfyn, *Aderyn bach mewn llaw*, Llandysul, Gomer, 1991.

[7] D. J. Williams, *The old farmhouse*, Carmarthen, Golden Grove, 1987.

[8] Kate Roberts, *Feet in chains* [*Traed mewn cyffion*], Cardiff, John Jones, 1977.

[9] D. J. Williams (as above).

[10] Mattie Thomas, *Collection of Welsh recipes for the preparation of meals commonly prepared a hundred to a hundred and twenty years ago*. (Translation of a typescript in the National Library, kindly lent to me by the Welsh cookery writer and restaurateur Bobby Freeman).

[11] Mattie Thomas (as above).

[12] Kate Roberts, 'Sisters' in *A summer's day and other stories*, Cardiff, Penmark Press, 1946.

[13] Augusta, Lady Llanover, *The first principles of good cookery, with an introduction by Bobby Freeman*, Tregaron, Brefi Press, 1991, p. 438.

CHAPTER 6

After Eden: attitudes to the language

Half a million people in Wales speak the Welsh language. That is a fifth of the population, but the proportion of Welsh speakers has been falling steadily for a century. At the close of the last century half the population were Welsh speakers, though in rural west Wales nearly everyone spoke Welsh as their first language. When George Borrow did his walking tour in 1854, he found Welsh the general language of the countryside. He met a young English couple who had taken a farm in mid Wales and felt totally isolated and miserable as a result of not knowing the language. Now it is Welsh farming families who are feeling depressed and isolated because their language is disappearing from around them as the young people leave to find work in a less depressed area of the economy, and the farms are bought up by English-speaking incomers.

Saunders Lewis gave his famous 'Fate of the language' broadcast on 13 February 1962, when the census returns showed that the percentage of Welsh speakers had dropped to 26%. He warned that Welsh would die out by the end of the twentieth century unless the people exercised 'determination, will power, struggle, self-sacrifice and endeavour'. His message led to the founding of *Cymdeithas yr Iaith*, the Welsh Language Society, in August 1962. Their non-violent campaigns have been successful in persuading public bodies like British Rail and British Telecom to go bilingual and make the language more visible in public services. *Cymdeithas yr Iaith* members are young and articulate, many of them students, and they make sure the media are present at their protests. They have enthusiastically carried out a continuing series of high profile campaigns. They have been instrumental in winning bilingual road signs, which have not led to additional carnage on the roads as the wiseacres predicted. They have used sit-ins in post offices

133

which have been effective in getting more bilingual forms and service for Welsh speakers, and they parade up and down regularly outside the big stores in Cardiff who refuse to develop bilingual policies on the grounds of economic hardship or lack of customer demand.

Of course people complain about their tactics, since they are intentionally high-impact and media-conscious, and prepared to go to prison for their cause (for spraying messages on public buildings or defacing monoglot road signs, for example). Many conservative respectable Welsh speakers of the older generation do not approve of their antics, though they may approve the cause. Many English incomers are irritated or uneasy when their attention is forced upon a language that is impenetrable (to them), and which they thought was in terminal decline. Some come to Wales not even knowing that it has got its own language, with a large body of literature and history behind it. There are also some ecologically conscious people who do not include the language in the ecology, and so see no need to protect it, though they will campaign vigorously on behalf of red kites or peaty wetlands.

There are problems too arising from the attitudes of English-speaking Welsh people in the south. There is a tendency among would-be cosmopolitans in Cardiff to see the language as backward looking, a drag on Wales' progress towards a European stance. If they are in favour of bilingualism they want it to be French or German and English, and see no room for a minority language which cannot be used outside the Welsh heartlands, and especially on mainland Europe. There is a minority who go further in their arguments against the language, on the grounds that it actually divides the nation, and may be used as 'a tool in the hands of mad nats'.

Cymdeithas yr Iaith's original manifesto is still a valid analysis of the language problem, though the situation has become more fraught with the influx of monoglot English speakers from the other side of Offa's Dyke during the 1980s. Between 10,000 and 15,000 a year (some Welsh returners, it has to be said) moved into the county of Dyfed, which contains the remnants of the most intensely Welsh-speaking rural heartlands. The small villages and scattered communities strung out

134

along peaceful country roads in beautiful scenery had already attracted incomers in the 1960s and 1970s, but the flow accelerated in the 1980s, as more people retreated from the urban rat race in Thatcher's Britain. *Cymdeithas yr Iaith* had warned in the sixties that failure to assimilate newcomers to the local language and culture would lead to steady anglicisation of local societies, chapels and churches, schools and shops and sub-post offices. But the Welsh did not (and for the most part still do not) see the necessity for English people to speak Welsh, and are reluctant for various reasons to help incomers learn the language. 'If they would stick to English I could understand them better', says one local farmer. Another is not emotionally ready to share his language with strangers, and others are at a loss what to talk about with incomers who have learnt the language but do not know the stories that are part of it, or the state of mind that is natural to it. Is it not another case of a dog walking on its hind legs, hearing the *Saeson* giving voice to the *Hen Iaith*, the beloved mother tongue? There is also a kind of shyness in rural parts, which does not make for easy talking in any language when strangers are present and their responses are not known. Will they laugh at the same jokes, weep at the same tragedies, get the little ironies and pleasant digs that the locals share with each other, to oil the wheels of everyday life?

So in rural communities in mid Wales from the 1960s public meetings switched more and more to English, even if there was only one English person present. The chapel culture was in serious decline, with Salems and Bethels closing and being converted to private houses (even holiday homes), and the old nexus of social activities centred on the chapel was giving way to a more mobile view of entertainment, where people went out to discos, pub, restaurants, concerts, in the nearest town. If they stayed in there was the telly, and the effects of the English media was another focus of discontent for *Cymdeithas yr Iaith*.

The struggle to get a Welsh language channel on the telly was successful in 1982, but only after Gwynfor Evans, Plaid Cymru's eminent statesman, had gone on hunger strike, a fasting unto death or until Wales got its own language channel. He was reviving an old Celtic tribal custom of shaming into submission those who had wronged you, by fasting in public in their courtyard until you received your due. *Sianel Pedwar Cymru (S4C)* is a success, in that for any minority language to survive it needs to have access to the most popular medium of all, the box in the corner of nearly every living room in the land. But there are problems. It does not attract enough young Welsh viewers, and there are many complaints about the quality of the Welsh used on programmes like *Heno*, a magazine programme scheduled at a peak viewing time every evening. Purists argue that there are too many English words and phrases used, even if they are often given Welsh endings or constructions. Social analysts have observed the rise, too, of a new class of Welsh-speaking 'media yuppies', whose values and life styles are not consistent with the traditional rural mores. It is one of the most expensive services in the world per head of viewer, provoking Bernard Levin's little joke in *The Times* about its average audience being eighteen, which provoked great ire among the *Cymry Cymraeg*, especially when *The Times* failed to print their indignant replies. The coverage of the Welsh-speaking culture in the British media is too often confined to ill-informed and curiously illiberal comment, often sitting cheek by jowl with rather better informed and more liberal articles on Estonia, say, or Lithuania.

Pace Levin, the view from the periphery shows *S4C* to be a significant cultural victory, for the English-speaking Welsh in Wales were moved by envy to begin campaigning for improved media coverage for the 80% who cannot speak Welsh, but want better coverage for English-language Welsh cultures. Some argue for sub-titling of Welsh-language programmes, and this happens occasionally, as in the film *O.M.* (the life of O. M. Edwards, who was a significant proponent of Welsh-language education and culture a century ago, and so part of the whole Welsh heritage). But many *Cymry Cymraeg* see sub-titling as a dilution or betrayal of their channel.

Another factor identified by *Cymdeithas yr Iaith* as contributing to the death of Welsh rural culture is the 'plague of holiday homes'. They warned back in the sixties that 'The Welsh countryside could easily become a social, cultural and economic wilderness, a mere playground for the English Midlands'. The problem is that tourism is one of rural Wales' chief sources of income, so the activities of the arsonists *Meibion Glyndŵr*, Sons of Glyndŵr, who burnt down their first English holiday home in 1979 and continue their campaign sporadically, can win only very ambivalent support, if any, in Welsh culture circles. It is easy for the well-known English language poet R. S. Thomas to support their aims in principle, and refuse to give holiday makers even local directions when they ask the way in English. It is not so easy for the mid Wales farmers who have been told to diversify into tourism because they are producing too many cattle and sheep. They need the income from English tourists. Even if they are not entrepreneurial enough to run a caravan site or holiday cottages themselves, they can offer bed and breakfast, and sell derelict cottages or out buildings for conversion to holiday complexes.

But there is often a two-way pull between economic need to make money by opening up *y filltir sgwâr*, the beloved locality, to outsiders, and so diluting the fragile culture; or keeping the locality closed to outsiders, with the result that the young leave because there is no work. It has to be said, however, that tourism is a very seasonal activity, taking on large numbers of people in the short summer boom, only to push them back on the dole by the end of September.

The idea of offering Welsh language and culture activity holidays on Welsh hill farms may seem far-fetched in the present state of tourism development, but it illustrates an important principle for culture-aware money making. When people go on holiday a lot of the fun is discovering differences, not samenesses, so why not a more positive marketing of the indigenous culture? Why not a culture and language interpretive centre in Aberystwyth, with audio-visuals and artefacts of the kind used in the National Museum's Celtica exhibition in Cardiff 1991, but not confined to the remote past, rather dealing with the cultural diversities and adversities of the present? Why not Welsh-language activity holidays in the natural setting of family farms, as well as in the language centre at Nant Gwrtheyrn? Learning a language and getting to understand a culture is the basis for an endless range of holidays on the continent, and the Scottish Highlands is now coming on the scene with Gaelic language

137

and hillwalking weeks in a scenic mountain setting. But the Welsh Tourist Board seems to be lagging behind in making a positive presentation of the culture and language of rural Wales *as it is now*, and not as it was in the past, which overemphasises the dreaded heritage concept. What is needed is a greater understanding of how to present a culture as seen from the inside, rather than packaged and seen from the outside.

The attractions of rural Wales for second home buyers are enormous. The scenery is wonderful, there is peace and quiet (except in honey pot areas like the mountains of Snowdonia) and characterful cottages tucked into the hillsides, which, until the late eighties, were relatively cheap for buyers on average English incomes. There is fishing and walking and birdwatching, and a surprisingly friendly and hospitable people, in view of the cultural tensions. But from the vantage point of *Cymdeithas yr Iaith* the increase in holiday cottages meant the decline of local communities where half the houses lay empty except in the summer and soon lost their local schools, shops and sub post offices. Their campaign *Nid yw Cymru ar werth*, Wales is not for sale, in the late eighties, was a response to this crisis. They called for a *Deddf Eiddo*, Property Act, to exercise controls over the building and disposal of houses in culturally sensitive rural areas. But the Thatcherite tenets of the late 1980s and early 1990s—'Let the market decide', and, 'There is no such thing as society, only individuals and families'—are not supportive of any such legislation. The most that can be done is for county planning departments to take account of cultural and language factors when considering development schemes. Gwynedd, for example, has refused planning permission for an estate of expensive houses, beyond the means of local people, on the outskirts of a Welsh-speaking village. The housing associations in *Tai Cymru*, Housing Wales, struggle to initiate schemes which will ensure a modicum of low-cost housing for local needs, but are operating on a fairly limited scale. The Welsh Office has made a modest sum available, for local authorities to draw on, to buy property in sensitive villages and make it available to local people, but curiously enough it is not fully taken up, although authorities complain that it is too little.

Rural Wales is not alone in the conflicts around holiday homes and the impact of incomers on local identity. Villages in the Pyrenees and the French Alps have suffered similar problems of losing their identity through an influx of urban escapees and large scale high-rise holiday apartments which are only used during the skiing and a brief summer season. I once spent a holiday walking in the Cerdagne, in the French Pyrenean foothills, and the picture that sticks in my mind ever since is of an old countrywoman driving her placid herd of cows along a village street on their cow-patted progress to the milking parlour. Their route had not changed from time immemorial, but their surroundings had. Now they wended their way past high-rise blocks of the new holiday village surrounding the ancient core. The village shop had been transformed from a community grocery and gossip exchange, where everybody knew everybody else and chattered in their strongly accented local French, to an Aladdin's Cave of exotic foods and parti-coloured Goretex leisure wear. The medieval Calvary in the village square had ceased to safeguard the community. It too had been diminished, and flickered weirdly in the coloured neon lights of the nearby 'Nite-Club'. The old countrywoman and her cows walked past the new phenomena with fatalistic indifference. Powerlessness is a terrible thing, especially when you know that the only way to have a say in what is happening to your community, is to get rich by selling your farm for even more development, just like your neighbours have done—before going off to live in the nearest city.

It is not always like that in the French Pyrenees. In another village they had not accepted overwhelming change as inescapable Fate. The community had formed a cooperative, raised money to buy up empty properties and abandoned farmhouses, and formed their own tourist management scheme. They determined the proportion of houses that could become holiday homes without reducing the permanent population to the crisis point where they would lose their shop and little school and bus service. They themselves managed the holiday cottages, which gave administrative and maintenance work to local people, and brought extra business to the village store during the season, so that it remained viable. There was financial encouragement for permanent incomers to set up craft workshops using local traditions and materials. Their wood-carvings and pots and needlework were sold in the Visitors' centre, so they had a local outlet and a start with their marketing.

In the Catalan speaking part of France there are, as in rural Wales, 'language problems'. Parisian visitors with strong centralist tendencies were heard to condemn Catalan as at best a quaint *folklorique* survival, and at worst as somehow subversive of the natural order of things (which was what went on in the Paris basin in the language approved by the Academie Française). Every self-respecting French citizen should be using the hallowed French tongue so sternly cosseted by the Academie to keep it pure, especially from the all-pervading intrusive influences of the world-dominant English language. 'Le weekend', 'le yuppy', 'le camping' have established themselves, although pronounced as if they were French rather than English (whereas in Welsh English words are pronounced the same, but transformed in spelling and endings and mutations, like *wedi'i gremato*, cremated, as I heard recently in this area).

Permanent incomers in French Catalonia are offered adult evening classes to learn the language, and there is a fair selection of Catalan reading matter in the local newspapers and bookshops. Among the inhabitants I found attitudes quite similar to the whole gamut of contradictions I come across among the people of mid Wales. Some who held their Catalan tongue in unquestioned affection, kept it for private family use, and were pained when the language became a political ball, bounced to and fro by ideologists on either side. Others could find no connections or empathy between the natural rural speakers of Catalan, like themselves and their village neighbours, and the media yuppies or alien incomers who speak an unnaturally perfect form of the language and take a sometimes intrusive interest in its natural speakers, or implicate them in an overt politicisation alien to conservative farming families. There were some enthusiastic incomers who wanted everything their new human-scale close-knit communities could offer, including the language and the culture. It was the absence of such secure certainties that had brought them to the countryside, and they were prepared to work hard and learn hard in order to gain access to this (from their

140

viewpoint) Schumacherian 'small is beautiful' community way of life, rooted in place.

It was clear that you cannot neatly divide off culture from politics. Who are the Catalan 'nationalists', anyway? The tradition-centred who run folk festivals, or the political activists who campaign for the language and culture in the fields of education, medical care, local government and the media? The conservative-minded locals who run little museums or cultural exhibitions which highlight things Catalan, or the left-wingers who fit the Catalan question into a theoretical perspective about civil rights for minorities? The intellectuals who write for the small presses and magazines, or the farming families who manage still to keep the culture alive on their own hearths and pass it on to the next generation?

The European Community in 1986 produced a summary report which emphasised that the treatment of linguistic minorities is a political problem, not just a cultural misfortune. It became clear that nation states like France and Britain might adopt more humane perspectives towards their minority cultures than they had done till modern times. Their histories reveal a tendency to eradicate small languages rather than to preserve or support them. They were, after all, spoken by mutinous or subversive peoples whom the governments wished to absorb into their just and progressive French or British empires. The official attitude was that these troublesome 'nationalists' were being offered the chance of education and economic opportunity through the medium of the superior, world-wide English language, so why should they go on and on about their impoverished little languages that held them back from material prosperity and technological development? These views were often internalised by the minority cultures, and there are continuing statements by English-speaking Welsh and also some Welsh-speaking Welsh at the present time, about the language as an impediment to progress and a turning the back on the wider world. European Community statements on the democratic rights of citizens to live their lives through their small languages are fine, and their strategies for the use of the languages in schools, public services and the media are practicable,

141

but ultimately it is personal attitudes that need to change if the languages are to survive.

The Irish experience illustrates the personal impact on individual sensitivities of a language that is dying or dead. In a television programme on BBC 2 in 1991 poets and novelists spoke movingly of how the death of the Irish language in their own past or present left them haunted by a silence or absence more palpable than any presence. But the poet Thomas Kinsella argued that it can be an enriching experience to be the inheritors of a dual language tradition. And the very way that the language was lost can become a dimension of an individual's writing or creative thinking. Thus Brian Friel in his play *Translations* (which has been translated into Welsh, interestingly), takes for his subject the British Ordnance Survey's visit to Donegal in the nineteenth century to remap the county and change the place names into their English equivalents. The task can only be carried out with the assistance of an English-speaking local willing to help. One of the English officers suffers the anguish of realising what his task means to the locals. The play includes all the paradoxes which polarised attitudes to minority languages often manage to evade. It also puts the language dimension back into the telling of history. The former prime minister of Ireland, Garret Fitzgerald, argued (on the same BBC 2 programme) that historians tend to evade their responsibilities to the language issue, by writing books and dissertations about a period when Irish was being replaced by English, without showing how this changed the everyday world for ordinary people, for it is language that shapes our everyday meanings. They can write effectively enough on language policies in education or put together convincing explanations for its decline, but still not convey the way the world is seen through the Irish language rather than the English language.

But we are now in the 1990s and the European Community has agreed on policies and strategies for safeguarding and preserving linguistic minorities in its member states. Governments are to avoid the 'fusion' effect, whereby they deny the differences between the dominant and the minority cultures. If you insist, say, that the Welsh are just the same as the English—they are all British—then they have no need of a separate culture or identity or language. But what this means in effect is that the Welsh are to become like the English, rather than that the English are to become like the Welsh. The dominant culture always provides the model, so it is not as simple or democratic as it sounds to say reasonably, 'Oh, we are all British these days—what's the fuss about?' 'Fusion pursued at all costs', warns the European Community Commission on Linguistic Minorities, 'is historically inequitable, culturally unjustified and politically equivocal'.

In Wales today, considerable progress has been made in developing an infrastructure for the Welsh-language culture, as recommended by the Commission on Linguistic Minorities. There is a Welsh-language television channel and *Radio Cymru*. There are bilingual schooling policies, and the language factor is woven into local government decision-making to a greater or lesser degree. But the problem of consciousness-raising remains. A minority language cannot be saved without the sympathy and support of the majority culture around it. But members of the majority culture cannot care if they do not know anything about the history and significance of the Welsh language. The Welsh Language Board, although much criticised for doing too little too late to save the language, has of recent years ensured a higher profile for Welsh, with the help of the Development Board for Rural Wales and the Welsh Development Agency. But, says Ron Jones of the Language Board, 'sympathy similar to that shown to some obscure and threatened species of butterfly is not enough'.

Welsh-medium schools, some in the more anglicised parts of Wales, are giving a greater visibility to the language, which encourages more adult learners, especially parents. *Sianel Pedwar Cymru* has attracted a huge surge of interest for its *Acen* programmes for adult learners, which have apparently won an audience among natural Welsh speakers as well. In the Welsh-speaking Swansea hinterland the Cwm Gwendraeth Project began at the end of the 1980s to support the language in the community, and ensure its continuing use when young people had left school and were at risk of finding no outlets for using the language in youth clubs and pubs, at work and in community activities. A concerted effort was made to win cooperation from local government officials, schools, leisure groups and community development groups, so that they could work together to resuscitate the language in every nook and cranny of Cwm Gwendraeth everyday life. But the problem continues of facing up to the existence of a surrounding population of monoglot English speakers, whose sympathy and support needs to be aroused, while accepting the probability that only a very small proportion of them will ever become Welsh speakers themselves.

In rural Ceredigion the focus in the 1990s is on Dyfed's bilingual schools, many of them kept open, ironically, by the influx of English-speaking incomers. If they brought up their children to be bilingual there would be hope, but why should they care? One group explained their views to *Wales on Sunday*, 1 July 1990:

> We are incomers into Wales who respect the country's life and native language. Our intention is to be an integral part of the communities into which we have moved. The Welsh language has been spoken in this land since Roman times, and we want to ensure that it continues to be the language of the community in the areas in which we live. Without that it cannot survive as a national language. But we realise this will not happen unless the language is acquired by our children in Welsh-medium schools so that they can become fluently bilingual.
>
> Those who have moved to Wales in recent years in their scores of thousands bear a great responsibility for the future of this ancient tongue and the rich culture which depends upon it. Welsh-speaking communities cannot survive in the face of the massive influx unless the children of incomers are fully integrated into them.
>
> We are therefore deeply unhappy that Dr Alan Williams MP should give the impression that English and other incomers oppose Dyfed's language policy. If we had chosen to live in Denmark we would have expected our children to be taught in Danish; if in Sweden, then in Swedish. It is just and proper that our children should learn through the language of the country in which we have settled. We are surprised and shocked that Dr Williams should describe Dyfed's policy as 'force-feeding in-migrant children' and that he should speak of the children as victims. Dr Williams accuses the Dyfed Education Authority of acting with 'Stalinist authoritarianism' but,

when the policy was being considered, we were free to take part in the discussion. Many of us did so.

The Carmarthen MP has given the impression that English and other incomers do not want their children to be integrated into the community. Such a misleading impression could lead to hostility to incomers and disharmony amongst the people of Wales.

Although English is the language of nearly all our homes, many of our children have gone on from Welsh-speaking primary schools to bilingual comprehensives, learning mainly through the Welsh language. They will be the fortunate possessors of two languages and two cultures, making easier the acquisition of others. Our earnest hope is that the Education Authority will stand firmly by its policy.

> Yours
> Irena Paxton and 68 others
> Llanybydder

The protests against Dyfed's policy of immersing four to seven year olds in the Welsh language (as the initial phase in their objective of achieving fluent bilingualism by the age of eleven) were organised by a pressure group of Welsh and incomer parents, called Education First. Their complaints were that Dyfed's policy was aimed more at the preservation of the Welsh language than at enabling children to achieve their full learning potential. Monoglot English-speaking infants from four to seven years old, if compulsorily 'submerged' in the Welsh language, were bound to lose out educationally, because, they argued, immersion strategies in language teaching only succeed when there is conviction (in parents, teachers and children) and therefore motivation.

Dr Alun Williams saw the policy as the 'English-Not' imposed on innocent children to stop them speaking their mother tongue, much as the 'Welsh-Not' used to be hung around the necks of Welsh children who spoke their mother tongue in the schools set up in the wake of the notorious 1847 Education Commissioners' Report, which condemned Welsh as an impediment to progress and civilisation. The Carmarthen MP's standing among the *Cymry Cymraeg* went down so low that he was mentioned in the same breath as Bernard Levin, who, not satisfied with attacking the Welsh television channel, set about sneering at the idea of teaching Welsh in schools, once more using the columns of *The Times* to reassert the hegemony of the dominant culture.

It needs to be noted, however, that Dr Williams was reselected by Carmarthen Labour Party to be their parliamentary candidate, after a number of rivals challenged him out of their pain and outrage at his treachery to the language. His own comment on the controversy was that 'Whenever anyone comments on the Welsh language, people divide into polar extremes. You are either pro-Welsh or anti-Welsh. It is black or white. You are either playing for Wales or you're playing for England'. He diverted to other rural issues, like supporting the Welsh-speaking hill farmers in their agricultural crisis, and was re-elected to Parliament.

Undoubtedly the fact that Dr Alan Williams was a Welsh speaker himself, and therefore seen as a traitor from within, caused him to be especially reviled for his opposition to Dyfed's bilingual schools. This stirs up racial memories of the long line of Welsh leaders, including Methodist ministers and teachers, who themselves used the Welsh-Not and told the people to give up the language if they wanted to succeed. The rationalist Unitarian Thomas Stephens of Merthyr, for example, had advised cultural deference to England a hundred years before:

> The Welsh should learn English in order to improve their chances in the material world. They could still cherish their own tongue in Chapel and in harmless eisteddfodic pursuits like writing, poetry . . . [1]

Thus was Welsh turned into 'the language of Heaven', but lost the race on earth. But it is too easy to revile historical figures who have spoken out of whatever misguided conviction about the precedence of material progress over cultural matters. They got obsessed by a partial truth, but a truth only too well confirmed by memories of older people I have spoken to about their families' experiences arriving in London as monoglot Welsh early this century. 'She had to wear a label pinned to her coat with the instructions where she was to go. In the hospital where she trained as a nurse they laughed at her funny way of speaking—even after she thought she had learned English . . . '

146

So it becomes easier to understand why many Welsh are reluctant to speak their language in front of strangers, and prefer to keep it for their private lives, for hearth and home. But that adds to the problems of adult learners who need to meet and mingle with natural speakers. There is a Welsh learners' Council (*CYD*) to bring together learners and native speakers for cultural and sociable activities throughout Wales. But as always such formal bodies need to be backed up by grass roots participation in the communities. It needs individuals who are prepared to have the courage of their convictions and support the language by themselves bringing learners into their homes or introducing them to Welsh societies and events, which many learners are too shy to go to on their own. The 1992 Eisteddfod in Aberystwyth received European Community money to organise an informal scheme of this kind, with *Cymry Cymraeg* receiving small groups of learners into their homes and teaching them enough Welsh to enable them to visit and enjoy the Eisteddfod, so perhaps it is possible to bridge the gap between formal institutional provision and community grass roots activity for adult learners.

Incomers who try to learn Welsh have to face up to the massive ambivalence of the Welsh on the language question. It is not very encouraging to read in Wales' one and only Sunday paper *Wales on Sunday*, that incomers' children are seen by some 'language fanatics' as 'school fodder' to keep 'our children's rural schools open' (an anecdote from the columnist Patrick Hannan). Nor is it motivating to be told that we have to choose between 'the factions promoting the Welsh language and culture, and the realities of a new fairly well-travelled multi-national society' (*Wales on Sunday* letter, 9 April 1989). Of course such extremes are usually counterbalanced by indignant rebuttals from equally sincere Welsh people taking the opposite stand. As often as Welsh is attacked as a drain on children's energies when they should be learning something useful like commerce or German, there is a response along the lines of Nia Rhosier's letter (*Wales on Sunday*, 23 April 1989):

Children Richer for Knowing Languages

Sir,

Your correspondent J. P. Cole of Clydach is sadly mistaken when he suggests that a bilingual upbringing is a 'severe disadvantage'.

It is generally accepted that persons who are already bilingual adapt more quickly to the learning of further languages; it is certainly true that children up to the age of about eight seem to cope with as many languages as adults care to expose them to.

And although there is always a period of mixing the languages spoken around them, children soon sort them out and are the richer for having reasonable command of those languages.

By all means teach French and German as well as Welsh and English, but please don't deprive Welsh children of their sense of identity by suggesting they do not learn Welsh simply because it will 'be of no advantage in Europe'.

There is more to having a language than merely commercial usefulness, and if the Welsh people of the future in Europe have no proper key to their own past literary heritage they will be poor specimens indeed.

Each nation and its language is unique, and civilised people everywhere are at last respecting this and preparing for a Europe and a world where respect for all is paramount.

That is the honest way forward for us all, and carries with it the hope of reconciliation and wholeness.

As a Welsh learner myself, I am encouraged by letters like that, because they are constructive and set in a wider context of human and cultural rights, a philosophy I want to identify with. It is sometimes unutterably painful to be present at the agonies of a language in decline, because for those who care it is not just a language but a whole way of life associated with family and close-knit community and nonconformist values, expressed through the *papurau bro*, community newspapers, the weeklies *Y Cymro* and *Y Faner*, and the more trendy weekly *Golwg*. And as the old people die, and non Welsh speakers move into communities, there are fewer neighbours left with whom to live daily life through the first language.

What discourages me is the kind of intemperate message I heard one Saturday morning breakfast time, when I was listening to *Radio*

148

Cymru's 'Dros y Sbectol', a personal viewpoint slot. The speaker said, in that tone of voice which people keep for serious things, '*heb iaith, heb ddim*'—without the language we have nothing, to lose the language is to lose all. He went on to recite a litany of the guilty ones, from the English incomers to Dr Alan Williams and other renegades who betray their own mother tongue. My Welsh was not advanced enough to be certain of the next bit, but I think his punch line was that despoilers of the language are in the same category as football hooligans, only worse, because football hooligans only invade other peoples' cultures for a short space of time and only damage their communities in a material sense, whereas the enemies of the language live in the communities and permanently undermine their culture.

It is hard to see how such viewpoints, however heartfelt, are going to make the situation any better. As I get older I apply my Humpty Dumpty test to people's utterances. I ask, that is, not how sincerely and wittily they moan and groan and hit their targets, but how well they put the pieces together again afterwards. There seems to be a constant danger in movements aimed at saving the language, of moving towards a defensive closing in, which is ultimately self-destructive, because it excludes outsiders who might be sympathetic, though in different ways than learning Welsh themselves. If the students of the Welsh-speaking hall of residence, Pantycelyn in Aberystwyth, for example, were to explain and promote their culture to the other students, would that not be more productive than sticking to linguistic purity and the dangers of ghettoisation?

If movements like *CYD* (to help learners cross the bridge into Welsh-speaking culture) and *PONT* (to build bridges between incomers and local communities) put too much emphasis on getting across the existing Welsh culture, and too little on the contributions that incomers can make to a developing Welsh culture, or cultures, then a great deal will be lost. It would be drawing up the covered wagons in a circle and waiting for the final onslaught, with nobody to play the part of the US Cavalry but the Welsh Office and the Welsh Language Board, and they are bedevilled by the fissiparous nature of Welsh society. When the Welsh

149

Language Board after many delays finally produced its draft Welsh Language Bill in 1990, it was caught in the crossfire between the CBI (denouncing bilingualism as a death blow to the Welsh business economy) and the Welsh Language Society (deriding the proposals because they allowed the private sector to escape bilingual obligations). When will inter-tribal warfare give way to a more modern pluralism?

And where can incomers who have learned the language find a comfortable niche in rural Wales? It has been observed that Welsh learners are often expected to become a certain kind of person, instead of being offered a range of different kinds of Welsh identity to choose from:

> Rather than regarding the Welsh language as belonging to each and every Welsh person, whatever his or her origins, colour, creed, interests or primary language, there is a tendency for Welsh speakers, unconsciously, to cultivate an ambience redolent of the values and assumptions of rural nonconformist Wales.[2]

The situation has changed since the late seventies, when that was written, due to an increasing number of professional jobs in the Welsh-language media and in local authorities, where in some localities staff such as social workers and teachers have to be fluently bilingual. But incomers only exceptionally become sufficiently fluent in Welsh to move in these circles. They are more likely to live in diminished traditional communities in country areas, and feel uneasy because they cannot subscribe to what remains of rural conconformist values. Clearly one important factor in the language's revival among adult learners will be the capacity of the Welsh-speaking world to offer varieties of Welshness, to enable different kinds of incomers to find empathic Welsh language-networks which express, say, local *and* national *and* inter-national concerns like peace work or feminism or greener ways of living. Welsh-speaking women were there at Greenham, and one of the leading Welsh-language poets is Menna Elfyn, a lively and witty feminist. The longest running organic farm in west Wales is a very successful business run by Welsh-speaking Rowlandses at Borth, north of Aberystwyth (Rachel's Dairy Products). The MP elected for Ceredigion and North Pembrokeshire in 1992 is Cynog Dafis, a Plaid Cymru man, but one who had been a green thinker since the 1970s, long before he was elected to Parliament as a result of a joint Green Party/ Plaid Cymru campaign. I cite these examples to offset the witty stereotypes beloved by Dylan Iorwerth of *Golwg*, and others, that greens are bound to be monoglot English incomers, bearded, sandalled and goat-keeping; or that feminism is a sort of She imperialism brought in by the English and irrelevant to Welsh-speaking women's experiences.

People talking about the language

'Little Nia, she's only four, burst into tears last weekend at the Christmas Party, because Siôn Corn [John Chimney, therefore Santa Claus] wasn't a proper Santa—he couldn't speak Welsh.'

'When Huw goes to the playgroup in the village he's one of only three Welsh-speaking children left, so their Welsh is submerged in a sea of English. There's been such a lot of English incomers just in the last ten years that it's changed things completely, especially for the local children. Some of the newcomers do very well with the language, but most of them give it up after a while. One of the playgroup helpers has succeeded and that's great; I really admire her. But it does not solve the problem of English becoming the dominant language, because the real battle is not in the classroom but in the playground. I'll be glad when Geraint goes to Penweddig the Welsh-medium secondary school in Aberystwyth because he's changed to thinking in English instead of in Welsh, though at home we only speak Welsh. It's because there's more English than Welsh among his school friends, and what do you do when it's his birthday and he wants to invite his best friends home, and everybody has to change to English in the house? I'm worried as well because his Welsh is not developing into a good thinking tool, it's got stuck at the level of simple talk with family and neighbours, and when you stop thinking in Welsh you lose a special way of seeing the world ...'

151

I asked her what she meant, but she just laughed and couldn't or wouldn't explain. But later, at different times, I was given two different descriptions of what it had been like in the valley when the hydroelectric scheme came in the 1960s, one from the viewpoint of an English engineer who had worked on it, and the other from a Welsh-speaking local, and they provided a striking contrast. Here is how the two men spoke of the workers on the scheme:

'Alun':
There were a thousand and eight men navvying to get the scheme done, and hardly one of them was Welsh. They were nearly all of them Irish, and they lived in big camps in the valley. A field of mud it was most of the time—you would sink to your knees in it. There were a few tough ones, and a bit of heavy drinking from time to time, but they were nice fellows and worked hard—till it came to harvest time. Then they would lay down their tools and go back home to see to their farms for a week or two.

'Jonathan':
You can estimate that on any big construction site in the UK 30% of the labourers will be Irish. They came over in the fifties and cornered this type of work. Add to that, if the scheme is in a remote part of the country, as in this valley, 60% will be Irish, for they have a tradition of being itinerant. A lot of the men leave their families back in Ireland and are free to go wherever the work is. In theory they work a lot of overtime and have plenty of money to send home. In practice they may drink it and/or abandon their families temporarily or permanently. But they can work hard, I will say that for them.

Incomers' voices

The people who keep the general store in our nearest village are from the West Midlands and came here, like so many others, because it was their dream to get away from urban hassles to a quiet friendly place in beautiful countryside. The village seems exactly that, with its chapel and small primary school, a *Siôn a Siân* (Derby and Joan) Club for the older folks, its own shop and sub post office, and a good bus service into town. But when you consider the place in greater depth, it is clear there are divisions in the small population, even if they all manage to rub along with each other on the surface. There are *two* women's societies, an English-speaking Women's Institute and a Welsh-speaking *Merched y Wawr* (Women of the Dawn). The *Merched y Wawr* movement, set up in the 1960s, helps to keep the language alive in rural areas at a time when dilution with English, or complete dominance by English, would otherwise be inevitable in villages like this. For the shop and post office are now run by people who speak no Welsh, and although locals can chatter to each other as in the old days when these were the gossip centres of the village, they invariably have to change to English to conduct their business, and pick up instant cues about which language to use with different people who are there at the same time.

There is considerable surface amiability, but a widespread consciousness of differences, too. The woman in the shop says resignedly, 'Well, it's no use just learning the Welsh words, is it? It's another world, like you have to have a different sense of humour—honestly I give up sometimes, trying to understand the Welsh. But it's great here, all the same'. That was a couple of years ago, but now the shop is up for sale, for the recession and the arrival of more supermarkets in Aberystwyth have proved disastrous for small village stores. It has been on the market for quite a while, but nobody, Welsh speaker or English speaker is rushing to take it on.

The *Siôn a Siân* Club in the village uses English at its meetings, for what else can you do when an increasing number of non-Welsh speakers join? You can see why the most dedicated defenders of the language argue that Welsh monoglottism is the only answer to English monoglottism, even if its inevitably leads to villages splitting into two distinct groups. But you cannot have two separate schools anyway. When the evacuees came here during the war, they went to schools where the other children spoke so little English that they soon picked up Welsh, with the enviable ease that small children absorb a second language. Children can still do this, and there are numerous examples of completely bilingual children in the homes of English incomers. But what happens to the grownups when faced with another language and culture from which they are excluded unless they can learn Welsh? And what happens to the 'mixed marriages' where one party is Welsh speaking and the other not? The following are voices from a number of Ceredigion communities, talking about the extent to which people see the language as divisive, or, on the contrary, enriching.

The mixed marriage of 'Ted and Enid'

Ted is an old-fashioned Englishman in every respect. He wears dark suits and silken cravats for evenings out, reads the *Daily Telegraph* and is proud to be a Conservative in all matters. He had one half-hearted go at learning Welsh a long time ago, but showed little aptitude and soon gave it up. 'In any case, who am I going to speak Welsh to?', he wonders. 'When any of them call here they speak Welsh to Enid till I arrive, and then most of them are very polite and change to English'. In fact Ted takes a certain amount of glee in teaching classic English expressions to a local man who does odd jobs for them and who is always on the look out for expanding his English, never mind his Welsh. Ted, however much he rationalises about everyday language changeovers locally, is quite aware of the significance of the language. 'In the early days whenever we had any difficulties with the locals, they blamed me and called me a ''bloody *Sais*''. If Enid hadn't been Welsh-speaking I doubt very much if we would have been accepted in any sense'.

I asked Enid if using her Welsh gives her more of a sense of belonging, even though in the home she mainly uses English. 'I think so', she said. 'I don't feel it right to speak English to Welsh people if I'm meant to be Welsh, and it's not an effort, for I was brought up to speak both English and Welsh in my family in north Wales . . . But it would be quite alien to be talking Welsh to Ted. There's nothing Welsh about him, is there? He's not any kind of Welsh character. It's natural for him to speak English, not Welsh, and it would seem very strange for me to speak Welsh to him'. She laughs, and pauses to reflect. 'Anyway, to be honest, English is my first language as far as speaking is concerned, though my degree was in Welsh literature and so I've read a lot of Welsh in the past . . .'

I asked her if she read any Welsh now. 'I would more naturally read English—including a lot of Welsh writers who write in English. I've read very few Welsh novels, I must admit. There's not much choice, and you don't feel there's any point unless you can talk about them to other people ... though I've heard there are groups in Borth I think, and in Llanbadarn, who meet (or used to) to discuss these novels. But I have very little incentive to do so ... so I can't say I'm propagating the Welsh language.'

She thought about the question of reading in Welsh for a while. 'Around here a number of people read Welsh books as well as speaking the language on a daily basis. Quite a few of them take Welsh books from the Mobile Library van, and many of the older people write and read well because of the influence of the Chapel. In days gone by you probably learnt better Welsh and read more Welsh books in the Sunday School than in the elementary schools. Because of course the influence of the 1847 Blue Books lasted for a hundred years, with the emphasis on learning to speak and write correct English, not Welsh. Good Welsh was lost during that period, and a language becomes kitchen talk, ''pidgin'', when it isn't written correctly. That's probably why there's such a gap between the written and the spoken forms of Welsh. And of course English was pushed as a way to get a job and get on in life, so Welsh became just a day-to-day communication device among the people you know well. That's why some Welsh people are shy about outsiders joining in their talk—they worry they're not speaking correctly.'

'Mary Truford', retired headmistress

'Mrs Truford' spent half her teaching career in schools in the North of England, and half in English-medium secondary schools in Wales. At one time she went to Welsh classes and learnt a certain amount of the language, but she does not speak it at all now. Like the vast majority of learners who have failed to achieve a working fluency, she has given up trying, but remains very aware of the difficulties and problems surrounding the language, and especially the nuances it carries for local

155

people, who are her neighbours. 'I have no need to speak it, so why bother?' She enunciates the issues systematically, ticking them off on the fingers of one hand. 'First you have to be aware that bilingual education isn't acceptable to a number of extremist parents on both sides. Some of the English come to live in Wales and are simply amazed to find there is a Welsh language in existence at all. They try to find all sorts of excuses to save their kiddies from learning Welsh, although the children find it all much more straightforward than the parents. On the other side are the extreme Welsh nats who reject bilingualism because they want their children to be monoglot Welsh, so as not to dilute the old-time cultural values. My own personal view is that the language deserves to be saved, and whether you decide to learn it yourself or not, you have a duty to support it in all the other possible ways—like campaigns for bilingual policies in public life and in business, subsidies for publishing and the media, and so on.

'Mind you, the Welsh themselves have a lot to answer for, in sorting out the blame for the decline of the language. It's true that three quarters of the primary school children in the village are now English-speaking incomers, and the language is under threat in the playground. But look at what happens at the carol service and the *Cawl Cennin* on St David's Day. Just because there are non-Welsh speakers present they hardly sing any carols in Welsh any more, or make any of the little speeches and votes of thanks in Welsh. They should stand up more for their own language if they want to save it, that's my opinion. But the people around here are not really nationalists. They feel it is impolite to inflict their language on English speakers, and they are quite confused when, as happens once in a blue moon, an incomer becomes fluent in Welsh and insists on their speaking it with him. I'm afraid there is still a deferential tendency to try and please, so they speak English and try to give the answers you want. If there's anything unpleasant to be said it's more likely to be said behind your back, not out in the open to your face.

'They speak of the beauty of the Welsh language and I am sure it can be, when properly used. I have been to some very lengthy funerals in Welsh in my time, as a matter of duty, and still remember the impressive cadences in the speeches about the dead, even though I had to sit through them for hours without picking up much of the meaning. However I gather that in the spoken tongue the language is mauled. They swallow beginnings and endings, shorten it, reduce it, and above all stuff it full of English words spelt in a Welsh way—like *siwgr* and *travelio* and *wats* and *tacsi*. I am not surprised that the academics and literati and nationalist glitterati go on so much about the purity of the language. They use Welsh because they are proud of it, but the majority of Welsh speakers seem to be still affected by the old pressures to use English to get on. They use Welsh any old way because it's not important to material prosperity. It's always been more associated with love and music and poetry and stories than with ruthless practicality and progress and achievement of a more worldly kind. Hearth, home and dreams . . . not enough in this day and age.'

Graffiti from the Ladies Loo, Aberystwyth Castle Grounds, 1991
'Why do the Welsh go on speaking the Welsh language when there are English people present? I think they are very rude, for they know how to speak English, so why don't they?

Anonymous
'What language? I thought Welsh was just a kind of English dialect.'

Incomer Kate from the North of England
Kate is into an alternative 'away from it all' lifestyle. Semi-settled in Ceredigion, having been here for about four years, she lives the simple life in an old cottage rented cheaply before the property boom. She and her mate have patched it up to be (only just) weatherproof. I asked her if she had ever thought of learning Welsh, since so many of the local community use it as their first language. 'Yeah, I'm quite happy to learn the language. But learning it—that's the biggest obstacle. I've even got the books to learn it. I nearly went on a four weeks crash course, but I had to go up to Lancashire and missed the enrolment, so I thought, well,

157

what's the use if you miss the first week ... When Dai (the local farmer who rents them the cottage) drops in, we talk Welsh a bit to him, but these beggars speak back in English to you. *"Nos da"*, *"Sut mae"*. Everybody knows those but you can't get any further. The language is one of the biggest hurdles. At the same time, though, everybody who lives around here speaks English, right? The way I look at it is, I'm a peasant on the land and these are all peasants on the land. We're all from the same level and there shouldn't be a language barrier ...'

James, the son of English incomers, now studying at an English university

'I hated having to learn the language at school. We came when I was twelve and I was self-conscious enough getting to know people without the extra barrier, and sensing it was a nest of vipers. There were Welshies and Lefties and I didn't want to be either. I was a victim of my liberal incomer parents at the time, though I now feel it's right to support minority cultures, but not through coercing incomer children into them. I'm doing politics at university now, and I can accept the principle, but it's very messy and emotional in Wales, and I found it quite alienating when I was growing up—all those stereotypes of Celts and Saxons, like primitive tribes—and no sense of humour ...'

'The Giffords', holiday home owners

The Giffords live in Hertfordshire, but Gwen's family still live around Aberystwyth, where she came from originally, and they bring their own family here regularly to keep up the connection and because they love the area. Teenage John became sensitive to things Welsh when he undertook to do a project related to the old lead mines for A level geography. 'I did a survey of all the mines and walked the old leats and tramways, and I got really interested in what it must have been like when it was all working a hundred years ago. I had to go into the National Library to look up information in the Manuscripts Department, and I felt awkward when they spoke to me first in Welsh and I couldn't reply. It was like I was excluded from some other dimension because I did not speak the

158

language. The National Library is one of the few places I've been to where you feel you ought to be able to speak Welsh. It's a bit of an eye-opener.'

His sister Susan is not so far affected like this. She tends to see Welsh as another language, and, 'I've got enough already with French and Spanish at school'.

Their Welsh mother can understand a fair bit of the language but can only speak a little, because when she was at school Welsh was not so strong in education as it is now. She regrets this, because she would like to be able to use the language with the local people, and with her own extended family and friends in the locality, many of whom use Welsh among themselves.

Their father bought himself a set of Linguaphone cassettes, *Teach yourself Welsh*, but these were a little ridiculed by one of the native speakers in Gwen's family, as the product of 'the mind of a Welsh speaker in Wolverhampton', so his efforts were inhibited, for one reason or another. But he continues to delight in Ordnance Survey Welsh, being a keen walker. He takes an intelligent interest in the etymology of local place names, and has worked out the colourful names of the old farms in the area. He is always prepared to have a rational discussion on the language issue, conceding that beyond a certain point the influx of English-speaking incomers on the delicate linguistic and cultural infra-structure of rural villages is bound to be negative, destroying more than it can contribute. But tourism is one of the economic bases of the locality ... 'Without the holiday industry of B & B and self-catering rural incomes would drop so low that the exodus of locals would increase. And that is the other half of what is called the problem of in-migration—the out-migration.'

It can be argued, indeed, that a modest proportion of holiday homes in a rural community is less destructive than permanent settlement by non-Welsh speakers. 'The Giffords', in any case, like many another, have bought a holiday home in Ceredigion to keep up their Welsh connection, and maintain close contacts with Gwen's Welsh-speaking family, as well as enjoying the scenery and the walking and the industrial

159

archaeology. It is naive to argue that holiday homes are a creeping paralysis spreading over the countryside, because the hill farm economy often depends on income from holiday lettings, and the absentee owners may well be Welsh exiles, and tourism is now Wales' biggest industry. Where the problem arises is when the proportion of holiday homes (particularly in villages) reaches a critical point, when there are no longer enough permanent residents to sustain the shop or the school or the post office or the village hall, all the year round.

An unused house lying empty except for a few weeks in the summer, can be, too, an offence to local people seeking a home in a time of housing scarcity and rising prices. The extremist response of *Meibion Glyndŵr*, the sons of Glyndŵr, has been to burn down holiday homes, and this invariably gets publicity in the British media, which tend to ignore more constructive aspects of Welsh life. So there has been a growing caution about buying charming Welsh holiday cottages among typical home counties clientele, even if they are not able to read the message on the tee shirts of some young language enthusiasts: '*Ta, Ta, Tŷ ha*', *Ha Ha*', Bye, Bye, Holiday home, Ha Ha', written above a picture of a cottage with flames coming out of the roof.

In Cwmrheidol the proportion of holiday cottages has gradually fallen during the last decade, as remoter cottages have been modernised and turned into permanent homes. Good news? Well certainly the rural depopulation of the 1950s and 1960s has been reversed, but from a strictly linguistic viewpoint it is bad news, because the proportion of Welsh speakers to English speakers in the valley has diminished significantly since the 1960s.

'Marie and Peter Robinson'
Marie and Peter are a dual career couple with grown up children who were brought up in Wales and have settled locally. Peter was born in Essex and worked there before moving to mid Wales in the 1960s. As a scientist, he sees no reason to use Welsh. He considers that the language of science is international, and it is English, therefore he would see it as an impediment to approach it through the medium of Welsh. 'You

simply don't have the range of up-to-date texts in Welsh that are available in English, and you never could have, because translating costs would be phenomenal'. His network of professional contacts and his political network (he is active in the Labour party) he sees as British, rather than English or Welsh. These contacts are all English speaking, so he sees no need to learn Welsh, and never has, during his twenty five years living in the Aberystwyth area.

'I'm basically a commuter', he says. 'Where I live is in many ways accidental, and not particularly significant to me. I don't have a strong sense of place. I use my home as my base, from which I go out into the world to do whatever I have to do, whether locally or in London or anywhere else in Britain that holds conferences or meetings in my interests. No problem. I've never wanted to learn Welsh, for where would I use it? To buy the vegetables from the farmer down the road? Hardly worth the effort, I think? Especially when I recall the misfortunes of some of my colleagues who have tried and been defeated by the unwillingness of their Welsh-speaking co-workers to speak Welsh to them. I distinctly remember poor old Jonathan hunting down the Welsh speakers in the coffee room, and having to nail them to the wall to get them to speak to him. He ultimately succeeded, partly because he was a Methodist lay preacher, I suspect, but also because he was an obstinate northerner, not easily discouraged. Whereas I'm a sort of Londoner—well, was once a greater Londoner, but probably still am and always will be. When I go back there it's so familiar to me, my old stamping grounds—like old slippers. Though of course I wouldn't want to live there now, with the rat race and the crime and what have you. I'll settle for around here—so long as I don't have to learn the language . . .'

Marie Robinson has more ambivalent views on the language, even though in the end she agrees with Peter about the problems for English incomers over learning it. She longs to put down roots in the place she lives, because she was brought up in a family which moved about the world, and she changed schools half a dozen times. But she does not see it as practicable to put down roots in rural Wales (or anywhere else) except through her children. 'That is how you get to belong to a community',

161

she insists, 'by having children and bringing them up to be part of it'. Their son and daughter both learned Welsh at school but never became good enough to use it in everyday situations. They now have children of their own who go to Welsh-speaking playgroups, so there is a reason for them as parents to use Welsh. Marie says, 'It is the children who bring their parents into the community. Then you can see the whole Welsh thing more from the inside than from the outside—through your children and the contacts they bring you with other parents'.

'But you, personally?' I asked Marie, 'have you never wanted to speak Welsh to feel a sense of belonging, in your work or in your counselling?' (Marie does voluntary marriage counselling). 'I've always found there's a problem about outsiders speaking Welsh with the real Welsh. They—the real Welsh, I mean—do not want you to speak Welsh, although they want Welsh to be spoken. It's like the language is a thing they have of their own and just because they value it so much they are wary of outsiders coming in and using it, like they were taking it over, I suppose'.

So a new problem emerges, if Marie's feelings are well-founded. Some native Welsh speakers are unhappy about incomers learning the language, because these new Welsh speakers may use it without insights into the culture and the values it stands for. It seems wrong to some to hear the language of Heaven coming out of the mouths of the English, who do not belong properly to the community or the inherited traditions, however clever they are at mastering the Welsh tongue as a tool for communication. There is perhaps a fear that even the language can be colonised in the end, and this innermost bastion of Welshness be invaded by the *Saeson*, the traditional enemies in Welsh history and mythology.

'Gerald Martin', writer
'There are the *Cymry Cymraeg* (the Welsh-speaking Welsh); and the *Cymry di-Cymraeg* (the English-speaking Welsh); and people who are Welsh by choice, which is my category. You always have a choice to make when you go to live in another country which has another

162

language. You can learn the language and (if you're English) stay English, as the majority of people going to live in France might do, because they have no need to be anything else. But in Wales the situation is different. There's no need to learn Welsh to communicate, because the Welsh-speakers are bilingual. Therefore the motivation for people to learn the language (and very often the result of learning the language well), is that they learn a value system, and are excited by a history and tradition and culture which they take on board. So you are learning not just a language but something wider and deeper, when you learn a language in a bilingual country where you've got one dominant language and one minority language'.

I pointed out that some people in Wales who are native Welsh speakers settle for a consumerist international culture, and abandon their traditional values and interests.

'Well, there's a negative identity as well as a positive identity you can take on. But in some parts of Wales now you have to be quite self-conscious in choosing or emphasising your Welsh identity, because the pressure of Englishness everywhere is so great that you are constantly faced with the alternative cultures competing with each other. That's precisely the problem—the number of unselfconscious Welsh speakers declines drastically every year, and that isn't going to be solved by people like me, who have chosen Welshness.

'Another problem is the dramatic decline in the quality of the language spoken by ordinary people over the past fifteen years, in my experience. It has been disastrous in south and west Wales. The only decent Welsh you hear from ordinary unselfconscious Welsh-speaking people is in Gwynedd, and not many of them'.

Why? I asked. Was it a result of the media?

'The media are only the sharp end of it. The culture is rapidly being assimilated into Anglo-American culture. When you use a language that has its roots in a culture that is no longer viable, you force the language to do things it wasn't meant to do. The most obvious things you hear are the literal translation of English idioms and aphorisms and so on into Welsh. The use of English *words* is in fact not so damaging, because it

163

seems quite appropriate when talking about English concepts to use the English word for them, and not to try to transpose them into a Welsh concept.

'What is more worrying is the decline in the structure of the language, because it is the grammar and the structure that incorporate the ways of thinking. A language can always absorb words, and Welsh has in the past—from Latin and Norman-French as well as from English. The problem is when the structure has become distorted to fit the word patterns of another culture. Once that happens the language just becomes a cipher for that other culture, and that's what happening to Welsh now'.

We moved on to the area of necessary consciousness raising. How can incomers become more aware of what is happening to the Welsh language and culture? I asked.

'When people come to live here, often not knowing about the situation of a language and culture in decline (though they are usually well enough informed about parallel situations in Europe), they usually sense something—that things are not as they ought to be. Most of them react not by saying, "God, I've got to find out about this", but by saying, "I don't want to know", or by turning awkward and bloody-minded about the Welsh, or by turning it into some big joke, so that they can laugh it off'.

'Well', I said, 'I suppose it's like a chasm opening up in front of you, when you're able to see that there is a different culture and language going on around you, that you're excluded from, because you're an English speaker. In a sense you're worse off if you can see this than the incomers who remain oblivious. Because if you're aware of it, you have to decide what you're going to do about it. What do you think people should do about it?'

'What you should do about it is learn the language if you've come to live in a Welsh-speaking area, because your whole relationship with the Welsh culture must be positive, not evasive or negative. It's easier if you have children, because you can express your commitment to Wales by speaking Welsh with them at home, and making sure that the children develop relationships with local people and not just with the children of other incomers. Too often what happens is that these children live primarily in a society of incomers, and so they remain English rather than becoming Welsh-speaking Welsh. If you come here and have children you must learn the language and use it with the children'.

My own story

Ken and I have lived in the valley for seven years, but long before that we decided we would live in Wales one day. It was a serious and positive choice, once we could arrange our lives to be able to live and work here. Ken's family moved from Anglesey to Merseyside in the nineteenth century, like so many other North Walians seeking work and wealth. He spent all his youthful holidays cycling round north Wales, talking to farmers and shopkeepers and the landladies who ran the modest B & Bs he stayed in. After we met, we used to come to Wales on walking and camping holidays every summer, and I got to know the country from a holiday viewpoint. But even that was an advance, for like a lot of Irish people, I had passed through Wales many times on the Dublin to London boat-trains, but had never stopped to explore it.

Once you have left the country you were brought up in, as I did Ireland, you have the freedom that mobility and widening perspectives give you, but also the uncertainties arising from being some sort of cultural mongrel, a displaced person, but from your own choice. You carry within you your original cultural baggage, but it is continually being modified and reshaped by current experiences of place and people. I have come to the conclusion that if you were brought up in Ulster, like me, it is much healthier to be a cultural mongrel, and the sooner you reshape your cultural heritage the better for yourself and the people you meet. I was heartened therefore to read the Raymond Williams Memorial Lecture 1992, in which Stuart Hall chooses the 'capacity to live with difference' as the coming question of the 21st century. It is an increasingly common modern experience to have 'to inhabit at least two identities, to speak at least two cultural languages, to negotiate and "translate" between them'.[3] Since we cannot get back to the old

165

certainties of a sense of belonging to a particular place and an undisputed culture, we should make a virtue of what Salman Rushdie calls 'the transformation that comes of new and unexpected combinations of human beings, cultures, ideas, politics, movies, songs'.[4] But that does not mean losing a sense of place.

There has certainly been an element of transformation for Ken and me as a result of coming and living in this valley. When we first came we had a modest collection of books (in English) about Wales and the Welsh, but I was amazingly ignorant of the everyday way of life in rural Wales, and of the implications of moving into a Welsh-speaking area. I remember well the first occasion it really came home to me. We were having a cup of tea with the ever-welcoming Mr and Mrs Davies Caihaidd. A neighbour dropped in to ask about something. They were chatting away in Welsh out in the hall, but as soon as they came back into the sitting room to introduce us to the neighbour, all three courteously and without fuss changed to English because Ken and I had no Welsh. I felt a terrible sense of embarrassment, and after that when I read the English-language books in our collection I was much more conscious of words like the following (from a former headteacher of Llanuwchllyn school, Ivor Owen):

> Because we are a polite and sociable people we will readily change the language to make a newcomer feel welcome. Perhaps Welshmen have been too polite for the health of the language. Once a nucleus of non-Welsh speakers is established in a small community the Welsh language is on the defensive. It is always we who have to build bridges out to the English speakers. They have rarely built bridges out to us.[5]

I began to talk to people about the valley, because it was a living way of finding out about this place I had come to live in, beyond a past fossilised in guidebooks and histories. Miss Nellie Jenkins told me about her childhood before the First World War, and about her father going down to south Wales to find work. I began to see the valley as my bridge to a better understanding of rural Wales, past and present, for it has been through an industrial past (the lead mining), suffered rural depopulation, a half-life of holiday homes, a 1980s rebuilding of derelict old farm houses and lead miners' cottages (by incomers), and a dilution of the traditional Welsh-speaking culture as the older generation die and the young leave.

It wasn't long before I realised I would have to learn Welsh, because Eirlys Davies lent me a book of local history by the former minister of Ystumtuen Chapel (Y Parch J. Henry Griffiths' *Bro annwyl y bryniau*), and there were a whole lot of references to the valley which I couldn't read, and I had to get a friend to translate them for me. And when Miss Jenkins showed me the old books in her living room and talked about what she was reading from the library, I couldn't read even the titles, and felt that here indeed was another world from which I was totally cut off. Once I became aware of this other world I saw evidences of it everywhere. I noticed *Sbec*, the Welsh equivalent of *TV Times*, and the news magazine weeklies *Y Cymro* and *Y Faner*, in neighbours' houses. I saw the local *papur bro, Y Tincer*, with its monthly local community news and neighbourly good wishes on marriages and 90th birthdays and examination results and *eisteddfodau* success. I realised there was a Welsh language women's organisation, *Merched y Wawr*, which local women belong to, as well as the English-speaking Cwmrheidol Ladies Guild set up by Mrs Margaret Davies in the 1970s. I noticed the page of Welsh-language reporting every week in the *Cambrian News*, and wondered what it was about. When I went to the public library in Aberystwyth I heard the librarians shifting, apparently effortlessly, from Welsh to English and English to Welsh, and wondered how they knew which language to address a reader in. I also saw there a section of Welsh books which I must have walked past blindly on earlier visits. I hovered uncertainly in *Siop y Pethe*, gazing hopelessly at the probably interesting magazines, like *Barn* and *Golwg*, and the yards and yards of Welsh titles, none of which could mean anything to me in my monoglot state.

I enrolled for a term of beginners' classes with Jaci Taylor in the Extra-mural Department in Aberystwyth that spring, and then went on the intensive *Cwrs Carlam* for nine days in July 1989. By this time, with the help of Miss Jenkins (who read children's stories in Welsh with me), and of Mair Stanleigh (who talked to me for an hour a week in Welsh slowly and patiently, that summer), I was beginning to read Welsh—enough to enable me to start subscribing to the monthly *Tincer*. But my modest reading ability meant I was graded too high on the *Cwrs Carlam*, and I sat in a haze of misery and incomprehension, till I could gather enough Welsh words to explain my predicament to the tutor (and overcome his natural reluctance for anyone to leave his group), and change to a lower class.

A year later, on the *Cwrs Carlam* in Llandovery, I had a far more rewarding time, for I began to experience a sense of progress in the language (relatively speaking). I could listen to *Radio Cymru* and watch *S4C* television, and follow the gist of it, though remaining blurry on the details when the speakers were too quick for me, or had a strong accent. Beti George, Hywel Gwynfryn and Sulwyn Thomas took their place in my litany of media presenters, alongside Dilly Barlow and John Humphries and Nick Ross. That other mysterious world on the far side of the language barrier was becoming peopled. Not just the living but the dead had something to tell me, since for the first time I was able to read what was written on the headstones of the former inhabitants of Cwmrheidol houses. I was on the road to exploring tentatively the hidden world of Welshness, though slowly and with difficulty.

For learning the language is not all plain sailing, in commitment or in practice. It is a bit like those early Celtic pilgrimages, where you set out to sea in a rudderless small boat, and knew not where you would end up, or if you would arrive at all, but that did not matter, for it was the voyage of discovery that increased your insight—if it increased at all . . .

[1] Thomas Stephens, Unitarian minister in Merthyr, quoted in Emyr Humphreys, *The Taliesin tradition*, London, Black Raven, 1983, p. 155.

[2] Harri Pritchard Jones, 'Mixed marriages', *Planet* 40, 1977, p. 6.

[3] Stuart Hall, 'Our mongrel selves', *New Statesman and Society, Borderland Supplement*, June 1992, pp. 6-8.

[4] Salman Rushdie, *Imaginary homelands*, London, Granta Books, 1991.

[5] Trevor Fishlock, *Talking of Wales*, London, Panther, 1978, p. 139.

Chapter 7

Blod and the Brush Salesman: approaches to learning Welsh

What can be the reasons for the extraordinarily high drop-out rate among adult Welsh learners? Nobody seems to have any precise figures of drop-out rates, but optimists have estimated that only about 5% succeed in mastering the language, and the first class I attended had sunk from 35 to half a dozen after one term. At the same time the language industry is booming. It employs large numbers of people preparing and publishing learning materials, taking classes and doing research projects, with ever-increasing sums of public money, including EC grants for minority languages. The teaching of minority languages gets more and more support, not just to help minority cultures, but because it may be a strategy for healing divided communities. Ulster Protestants have been offered Irish classes at the tax-payers' expense, for example.

Why then is this well-motivated and reasonably well-financed infrastructure not turning out more linguistically born-again incomers who can integrate with their communities and help solve the problem of a dying culture in the Welsh-speaking heartlands? Look around rural Wales and you can see that the country is littered with furtive failed learners, or the not-so-furtive who are still trying, from time to time, but who almost justify the bitter comment by R. S. Thomas that after ten years of Welsh classes all the English incomers can say to the locals is *Bore da* and *Diolch yn fawr*. In these circumstances a stab at a few classes is no more than a symbolic gesture to salve consciences about coming to live in a beautiful countryside, where the local culture is still clearly intertwined with the language or else haunted by the bitter ghost of the lost language and the guilt that gnaws on losing it.

From my personal experiences as a Welsh learner I would like to suggest that too much effort has been going into functional and mechanistic approaches, and not enough into organic approaches that take account of different learning needs and ways of supporting learners in their communities. It is a basic educational tenet that you start where the learners are. The problem with Welsh classes for adults is that they tend to assume a homogeneity among learners which rarely exists. I have met a fair number of people whose primary need is to read Welsh, yet all the classes seem to be conversational Welsh. Since the two are very different because of the endless elisions, abbreviations and local varieties of spoken Welsh, you cannot easily teach them together. Also, quite a few people want (or could use) Welsh in their everyday work in catering or other service jobs. Others have come to learn the language for cultural or social reasons, from varying degrees of conviction about the significance of the language in the communities where they live and want to belong. Still others choose to come to classes for more specific purposes, like needing a bit of Welsh to be able to take part in local political action, or to be able to have a say on the Welsh media, like the phone-in programmes on *Radio Cymru*. There are those who have rather vaguer motivation, and treat the language classes like any other evening class—to provide another interest, which they have always meant to take up when they had time. Or because, like *Yr Wyddfa*, Snowdon, the language is there in the background, looming when not shrouded in mist, and one becomes aware of it, like it or not.

The cultural and political implications of learning the language are usually more implicit than explicit, or not obviously there at all, in classes for adult leaners, which seems a strange lacuna when you consider the heavily publicized crisis of in-migration into rural Wales, and the increasing attention given to the 'lesser-used languages' within the European Community. Languages are not just neutral tools for exchanging information (except perhaps when you go on the continent for holidays, and can only operate at a frustrating minimal level of communication, buying goods and services). They are ways of seeing the world around you, through perspectives that have accumulated throughout the history of the language, and go on being constantly changed by present circumstances. You can still trace the impact of the Roman occupation in the considerable number of Welsh words that go back to Latin (like *ffenestri* for windows, *eglwys* for church, and *mil* for a thousand). You can trace too the waves of infiltration of English words from the Anglo-Saxon period onwards, and after the Act of Union 1536, when Welsh was exiled from public life, the law courts, the schools and the coroners' courts. But English infiltration was not confined to official or bureaucratic vocabulary. For some reason Welsh very early on borrowed from English basic everyday words like kissing (*cusanu*) and socks (*hosanau*).

It continues to borrow English words quite unnecessarily, because that is the fate of minority languages when spoken alongside a world-dominant language like English. So in reports from the Gulf War on the Welsh-language media, reporters used *bomio, tanciau* and *byncer* (bunker is probably itself borrowed by English from Old Norse). They mixed these with genuinely Welsh war vocabulary, like *taflegryn* for missile and *awyrennau* for planes. Such borrowings obviously increase in colonial or post-colonial situations, but there are examples round the world far more extreme than the Welsh case. One of the most interesting is in Papua New Guinea, where the Chimbu people regularly perform an ancient tribal courtship ritual in which the men dress up and perform music for the women, who then choose the man they want for a partner. The ceremony is now called '*Turnim Hed*'.

There are other reasons why Welsh takes on so many English words. The flourishing Welsh-language rock music scene sometimes wilfully uses English borrowings for the sake of 'style'. It is cool to be able to take it or leave it, use or not use English words without feeling colonised as your elders warn you will be. You can appropriate the appropriators by bending their language to your own purposes (like James Joyce did with English in *Finnegan's Wake*, and Synge did in *Playboy of the Western World* or *Riders to the Sea*.)

It would be helpful for learners to know some of this, because they might then speak a more acceptable form of popular Welsh, rather than the too goody-goody Welsh taught in adult classes. This would be especially valuable for the many incomers who want to use the language as a bridge across into the rural communities they have come to live in. Those who have chosen to live in rural Wales for idealistic reasons, to escape the Anglo-urban rat-race, have to a greater or lesser degree a vision of their new country. Many have begun to run a smallholding or a small business, hoping to become part of a close-knit neighbourly community. They see the language as a help in developing this new sense of identity, because it could bring authentic contacts with the traditional place and people. But where is the map of this new country? Where are the bridges to cross the great divide between incomers and locals, even as you attend adult Welsh classes? There are bodies out there somewhere trying to help, like *CYD* and *PONT* and the Dyfed Working Party on Bilingualism. But it is all still rather formal and contrived, when what one wants is an organic web of connection and support between individuals in the communities.

Perhaps the luckiest learners are the parents of nursery school children, for in a number of places there are classes linked with what the children are doing in the local playgroup, and there are excellent published materials for parents and children to use while learning the language together. Gomer has published the *Dysgu Dau* books, for example, where each lesson is followed by suggestions for reading stories with the child, and listening to tapes of songs and traditional tales. It is also non-sexist unlike a lot of the adult learning materials (see below). This approach fulfils the need to start where the learners are, to focus on their immediate interests, and to provide attractive and varied backup materials.

For the learners without nursery school children the situation is not so promising, unless they are lucky enough to meet a *Cymro Cymraeg* or a *Cymraes Gymraeg* who is prepared to see them regularly, to talk and read and explain the background of the Welsh-speaking world. Learners still need the many simplified stories for adults, like *The Mabinogi for learners*, with vocabulary at the bottom of the page to save the boring experience of looking up the *Geiriadur* every time. Alun Ifans' books are a good example of attractive simplified reading related to the culture. But the problem is getting access to information about such help, and about how to move on from simplified stories to genuine current Welsh writing. If you are not a school student, or prepared to spend hours in the town library sifting the shelves to find something on the Welsh culture which is within your reading ability, you need personal guidance and advice from the *Cymry Cymraeg* world.

The British Adult Literacy Scheme back in the 1970s had a parallel problem of providing literacy classes with simple reading materials that yet appealed to adult interests. The gap was soon filled by keen librarians and publishers. Can the same thing not happen for adult Welsh learners? Libraries could do a lot by compiling reading lists for various levels, and doing displays, and drawing learners' attention to suitable material in the children's library. Why not an adult learners' corner, which could also include information on local language classes, Welsh theatre in the area, and a display of magazines like *Golwg*, which have a policy of including material to help learners. The more ambitious local library might even try organising an 'adopt a learner' scheme, inviting Welsh-speaking readers who have a bit of spare time, to put their names on a panel for a weekly chat with a learner, or a visit to a Welsh play or Welsh-language local society.

The main thing is to get a more personal one-to-one approach for bringing together adult learners and local Welsh speakers. *CYD* looks after the more general get-togethers, though their success depends equally on enough participation by locals, for the ever-present problem for learners is that they find themselves in the self-conscious position of only having other learners to speak too, and that is not the point at all. There must be many local people who would shy away from the formality of a public gathering (however informal the *CYD* gatherings are in practice), but who would be glad to spend an hour a week in their own homes chatting with a learner, or reading the *papur bro* with them, or tackling a bit of *Golwg* or the women's magazine *Pais*. This would begin to create the social contacts that learners so often lack, as well as improving their linguistic efforts, and getting them accustomed to hearing a natural Welsh speaker using the variations from formal Welsh which make understanding such a nightmare at first. As it is, too many learners have to develop the nerve to invite themselves into Welsh-speaking homes, go chapel-creeping, or loiter compromisingly in *Caffi Morgan* or the National library, in order to hear the real lingo being spoken.

Another problem is that it is far too easy for learners to revert to English at the first hesitancy or slightest difficulty, because a great many Welsh speakers tend to be over-considerate (or bored out of their minds by the half-witted stumblings of the learner?) and change back to English. When another non-Welsh speaker joins them, the Welsh person automatically seems to turn to English, too, instead of continuing to speak Welsh with the learner (or a mixture of Welsh and English to include the newcomer). If they were not so quick to turn to English, learners would improve no end, and others might be encouraged to begin learning. You cannot save a language by making it invisible. It needs a high profile, a pride taken in it, a Saatchi and Saatchi (well, almost) promotion of a good cause. But there is always the enemy within, lurking to do down the language and to argue that bilingualism is a waste of time and effort in the modern world, the Wales of tomorrow in Europe.

Whatever the future of rural Wales in Europe, how is the host culture helping incomers to become part of it, by sharing their hopes and fears, their projects and visions with the newcomers who have committed themselves to learning the language? The social context of learning Welsh is paramount in motivating people.

That does not mean you can get by without good learning materials. Until the excellent *Acen* programmes began in 1990 (*S4C* telly programmes for beginners and experienced learners, backed up by cassettes, booklets and a network of local groups) there was a curious sameness about learning materials. There were plodding sets of conversational drills with crashingly obvious exchanges like, 'Is Snowdon higher than Everest?' 'No, Snowdon is not higher than Everest.' The *Acen* approach was to incorporate visits around different parts of Wales, and show things interesting in themselves, a narrow gauge railway or a little country town

174

like Machynlleth, where some of the inhabitants were actually brought into the programme as amateur instructors. The presenters are lively and intelligent and the content of such general interest that the programmes went to the top of the charts for *S4C* viewers within the first year. Over 100,000 watched it, including many natural Welsh speakers, who didn't need to learn the language, but simply enjoyed the coverage and attractive presentation.

The more stodgy traditional materials can of course be enlivened by the tutors who use them, but that is leaving too much to stray genius, and leaves less experienced tutors in the lurch. Can tutors not be trained to supplement the drills with more 'live' material? There are plenty of bilingual leaflets and free handouts in tourist offices and banks and local government offices and libraries (even income tax forms, but that may be going too far in realism). If these were thought of as real-life learning materials, groups could have more choice of using material close to their daily interests, whether arts centre programmes, political party leaflets, CND or Friends of the Earth handouts, Urdd or Eisteddfod guides, supermarket or laundrette notices in the domestic sphere, or bilingual holiday brochures about Wales.

And what about the sex stereotypes? Again *Acen* is the exception, with quite a fair division and good role models both in presenters and coverage. But the more traditional learning materials are often impossible for 1990s women to identify with. One of the off-putting things is the excessive amount of *pêl-droed, rygbi* and *tafarn* talk women have to put up with on many Welsh courses. These I know are sacred to all male chauvinist Welshmen, but we women are half the human race and it is a very curious experience to be given a vocabulary for chatting up 'girls', which includes phrases like 'The barmaid is quite a piece. She has excellent breasts'. I've never come across the reverse sexist equivalent, even, in Welsh phrase books: 'The barman is quite a fella. He has a lovely tight little arse'? Then there are the women depicted solely as those who beaver away with Hoovers, iron men's shirts, and occasionally demand new washing machines. Just occasionally, to add 'humour', we get a 'sexy' Welsh-woman making advances to whoever knocks on the door. This is music

175

hall stuff, as in *Welcome to Welsh*, where Blod nearly has it off with the brush salesman, but the husband comes back early from work . . . Well, come back Delilah!

Show me a phrasebook, pre-*Acen*, where there are women with professional careers (much less mothers with professional careers), or where women are responsible for, instead of just nagging the man about the garden or the family holiday. That's another thing—the Family. It is fairly clear by now, except to the writers of Welsh phrase books, apparently, that the nuclear family of domesticated mum, breadwinning dad and two schoolgoing kids, only exists now in a minority of households. Yet here it is, much larger than life, in phrase books intended both for adults and, worse, for the coming generation of school children. Here is Dad doing men's things and Mam doing women's things so exclusively that you wonder they have anything to talk about at all, so little can they have in common. But in any case they do not usually so much talk as engage in endless bickering about the goods of the great consumer dream—the holiday on the continent, the new car, the swish suite for the lounge, *ad nauseam*. Is this ALL that Welsh culture today has to offer (besides of course *rygbi, pêl-droed* and the *tafarn*)? What a set of role models to offer to the away-from-the-consumer-rat race incomers who are often the ones who decide to learn the language!

In a class I early on attended, we were working in pairs practising the drills for 'I have . . .' and 'Do you have . . .?' The poor fellow I was practising with was left practically speechless by the vocabulary provided, since he was not materialist enough to fulfil any of the consumerist assumptions of the learning materials. He hadn't a car or a house or a telly. Nor did he fulfil the family stereotypes either, being without a wife or a child. He was a wandering minstrel really, with a bike and a guitar. He travelled around the countryside entertaining people with his own songs. It rings a bell, doesn't it? Remember those real life medieval Welsh bards? If there's no place for their modern equivalent in the phrase books, this world of Wales is a poorer place.

The greatest hurdle of all, perhaps, in learning Welsh, is that everyone tries to get you to speak a purist form of the language that makes it

176

impossible for natural speakers to understand you, because their Welsh is a liquid flow of elided words and phrases bearing little resemblance to the neat, disparate parts of speech set out on the pages of grammars and phrasebooks and learners' handouts. 'Poor man', said a churchwarden in the Tregaron area to me, 'our last vicar—he learnt Welsh, for we have bilingual services in our church, and he was a conscientious young man. But it was a pity he learnt it so well. He spoke such a pure form of Welsh that nobody around here knew what he was talking about . . .' Why do teachers impose such a burden of perfection on learners, who then, if they persist with speaking the language, have to unlearn a great deal of the hard-won basics? Even the basic pronunciation is often different from what is taught, since the ends of words get speeded up or dropped off, like the -au plural ending which usually is pronounced -e, as in *Siop y Pethe* (not *Pethau*). With placenames like Dolgellau, it can paradoxically be more helpful to have a Victorian map with anglicised spellings, as far as pronunciation is concerned, for they used to spell it Dolgell*ey*, and that is much nearer the way it is said than Dolgell*au*, the correct Welsh spelling.

No wonder they say the learner's biggest problem is understanding what people say back, in response to his or her faltering overtures. Sometimes on Catchphrase broadcasts you even hear one of the tutors slipping momentarily into ordinary parlance, and then hastily correcting themselves, to impose on the hapless learner the 'correct' form, which he or she will rarely hear spoken outside the programme itself, unless they move in educational circles.

Is this search for purity something to do with the guilt a lot of Welsh speakers feel about the decline in good spoken Welsh? Are they sublimating their own guilty consciences by trying to ensure that adult learners at least will bear the burden of perpetuating 'proper' Welsh? Whatever the reason, learners beware! When I went for some conversation practice to a kind friend who helped me in my early struggles, she said right at the start, 'I hope you are going to learn the right way of saying things—it is a crime the way everyone treats the language, mutilating it and mixing it up with English words half the time'. But

177

later on, when I found I couldn't understand a word of *Pobol y Cwm* on the telly (the daily soap opera that is so popular it has been sold to small countries on the continent), another friend showed me a copy of an old script and explained some of the astonishing elisions. The very simplest of these were *sa i'n gwbod*, which learners are taught as *faswn i ddim yn gwybod*!

The greening power of the Welsh language

The central question on the future of the Welsh language is not how well it can imitate English (by developing scientific and technical vocabulary, for example), but what kind of unique contribution it has to make. In a bilingual country few can doubt the value of knowing English, the world's leading communication medium. The flaw in the argument comes when people go on to argue that therefore Welsh is a hindrance to modernity, progress and national achievement (by which they may mean either British national achievement or Welsh national achievement). Some opponents of the language concede that there is a Welsh-language cultural heritage to be conserved. They see it, however, as a backward-looking cluster of values to do with the declining nonconformist religion, traditional strict-metre poetising and a peasant way of life that has to give way to cost-effective agribusiness. The defenders of the language point out what Welsh is quite capable of developing technical terminologies which can make it feasible as a scientific or commercial medium. This is undoubtedly true, but may not be as important as arguing that the minority languages of Europe could have a role in restoring to people a way of seeing the world that gives them back a sense of community, of a culture rooted in place, of a 'small is beautiful' mentality.

Of course there are grave risks in such an approach. The 'small is beautiful' mentality can become a narrow parochialism, a turning in upon oneself, a desperate clutching at old-fashioned ideals, in order to keep change at bay. But it can also be a new way forward for individuals and communities suffering from an excess of multi-nationalism and a mega-technology that threatens human life and the very environment of our planet. To be cosmopolitan can be an experience of rootlessness and alienation, unless it is grounded in a strong true belongingness, at an individual and local level. To achieve that we need to revalue what is left of our small-scale languages and cultures, and give them a protected place within or alongside the dominant cultures, not only out of respect for the past, but for our future too.

The Welsh language has a number of features which I as a learner and not a native speaker, find very different from English, and these suggest to me that it may offer greener ways of seeing the everyday world. Some of these features are currently used to put down the language, either by incomers or the Welsh themselves, but I would suggest that we need to look again for what they may tell us about how a language shapes our way of seeing the world around us. It is a complicated matter, raising the old chicken and egg question as to whether our language is shaped by our culture, or our culture moulded by the ways we describe and analyse our world, using the constructions of a particular language.

Welsh seems to be in many ways a more participative language than English, perhaps by the very fact that it is less terminologically developed. When you need a concept you can devise it by a DIY process from a kit of abstract noun endings (*ffeministiaeth* for *feminism, benywdod* for *womanhood*, for example), if it is not in the dictionary. When you need a descriptive word you can add standard endings denoting doer or the tool, to a verb stem. So during the Gulf War Scud missiles emerged as *taflegrau*, from the verb stem throw or hurl. The pity is that this potential for creative initiative in Welsh is often dismissed as poverty rather than opportunity, and the English word dropped into the dictionary hole, instead of making up the Welsh one. Perhaps the teaching of the Welsh language needs to go a step further than structure and vocabulary, and give learners their own kit for developing the language where the need arises in their own experiences.

The uncertainty of finding abstract concepts in Welsh, as compared with English, suggests that its usage has been more rooted in everyday concrete activities and emotions. That is of considerable interest to those on a modern spiritual quest, looking for ways of seeing the world whole,

179

rather than abstracted and fragmented. There is, currently, a strong interest in revivals of Celtic Christianity, outside as well as inside the Celtic lands, because it is seen to offer what Esther De Waal calls 'a world made whole':

> This is an approach to life in which God breaks in on the ordinary, daily, mundane, earthy. It is very much a down-to-earth spirituality. The sense of the presence of God informs daily life and transforms it, so that any moment, any object, any job of work, can become the time and the place for an encounter with God. [1]

I discern in early Celtic Christian hymns and blessings a concreteness of feeling and expression, allied with a sense of the abstract rooted in the concrete, that is very attractive to modern seekers. It is the kind of language which does not allow a retreat to the abstract, which discourages the distancing that our contemporary world so often uses to justify official violence or war. I have not got an example from the Welsh tradition, but I have got an example from another branch of the Celtic family of languages, Scots Gaelic, which I hope will illustrate my point. It is a Peace prayer from the Western Isles, handed down orally over, it is thought, many centuries:

Peace between neighbours,
Peace between kindred,
Peace between lovers,
In love of the King of Life.

Peace between person and person,
Peace between wife and husband,
Peace betwen woman and children,
The peace of Christ above all peace.

Bless, O Christ, my face,
Let my face bless everything:
Bless, O Christ, mine eye,
Let mine eye bless all it sees. [2]

A newcomer to Welsh is soon conscious of very different sentence constructions, which seem to lack the familiar logic of English grammar. A double negative reinforces rather than cancels out, as happens in English, so one learns a different logic. Welsh too seems to put words 'the wrong way round, or back-to-front', from an English language stance. *Bore da* is literally Morning Good, and *Daeth y ffrindiau* is Came the friends. But recently I was speaking to someone who does research in developing computer languages and he pointed out the value of language constructions for dispelling any view you might have about the existence of one superior and universally acceptable logic. He then added that in fact computer languages put the substantive word first and the refining or descriptive word later, which follows the Welsh word order. A minor matter, perhaps, but it may hasten acceptance of the 'back-to-front' problem.

More significant is the phenomenon of words that change their meaning according to their context. *Dysgu* can mean either teaching or learning. *Benthyca* can be either borrowing or lending. When I got beyond the initial reaction of being irritated by this, I was moved by the interdependence it implies. Can you really separate lending from borrowing, teaching from learning? Well, yes, on occasions it is clearly quite vital, but philosophically the phenomenon reminds me of the modern revolution in educational thinking, which has tried to make the processes of teaching and learning more reciprocal, mutual, inter-dependent, and to see the particular context as an important factor.

The 'verb-noun' in Welsh is a striking feature which gives rise to quite different constructions from those familiar in English, Latin and Greek. 'To be struck' is literally in Welsh 'to have your striking'. 'We will see' is literally 'we will have the seeing' (*cawn ni weld*). 'Buried lives' is 'lives after their burying'. It is a vivid and immediate form of expression found elsewhere in the Celtic family of languages, for it reminded me of the Synge plays that reproduce the speech styles of the West of Ireland, though in English. In *Riders to the sea*, Cathleen says of the sorrowing old woman whose sons have all drowned, 'and isn't it nine days herself is after crying and keening, and making great sorrow in the house?'

The nature of the verb-noun can be observed in the following extract from Caradog Prichard's *Un nos ola' leuad*, literally translated (with apologies for diminishing the beauty of the Welsh original):

> ... fine was it to have our walking on a level place along the sheep path through middle of bilberry bushes, in place of climbing on a slippery place still. And after reaching the place of picking bilberries, here we all are sitting down and everyone opening their food tin and taking their piece ... [3]

There we have the concrete immediacy of the Celtic languages, marked by the personalising of actions, the flowing looser connections between main clause and subordinate clauses, the central use of the verb-nouns (walking, climbing, sitting down, opening, taking). The verb noun seems to me to combine the idea and the action, and, as Yeats reminded us, you are on the way to seeing things whole when you cannot tell the dancer from the dance. How far is that, I wonder, encouraged or inhibited by the language you use to describe your world?

My experience of learning Welsh has stirred echoes in me of certain ways of speaking that I must have learned in Ireland as a little girl, before I was taught in school to speak 'correctly' and 'grammatically'. There was a story-telling vividness and directness in everyday chat, which probably went back to an oral culture that came to be despised in formal schooling, but survived outside the education system. So to this day the kind of English spoken in Ulster folk's 'brave crack' uses Irish and Scots constructions, even when Irish has almost died out. Indeed perhaps because Irish has been dying, Irish English has become more Irish, as it has to bear a linguistic heritage of translated idioms and constructions, though not an actual vocabulary and grammar.

So in Belfast, whether it accords with people's ideologies or not, the English spoken is a Gaelic English, from the same stable as Synge's translations from the Irish (as patiently collected by putting his ear to the floorboards of his sleeping loft night after night in the west, and recording the talk in the kitchen below), if not always reaching the same poetical heights. People say 'I have a cold on me,' which is very like the Welsh construction *Mae annwyd arna i*, there is a cold on me. They say, 'Are you for staying the week?' as in Welsh *Ydych chi am aros?* Not quite correct English, but perfectly correct in the Celtic languages. Individual words too, in Welsh, stir memories of my own early days. I never could understand why people in Belfast said 'Brave day' to each other, because there was nothing courageous about the sun shining, was there? The meaning of '*braf*' in Welsh is 'fine', so that sorted that out for me, though I was later given a more scholarly gloss on the word '*braf*': it was borrowed, apparently, from French into English and Welsh, has kept its original meaning in Northern Ireland and in Wales, but only very exceptionally in English, as in 'a brave show'.

My personal conclusions on the nature of Celtic-language constructions, (which I put forward with trepidation, since they are based on pragmatic speculation only) are that these languages retain patterns conducive to oral story-telling, and that could be a useful defence for us in an age of mass culture, when each of us needs to be able to tell his or her own tale. Maybe Celtic languages have retained certain medieval qualities which support the story-telling mode of speech—stringing out anecdotes by extending the sentence till the main clause has been forgotten; a rich anarchy of local dialects; an elaboration of speech which is more like embroidery than architecture. The hearth focus shows in the concrete and personal modes of expression, which may be too inturned, romantic verging on the sentimental, but are a useful antidote to brilliant but cold Renaissance ideals of construction—in buildings or language or art. For in reviving those old Greek hierarchies which put abstract thought at the peak of human achievement, the Renaissance did humankind a very ambiguous service.

The Celtic peoples, however, by virtue of their struggles to keep their languages, their religions and their identities alive during the centuries of cultural and economic colonisation, had neither the leisure nor the instinct for Renaissance civilisation. The languages were at various times publicly proscribed and banned from public discourse. The only way they survived in literature and in the home was because they were beneath the contempt of most of the colonists, who saw them as a kind of rude patois gabbled by the natives, not a civilised language with a literature of its own. So when, for example, the historian Lecky wrote of the history of Ireland (in his great classic *The history of England in the eighteenth century*, of course), he omitted all mention of Gaelic literature. His social and intellectual analysis did not see fit to consider the state of the Gaelic imagination or its forms of expression, but only their (monotonously wretched) material state. If he had bothered to tackle the barriers of language and culture, he would in any case have simply confirmed England's worst suspicions that the Celts were obsessed with Religion, Nationalism and Rebellion—for quite sound historical reasons. But it was left to Daniel Corkery in *The hidden Ireland*[4] to tell the story of the Gaels that Lecky had left out. Corkery in turn can be criticised for an extreme form of cultural and linguistic nationalism which alienated many of the Irish intelligentsia from their own language in the early history of the Republic, when so-called freedom had dawned.

Why bother about such old forgotten far-off things? Because the colonial and anticolonial attitudes live on, internalised, and making similar attacks on, or defences of the Welsh-language culture today. This is a serious obstacle in the path of every Welsh learner, and it sometimes feels that the burden is too great for an outsider to try and speak or read a language which its own natural speakers do not care about enough to save. Behind every member of the Welsh-speaking intelligentsia, even, is the ghost of another one who has abandoned the language as part of his or her education or sophistication, just as in Seumas Heaney's poem on the Irish-language question, the ghost of James Joyce tells the poet:

> The English language
> belongs to us. You are raking at dead fires . . .
> That subject people stuff is a cod's game,
> infantile, like your peasant pilgrimage.[5]

It is only the principle that keeps me going in the face of such native ambivalence. For me the principle is that progress is not uniformity but diversity; not centralization but devolution to localities. People today need to have a locally-based culture in which to root the otherwise cold verities of Rational Man, or International Man.

But anyway, how is it possible to watch a language and culture under threat of extinction, without being as concerned as your average Irish or British leftie is by endangered species (wild-life), the loss of Amazonian rain forests, the death of another American-Indian culture, or the (now unexpectedly past) Russian threat to the language and cultural identities of the Baltic republics? Language is part of the ecology.

[1] Esther De Waal, *A world made whole*, Harper Collins, 1991, p. 11.
[2] Esther De Waal, *The Celtic vision*, London, Darton, Longman & Todd, 1988, p. 113.
[3] Caradog Prichard, *Un nos ola leuad*, Caernarfon, Gwasg Gwalia, 1988.
[4] Daniel Corkery, *The hidden Ireland*, Dublin, Gill & Macmillan, 1967.
[5] Seumas Heaney, *Station Island*, London, Faber & Faber, 1984, p. 93.

CHAPTER 8

Mr Crow v The Secretary of State for Wales: hippy travellers

The first wave of hippies who came to our valley put up half a dozen benders in the Forestry Commission Woods at the head of the cwm, and were eventually moved on by an official court order repossessing the land and giving them ten days' marching orders. Crow, a solitary contemplative who carved wood and wrote stories and poems, left a valedictory poem pinned on a fir tree by the clearing where he had lived for nearly a year. It was called 'Crow base '90—Farewell':

Are we the last stand of the oppressed of this land?

Are we the reincarnate Celt who was called for aid
When the initial invasion of this nation was made?

What do you see?
Think about it if you dare.

They don't want us
They don't really want you
Except to do as you've been told to do.

You pull down our homes
And make us move on
But you'll be the target when

We have gone.

Can you not understand that they
Are the spoilers of your beautiful land?

What will you do
When they've killed the soil
Wasted your valleys and
Ancesters' toil?

When they move you on—
As you once did us
What will you do?
Live in a bus?

But the residents were inclined to side with the Secretary of State for Wales, and breathed easier after the departure of the hippies, who were alien to the nonconformist ethnic in their apparent idleness and unwillingness to stand on their own feet instead of living off other people's land and firewood and social security handouts. Besides, this is sheep country, and some of the hippies allowed their dogs to wander free, as they themselves assert the right to wander free. But in the traditional ranking of rural virtues individual freedom comes near the bottom of the list, after neighbourly responsibility and hard work and duty.

To the locals the hippies themselves were the invaders of their useful (and beautiful) land. They did not belong, they did not mix or try to understand the local life, and their exotic appearance of eldritch locks down to their shoulders, and dark multilayered clothing, was a constant reminder along the single track road of the alien presence in the woods.

The folk memory failed to make any connection between these round hippy benders with their framework of saplings, and those *hafodydd*, summer huts, which were thrown up as temporary dwellings in the Dark Ages. Even before that, Iron Age people had made similar structures of saplings covered with animal skins (The Ferrycerrig Museum outside Wexford has some reconstructions that look very similar to New Age benders). In post Roman times the poor lived in huts made by piling up turves on an inner frame of stout branches cut from the birch and oak woods that thickly clothed the hillsides (the Cwmrheidol oak and birch woods are now conserved by the Countryside Commission).

187

As late as the twelfth century Giraldus Cambrensis observed that the Welsh:

> ... neither inhabit towns, villages nor castles, but lead a solitary life in the woods, on the borders of which they do not erect sumptuous places, nor lofty stone buildings, but content themselves with small huts made of the boughs of trees twisted together, constructed with little labour and expense, and sufficient to endure throughout the year. [1]

The makeshift round cabin on the edge of the woods continued to be put up by poor squatters in rural Wales right up to the early nineteenth century. The *tai unnos*, one night houses, were round or rectangular huts built of turf clods to a certain height, then roofed with branches woven together, and thatched with straw or rushes. Often they would have no windows, only a door hole which could be closed off with a wattle hurdle, and a chimney hole through which (eventually) smoke from the central fire would drift out. The tradition was that if the *tŷ unnos* could be completed and the smoke coming out of the chimney by dawn, squatters' rights were established. The possessor could then lay claim to as much of the common land as he could encompass by hurling an axe from the door of the hut to the north, south, east and west. But the old squatters worked to live, and they had no choice, whereas these New Age squatters fulfilled neither of these conditions of local acceptability. But there was one notable exception—Jan and Billy, who have become our own community hippies in the valley. Jan and Billy, who have given up travelling and have lived in their bender in Cwmrheidol for the past five years, know these stories from the Welsh squatting tradition, but most New Age travellers do not. They are grounded rather in the traditions of North American Indians.

Few stay in one place long enough to cultivate a particular patch or to put down any roots, however deep their attachment to Mother Earth in general. The hippy life centres on the bender or tipi, a deliberately circular dwelling (for that is an organic shape), close to the earth, and with a living fire at its centre. But you should always be able to up sticks and move on, so as not to get overattached to possessions, and be free to

188

make journeys to the sacred places as the cycles of the year unfold (like Glastonbury for the summer solstice). So some itinerant hippies consider Tipi Valley near Llandeilo an elitist place, because many of the inhabitants have been there since the seventies, and they live in posh tipis modelled on the original Indian wigwam, and are frequently visited by the media looking for colourful copy on alternative life styles.

In Tipi Village there are over a hundred men, women and children trying to work out a life style that is nurturing and sustaining, to themselves, to other people and to the planet. They teach the children themselves, treat illness as far as possible with natural remedies, grow their own food, and live by a series of unwritten precepts taught by example, for there is no formal government. 'No rules' is an important element in the escape from the heartless bureaucracies of the outside world, but it does not mean anarchy. It is meant to be about taking personal responsibility for all aspects of your own life, and doing what you can for the rest of life on earth. So there is no cutting live wood for fuel, no littering the place with rubbish, no shitting on the pathways, no polluting of water supplies, no consumerism.

At the centre of Tipi Village is the community tipi, Big Lodge, but it is not a mirror image of outside authority, where officials meet to make decisions for other people. Instead it is the convivial core of the community. The tipi people gather there to celebrate the old earth-centred festivals of summer and winter solstice, and the phases of the moon. These are reminders that human life needs to keep in touch with the cycles of nature, and respect the earth. So money-driven consumerism and earth-polluting technologies are the greatest evils, replacing traditional religion's obsessive concern with the sins of carnality. To be in touch with the earth is to be in touch with one's own carnality, and to be in touch with one's carnality is to be in touch with the earth, to be part of the whole creation.

Could such a life style exist without the underpinning of dole money, though? Well, they say, they could give it a go, but as long as the dole money is there why refuse it? It's only money, after all, and money is not as important as straight people think. It's far more important to work at

189

opening yourself up to your instinctive natural rhythms, and be ready always to share what little you have of food and shelter with a stranger who needs it. In any case some of the Tipi Village people work at crafts and are not averse to small scale business enterprise, so long as it keeps to the Spirit. To be in the Spirit is to be able to relate, person to person, to help people give expression to their whole selves, body, mind and spirit. That means getting rid of the repressions and aggressions and prejudices of straight society. Officialdom never solves anything; it is the Spirit that gives the answers, if you are in touch with it. Tipi Valley hippies are trying to work at freedom, that freedom we all need if we are to take our problems into our own hands and not go on waiting for official experts to solve them for us. Because the experts will never solve our problems. It is the experts of so-called Progress who have brought our planet to crisis point, and us with it. There have to be alternatives, and Tipi people are engaged on the quest, however hampered by a certain new tyranny of structurelessness, which sometimes gets in the way of living up to their own practical ideals. But by no means always, for you can run a word processor on power from a wind generator outside your tipi, as Brig Oubridge does, and be an activist in local politics. In 1992 he even organised a cricket match between the Tipi Village team and a local team.

But Crow and our resident local hippies are suspicious of even such modest organisation as exists in Tipi Valley. They go their own way and explore their own things, keeping strictly to their own world.

Crow is small and neat and has calm pale blue eyes. He wears his light brown hair in a pigtail and has an ear ring in his right ear. He is versed in the lore of the American Indians, and left behind him various symbols of peace and celebration of Mother Earth, around the dismantled site of his bender in the woods. There was a circle peace sign marked out on the ground with white quartz stones, the four cardinal points of the compass marked by sticks adorned with bunches of crow feathers tied on with red ribbons. There was a six-foot totem pole with a squirrel's head on the top, twined about with coloured ribbons and beads. Another white quartz stone marked where the bender entrance had been, signifying primal energy. When he extinguished his last fire he scattered the wood ash round the site and covered up the dying embers with a stone cairn to commemorate the living fire.

Crow is known to have healing lore, using natural remedies made from herbs and trees. He follows in the footsteps of Dr Bach, whose healing centre still goes on at Mount Vernon, and whose Bach Flower Remedies are to be found in every wholefood and health shop. It was said, when Crow left the valley, that he was walking to Mount Vernon, en route to the Beltane celebrations at the Uffington White Horse in Oxfordshire. The basis of these flower and tree remedies is that Edward Bach would experience in himself the negative states of mind which he believed give rise to our physical ills, and he would develop the physical symptoms in his own body. Then he wandered the fields and woods of Oxfordshire around his home till he instinctively found the plant that would restore peace of mind, and in a few hours the physical complaint too would be healed. His discoveries are now fully catalogued and the essences distilled and on sale, but Crow and the few to whom he reveals his healing secrets prefer to wander the woods and use their instincts and make their own variations on the original Bach distillations:

Agrimony for those who hide worries behind a brave face
Aspen for apprehension without reason
Beech for moods of intolerance to others
Centaury for the weak-willed, the imposed upon
Cerato for self-doubt and the need to be always seeking confirmation
   from others
Cherry plum for uncontrolled irrational thoughts
Chestnut bud for continually repeating the same mistakes in life
Chicory for clinging and overprotectiveness to loved ones
Clematis for dreamy escapism
Crab apple the Cleanser for self-disgust and shame at own ailments
Elm for being overwhelmed by inadequacy and responsibility
Gentian for despondency
Gorse for pessimism and defeatism
Heather for obsessive talkers who go on about their own troubles
   the whole time

191

Holly for hatred, envy, jealousy and suspicion
Honeysuckle for living in the past—nostalgia and homesickness
Hornbeam for procrastination and Monday morning feeling
Impatiens for impatience and irritability
Larch for lack of self-confidence and fear of failure
Mimulus for fear of known things, shyness and timidity
Mustard for the dark cloud that descends, sadness and lowness for
   no known reason
Oak is for those who are normally strong and courageous, but no
   longer able to struggle against illness and adversity
Olive is for a draining of energy
Pine for a guilt complex and constant apologising for oneself
Red chestnut for obsessive care and concern for others
Rock rose for sudden alarm, panic and scares
Rock water for rigid minded, self denying people
Scleranthus for indecisive, fluctuating, uncertain people
Star of Bethlehem for the effects of bad news or fright following
   an accident
Sweet chestnut for utter dejection and bleakness
Vervain for overenthusiasm and fanatical beliefs
Vine for the dominating, inflexible, tyrannical, autocratic and arrogant,
   the 'good leaders'
Walnut helps through changes—puberty, menopause, death or
   divorce, new surroundings
Water violet is for the proud, the reserved, the ones who enjoy
   being alone
White chestnut for persisting unwanted thoughts and preoccupation
   with some episode or experience
Wild oak helps determine one's intended path in life
Wild rose undoes apathy and resignation
Willow undoes 'Poor old me' feelings of bitterness and resentment
   against the world . . . [2]

From the alternative perception of the world, Crow is a healer and story teller who moves lightly across the land, leaving behind him recipes for healing ointment and a squirrel totem or a cairn of quartz stones. But in the eyes of Officialdom he becomes 'a person seen in the forest', a trespasser against whom court action is required. So where Crow's

192

bender had been, pinned to a tree adjacent to the tree with Crow's poem on it, was the following notice:

Affidavit sworn by the forester in the matter of land known as Coed Pen Rhiw in the Ceredigion Forest District ... between the Secretary of State for Wales and Mr Crow and other persons ...

In October/November I was informed by a member of the public that there was some 'hippy' activity at the top end of the Cwm. I visited the area and found 6 tents (benders) on the site of the old mine buildings, but at the time I didn't see any on Forestry Commission land.

In December a tent was seen on Forestry Commission land opposite the waterfall. A person was seen in the forest who said he had been there since September.

On 24 January my ranger visited the area and found 3 benders which he reported to me. He told one of the persons in the vicinity that they were trespassing on Forestry Commission land and should leave immediately. A negative response was received.

On 25 January I visited the site accompanied by a forester and found 3 benders. We met the occupant of the first one, who said he had been there since December and had no intention of moving on because his van had broken down and he wished to stay for the winter. It was pointed out to the traveller that he had no right to be on Forestry Commission land and unless he vacated the site legal proceedings would commence for his removal. The traveller said that was OK by him.

On 19 February I visited the site again and met the occupants of all three benders. The traveller I had spoken to on my previous visit, when asked, declined to give his name, but accepted a notice to vacate ... The second person who had said he had been there since September, accepted the notice and gave his name as Crow ...

Save for the rights of the public to pass and repass over and along public footpaths and other public rights of way within the land, no-one has any right to come on to and remain on the land ...

193

In the circumstances I invite the Court to make an immediate order for repossession of the land so that the Defendants may be removed therefrom forthwith.

Signed . . .

On behalf of the Secretary of State for Wales

The Court duly made the order, and Crow and the others took down the benders, leaving bare circles of beaten earth and piles of curved branches which had formed the bender frames. Crow was the last to go as he had been the first to arrive. A solitary, he yet draws others after him, and that proved his undoing, for it made him visible to Officialdom.

The story of 'Lyn'

Lyn had come to the valley long before Crow and the others, and resented their arrival because it threatened the fragile acceptance of her own birch-embowered enclosure up in the woods. But Crow became her friend and added to her store of lore on natural remedies to cure headaches and period pains, to relax tension or heal bruised or aching limbs.

The first time Lyn ever came into our house she unerringly picked up from the household collection of books the one that most aptly spoke of her own way of seeing: *Touch the Earth: a self-portrait of Indian existence.* She knew it already from her own experience, but to read bits of it out was like talking to a dear friend she hadn't seen for years—or never in the flesh, but only in the imagination.

> . . . they sat or reclined on the ground with a feeling of being close to a mothering power. It was good for the skin to touch the earth, and the old people liked to remove their mocassins and walk with bare feet on the sacred earth. Their tipis were built upon the earth and their altars were made of earth. The birds that flew in the air came to rest upon the earth, and it was the final abiding place of all things that lived and grew. The soil was strengthening, soothing, cleansing and healing. [3]

'That's it, that's it', she said when she had finished reading.

194

When Lyn and Jimmy came to the valley five years ago and built a bender in a remote clearing on the wooded hillside, she had caused a bit of a scandal by going barefoot and wearing a shift or less as she went about her domestic tasks on hot summer days. Our respectable culture had only one explanation—she was indecent Eve, surrounded by an aura of carnality that was actually more in the mind of the beholder, rather than in any intention of hers. What *she* wanted was to feel kinship with the life-giving forces of nature, to touch and be touched by the earth, the light of sun and moon and stars, like her beloved North American Indians. For her there needs to be connections between all forms of life, and respect for all living beings, and that means always staying close to nature and to the earth energies.

'I can't live in a house. I'm not ready to live in a box', she says. 'I need to live in a round place like this'. Her gaze takes in the peaceful interior of the bender. The first time I spoke to her, shortly after their arrival in the woods up the back, I had no inkling of any of this, and asked (I could see later with guilty hindsight) crude questions in a spirit of uncaring curiosity. 'Could I photograph your place?', I said, and was all set to conduct some kind of interview on where they had come from, why they were there, what the sheep skulls at the bender entrance meant, why was there an eight foot high wooden cross outside, and bells blowing in the wind . . . But all she said to me on that occasion was, 'No photographs —this is where I live, my own space'. And in response to 'Where have you come from?', she simply stooped down and touched the ground with the palms of her hands. It began to dawn on me . . . 'Mother Earth?' I queried cautiously, and she smiled and agreed without words.

Now that I know Lyn a bit better I understand that, for her, good energies work in circles, and while we keep the circles unbroken we have peace in ourselves and in our worlds. The seasons form a circle in their turning. The life of each of us is a circle from childhood to prime to second childhood. The earth is round, the moon and sun are round. The wind at its greatest strength whirls, and water forms whirlpools. Everything has its seasons as the circles of life move in their proper courses. It should be like this, too, for individuals and for communities

195

and whole peoples, which are the wider circles that embrace us. Imagine the flowering tree at the centre, the tree of life, and the circle of the four quarters nourishing it and nurturing it. From the north we can draw on strength and endurance, from the west rain for growth and refreshment, from the south warmth and richness and ripeness, from the east light and peace and a fruitful stillness. The two-leggeds and the four-leggeds need to live together like relatives, rather than isolated on their own little islands, surrounded by rules, lies and greed.

So up at the bender there is not just Lyn and Jimmy, but the cats and guinea pigs, rabbits and chickens, and Rambo the adolescent ram rescued by Lyn when he was a tiny lamb rejected by his mother. The cockerel wakes up every living being at dawn, which varies as the cycle of the year goes round, so in the wintry dark days the little household get up later and retire earlier, eating their main meal of the day as the sun goes down, so that dinner time too is in harmony with the revolving seasons.

There is no sentimentality towards the animals, as you might first suspect when you hear of these back-to-Mother-Nature ways. The rabbits are due for the cooking pot soon, because they have against all the odds failed to breed. Rambo has had a good life, first in his own little enclosure, and later collecting his own harem of ewes in the unfenced woodland pastures where stray sheep have wandered over the years. He has been marked down for a Spring Equinox feast, and a sheepskin for the bender. The cats are trained to hunt not just for themselves, but for the cooking pot too. They bring back rabbits and squirrels, so everything is shared out. The animals include us, and we include the animals, and all of us are included in the cycles of Nature.

The animals, besides, can teach us how to live better than any book or school can do. An animal is aggressive only under threat, kills only to eat, lives out its *tao* or Way without worrying about its self-image. It does not pollute its environment unless it is caged or cruelly treated. Lyn's cats know how to be. She has taught them and they have taught her. Whereas Educated Man often, as the Hopi Indians observed, rejects the spirit of being:

The white man's advanced technological capacity has occurred as a result of his lack of regard for the spiritual path and for the way of all living beings. The white man's desire for material possessions and power has blinded him to the pain he has caused Mother Earth by his quest for what he calls natural resources. And the path of the Great Spirit has become difficult to see by almost all men, even by many Indians who have chosen to follow the path of the white man.[4]

The Indian perception was that when their people went through the white man's colleges they came back good for nothing. They had become ignorant of the ways of living in the woods, unfit to hunt, useless as counsellors to their people. They only knew about the work that kills the imagination and changes the face of the Earth, without respect. They could uproot trees, blow up rocks, 'tame the wilderness'. But what is a wilderness? Is it the place before man comes, or the place where man has been, that is a wilderness?

When I go up to the bender to see Lyn I may find her ready to speak, or wanting to be silent. When she first came to the valley she spent many weeks in silence, just writing down the few necessary things she had to communicate. When in one of her silent phases she is always courteous, carrying a little scribbling pad so that she can let you know. I think her selected silences come from the need to be calm and still within herself, like the leaves on trees between storms, or the ripples on the water stilled to a mirror pool where you can see every detail reflected in perfect clarity. It is a silence to offset the outer babble that goes on all the time around us, so as to give room to the unspoken. It is in the good hermit tradition, but these days hermits are not much in people's minds, and for a while it was assumed that she had a speech impediment!

On the day of the winter solstice (*Alban Arthan* is the New Age Celtic term for it), Ken and I went up through the woods to the bender, with a gift of mince pies and a card to celebrate the turning of the year. Jimmy, who has green fingers and has had forestry jobs from time to time, showed Ken around the terraced vegetable patches he has patiently built up on the steep hillside. He has a tiny tree nursery of nine-inch high chestnuts (grown from some halloween leftovers). He has made a miniature rock garden and a pool made by diverting some water from the stream that provides their water supply. He is developing a flower bed behind the shelter of the scrub birches that were the only things growing on the site when they first came. He uses the cab of the old ambulance they arrived in, as a greenhouse for bringing on his seed trays. In another section of the thirty by twenty yard enclosure there are blackcurrant cuttings and crowns of rhubarb, and beyond that, the hen run and guinea pig pens. Rambo the ram has his own special enclosure.

While the men were doing the rounds outside, Lyn led me into the warm dusky interior of the bender for the first time, and put the kettle on the wood stove, to make tea. The whole atmosphere took my breath away. Outside the bender is not at all beautiful, because it is water-proofed with black polythene sheeting over the traditional tarpaulins. But going inside is like stepping back in time to some medieval nomad yurt. The frame is made of saplings curving in to the apex of the roof, forming a domed interior about five metres in diameter. Cross struts strengthen the wooden framework, and a stout central pole supports the whole.

The inside is cosily lined with old faded rugs and a few sheepskins. The sheepskins are a bonus, the result of Jan finding dead sheep which had been trapped in a barbed wire or other misadventure, too late to be rescued, too early to have rotted, and therefore in a moment of ethical nicety. On the way in you pass through a polythene porch on a slatted wooden frame with animal skull finials. This is where the boots and animal feeding bowls and water buckets are kept, and it also serves to keep the south westerlies out of the living space. The bender is heated by a stout old cylindrical iron stove, with a chimney pipe projecting up through the roof. This is also the means of cooking. A pot of stew can be kept hot close to the ash pan, while the kettle is boiling up on the top for tea.

The bender is all one circular space, but as one's eye gets accustomed to the candlelight and the stove glow, it's clear there are living, sleeping and kitchen subspaces. The kitchen corner is near the entrance. A row of spoons and ladles hangs from the curving wall, and little jars of home-dried herbs are tucked away above on part of the bender's inner frame of branches. There is a working bench of rough wood, and storage above the doorway for fresh food that has to be kept cool and as far as possible out of reach of Spit, the one greedy cat.

The sitting area is foam rubber slabs covered with draperies, and there are more of these forming the sleeping accommodation, with a heap of blankets and quilts and spreads lying over them. Possessions (which are modest, since the whole point is to be non-consumerist) are stored in boxes against the curved walls, or hung from the branchwork of the bender's frame. There is a window of opaque white polythene giving just enough light to move around to find a place to sit, while more candles are being lit.

The air is scented with one of those bitter-sweet oriental incense sticks, perhaps sandalwood or patchouli. It is very peaceful and enveloping and womb-like, in spite of, or maybe because of the wealth of comfortable clutter, all with some useful purpose, crowded in a relatively small space. Every object is precious and has its own place in the internal logic of the bender, as we discover while drinking mugs of black tea. For this is our first visit and we are shown the treasures of the house. Lyn opens a flat tin box and passes it over. It is full of tiny vole skulls and rabbit skulls, the bleached remains of the black tomcat's hunting expeditions. From the same source come the finch's wing and the bright blue chest feathers of a jay that mocked once too often. Then comes a fox skull to examine, and a minute dried bat body of infinitesimal lightness and perfection. And oval stones from the stream worn smooth, and rough pieces of energising white quartz . . .

The two cats behaved in their respective fashions while we sat drinking tea. The mischievous Spit, a near replica of an ancient Egyptian tomb cat (and so nearly called Bubastes, only it was too much of a mouthful), darted around exploring and leaping onto shoulders, disappearing into dark corners on mythical hunts, trying to steal Twt's dinner by creeping up on the serious black tom and snatching from behind. Twt, who had of late been visiting our house daily to suss out the possibilities of a more bourgeois home free of rival pets, sat carefully with his back to the company, guarding his own space, pretending he had never seen us before in his life. Clearly he hadn't finished working out whether he should adopt us as his new owners, and found it embarrassing to be faced with old and new relationships in the same time and place.

Since then the black tom has, in fact, being a jealous and exclusive cat, fled from the sharing of Lyn's affections with Spit and Rambo, the guinea pigs and the cockerel. He took several months to move his territory down to our place, and he planned the whole strategy with the cunning of a guerilla commander. First he accepted an occasional saucer of milk, then slipped effortlessly into the habit of a daily snack, always going back to the bender for evening dinner. The next stage was full of heart-rending pathos—we found him sleeping on a heap of old painting rags out in the shed, as if he had no home to go to, although he had a perfectly good bed up in the bender. As winter came on we felt obliged to make him a makeshift bed in the shed by lining an old box with cushions. Then he infiltrated the house during the day, luxuriating in the sensuousness of the corduroy sofa by the wood burning stove. He still went up to the bender when he heard Lyn's whistle to summon the animals to dinner—for a week or two, but then he pretended he didn't hear her whistle and he stayed on to share our dinner occasionally . . . then often . . . then every day . . . He is still with us. But on that first visit to the bender all we could do was admire his sheer acting ability, his assumed indifference towards his adoptive fosterers—he being the adopter, rather than us. We were only the innocents he had fixed his sights on, once he had glimpsed another Eden, free of animal competition.

Lyn is averse to putting any kind of labels on people, but those of us who are in the habit of categorising and naming would probably be accurate in describing her as a Taoist. She keeps a small stock of Taoist books on a shelf behind the sleeping space, and one day she showed me her favourite—the *Tao Te Ching* and Wieger's *Wisdom of the Taoist masters*. I opened the *Tao Te Ching* at random and (fortunately) hit on one of her favourite bits, which we read out together:

The highest goodness is like water. Water is beneficent to all things but does not contend. It stays in places others despise. Therefore it is near Tao.

In dwelling, think it a good place to live;
In feeling, make the heart deep;
In friendship, keep on good terms with men;
In words, have confidence;
In ruling, abide by good order;
In business, take things easy;
In motion, make use of the opportunity.
Since there is no contention, there is no blame.

This explains a lot about her way of life. Before she met Jimmy, and they came to live in the valley, she had travelled about in an old ambulance on her own. Sometimes she still goes off travelling for a week or two to meet up with old friends ('my little sisters'), or to visit her mother in the south-east of England ('we are close, we don't have to explain things to each other'). But her daughter in Milton Keynes, with a 'proper house' and baby, doesn't approve of Lyn. 'She tells her friends her mother's a witch', she says sadly. I tell her most witches have been white witches right through history, and we talk about the women in the past who were burnt at the stake for no reason than that they were different and their ways of seeing were a threat to the official ways of seeing in the church and state. Many of them were healers and midwives and handed down traditional knowledge about herbs and soothing potions from mother to daughter over the generations, but that did not save them . . . Their beliefs were indeed a strange jumble of pagan and Christian, but then even official Christianity had to absorb some of the old ways when it was rooting itself in a specific place . . .

Lyn continues to be an eclectic in religion. Friday mornings she catches the weekly bus into town to go to the Bible study in St Michaels. At regular intervals a couple of dedicated Jehovah's Witnesses call on her and push their point of view. Neither lot approves of her connections with the other. She gives both of them Taoist quotes which she has painstakingly typed out on her latest acquisition, an ancient manual portable. Alongside her Taoist text she keeps a copy of the Bible, and mingles the two together happily as a way of figuring out how to live—close to nature, caring for as many creatures as gather round her, quite immune to the endless consuming and throwaway life style, sad that in Milton Keynes they've lost interest in magic mushrooms and gone in for chemical highs on 'speed', trying to live always in the present moment ... in What Is ... 'I sometimes spend hours chopping vegetables for the dinner and putting my attention into that or whatever else needs to be done, like going around feeding the rabbits and the guinea pigs and the cats and Rambo. It's like you should pay attention to whatever you're doing and do it properly and then you are alive. I do bits of tapestry too when I want to put words down that have stuck in my head from the books. You can work at a six inch square for days before it's finished but that doesn't matter—it's the doing that counts ...'

She has given us a few of her tapestries from time to time. There is the one which has the words emerging from a darker background, green against green, grey against grey and brown against brown: 'If God be for you, who can be against you?' There is a pale and dark purply one: 'Being is Non-being, Non-being is Being; in the realm where this does not obtain it is ill to dwell'. One of the most painstaking has a purple border and within it are black letters on gold:

> Not knowing that one knows is best
> Thinking that one knows when one does not is sickness
> Only when one becomes sick of this
> Sickness can one be free from sickness
> The Sage is never sick, because he is sick
> Of this sickness,
> Therefore he is not sick.

Since coming to live in the valley she has moved in a new direction with her tapestry work, and now sometimes works in the Celtic knots and interlacing patterns that symbolise the inter-dependence of all things, without words. She has a strong sense of this place as the place she has come home to, after all her travelling, and it has an effect even on her sewing.

One night she was thinking about the words of an old American Indian woman (at the turn of the century, when the land developers were moving into her homeland). She read me out these words:

> You see that Eagle-nest mountain and that Rabbit-hole mountain? When God made them he gave us this place . . . We do not care for any other place . . . How can we go away? If you give us the best place in the world it is not so good for us as this . . . This is our home . . . We cannot live anywhere else . . . There is no other place for us. We do not want you to buy any other place. If you will not buy us this place, we will go into the mountains and die there like quail, the old people, the women and children. Let the government be glad and proud. If we cannot live here we want to go to the mountains and die. We do not want any other place.

'That's it', said Lyn, 'that's what I feel about up there where we are now, in this valley. I never want to go anywhere else. I have come home'.

The bus called Hassle Street

In case there is a danger at this point of idealising the hippy subculture and ignoring the stresses and strains on the rural communities who have experienced their influx, it is time to move on to the less happy episode of the hippy convoy who moved in to the old Cwmrheidol Mine at the end of the valley in 1991.

Over the winter they came in dribs and drabs, as the news spread through the travellers' network that Cwmrheidol was 'the best park-up in the Aberystwyth area'. First there came a couple of 'rainbow buses', one brightly adorned with Glastonbury symbols of the New Age, another with 'Hassle Street' on its indicator board as a destination. They were joined by a variety of old caravans and converted horse boxes, all of which conveniently broke down as soon as they got here, so there was 'no way' their occupants could move on that spring. Gradually the travellers spread out into the unfenced grazing land around the mine, cutting young saplings to make their bender frames, and letting their dogs roam free during lambing, for 'Look at them, they wouldn't hurt a fly', they said. But the sheep did not know that and panicked anyway. And from time to time the dogs' primeval instincts were clearly aroused, for there were sheep savaged at the throat, but it was impossible to prove that a hippy dog had done it.

Eventually there were more hippies in the upper cwm than permanent residents, and their presence became strangely oppressive, whatever liberal intentions we might have towards alternative life-styles. They formed their own defensive knots, establishing a completely alien subculture which remained obscure and apart, sending out no messages that could be understood by the people of the valley. They went against the grain of nonconformist expectations of hard work and 'making something' with whatever you have in the way of a patch of land or a skill or a gift. For, like the lilies of the field, they toiled not, neither did they spin, beyond the everyday necessities of collecting their firewood from somebody else's woods, and fetching water from somebody else's spring. They did not believe in the concept of private property, they carefully explained, and considered that anyone who asked them politely to move on, was just another of the filthy landowning classes who were destroying the earth. 'Who needs all these sheep, anyway?' one asked. And it is fair to add that some of them were indeed vegetarians, for when in the end it was necessary to get a legal injunction to move them on, the judge at the Crown Court in Aberystwyth asked them about lavatory arrangements, and showed concern on hearing that they simply walked as far as possible away from the benders to do it. 'It's natural', said one young woman, 'The sheep do it'. 'Sheep are herbivores', the judge reminded her. 'I'm a vegetarian myself', she retorted.

It was probably the invasion of community space that was at the root of the matter. To the travellers the upper cwm looked like an empty place, but to local people it is part of their *bro*, their community land. And just because it was unfenced did not mean it was unused. There were grazing animals, locals and visitors driving up at the weekends for a quiet walk or a picnic by the river, amateur industrial archaeologists exploring the old mine, school and college minibuses debouching groups doing field work for science projects. Or rather, there had been, till the hippies took it over. Then people would drive up to the top of the cwm, be faced with the bender encampment, and in many cases they would drive away again, not even stopping to have tea in the valley cafe, which lost customers as a result. Not all, however, for the hippies said indignantly to local residents jaded by the whole experience, 'Some people take an interest in us—a chap came over from somewhere and asked a lot of questions about how we live . . .'

During that time it became very clear that there are hippies and hippies, for Lyn and Jimmy's lives were adversely affected by the new arrivals, although they had reached the status of some kind of 'community hippies', known personally and accepted by people in the valley. The police came up from time to time to check for drug trading, and included the bender up the hill in their search, as well as the benders on the mine. A few of the new arrivals were 'OK', in Lyn's judgment. Mick and Reg from Bermondsey, who were horse-drawn hippies and whose stay was limited by the amount of grazing available, got a farewell Sunday lunch of roast guinea pig and freshly grown vegetables. But to a lot of people all hippies are alike, so Lyn and Jimmy sometimes got included in the general disillusionment with the travelling classes. There were benefits for them, too, however. When the convoy finally left the mine, they abandoned (as well as the Hassle Street bus, cut down into small pieces) an old Rayburn stove which enables Lyn to cook things in the oven instead of just on the stove top.

One of the little talked of effects of going into Europe in 1992 is an increasing influx of travelling folk from France and Spain, as the French and Spanish governments apply their resettlement programmes, which threaten the nomadic life-style of their itinerants. The National Gypsy Council also foresees flight to the British Isles by Romanian and other East European travellers facing persecution at home, for British law, in spite of the efforts of farmers' unions and Country Landowners Association members, is 'soft on squatting'. The extra pressures on the diminishing areas of unfenced land and abandoned mines in rural Wales are likely to be severe. And, say local residents, these old sites are already overused by the travellers. The problem is aggravated, ironically, by EC grants for reclamation schemes on former mines. As these are landscaped the remainder come under even heavier use. The solution proposed by travellers' spokespersons is for local authorities to set aside special sites for travellers' use, and a place in every county where they can hold their festivals without being hassled by locals or police. But many travellers do not want the regimentation of selected sites, for freedom is all, and locals never want even a designated travellers' encampment in their locality. 'Not in my back yard' (NIMBY) instincts are well to the fore on this proposal. The situation remains obscure, but community action seems to be increasing in the countryside. This year in Cwmrheidol there were indications of an informal early-warning system operating in the valley, when remnants of the Castle Moreton Festival of travellers and ravers arrived in the Aberystwyth area.

In parts of Dyfed the locals sometimes take their own particular initiatives. A sheep farmer from Crosshands told me:

'The only way you'll shift them is with dynamite. They moved in on us from Tipi Village. First there were only a couple of them in an old derelict ruin with a bit of rough grazing around it. Then more and more turned up with, like, gypsy caravans covered in tarpaulins. They were all over my land till I took out my shotgun and warned them off. They even sent their kids wandering over the fields picking bits of wool off the hedges and barbed wire, and the women sat there spinning it on hand spindles—though I never saw that they made much out of it, for they spent so much time spinning they never got to knitting. But anyway they didn't seem to care what way the kids were dressed. They put the boys in frocks like the girls—those poor kids will grow up bent as a clockwork orange ... They were cutting down my trees to burn, as well, and the police did damn all, so I warned them off politely, and when that didn't work I went out shouting and yelling with my shotgun ...

'The trouble with Wales is there's so much land that nobody can prove ownership to, so once the hippies are in, you can't get them out, and they all know it—that's why they're pouring in, in their thousands. They're the latest lot of vultures in the countryside, and it's my taxes pays their dole money, so they can swan around while the wife and I struggle to make ends meet, with the sheep prices falling all the time. They say there's no such thing as a free lunch. Well, the hippies have the next best thing—only it's us who's paying.'

People in Cwmrheidol were never so Draconian. If anything they avoided direct contact with the hippies, but there were many real-life stories added to the gossip network as long as they remained on the old mine. There was the day that one of the young women was seen begging on the pavement outside Woolworths, her eyes downcast, and a black puppy dog (which had earlier been chasing local lambs) in her lap. In front of her she had propped up a cardboard placard with 'Hungry and Homeless—Please Help Me' scrawled on it with crayon. By lunchtime she had collected enough cash from the good citizens of Aberystwyth to buy a number of bottles of Rheinhessen in the off-licence. For she was observed again on the beach in the golden noon, quaffing the easily gotten gains with other hippies from the valley. A lucrative morning begging, an afternoon of wine and roses, and back to the sky-blue bender for an evening of Jimmy Hendrix tapes and camp-fire socialising on the idyllic banks of the Rheidol—one woman in her day plays many parts. 'And', someone said, 'she gets an extra £5 a week from the Social Security for the puppy dog!'

The tale of 'Hungry and Homeless' was quickly woven into the warp and woof of local satire, even though we no longer have a *bardd gwlad*, folk poet, as in the old days, to celebrate our happinesses and castigate the follies of others. Nowadays it's all done through story telling and gossip.

During the summer of 1992 the hippies reached a new level of public visibility, because 10,000 of them congregated near the small rural community of Kerry near Newtown in Powys, and they were taken up by the media. Investigative journalists revealed that they had a secret programme of summer festivals (rave-ups), and indignant farmers and other rural dwellers complained that the police and indeed the whole legal situation seemed powerless to prevent these rave-ups, or the mass encampments on private land which accompany them. The ultimate outrage to traditional values was the appearance on the small screen one night of social security officers driving out to the Kerry hippy encampment to distribute dole money on a mass scale to the travellers. A government spokesman soon afterwards announced that there would be a tightening up of social security payments to travellers, and that they would have to prove their availability for work before being given their dole money (except for those with children or disabled partners to support). But the Archdruid of Wales then delivered a controversial speech at the National Eisteddfod in Aberystwyth warning that such cuts in social security handouts would 'open the floodgates to an unprecedented influx of deprived people from English cities to rural Wales . . . They will not just be looking for somewhere to camp but will plunder the fields because they are hungry'. He went on to compare the New Age travellers with the Old Testament Midianites who once were such a thorn in the flesh of that other pastoral people, the ancient Israelites. For, he reminded his audience, 'The Midianites encamped against them. The Midianites came up with their animals and their tents, and they came as locusts and were without number . . .'

There were those among the Archdruid's Eisteddfod audience who remembered their Old Testament in some detail, and were worried. For had not the Isrealite folk hero Gideon pursued the Midianites so ruthlessly and without mercy that their numbers were reduced from a hundred and twenty thousand to fifteen thousand by fierce slaughter—albeit with the approval and help of the Lord God of Hosts?

[1] Giraldus Cambrensis, *The itinerary through Wales*, London, Dent Dutton, 1912, p. 184.
[2] Bach Flower Remedies Ltd, *Information leaflet for the public*, c. 1990.
[3] T. C. McLuhan (compiler), *Touch the earth: a self-portrait of Indian existence*, London, Abacus, 1986, p. 6.
[4] T. C. McLuhan (as above), p. 170.

CHAPTER 9

Storytelling and gossip

John Berger has a theory about gossip in rural communities, which seems to fit rural Wales as well as that remote part of the French Alps which inspired his *Pig Earth*. The function of gossip, he argues, is to allow the whole village to define itself in its own terms. Gossip is personalised oral history. The stories that circulate when the inhabitants meet and pass the time of day are not just trivial talk, as they may seem to outsiders. They are an important way of giving a place its own identity, as seen from inside the community, and in the everyday language of its own dwellers. This provides an antidote to outside analysis—by journalists or tourists, sociologists or economists, whose analyses only scrape the surface of what it means to belong to a particular place.

So gossip is ever at it, building up a continuing unfinished portrait of the community, where everyone is able to add to the picture, and everyone is also part of the picture. But instead of the mutual clicking of cameras to freeze scenes in time, there is an endless weaving of words into anecdotes made up of memories, opinions and prejudices, hearsay and eye-witness accounts, overheard conversations and phone calls starting with 'Have you heard . . . ?'

Gossip is an organic part of community life, without which the sense of self-identity blurs and fades. When everyone knows everyone else inside out, nothing can be hidden for long, and the portrait has unity and cohesion, even when it includes conflict, scandal or simmering quarrels going on from one generation to another between neighbouring farmers. But such cohesive communities are becoming very rare in rural Wales, so what happens when communities become fragmented as a result of locals leaving and newcomers arriving?

When the number of newcomers increases beyond a certain point, they cannot be absorbed into the existing picture the community has of itself, and the self-portrait of the village fragments. There are increasing areas of ignorance and uncertainty, where newcomers are not sure what to make of the locals, and the locals are not sure what to make of the newcomers. Incomers see the place in terms of their outside experiences, and make judgments on that basis which would never be made by locals. They criticise lovely new bungalows, or invoke official planning guidelines without considering the personal and local circumstances of, say, an old farmer wanting to retire to a nice easy-to-run place and let his children take over the farm. And incomers' thinking is a mystery to the locals, too. Why do they want to do up an old wreck of a place at the back of beyond, when they are not even going to farm the land, but are trying to let it to a local farmer? Why do they do all that walking about in the countryside, when no self-respecting local would walk if he could use the Landrover—even for driving sheep in the fields? Exercise, is it? Beautiful scenery? Well, if you're a farmer you get plenty of exercise at your work and you keep your head down to your job, and you never think of *y filltir sgwâr*, your own patch, as 'scenery'. It is the place where you live and work, and is peopled with past and present stories of success, of struggles and setbacks, schemes that flourished for a while, others that you prefer to forget . . .

So the community's continuing story fragments, and the picture you get of the place depends on who you speak to. People can use the same words, even, and mean something different by them, for there are degrees of politeness and evasion at work, when there is a growing sense of difference. From being like a Victorian narrative painting (with Hogarthian touches of satire), the picture of the place can easily splinter into a cartoon collection of stereotype characters—hippies and respectable residents, English speakers and Welsh speakers, Them and Us. But there are countervailing forces at work, too, for there is still a great longing for a place to have its own identity, and this is as strong among many incomers as it is among locals, for one of the reasons they come to rural Wales is to find community and get away from anonymous places with no character of their own. So bridges are built between many different kinds of people, and the news is passed on in a continuing flow of gossip, even if the stories now have different meanings for the people who tell or hear them, and different kinds of jokes are going the rounds.

Individual story-telling used to be the ordinary way to hand on a place's history and imaginative life from one generation to another, in the rich oral culture of the Celtic lands, before the days of formal schooling and the media. But with the coming of the global village of video and telly and radio, community storytelling often gets reduced to a thin gruel of current gossip, for we have come to rely on the daily soap operas for our regular dose of well-crafted anecdote, and are subject to a relentness bombardment of news and comment on the news and comment on the comment. But it is underestimating human resilience to see people as helpless victims of mass communication. In a small country like Wales the media themselves become personalised vehicles for ordinary people's story-telling. On Sulwyn Thomas' *Stondin Sulwyn* on *Radio Cymru* there is an interweaving of the listeners' own experiences with issues of the day, as people phone in and tell it their way, whether the topic be farming, the National Eisteddfod, schooling, or wind-generators. One of Hywel Gwynfryn's phone-in programmes has gone a stage further, with unsuspecting (?) individuals being phoned up by him and given their moment of fame on the airwaves, as a result of family or friends setting them up as having an interesting story to tell. This can sometimes be quite embarrassing, for not everyone has the story-telling skills that enable them to link up the little tradition with the great tradition, to raise the personal above the level of the mundane to the heights of myth or moral tale.

The difference between these levels is best shown by looking at a few examples of classic storytelling from Ireland and Wales. Maurice O'Sullivan's *Twenty years a-growing* is one of the perennial classics of Irish traditional story-telling, from around the turn of the century, in which the oral culture still exercises a dominant influence, even if it has been transferred to printed form:

Wait now till I tell you a story about the Irish . . . I saw times when I was at school, and if the master heard a word of Irish coming from your lips, I tell you, you would be singing Donal-naGreine by the end of the day. Would you believe it, I had a little board tied behind my back with these words written on it, 'If you speak a word of Irish you will be beaten on back and on flank' . . . but praise and thanks be to God above, it is not so today. And if so, do you know who we have to thank for it? The soupers. Because when they were here in Bally-na-Raha with their big Irish Bibles, giving half-a-crown to every man who would come and read a line or two, without lie or mockery there wasn't a man in the parish but would be going to them every night, until they were all able to read Irish fluently. And so it is they who revived it and restored it and raised it up—and good day to you . . .[7]

This is Liam Beg speaking, 'a thin worn man, nothing but skin and bones but as healthy as a herring'. He greets the island men with the usual question asked in country encounters, 'have you any news from the west?' 'Indeed we have not, Liam', is the reply, 'unless you have some yourself'. 'I have not, my lad', retorts Liam. Whereupon both parties proceed to exchange news not only of present concerns (the wedding they are going to) but of past stories like the one quoted above. This is a procedure still current in rural gossip—a certain jockeying for position and assumed modesty about the newsworthy items one may have in one's possession, in case the other has better. Also past and present are interwoven, to keep the connectedness of a place going in the imaginations of its inhabitants. And history is made alive through personal anecdote and feelings—which are a bit suspect in what we now think of as history.

There are similarities between the Irish and the Welsh story-telling traditions. Caradog Prichard's *Un nos ola' leuad, One night when the moon was full*,[2] is a treasure house of rich storytelling, which moves between everyday tales of a rural community in Gwynedd to a surreal dimension where angels hover outside the sickroom window to take up a boy's soul, and a mother goddess can be seen (if you know how) stretched out along the ridges of *Yr Wyddfa*, Snowdon. The boy at the centre of the tale is taken on a bilberry gathering outing, and from the top of the slope

Guto shows him the crest of Yr Wyddfa standing out clear in the blue distance:

> You can see Yr Wyddfa from here. There she is, look, with her head in the clouds . . . But I bet you cannot see the Queen of Wyddfa?
>
> I can't see a Queen anywhere. You don't either. Joking you are.
>
> No, I'm not. I am looking at her now. But not everyone can see her.
>
> A real lady is she, Guto? I see nobody.
>
> No, indeed. The mountain over there makes the shape of a woman against the sky, and only on a clear day like this does she come into sight. Lying along the crest of the mountain she is. Look now.
>
> (Guto points to the mountain by the side of the summit)
>
> Do you see the crag there where the sheep are grazing?
>
> I see it.
>
> Well, look over there, along my finger, a little bit to the left of the summit of the crag. Do you see the shape of a woman's head lying along it?
>
> I do. I think so.
>
> Now her breast a little bit lower down.
>
> I see.
>
> And then her stomach that is swollen . . .
> And then her feet showing a little from under her skirt?
>
> Yes, I can see her all now.
>
> There you are, then. That is the Queen of Wyddfa. After you see her once, you can see her for ever after.
>
> Why do they call her the Queen of Wyddfa?
>
> Because it is on the summit of Wyddfa she is, of course.
>
> Yes, but why do they call her Queen?
>
> Because Wyddfa is hers, of course. And they say if she rises and comes down from Wyddfa it will be the end of the world.

This is the mythical aspect of storytelling, but Caradog Prichard is equally direct, personal and vivid, in telling the everyday stories of his human characters. The young boy gets an insight into the facts of life through an anecdote about one of the village girls. Who is she? He points, and his friend Huw says:

> Grace Elin Shoe Shop ... Do you remember we saw her with Frank Bee Hive a while back in the sheep pasture?
>
> I do, sure. When we were gathering earth nuts.
>
> Yes. She's had a baby and nobody knows who the father is.
>
> Go on. Why is that?
>
> She will not tell anybody.
>
> Perhaps she doesn't know herself.
>
> Perhaps not. She used to go to the sheep pasture with someone every night nearly, they say.
>
> Maybe Frank Bee Hive is the father.

Caradog Prichard presents us then with two levels of story-telling, the everyday gossip that gives the community its self-identity, and the myth-making element embodied in the Queen of Wyddfa and the Queen of the Black Lake, whose voice is heard in the middle and at the end of the novel, uttering first her song of hope and expectation, and then her song of despair and disillusion, both in the style of the Song of Solomon. The Queen of Wyddfa expects her fulfilment in giving birth to a son-lover. The Queen of the Black Lake awaits the coming of the holy bridegroom, who will be both son and lover to her. But the theme of the novel is the unfairness of life that drives the characters to madness or suicide, so the awaited bridegroom never comes; the Queen of the Black Lake is rejected and her search doomed. Search for what? The meaning of life, no doubt, and the fulfilment of one's potential. But it does not happen in the Gwynedd community where *Un nos ola' leuad* unfolds. The boy loses his mother to madness and the Asylum. Grace Elin Shoe Shop utters the bitter words: 'I hungered for the bread of life and my greed was satisfied; I thirsted for the living wine and I was cast out into the drought'. The boy finally at the end of the story suffocates the girl who initiates him to sex.

There is, it seems, a dislocation in *Un nos ola' leuad* between the everyday and the mythical stories, which may well be deliberate, a device used by Caradog Prichard to attack the conventional rural life which restricts and inhibits visionary potential. Those who glimpse a vision beyond the everyday are punished by madness and disaster, since the circumstances they live in are not conducive to fulfilment of visions, and they are stepping outside their normal roles.

Modern gossip in rural communities can also suffer a parallel dislocation between the everyday anecdotes, the surface chatting, and any deeper significance they might have—the mythical element, if you like. We have lost the art of turning everyday stories into myths about humanity, and tend to operate on the soap opera level. What makes soap operas so popular on the box? Hilary Kingsley, author of *Soapbox*,[3] says, 'Soaps are comforting. Viewers enjoy seeing other people's problems. It's a bit like having neighbours and watching them have their fights'. It's about escapism from real life into a never-never community which is a very selective and slanted picture of what was once a genuine close-knit community, with all its thrills and spills and authentic connections between the people telling the stories against a shared background of values and beliefs.

Although gossip has largely lost its myth-making potential, it still tries to hang a moral on every tale. Only now the morals are more various, and the same story will be told with quite different moral overlays as it passes around a community that still shares the same locality, but not the same values. The universal truths embedded in storytelling from Homer to the *Mabinogi*, and then found again in Irish or Welsh folk tales passed on into the present century, have however acquired a new role in therapy, where sufferers are encouraged to tell their own stores in the manner of a fairy tale, in order to get in touch with their psychological problems. But they have dropped out of the popular consciousness, and the majority of people who think about folk tales at all, tend to slot them into the categories of children's stories or branches of academic study.

215

So what is the nature of modern gossip? It still bears the burden of weaving the identity of a community, so it includes the good and the bad, the exciting and the dull, the traditional and the transitional and the shockingly new and different. A good gossip usually starts off in a low key way, with neutral exchanges about the weather and local events of a public kind. An element of mutual trust encourages further exchanges on the doings of people, known to one or both parties, but judgments are suspended until there is a real familiarity and ease between the talkers, for fear of social solecisms or worse—moral abysses opening up at one another's feet. There are also unwritten rules about gossip which apply over large areas of the world and not just in rural Wales. The first rule is that everyone who lives in a place is included in the gossip, whether he or she belongs to the gossiping network or not. A person arriving in a remote country area is far more visible than in an anonymous urban environment (as drug smugglers attempting to land their contraband on 'remote' Welsh coasts have found to their cost, when the police are speedily informed). A stranger is immediately spotted and his or her purpose sought. Every house and barn stand out in the landscape, and there is much speculation about unknown callers or even strange cars. Perhaps this is a carryover from the time when a stranger could be a potential enemy (a prying official or unwanted inspector of local enterprise), or a welcome traveller from the outside world who would entertain with news and fresh stories, in return for bed and board. Either way it was important to find out about strangers. It still is, though the reasons may be changing. Newcomers have a big impact on thinly populated fragile communities, for better or for worse. So when a house is sold the news flashes round, and clues are sought as to the nature of the new owners. Disappointment sets in if the clues suggest it's going to be a holiday home—they have not put in a regular milk order, and they only appear at weekends. That's another house gone out of permanent occupation, no smoke coming from the chimney or lights in the window at night. The house will die a little and the community feels a kind of bereavement.

But the holiday-home owners will never hear of this sense of community bereavement. They are indeed likely to be treated with the kindness and courtesy that is traditional in long-standing rural communities, and given a cup of tea and a bit of chat (if they are not stand-offish). This illustrates another rule of gossip, which is that the people talked about are the last to know. 'Most people are very cagey about what they say to you face-to-face, but they all have their binoculars!' There is, too, an irresistible fascination about newcomers whose activities are not 'our ways', and therefore offer new possibilties. I was told of a shy bachelor farmer Humphrey, whose inhibitions did not operate with 'incomer women' among whom he roved with new zeal, and, yes, dear reader, he married one. Then there is the Englishman who has for twenty years been using a redundant farmhouse in mid Wales as an occasional meditation retreat centre. The locals have grown accustomed to colourful track-suited retreatants doing their walking meditations on the steep green hillside behind the house, but in the early days the neighbouring farmer said in wistful tones to the organiser, 'That's a fine lot of young women you have there at the weekend . . .' The tip of the iceberg of local gossip?

In the old days of traditional rural communities satirical gossip was turned into good story-telling by the *bardd gwlad*, folk poet, but there are few left today, and they are under threat from the competition of the mass media. A local farmer or craftsman, embedded in the community culture, usually born and brought up in the immediate locality, *y filltir sgwâr*, would take on the job of chronicler and conscience, and use his skills to entertain at local events and celebrations. He would draw on local events and known characters, to memorialise, from his insider position, the changing face of the district, whether it was the arrival of a new minister, the passing of a well-known character, the rise and fall of farming subsidies, the beauties of local waterfalls or woods, the weddings and christenings or the caprices of nature in the way of floods and lightning strikes.

Satire was a continuing tradition from the time of the pagan Celts, whose bards could curse a man to death, as well as build him up to fame and fortune, such was the power of words. The *bardd gwlad* of more

217

recent times is not averse to well-honed poetical barbs, directed, say, at wealthy drapers returned from London with big fortunes but little of their culture left; or at those of conspicuous life-style or piety but little charity. Satire works through sending up the Outsider (who may have been an insider once but failed the tests of acceptability), and the Outsider is a prime element in traditional storytelling. For the basic plot is often focussed on pompous overweening outsider who threatens to undermine local ways or local schemes, but is eventually defeated by the modest cunning and ingenious wit of insider person, to much community applause. The film *Local Hero* is a good example of the upmarket Scots version, and attracted huge audiences presumably because it tapped this fundamental human need for insider/outsider epics.

The community newspapers in the Welsh-speaking culture, the monthly *papurau bro*, have not taken on board this longstanding satirical tradition, though they would seem to be the obvious inheritors, set up as they were in the 1970s to tell the ongoing stories of the rural communities, by their own people, from the inside, and mingling past and present with concern for the future of their people. They are made up entirely of news from within a ten mile radius, and give personalised reports of the achievements and celebrations and passing of local people, of local societies and competitions, of eisteddfodau and sporting fixtures. They are written in a warm hearted style, but are strangely anodyne, avoiding controversy and conflict of the old-style satirical tradition. Even the local history columns, which show a nowadays rare enthusiasm for the past of their communities, are cautious about what they say of the dead. After all, their descendants might still be living in the area and take offence, even after a century had elapsed. Perhaps the situation is changing a little, for our local *papur bro*, *Y Tincer*, has recently begun a personal opinion column, *Meddai Fi*, which occasionally tackles troublesome rural issues, like conservation or hippies. But it seems that satire is approved of still, only when it is oral (it began after all in an oral culture). It is too stark and direct to put it down in cold print. So gossip gets a new lease of life, to say the things that cannot be said openly without offending, but which need to be circulated by some means or other, for they are part of the story of a place.

Age-old themes of storytelling

Joseph Campbell says that one function of myth is 'to support the current social order, to integrate the individual organically with his group'.[4] Maybe in the traditional rural culture storytelling and certain kinds of gossip succeeded in doing this. They gave everyone a chance to picture their place in the community and see themselves in relation to others. The place you lived in was peopled by those whose stories you knew, and who knew your story. There was also scope for exaggeration, satire and fantasy, through the license that familiarity and intimate knowledge allow. You can wash your own community's dirty linen, but you do not want outsiders to take part in this activity.

Now there is a problem of lack of cohesion in communities, and story telling might divide rather than unite, offend rather than entertain, if the old robust tradition were openly followed. But as Giraldus Cambrensis said in the twelfth century, the Welsh 'love sarcastic remarks and libellous allusions, plays on words, sly references, ambiguities and equivocal statements. Some of these are just for fun, but they can be very bitter . . .' So gossiping and story-telling go on, and it is even possible to detect the age-old universal themes in some of the gossipy local stories.

The return of the prodigal son?

'The ne'er do well son has come back, with a different woman. They're sleeping in the haybarn, because the old man won't have them in the house, in case they get their feet under the table for good. But they sit there all day by the fire, not doing a hand's turn (though there's plenty to do about the place, even in winter isn't there?), except to raise a glass from a bottle they haven't paid for . . .'

The eternal Eve?

'Walking about bare as the day she was born, for all to see . . . She thinks she's back in the garden of Eden, maybe. Being natural before the

Fall ... but I've heard preachers say that nobody can be that natural without doing wrong. It's Original Sin ...'

The battle between the sexes?
'I'm very fond of them both—when they're not together, but I don't know why they stay with each other, for all they do is scream blue murder and when they've finished the bottle they're drowning their sorrows in, it becomes another weapon ... And they don't thank you if you try to help, when you can't get to sleep for worrying that at last one of them has killed the other ...'

Beauty and the Beast?
'Not looking, just walking past the house we were, and the door was open, and there she was sitting on his knee ... He's old enough to be her grandfather, and they say he's not taking a penny piece for renting the cottage to her, either—but that's hard to believe when he hasn't a sock left to put his foot in, he has them all stuffed with every penny he can get his hands on ...'

These scraps of gossip illustrate the judgmental side, the role of gossip in asserting or confirming a particular group's value system, its particular forms of respectability. This can easily slip over into character assassination, idle gossip with a cutting edge, which every group—village, work group, friends or professional networks—indulges in from time to time, with or without faint twinges of guilt because of the unfairness of talking about people behind their backs and giving them no chance to reply. But gossip also makes people feel good, because it is about belongingness, and takes place among people with shared concerns, a shared place, or a shared cause. We owe it to each other to make our own picture of our community, and not leave it to experts or outsiders to impose their meanings or abstractions on our ways of living. Their analyses never present the whole, but the endless weaving of gossip can, for nothing is excluded—homes, jobs, trips, relationships, feuds and quarrels, good deeds and bad, love and sex, births and marriages and deaths, the coming of strangers with their incomprehensible ways, the activities of officials as they go about their enigmatic investigations of water supplies or river pollution or building inspection work ...

So although gossipers can be malicious, dishonest or get things wrong because they do not even give a fair hearing to other people's stories, the importance of gossip for knitting up communities is that it can, at its best, tell the whole human story of a place, with all the different ways of seeing that these days make the final picture such an intricate mosaic. The lowest level of gossip is an escape from reality, the highest encourages us to face reality. There is a good story in the *Mabinogi* about the importance of avoiding self-indulgent fantasy in our lives and facing up to reality.

After the war between the Welsh and the Irish over the ill-treatment of the Welsh princess Branwen by her husband Matholwch King of Ireland, there were only seven Welsh warriors left alive to return to their native land. They landed on the island of Grassholm in Pembrokeshire, and there feasted and indulged themselves for four-score years in a fine hall that had two open doors and one closed door in it. 'And notwithstanding all the sorrows they had seen before their eyes, and notwithstanding that they themselves had suffered, there came to them no remembrance of that or of any sorrow in the world'. But in the end one of the company dared to open the Third Door, and they saw reality once again, so that 'they were as conscious of every loss they had ever sustained, and of every kinsman and friend they had missed, and of every ill that had come upon them ...' With that revelation of true reality, however, they were released from the blandishment of wishful thinking, of escapist fantasising, and were enabled to return to authentic existence, and resume their own life quests.

And the moral of that story is surely that it is not enough to be a gossiping spectator of other people's lives, but you must get on with the work of making meaning in your own life, of telling your own story as part of your community's story. The Higher Gossip is storytelling that is interdependent, and everybody has their turn to make and tell their own stories in their own voices. But we are left with the dilemma introduced at the beginning of this chapter. Many rural communities no longer speak with a common voice nor tell their stories from a sense of shared values, though there may be a surface amiability covering up the buried divisions. The pressures of convention have lightened, and there is no longer consensus on 'the right thing to do'. People from different groups in the community are uncertain about what to say to each other, beyond the initial greetings, because of the loss of the traditional certainties, expressed in the traditional language. The audience for a person's stories has become a lot more unpredictable in its responses, but everyone needs to contribute to the ongoing story of the place, to keep its identity in existence, even if nobody knows any longer the whole story. Is this what sociologists mean by a pluralist society?

[1] Maurice O'Sullivan, *Twenty years agrowing*, London, Oxford University Press, 1983, p. 208.
[2] Caradog Prichard, *Un nos ola' leuad*, Caernarfon, Gwasg Gwalia, 1988.
[3] Hilary Kingsley, *Box of delights*, London, Macmillan, 1990.
[4] Joseph Campbell, *Occidental mythology*, New York, Viking, 1970, p. 520.

CHAPTER 10

The Grammar of the Rose: sex v respectability

In 1990 a top women's magazine, *Cosmopolitan*, published the results of a poll they had carried out among their readers on women's sexual behaviour. It suggested that the women of Wales are the most sexually active in the UK. Six out of ten said they had made love on a first date. Over a third said they made love three to five times a week, and one in a hundred confessed to doing it twice a day. According to the claims made in the poll, women made love to other women's husbands and to strangers with equal enthusiasm. Six out of ten said they were unfaithful to their longterm partner—a third by having affairs with married men, and another third having sex with a stranger. Surely this could not represent the situation in rural Wales, with its clinging on to traditional values about the family and respectability? It must be about the women of the South, of urban areas . . . ?

The popular press in Wales responded in ways that reflected their conflicting needs to give a good spread to 'hot copy', while not offending traditional notions of respectability to which their readers mights still subscribe, in theory or practice or both. *Cosmo* readers in Wales who had taken part in the poll were likely to be 'sophisticated' women in their twenties and thirties; beyond the *Cosmo* catchment area there must be decent Welshwomen continuing to conform to the stern sexual ethic of Methodism, whether or not they still go to Chapel. *Wales on Sunday* took a more sociological line, highlighting the sad truths behind the statistics—the poll revealed that half the women who did have sex on a first date were heavily under the influence of drink or drugs, and a third did it because they were lonely and sex seemed the easiest way out, even if it might just confirm their loneliness. There was the heavy jocular line, too, that this was really good news for Welshmen

—were they aware of all those sexual opportunities right here in their own communities? But many rural newspapers simply ignored the findings, because they do not discuss sexuality unless it becomes the subject of a court case (rape or domestic violence), or forms the background to a planning application (who wants a Women's Refuge in their locality?).

There seems to be an element of puritanism in rural Wales which betrays a rich heritage of sexual lust and full-blooded love-making going back to the beginnings of history. There seems to be a need to deny this sexual heritage, which sometimes leads to curious hypocrisies, as in the following letter from the Welsh-language weekly *Y Cymro* (or is it a joke targetted at this kind of hypocrisy—who can tell?):

I am writing to you to complain about the advert which I saw in the last issue of your *previously* honourable paper. Condoms, forsooth! To see this sort of thing advertised in a Welsh paper and in the precious language too!!!

It is disgraceful enough to see such things on sale in any language—but through the medium of Welsh and in *Y Cymro* too!!!

The moral standards of our nation are being undermined—everything Welsh that is pure and holy is busy decaying and now *Y Cymro* is joining in the process.

Shame! Disgrace! (*Y Cymro*, 7 June 1987—my translation)

This is in fact no joke, especially in the age of AIDS, and in the light of a further recent statistic that over a quarter of young people in Wales do not use any contraception when making love. The hospitals in rural Wales conscientiously display AIDS counselling posters, but if the risks are present in popular consciousness at all, it is usually only as some distant threat which is nothing to do with Us, because We are not promiscuous, or drug users, or gay . . .

It is salutary to consider the history of sexuality in rural Wales before jumping to any conclusions about decline and deterioration in the nation's moral standards at the present time. The permanence and stability of marriages in early Wales were threatened by problems familiar in modern times, as a study of the tenth century Laws of Hywel Dda will reveal.

In Hywel Dda's *Laws of Women*[1] there is detailed provision for pooling the matrimonial property in the event of a marriage breaking up, and thoughtful distinctions are made between marriages that have lasted less than seven years, or are of longer standing. No need to argue over the cat or the bedclothes or the household debts, for the laws laid down that the bedclothes over the matrimonial bed belong to the woman and the under bedclothes to the man. The man gets the hens and one cat, and the woman gets the rest of the cats, the sheep and the salted meat (not the hams hung up to smoke—they go to the husband). Of the sons, two thirds go to the father and one third to the mother. Daughters are clearly of less value, for they are not mentioned, so at least the parting couple could argue over them.

The Laws acknowledge that men and women are prone to behave adulterously, and elaborate degrees of compensation money are specified, depending on whether the insult to the spouse is limited to kissing and fondling, or extends to a man 'lying between the two thighs of a woman'. As for sex with a stranger, it seems that men from a far country were safer lovers to have, for a husband could not claim compensation for his wife's infidelity with a man who fondled her 'before knowing the law of the country'.

Outbursts of romantic lust which did not last beyond a few nights were seen as more damaging to the woman than to the man, so 'whoever sleeps three nights with a woman from when the fire is covered until it is uncovered on the morrow, and from then on wants to leave her, let him pay her a steer worth twenty pence and another worth thirty pence and another worth forty pence'. But if the affair went on and became a common law marriage lasting seven years, they share from then on in just the same way as if they were formally married.

The women 'of bush and brake', who had no kin to exact compensation for their sexual misfortunes or misadventures, were humanely considered in the Laws. 'If it happens that a person makes pregnant a woman of bush and brake, it is right for him to maintain the child, for the law says that through she may lose the man, it is not right for her to suffer want from him or because of him, while not getting any benefit'. If a woman

225

was raped, however, there was less consideration given to her feelings. If she wanted to bring a legal charge against the man, she was required to take his member in her left hand in the public gaze, put her right hand on a holy relic, and swear by the relic that the member she held had penetrated her by force. There was evidently a similar problem to that experienced by women today in convincing the powers that be that rape had taken place and not consenting sex. Many women must have been discouraged from pressing the charge by the provision made in the Laws for a man denying the charge. He could bring to the hearing fifty stout fellows to give oath on his behalf. But that in the context of the time signifies the vital importance of kith and kin in the process of the law. Family and tribe were invariably involved in claiming or in paying out compensation for insults (sexual or property or personal violence) to the extended family. In practice this often meant taking the law into their own hands, for there were no police to administer it, of course. It is still said in rural Wales today that 'When you take on a Welsh person, you take on a whole family', and feuds are known to be perpetuated from one generation to another through being handed down in the family.

Living with your chosen mate before you were married was common practice as far back as the Middle Ages. Giraldus Cambrensis, the part-Norman, part-Welshman who was one of the most colourful churchmen of the twelfth century, says that the Welsh of his day 'do not engage in marriage until they have tried, by previous cohabitation, the disposition, and especially the fecundity, of the person with whom they are involved'.[2] There was a down-to-earth understanding that marriage is something different from either courtly love or the fires of lust. These could burn themselves out, but marriage to succeed had to produce children to help with the endless work, and to care for the parents in their old age. It also had to be based on some measure of compatible temperaments, to make everyday living together tolerable, at a time when the household was the place of work as well as of domesticity (as it still is in farming areas).

Giraldus Cambrensis also claims that the Welsh 'have long had the custom of buying young girls from their parents, with a penalty-clause in case they run away, not in the first instance with a view to marriage, but just to live with them'.[3] It is not recorded how often this happened or the subsequent fate of such young women. Did they become fodder for medieval brothels, or, in small communities, a consolation for lustful apprentices, old bachelors and widowers? Or, if they were more fortunate, did they join that band of young women who in the larger households were assigned the job of entertaining guests?

> Those who arrive in the morning were entertained till evening with the conversation of young women, and the music of the harp; for each house has its young women allotted to this purpose . . . as no nation labours more under the vice of jealousy than the Irish, so none is more free from it than the Welsh.[4]

However, in spite of the apparent sexual tolerances, 'corrupted maidens' could be spurned where formal marriage was concerned, another example of the double standards for women and men which often apply even in sexually liberal cultures. The Laws of Hywel Dda advise that if the husband finds, when he takes the alleged maiden to his marriage bed, that she is not a virgin, he either puts up with the situation and keeps her in his bed all night (which is taken as acceptance); or, on finding his bride not a virgin, he testifies with penis erect before the wedding guests that he found her corrupted and so she is not entitled to anything from him.

While the early laws give a useful insight into what was seen as the legal rights and wrongs of sexual behaviour, they fail to convey people's personal responses to these varieties of love and lust that went on inside or outside formal or common law marriages. For that we need to turn to the poets, and then it becomes touchingly clear that people's feelings on love and sexuality do not change all that much over the centuries, whatever the formal inhibitions imposed by church or state.

The problems of medieval men and women in love can sound amazingly like some of the letters on today's Problem Page in *Wales on Sunday*. Here we go again—jealous spouses, shy lovers, the agonies of secret love affairs, the terrible pangs of unrequited love, women as objects of desire, men as absent heroes with a horrid tendency to abandon love for war and fame and fortune . . .

227

Dafydd ap Gwilym[5] is the best known love poet of medieval Wales, and among the finest in fourteenth-century Europe. He frankly reveals himself as an untiring lover, flitting from one mistress to another, for ever pleading his undying passion for each one in exquisite and yet earthy language:

> A blameless art is it for my woman to walk the woods with her lover, to be face to face, to smile together, to laugh together lip to lip, together to lay ourselves down by the grove, together to escape the crowd, together to lament our secret love, together to pass time in pleasure, together to drink mead, together to make love, together to lie, together to keep up our hidden passion . . .

As for jealous husbands, they are sour fellows who try to keep wives for themselves alone, have no spirit of play, and are enemies to all that represents life and vigour and beauty in God's creation:

> The talk of the thrush and the proud nightingale under the greenwood is what he hates. It is odious to the feeble Jealous Husband to hear the hounds and the harp-string . . . the Jealous Husband, boorish and livid, is odious to me. Let the fair girl whose brow is as white as dice, desert her mate within six months, and *I* shall love her henceforward; I love none but married women.

And it is not only men who desire young lovers, for in Dafydd's poetry women too are portrayed as having their own yearnings for young and tender males:

> They serve their own hearts, they love a man slender and sound . . . An old fat greybeard they do not desire a tryst with—dearer to them is a young lad, however poor.

The interesting question is: what happened to this heritage of sexual and romantic energies when the Great Awakening took place in eighteenth-century Wales and Calvinist Methodism became the dominant ethos from then until the mid twentieth century?

The early Methodists were made fun of for their long faces and their emphasis on sin rather than salvation, and especially carnal sin. They did away with the rural pastimes of dancing and Mayday frolics between the sexes. Yet at the same time it was observed that converts often experienced a spontaneous joy and release of energy which could sometimes get channelled towards unworthy sensual ends. And when preachers like Hywel Harris were attractive to women as well, it was not always clear whether it was the message or the messenger that was winning souls. In one of William Williams Pantycelyn's works of 1762, the pastor 'Philo' gives this response to a young woman's worries that her ecstacy in Christ may only be 'the heightened excesses of nature':

> Salvation in Christ is the only pleasure . . . The country's young people have become estranged from fancy clothes. Sleep has fled. Craving for meat and drink is swallowed by praise and song. Hymns and psalms and spiritual songs are the only nourishment at the saints' love feasts.[6]

Inevitably a tension developed in Methodism between the rapturous conversion experiences which transported people out of their normal selves, and the uncompromising insistence on the virtues of sobriety, industry, thrift and honesty in every aspect of daily life. The Holy Spirit caused 'unspeakable raptures of the mind' which bore sufficient resemblance to carnal rapture to be of concern to the leaders of the movement. An 'excess of emotion' was noted and condemned in every major revival from the eighteenth century till the last large scale revival of 1904. The problem was that 'Man is prone to licentiousness and needs to repent', but to be plucked by God from the burning fires of sin (the carnal raptures of the World, the Flesh and the Devil) was to be fundamentally aroused, transported. In some cases this holy ecstacy toppled over into unholy sensuality, as men and women felt released from conventional controls and were moved to give direct expression to their inner feelings. Thus the warnings of the leading preachers against excessive emphasis on the emotional traumas of sin and conviction and religious ecstasy, at the expense of a good grasp of the Scriptures which helped the convert sift the gold from the dross in the aftermath of the conversion experience.

229

The most common offences leading to expulsion from chapel membership were unchastity and drunkenness. Moral discipline was strict. The first stage was to be reprimanded publicly in front of the other members, to bring a sense of shame on the wrongdoer. If that was insufficient communion could be withheld until the sinner was expelled entirely or restored to right thinking and correct moral behaviour. The final decision was always a community judgment, done through a show of hands by neighbours and kindred who knew the individual personally. It is impossible to keep secrets in a face-to-face community where gossip is a prime input to conversation and the folk subscribe to the ideals of sexual restraint and sobreity. So a certain amount of hypocrisy became inevitable to accommodate irrepressible sensuality to the new tone of pious morality.

In the sphere of sexuality the problem was exacerbated by a failure to follow the open good-hearted guidance of the great leader of the early days, Williams Pantycelyn. In 1777 he published a *Guide to marriage*, which takes the form of a counselling dialogue between Mary (happily married) and Martha (unhappily married). There is no hypocrisy here about women not having natural sex drives, of being only passive responders to male 'needs'. Martha's predicament arises from the fact that she succumbed to sensual yearnings and forgot about spirit and reason:

> O the hellish fires of natural love! What a host of virtuous young women like me weep bitter tears for following their own desires instead of the will of God and their parents.[7]

She now finds herself stuck with a failure of a man, who is not even interested in her any more, now that she is ugly with pregnancy ('My belly swollen, my stomach sick, my womb having eaten the flesh from my face, till I look like death from the waist up, and like a hayrick from the waist down'). The good wife Mary on the other hand is presented as enjoying matrimonial love within the blessing of God's love, so good sexuality is given an honourable place, provided the lovers are properly married.

Williams Pantycelyn indeed put such emphasis on positive sexuality within marriage in his guide that Victorian Methodists suppressed it because they detected in it elements of indecency. Wives who have quarrelled with their husbands for instance, or whose husbands are neglecting them, may need to take sexual initiatives as part of the conciliatory process. This may have appeared faintly shocking to late nineteenth century Methodists, but it followed the sexually more even-handed attitudes of the great Puritan divines on marriage. They had quoted 1 Corinthians 7.3 - 5, which is certainly more supportive of the basic human instincts than the more often quoted words of Paul about it being better to marry than to burn. In a modern translation this reads:

> The husband should fulfil his marital duty to his wife, and likewise the wife of her husband. The wife's body does not belong to her alone but also to her husband. In the same way, the husband's body does not belong to him alone, but to his wife. Do not deprive each other except by mutual consent and for a time, so that you may devote yourselves to prayer. Then come together again so that Satan will not tempt you because of your lack of self-control.

Williams Pantycelyn then is seen to be following in the more liberal Protestant tradition, in which, according to the Scriptures, we should beware both a deficiency and an excess of sexual expression. At the same time he was vigilant against the dangers of sexuality, being well aware of allegations that the fires of religious conversion could easily turn into the fires of concupiscence. The intimacy and warm feelings in the early Methodist communities could readily lead, he saw, to immoral behaviour, for young women are led astray '*gan rym tân natur*', by the power of nature's fire. But that was no reason for inhibiting sexuality in the right place, within marriage. Indeed the unhappy wife Martha in *Guide to Marriage* is advised to mend marriage in the matrimonial bed as well as in the other parts of the home.

At the same time as Methodism was becoming firmly rooted in late eighteenth-century Wales, there was an influx of outsiders pouring in to get work in the mid Wales lead mines, and many of them showed little concern for respectability. They developed the custom of the *priodas fach*, the little wedding, described by Lewis Morris:

> Sometimes half a dozen couples will agree at a merry meeting, and are thus wedded and bedded together. This ... is frequently made use of among miners and others to make sure of a woman. [8]

The little wedding was considered to be binding only for a month, and if after that time the couple parted by consent, there was no obstacle in their way. Lewis Morris worried about the position of the women who might be abandoned by their miners after only a brief fling, but he was reassured by observing that in Ceredigion 'the girl was not worse looked upon among the miners than if she had been an unspotted virgin', because the custom had taken a firm hold in the mining areas. It was common for miners to arrange simply for a man to conduct the weddings in the local pub, and he would charge them only a few tankards of ale for his services. The persons most vociferous in their complaints about the *priodas fach* were the ministers of the parish, who suffered the loss of their marriage fees as well as disapproving on principle. In one small Ceredigion village the minister complained that fifty or more couples had taken the 'little marriage' rather than the 'great marriage', though a few did come later to his church for a confirmation of the informal ceremony.

At the beginning of the nineteenth century the country districts around Cwmrheidol and Ystumtuen were not noted for their civilised behaviour or respect for religion. Church services would be interrupted by noisy games in an adjacent field, and after the services there would be stone-throwing games. In the church at Ysbyty Cynfyn wrestling competitions took place into the early hours, during which the girls egged on the boys, and some of them were ready and willing to take part themselves in the wrestling. [9]

The conflict between chapel culture and tavern culture which surfaced in the lead mining areas at the end of the eighteenth century continued unabated through the Victorian era, when much effort went into the temperance movement and the saving of 'fallen women'. Women's sexuality entered it's worst period of repression in the latter half of the nineteenth century, at least on the surface, though as usual popular culture was more live-and-let-live than the dominant Methodist ideology might suggest. The images of Welshwomen held up as models to follow, in the first women's magazine in Wales, *Y Gymraes*, 1850, are of 'faithful maids, virtuous women, thrifty wives and intelligent mothers'. The aim of the magazine was 'the elevation of the female sex in every respect—social, moral and religious'. There had been an agonised debate going on since the 1847 Education Commissioners had cast doubt on the morality of Welshwomen, as well as on the value of the Welsh language, and the magazine was intended to ensure that such criticisms could never happen again. The alleged unchastity of women had been seen by the Commissioners as responsible 'for all other immoralities, for each generation will derive its moral tone in a great degree from the influences imparted by the mothers who reared them'. Lady Llanover was the new magazine's patron and helped to create this image of the ideal *Cymraes* as wife and mother, chaste and sober and thrifty, bringing her children up in the Welsh language and, preferably, wearing the Welsh flannel dresses and tall beaver hats which Lady Llanover urged as the native dress. Women were to be the angels on the hearth, and the language was to be a means of moral rejuvenation and revival.

Since the magazine was largely produced by men, it is not surprising that it ended up being mainly read by men, and that it ignored vital women's issues and viewpoints:

> . . . the main occupation of Welsh women, domestic service, was romanticized and seen as the ideal opportunity for women to exhibit their natural feminine instincts of service and deference . . . themes central to working women's lives, such as illness and childbirth, were not mentioned. All discussion on sex was from a male standpoint: 'fallen' women who succumbed to temptation should bear the consequence of their foolishness. [10]

But women who wrote for it followed the same line as the male editors, urging that women should be submissive and hard-working, pure and godly, mothers first and foremost who had a responsibility not just to their families but to the nation, in bringing up its future citizens. By the end of the century there were a great many women in the chapel culture. living out these ideals, by reading the Bible, being active in chapel life, and handing on the Welsh language, which was seen as a barrier against the penetration of inferior moral values, to the next generation. This was the apogee of respectability, for with the 1914-18 war began the first steps in the decline of the Nonconformist ethos which has been going on ever since.

The Respectable approach to sexuality and drink comes under increasing satire in the twentieth century. The promiscuous spirit of Dafydd ap Gwilym lives again in the lyrics of Dylan Thomas, who soaked up the atmosphere of rural Wales during boyhood summers on his aunt's farm in Carmarthenshire. There he struggled, unsuccessfully, to reconcile in himself his burgeoning romantic sensuality and the Nonconformist attitudes to morality he sensed around him. He opted openly for the love of women and the love of drink, and his poetry profoundly echoes his choice. His Gossamer Beynon dreams she is digging deep in a hummock of chicken feathers in a slaughterhouse with chintz curtains and a three piece suite. There she finds, 'with no surprise, a small rough ready man with a bushy tail ... At last, my love', she cries, and 'the bushy tail wags rude and ginger'. There is, too, Polly Garter, for whom 'Life is a terrible thing, thank God'. She gives her shapely breast to yet another new baby, whose father like all the other fathers of her children, lives over the hills and far away. And there is the young girl Mae, who 'peels off her pink and white skin in a furnace in a tower in a cave in a wood and waits as raw as an onion for Mister Right to leap up the burning tall hollow splashes of leaves like a brilliantined trout'.

Thomas both sings the praises of sexuality and conducts an onslaught on respectability at the same time. There is Jack Black with his nightshirt tied by elastic to his ankles, but dreaming in his 'bible-black airless attic' of 'chasing the naughty couples down the grassgreen gooseberried double bed of the wood ... driving out the bold bare girls from the sixpenny hops of his nightmares'.

While respectability and sensuality carried on their ideological battles, the innate conservatism of the countryside ensured that some medieval love customs lived on into the twentieth century. Night courting, or 'bundling', or courting on the bed was a widespread custom right across Europe in the Middle Ages. There are descriptions of it in such varied sources as old Norse sagas, Arthurian legends, and in Welsh medieval literature (including of course Dafydd ap Gwilym). The custom travelled to South Africa with the Dutch colonists and is described in Olive Schreiner's *African farm*. In Wales it remained a common practice in rural areas during the nineteenth century, bringing down the accusations of immorality from the Education Commissioners in 1847, which put pressure on women especially to prove their purity during the remainder of the century.

In night courting the man turns up at his beloved's house and attracts her attention by striking on the window or throwing small pebbles against the glass. If the window is opened to him, the two engage in verbal dalliance which may or may not gain him entry to her room. If the lover was admitted, what happened? There begins the great controversy. When the Education Commissioners of 1847 reported on the practice as evidence of unchastity and a frequent cause of illegitimacy, there was an indignant rebuttal from the *Cymry Cymraeg*. All that happens, they asserted, was that the young couple, in a romantic Romeo and Juliet spirit, sit up together for the greater part of the night, and the charge of 'bundling' together is a gross calumny. Others said that a bolster was put down the middle of the bed, like the Arthurian sword of honour, and only removed by mutual agreement of the lovers. It was also argued that country folk worked such long hours and had so little privacy that the only time they could do their courting was in this manner during the night, but that should not be taken as an irretrievable loss of innocence.

Nobody seems to have defended the practice of night courting as a romantic celebration of love which carried on the fine medieval love tradition of Wales. There was too strong a grip by the puritan Christian ethos, which fulminated against the flesh as of the Devil and not of God, though this is dangerously manichaean, for the body as well as the mind and the spirit, is part of God's creation and therefore is not inherently evil.

But what happened if the practice led to women being left with fatherless babies? In close-knit rural communities this was catered for in a number of ways. If a baby was on the way it was the done thing for the young couple to get married, and gossip always ensured that people knew who the father was. If a girl did have a baby outside marriage, it was the humane practice to bring up the child as one of her mother's or aunt's own brood, and in the days of large families the new baby would just be another step in the staircase of curly heads.

For the woman, courting on the bed gave her a certain control over her sexuality. It was she who decided whether or not to admit the lover to her room, and after that, to her bed. Both the lovers could discover a great deal more about each other this way than in walking out (the weather must have been better in Dafydd ap Gwilym's time than it is now, for many of *his* love nests are bowers in the woods), or going on chapel outings with the rest of the crowd. There was probably, too, an element of practical anxiety to make sure a future partner was able to have children, for it was just as important to have extra hands in the smallholdings and quarries and lead mines.

But bed courting came under the strictures of a brand of Christianity more concerned with original sin than with original blessing, with repression rather than celebration of the body and emotions, as well as the mind and spirit. The question that was often asked in the chapels and the schools was, 'Is it respectable?' Bed-courting was pronounced *not* respectable, and the upper echelons of rural communities set about trying to eradicate it. The Agricultural Commissioners reported in the 1890s that:

> The farmers' daughters who were sent from home to school, learned that the old fashion to which we have alluded was disgraceful, and that it was regarded so by educated people. So they set their faces against it when they

returned home. In time the better-behaved of the farmers' daughters would tend steadily to establish a better fashion among the maid-servants too. [11]

In the 1990s a new cycle of 'unrespectable' love and romance is well established. More and more young people decide to live together before, or instead of, getting married. Well, *'Nid oes dim newydd dan yr haul'*, there's nothing new under the sun, says a former minister of Ystumtuen Chapel, as he compares the so-called new modern mores with the *priodas fach*, or temporary marriages among the old lead miners in this district. In the old days there was a complicated extended family usually made up of parents and children and *plant siawns*, love children, sometimes, and farm servants. When life expectancy was shorter, it was common to have more than one marriage partner in a lifetime, as a result of accidental death or disease or perinatal mortality removing the first spouse, so there could well be stepbrothers and sisters in the family. Also families helped each other out in periods of financial difficulty or illness, so there might be a nephew or niece being looked after in the household, or they might be sent to help when the people of the house got too old to keep up their place themselves. The modern extended family also means a complicated network of step parents and stepchildren, step sisters and brothers, but for very different reasons, to do with the increasing rate of divorce and remarriage or of serial relationships not formalised as marriage.

Gay rights have, since the eighties, been building a higher profile in rural Welsh-speaking Wales, and this is something of a shock for those traditional nonconformists who regard homosexuality not as a sexual preference but as a perversion condemned in the Scriptures (where the Lord God destroyed the city of Sodom to punish the Sodomites for their wicked practices). Homosexuality has been an inherent part of certain respected cultures—as in ancient Athens when Plato and Aristotle and Socrates were perfecting their philosophical systems. But it seems to have had a negative image in the history of Wales. The somewhat scurrilous Giraldus Cambrensis (three quarters Norman, one quarter Welsh) goes so far as to say:

It was because of their sins, and more particularly the wicked and detestable vice of homosexuality, that the Welsh were punished by God and so lost first Troy and then Britain ... In the *History of the Kings of Britain* [Geoffrey of Monmouth] we read of Malgo, King of the Britons, who practised homosexuality, and many others with him.[12]

But, he adds, homosexuality had for a long time ceased by his time (the twelfth century) and 'hardly anyone can remember it'.

By the 1980s the statistics suggested that one in ten of the population are gay men or lesbians. At the 1990 AGM of *Cymdeithas yr Iaith*, the Welsh Language Society, in Aberystwyth, there was a motion calling for a working party to further lesbian and gay rights. The argument was that 10% of Welsh speakers are gay or lesbian, and they suffer from reactionary prejudice in the community which puts pressure on them to leave the Welsh-speaking areas for more liberal urban scenes. So if the *Cymdeithas yr Iaith* was serious in its intention to build a radical front in Wales, they should support gay rights. But they ducked the issue in Aberystwyth in 1990. The retiring chairman Siân Howys argued that 'she realised the proposal was concerned with someone's personal identity but it was unfair to use the Society as a platform to put people on trial'. It was another of those moments in history when self-confessed political radicals fail to connect the personal and the political.

Alongside these trends towards sexual liberation there continue the old conventions surrounding marriage, and of these certainly the most striking is the sumptuous white wedding costing anything between two thousand and seven thousand pounds, which even only modestly well-off parents are determined to offer to their daughters, to make it a good send-off and an occasion to remember. Aberystwyth has its own special wedding shop, Carol Ann, to take care of the fashion side of things, and its window is a feast of romantic billowing white dresses and satin stilettos, beaded bags and gorgeous lacy undies. There are vivid two-pieces and cartwheel hats for the mothers and aunties, and fine silk hankies for them to cry into. Without the wedding functions, too, Aberystywth hotels would be in a bad way, after the tourist season is over. When *The Observer* colour supplement did a special feature on 'Weddings Today' in 1989, they sent a camera crew to Aberystwyth to film a typical local couple on their Great Day. Sandra and Gary said they had spent so much money on this wedding 'there was no way either of them could back out (*jôc*)'. They had a full-blown church wedding, with three bridesmaids, a pageboy and a flower girl, all dressed to the nines in frilly long dresses or little Lord Fauntleroy suit. There were eighty guests at the wedding breakfast, that is lunch, in the Marine Hotel afterwards, with her relatives sitting on one side and his on the other, as in the church ceremony. There was soup and roast fowl, black forest gateau or cheesecake, followed by coffee and pieces of the three tier wedding cake. There were telegrams from absent friends read out, and toasts drunk, and funny stories from the speechmakers in the families, and a mixture of Welsh and English being spoken down the long tables . . . After a lull in the afternoon there was a disco for 200 people and another enormous meal laid on, this time a buffet of ham and chicken and all the trimmings. The celebrations went on till midnight, petering out eventually after a singsong of favourite hymns and rugby songs. Then there was the honeymoon . . .

So romance is alive and well, but wears many different faces these days. You have to pick your way with care between the idols of Respectability, Sexual Liberation and Consumerism, to get to the heart of the Rose.

[1] Hywel Dda, *The law of Hywel Dda, translated and edited by Dafydd Jenkins*, Llandysul, Gomer, 1986. (See 'The laws of women', pp. 45-61).

[2] Giraldus Cambrensis, 'The description of Wales', in *The itinerary through Wales*, London, Dent Dutton, 1912.

[3] Giraldus Cambrensis (as above), p. 263.

[4] Giraldus Cambrensis (as above), p. 236.

[5] Dafydd ap Gwilym, *A selection of poems translated by Rachel Bromwich*, new ed., Harmondsworth, Penguin, 1985.

[6] William Williams, Pantycelyn, *Llythyr Martha Philopur at y Parch Philo*, Caerfyrddin, E. Powell, 1762.

[7] William Williams Pantycelyn, *Ductor Nuptiarum*, Aberhonddu, E. Evans, 1777.

[8] Lewis Morris, 'Morrisian Miscellany', *Gentleman's Magazine* LXII, 1792, p. 325.

[9] J. Henry Griffiths, *Bro annwyl y bryniau*, Aberystwyth, Cymdeithas Lyfrau Ceredigion, 1988, p. 63.

[10] Siân Rhiannon Williams, 'The true Cymraes' in Angela John (ed.), *Our mother's land*, Cardiff, University of Wales Press, 1991, p. 69-91.

[11] Royal Commission on land in Wales and Monmouthshire, Report. London, Stationery Office, 1896.

[12] Giraldus Cambrensis, *Itinerary through Wales*, London, Dent Dutton, 1912, p. 264.

CHAPTER 11

Ways of seeing the scenery: the meaning of tourism

'People come from afar to admire and enjoy the wonders of our valley', said oldest inhabitant Miss Elinor Jenkins to the *Cambrian News* reporter, on the twenty-fifth anniversary of the opening of the Cwmrheidol hydro-electric Power Station. There had been a steady trickle of determined tourists to the valley in the nineteenth century, to enjoy the picturesque cascades and the 'alpine' upper reaches of the Rheidol. But travelling was slow and uncomfortable on the single track road up the valley until the coming of the CEGB power station in 1965, when Cwmrheidol was opened up to modern tourism. The CEGB built a visitors' centre with landscaped grounds and a large car park. There you can see a video on the development of the hydro-electric scheme. There are picnic tables in the lay-bys overlooking the reservoir, and guided tours of the power station and fish farm. A nature trail extends for two and a half miles around the reservoir, and there is a printed guide to enable visitors to identify typical natural features of the valley—the oak and birch woods, the liverworts and lichens, the rich assortment of woodland and water birds (said by some local wildlife enthusiasts to be more easily spotted than those in the Ynys Hir RSPB sanctuary further north). So now on summer days coachloads of tourists from as far afield as Germany and the Netherlands come to savour the organized beauties of Cwmrheidol, and the more adventurous car borne visitors make their way along the still single-track road beyond the Power Station, to explore the upper cwm, with its network of ancient tracks and long abandoned lead mines.

What do they come for? Modern tourism can easily turn into an exhausting and not very meaningful experience, although it is supposed to be about relaxation and refreshment of body and spirit. There are of course perfectly rational needs which send us on holiday trips to remote places—to escape from everyday pressures, to find renewal of basic energies, to get fit for a return to the daily slog, to satisfy some ill-defined but profound need for exploring unknown places and meeting different kinds of people. But there are also irrational worries and disappointed expectations experienced in having a holiday in an unknown place. And there is increasingly a snobbish distinction made between common tourism and serious travel, even though serious travel is clearly such hard work that it can hardly be considered to be a holiday in the popular sense.

There were and still are serious travellers in rural Wales, but now they are few and far between. The basic drive of the old-style traveller, like Thomas Pennant or George Borrow, was to find out about the way of life of the country by questioning the inhabitants about everything under the sun. They kept voluminous diaries of conversations along the way (which were numerous because they were travelling on foot), and made more or less well-informed observations on the agriculture and folklore and architecture of the regions they passed through. They exercised their artistic skills by sketching or doing water colours of the scenery, according to the prevailing aesthetic canons. They tended to have an aristocratic self-confidence, and therefore an insouciance, or limitless effrontery (depending on how you see it), in stopping complete strangers and extracting detailed information on their way of life and attitudes. Serious travel is hard work, and perhaps a grosser invasion of the privacy of local people than the more superficial tourism that prevails today. But at least it enables visitors to face up to the reality of life in the countryside, and discourages their romantic illusions.

Till the end of the nineteenth century tourism was confined to the few who had money and chose to travel. Now it has become a mass consumer activity, and the pressure is on us all to have regular holidays and to enjoy them. But it is not entirely straightforward enjoyment on holiday. To travel to strange places is sometimes to be threatened by the very differences we think we will enjoy, so some tourists prefer to be insulated from any real impact with the local way of life, even while they feel they want to get through the barriers and enlarge their understanding. To cater for these ambiguities mass tourism provides special activity centres or heritage centres which package a place for holiday consumerism, while sparing visitors any serious confrontation with the realities as lived by the locals. This has advantages for locals too, since it provides at least seasonal jobs as guides and curators and wardens and caterers, while maintaining an essential privacy and apartness in their own community life. But have we lost something important in our twentieth century brand of consumer tourism? One way of finding out is to compare what happens now in mid Wales to what happened in the past when serious travellers came here on their quest to discover rural Wales.

The quest for Romantic Scenery

Towards the end of the eighteenth century the trickle of tourists to Picturesque Wales became a spate. They were motivated by the prevailing Wordsworthian taste for Sublime Nature, which was supposed to elevate the spirit and free the soul from more humdrum daily concerns. It was also becoming more practicable, for pioneering travellers had published their guides to the terrain. Thomas Pennant's *Tour in Wales* came out in 1778, and many lesser men imitated his well-observed account in their own often plagiarist responses to Snowdon, Cader Idris and the Vale of Ffestiniog. The usual trips to the continent which gentlemen were expected to make as part of their education were prevented by the Napoleonic fracas from 1790 to 1815, so many looked nearer home for their travel diversions. All of this helped to dispel the common prejudice in England that 'the Welsh roads are impracticable, the inns intolerable, and the people insolent and brutish'. On the contrary, says the traveller H. P. Wyndham, the turnpikes are excellent in the low-lying areas and the mountain roads as good as the nature of the country permits; the people are 'universally civil and obliging', and 'the inns, with a few exceptions, comfortable'. [1]

Wordsworth, Shelley and Coleridge all came to Wales in the 1790s to exercise their romantic imaginations face to face with Aweful Nature. It became fashionable to climb mountains by moonlight, with the help of a local guide, usually a shepherd who was unceremoniously roused from slumber to be at the service of the tourists:

> I left Bethgelert's huts at couching-time
> And westward took my way to see the sun
> Rise from the top of Snowdon. Having reached
> The cottage at the mountain's foot, we there
> Rouz'd up the Shepherd, who by ancient right
> Of office is the Stranger's usual guide;
> And after short refreshment sallied forth.

Thus wrote Wordsworth in *The Prelude*. The object of such exercises as these moonlight climbs seems to have been not so much to get in touch with the country that was reality for their shepherd guides, but to select examples of picturesque landscape that would best elevate the soul of the contemplative traveller. So on this particular excursion up Snowdon, Wordsworth describes how, 'after ordinary travellers' chat with our Conductor, silently we sank Each into commerce with his private thoughts'. Finally there came the moment of Romantic Illumination they were seeking, when the moon came out from behind dark clouds and they beheld:

> A deep and gloomy breathing-place through which
> Mounted the roar of waters, torrents, streams
> Innumerable, roaring with one voice.
> The universal spectacle throughout
> Was shaped for admiration and delight,
> Grand in itself alone, but in that breach
> Through which the homeless voice of waters rose,
> That dark deep thoroughfare, had Nature lodg'd
> The Soul, the Imagination of the whole.

Although occasionally roused from his inner musings (by the shepherd's dog unearthing a hedgehog among the crags, for example), Wordsworth and the rest of the Romantics remain strangely insulated from what is happening around them in the countryside. The 'lowly Welsh cottages with thatched roofs overgrown with plants' are not observed as living homes, but as elements in the composition of a Picturesque Scene, providing foreground interest to the beetling crags behind. When Dorothy Wordsworth notices that the corn has been cut it is not her concern that the harvest has been got in to sustain families for another season. Rather she is seeking her own personal enchantment, which depends upon an inner sensitivity to the Beauties of Nature. So the corn-cutting is of interest because there is a new 'mellowness of colouring which seems to impart softness to the forms of hills and mountains'. The people who live there tend to be interruptions to the romantic imagination. Dorothy writes for example in her *Journal*:

> It is now 7 o'clock—I have a nice coal fire—William is still on his bed. 2 beggars today. I continued to read to him. We were much delighted with the Poems of Penshurst. William rose better. [2]

The seeds of modern nostalgia for the rural idyll that urban people have lost were thus planted in the early romantic phase of tourism. Getting back to nature and rural simplicities has continued to be an important holiday ideal ever since. And, as with the romantic poets, the tendency continues of seeing the country in a way that filters out reality and keeps a safe distance between the visitor and a possibly alien place with its enigmatic inhabitants. Some idyllic holiday cottages in rural Wales are awash with this romantic nostalgia for the imagined rural dream. They maintain the old slate slab floors and lovingly replace the fishtail slates on the curving roof beams, where locals would put on a new roof and install a more washable floor surface. The interiors are full of lovingly collected objects from the rural past or from nature. There are nice hangings on the wall, or old quilts and rag rugs decorating the sitting room. There are *objets trouvés* of great beauty and fascination—drift wood, coloured boulders from a stream bed, dried grasses and pheasant feathers in lovely terracotta jars on the floor. In the deep window embrasures stand old oil lamps and brass candlesticks with snuffers, and the occasional old delft or china jug or plate found in an antique or bric-à-brac shop. There are RSPB and World Wildlife Fund posters on walls, to assist the identification of birds and beasts. There is usually an interesting collection of reading matter—Ordnance Survey maps for walking; bird and flower and insect handbooks, well thumbed with use; and some of that genre of getting-away-from-it-all books, which describe personal struggles to realise the rural idyll in the Welsh countryside—Ruth Ruck's *Place of stones* and Elizabeth West's *Hovel in the hills*. Both of these last, it is worth noting, have been reprinted again and again over the last decades, an indication of the continuing appeal of the country idyll for visitors, even if only a tiny minority will ever try to realise it on a permanent basis.

But for those who live in the countryside the perspective is very different, and it is worth considering their observations on the same places, and on those who come as tourists. Lord Lyttleton, whose travel reminiscences were published in 1781, was remembered by a farmer's wife in the Vale of Ffestiniog like this:

Aye, he was always scribbling, poor dear gentleman, when he was within doors, and when he was without he ran up and down hills and dales in such a manner, though neither young nor strong, that folks hereabouts thought him a madman; but his valet de sham told us he was only a poet, and making a book about the Welsh people and our country; though what he could find here worth putting in a printed book, I cannot think, yet he was quite beside himself with joy and often told my husband that we ought to think ourselves very happy, as we lived in Paradise: for that matter we do not live amiss, considering a poor lone place; we get fish and game of all sorts in plenty, and now and then can shew a joint of meat with any-body.[3]

Until the end of the eighteenth century the Welsh tended to look on their own mountainy land as a farming misfortune, because they had to make a living from its harsh climate and unproductive soils and steep gradients. They saw their struggle for subsistence and their poverty-

246

stricken agriculture as the forefront of their lives, naturally enough, and had little leisure for pondering on the beauty and peacefulness of the scenery. The moorland peat bogs were not so much the haunt of snipe and curlew, but the source of much-needed turf for fuel, which had to be dug in driving rain and carried often over long distances to their damp and draughty cabins. Groves of trees were first and foremost shelter belts from the prevailing westerlies, which could be coppiced for fencing and crooks and the like. The charming pattern of little fields in the valleys were reminders of hard graft to clear stones and bracken and wring a bit more arable or pasture from the stubborn earth. A babbling stream, however exquisite, had to be judged in practical terms for its reliability in giving water during drought. A lake might even be drained in the hunger for more land. Thomas Pennant tells of attempts by one of the Lloyds of Cwm Bychan to drain a lake on his scenic holding below the Rhinog Mountains. He failed in his scheme, Pennant adds in relief, for, he says, a beautiful stretch of water was saved from extinction.

The same contrasting attitudes are to be found today, with farmers who have a living to earn in the national parks complaining of the restrictions put upon them by the Park Authority, and of being overrun with walkers when they're not being brow-beaten by officials. There may be a psychological impediment, too, which deters some from diversifying into tourism in spite of the economic pressures. One old farmer said to me, 'I cannot understand all these people coming to a place like this every summer. What is there to see? I've lived and worked here most of my life, and I know every inch of this ground, and for me it spells endless struggle. Where's the beauty in that?'

Nineteenth century popular tourism

As the nineteenth century advanced the traveller's journal gave way to the popular tourist guide book, a compendium of factual information about the best places to visit and where to stay and how to get there. The earliest of these guides were imbued with firm notions of 'correct taste' in looking at landscape, derived from ideas about the Picturesque, filtered down from William Gilpin's *Observations relating to Picturesque*

Beauty. [4] Scenery, he declared, should be selected for its closeness to the paintings of Salvator Rosa, Claud Lorrain and Richard Wilson. The tourist with any serious aesthetic pretensions could not just ramble about the Welsh countryside responding to whatever was there. He or she should engage in a deliberate search for the ideal ingredients for landscape: 'a variety of garnished rocks, shattered precipices, rising hills, ornamented with the finest woods, thro' which are opened the most elegant vales ... terminated by the blue hills at a distance'. Movement added interest to the basic components, so passing clouds, cascades and drifting flocks of sheep were desirable features. The great thing was to have the correct emotional responses to scenery. It was right to feel melancholy under lowering thunder clouds and wind-driven rain; to be rendered puny and vulnerable by mountainous crags and overhanging cliffs; to sense an uplift in the spirit when sunlight bursts from cloudbanks and lights up a hitherto dreary stretch of water. These were the correct responses because they acknowledged the interaction between nature and the individual sensibility. In the Wordsworthian perspective to appreciate landscape was almost a religious meditation, and the real scenery out there took second place to a dream landscape, the realm of the refined spirit, with 'sensations felt in the heart and felt along the blood ... till we are laid asleep in body and become a living soul'.

Landscape painters, whose engravings are sometimes found in the tourist guidebooks, reshaped the Welsh scenery to fit the requirements. Early engravings of Cwmrheidol exaggerate the height of hill and steepness of wooded crag, the profundities of the valley depths, the verticality of the waterfalls and the white waters of the cascades, while they understate the sheep and shepherd in the whole creation.

The Victorian guidebooks which describe Cwmrheidol retain a great deal of the Search for the Picturesque as the aim of tourism, though they do not insist on the fanatical approach of the purists who had recommended that visitors had to stand in a particular spot and look in a particular direction in order to thrill to the right combination of crag and tree and waterfall. This had led to the really conscientious tourists spending so much time checking up in their guidebooks that they scarcely had energies left to confront the reality before them. But by 1848 we find the Aberystwyth Guide more moderate in its advice to visitors, though still couched in the language of the Romantics. Here is what it says, starting with the bridge of Pompren Plwca in Cwm Rheidol, where the road gives out by the old lead mine:

> Within a mile and a half of the Devil's Bridge is Pompren Plwca, a singularly striking and romantic spot, where the river is crossed by one of the simple wooden bridges of the country. The river here struggles through vast fragments of rock, which, in angry and tumultuous roar, obstruct its course. On one side the banks rise to nearly four hundred feet in elevation; these are opposed on the other side by inferior cliffs. Through an intervening chasm issues the river, which here forms a delightful cascade. Below the fall and impending over the pool, is a bridge of the simplest construction, consisting only of a single plank and a handrail, and the fall is called Ffrwd Ddu. The river then continues its course down the vale, still bounded on either side by lofty banks, generally well wooded, discovering in many places the levels of the industrious and enterprising miner. After passing the modern house of Ty Llwyd, and on the farm of Neuadd, is again a fine fall of the whole river, of considerable height, over another ledge of impeding rocks, with the accompaniment of a mill, to give it character in the eye of the painter . . .

It is hard to believe from this description that the valley was then undergoing a lead mining boom, and its scenery rapidly giving way to an industrial landscape. The brief reference to 'the industious and enterprising miner' is hastily skated over, and the problem of everyday life intruding on the tourist beauties turned lightly aside. Similar evasions occur today. As Roland Barthes asked in his 1960s critique of the Blue Guides, why is it that the cement factories and the tower blocks are ignored, and the cathedrals and chateaux included, so that the tourist is ghettoised in a dream world, as if the real world of everyday life did not exist? Because, presumably, the real world is not sufficiently Picturesque, and holidays are about escapism, anyway.

By the second half of the nineteenth century the holiday guidebooks were trying to popularise their style, to extend their appeal to the increasing numbers of more ordinary folk whom the expanding rail network was bringing in from the West Midlands. But the rhetoric of the Picturesque was hard to shift, and in *The Popular Guide to Aberystwyth, the Devil's Bridge and Mid Wales*, 1880, it is still said of Cwmrheidol that:

> God in his providence has made everything for the comfort and enjoyment of man. The towering crags, the precipitous hills, the shady dells, the rushing torrents flowing down to the sea, are all created by the same beneficent and powerful hand.

References to the lead mines are carefully segregated and made acceptable in two ways. The visitor with an enquiring mind who wishes to be well-informed should take a 'very pleasant walk through a mining district', and he will find that it is not spoiled by industrial activity because water power is used, and produces none of the grime and smoke associated with industrial development. The local mining captains are obliging fellows and will be glad to show off their works to tourists.

The second approach to the blot on the landscape produced by lead mining, was to depend upon the Victorian tourist's interest in what we would see as tedious and longwinded factual information. It was obviously aimed at the Victorian paterfamilias who was eager to have himself and his family instructed rather than entertained even on holiday. So the entire history of lead mining in Ceredigion from Roman times is set out, ending in over-optimistic hints about the value of lead mining shares as an investment (another appeal to the Paterfamilias, no doubt): 'from the great returns which are being made from all [the mines] as are worked with spirit, public attention is justly awakened to their value'.

Scenery as God's creation: religious ways of seeing

The lead miners and small farmers who lived in Cwmrheidol when the early tourists came visiting were for the most part members of the Calvinist Methodist Chapel in Aberffrwd or the Wesleyan Chapel in

Ystumtuen (and later in its daughter chapel, the Bethel built in the valley in 1872). Their faith was founded in struggle, for they were attacked with sticks and stones when they held their first meetings in the farmhouses of the district. But Methodism gave them an ethos of hard work and self respect to be derived from just dealings among themselves and with the outside world. It also provided them with a philosophy of nature, in striking contrast to the Picturesque ideal pursued by the passing tourists. Many read their Bible daily and attended several meetings a week in their chapel, which was the centre of their outings and entertainments, as well as their centre of instruction in matters of religion and morality. From their religion they learned that Nature is the book of God's creation, and to be reverenced accordingly.

The Psalmist sings, 'The heavens declare the glory of God and the firmament showeth His handiwork'. So nature is an instructor of humankind, even as the Bible is. The Creator has given us two books for our edification, and these are the Book of Nature and the Book of the Scriptures. These ideas were most fully developed by Ieuan Glan Geirionydd, 1795-1855, who was brought up as a Calvinist Methodist, but later became an Anglican priest, well known for his hymns and poems as well as his theological writing.

Nature, says Ieuan Glan Geirionydd, teaches us through our bodily senses, whereas the Scriptures teach us through the rational faculty. Since nature displays all God's attributes, it is an endless resource for learning about God's omnipresence, his omnipotence, and about eternity and wisdom. Wales in particular, he believed, was by nature endowed with special qualities which helped its inhabitants to consider God's work, for in it are to be found every variation that adorns and beautifies the natural world. There are the mountains to remind us of the divine majesty, abundant water sources to recall the living waters of His mercy, the steep and stony pathways by which we must learn to struggle to the heights, the passing storms followed by sunlight breaking through which represent our personal pilgrim's progress. The godly man is 'like a tree planted by the rivers of water, that bringeth forth his fruit in his season; his leaf also shall not wither', whereas the wicked man

251

is 'like the chaff which the wind driveth away' (Psalm 1). The Lord is, above all, our shepherd, and that has a homely meaning in a country like Wales where the sheep have always outnumbered the people and the shepherds still use biblical crooks in modern times.

This philosophy of nature was not entirely original (Shakespeare had talked of 'sermons in stones, books in the running brooks . . .'), but the Calvinist Methodist version carried practical precepts with it, which were regularly spelt out in chapel sermons. 'The lilies of the field,' for example, that 'toil not, neither do they spin', warned against hard work becoming an obsession with material things, to the detriment of the things of the spirit. On the other hand idleness was to be avoided by considering the example of the tiny ant and its unstinting toil for the sake of its community. By looking around anywhere in the countryside you could see examples of divine precepts embodied in nature, and these you should ponder and follow in your own life.

So while the early tourists looked for the Picturesque and for personal spiritual enlightenment in nature, the devout rural dwellers looked for the hand of God and for practical precepts by which they could order their lives. Wordsworthians might use nature to reach sensitive states of meditation, but the Methodists were always suspicious of any kind of spiritual trances, as smacking of popish saints, and sought parables for practical guidance in everyday life. 'Fair daffodils, I weep to see thee haste away so soon', would not be an appropriate response for the Welsh Methodist, for he or she should rather remember that there is a time to be born and a time to die, and in any case death is a coming home to God and a world that is superior to this one. Which is not to say that the Methodists had no celebratory strand in their religion, for Ieuan Glan Geirionydd reminded them that one result of being familiar with the bounty of God in nature is that we have more and more subjects for which to glorify and praise Him.

The hymns of the two best known hymn writers in Wales, Williams Pantycelyn and Ann Griffiths, reflect this concern in Methodism to merge their knowledge of the Book of Scriptures with the Book of Nature so magnificently seen around them in rural Wales. Whereas the

Romantic poets engage in nature mysticism, the Welsh hymn writers use endless pictures from their own beloved landscapes, but merge these with their biblical equivalents to push home the Christian messages. Clouds gather and darken round us, as they do over the hills of Mid Wales for most of the year, and remind us of the sins and troubles of our earthly lives. Spring days come at last after the long and trying cold wet winters, and this teaches us that our salvation in Christ comes after the miseries and depressions of our unsaved selves. Yellow cornfields and peat-brown torrents gurgling down bouldery hillsides are signs of summer, just as summer comes to our hearts at last through God's grace.

Another strand in the Welsh protestant view of nature is the idea of stewardship, which is being revived currently as Christians address the urgent ecological problems of the destruction and pollution of nature by modern technology (including overuse of chemical fertilisers in farming). In Genesis God made man responsible for the lower creation of plants and animals, but it is not possible to be responsible in practice without conscientiously learning about their conditions of survival and conservation. And in both the Anglican and Methodist traditions nature theology is inseparable from the idea of Christian humility. In the face of God's mighty creation it is fitting for humans to be respectful and pay attention to nature's ways of doing things, even, or especially when they have the technological power to destroy the whole planet many times over. The Psalmist says, 'When I consider the works of thy fingers, the moon and the stars, which thou hast ordained; what is man, that thou art mindful of him?'

Even this brief excursion into religious ways of seeing nature in Wales, suggests some attitudes relevant to our own ecological dilemmas. Here we have a sense of stern duty allied with conscientious attention to the non-human creation, which is in striking contrast to the often voyeuristic admiration of Victorian tourists, or the slightly egotistic nature meditations of the Romantics, neither of whom seem to engage in much authentic interchange with the country they visit. But there are some notable exceptions, like George Barrow.

Travel as dialogue: George Barrow questions the natives

George Borrow's *Wild Wales* was first published in 1862, and is still a popular classic, on sale in the bookshops today. The author was one of the great English eccentrics of the Victorian era, who despised fashionable travel and sought rather to get in touch with the life and people of the places he visited. In 1854 he set out on a walking tour of Wales, which eventually brought him to the valley of the Rheidol, where, in the Hafod Arms Hotel in Devil's Bridge, he recorded his impressions of the area. He was one of the few travellers who was able to converse with the locals, the majority of whom spoke Welsh and knew no English, for he had learned Welsh with the help of a Welsh groom who happened to be working in the same part of East Anglia where George Barrow was serving his time as an articled clerk. Not content with a grasp of conversational Welsh, he had studied the literature on his own, and held the considered opinion (well ahead of his time) that Dafydd ap Gwilym was 'the greatest poetical genius that has appeared in Europe since the revival of literature'.

He went everywhere on foot, despising the newly come railways which, as he saw it, brought 'the scum of the Liverpool and Manchester manufacturing districts' into north Wales every weekend, ruining it for the bona fide traveller like himself, who wanted to talk to the real inhabitants and not his fellow countrymen from the north of England. Borrow was an indefatiguable conversationalist, and, since he had left his wife and stepdaughter installed in a holiday house in Llangollen, he was entirely dependent on the people of the country for his entertainment and instruction. He remorselessly questioned everyone he met, in inns, or walking along roads and lonely hilltracks, or in isolated cottages where he stopped, ostensibly to ask the way or to persuade someone to guide him over the next range of hills. He asked them about their family, their means of earning a living, their knowledge of Welsh language and history, their bards past and present, and their opinion of the English. He then scribbled down his findings in a notebook before retiring every night, having walked thirty or forty miles in all weathers, and worked up a good appetite for his usual dinner of fried veal and chops, with potatoes and ale, or, in humbler establishments, bacon and eggs with home-made bread and butter.

The result, *Wild Wales*, is fascinating because it faces up to all the questions the rather po-faced Victorian guidebooks do not even ask. Though they are encyclopedic in a factual and historical way that far exceeds any modern equivalent, they fail to raise the perennial issues of Welshness. What is the state of the language? What is the latest score in the eternal cultural conflicts between Celt and Saxon? What happens to English people who settle in Wales, and to Welsh people who go off to work in England? How do the Welsh see their own culture (their bards and their music and their religion and history)—as something to cling to for ever, or as a burden to fling off in pursuit of 'success'? George Borrow tackles all these questions fearlessly and with a partiality for the Celts that inspires him to cry out, on the summit of Snowdon (on being mistaken for a Breton as a result of reciting an *englyn* in an unfamiliar Welsh accent):

> I wish I was, or anything but what I am, one of a nation amongst whom any knowledge save what relates to money-making and over-reaching is looked upon as disgrace. I am ashamed to say I am an Englishman. [5]

He directed this remark particularly at a party of English visitors who sniggered and jeered on hearing the Welsh tongue, as is the way of many monoglots, taken aback to find that the full range of human meanings can be communicated in a language from which they are excluded. It still happens today in Wales.

Borrow, in spite of his fluency in Welsh, still looked to most people unmistakeably an Englishman, and this caused him problems in collecting his data on the state of the nation. In Bala when he appeared the locals' conversation dropped to a whisper and people edged away. He concludes from this incident that all conquered people are suspicious of their conquerors, and while the English have long forgotten that they conquered the Welsh, the Welsh are still afraid that the English should know their language and find out about their private affairs, however trivial. The Welsh grudge against the English, says Barrow equably, is understandable if unChristian, after such incidents as the Night of the Long Knives (when British chiefs were stabbed to death by Saxon hosts during a feast—in the ultimate violation of the laws of hospitality). One should be grateful that the two sides are becoming more humane towards each other, for in the old days, as a Calvinist Methodist reminded him, it was customary for the English to cut off the ears of any Welshman found east of Offa's Dyke, and for the Welsh to hang any Englishman found to the west of it.

The concern about English incomers buying up Wales and changing it for the worse, a burning issue in our own time, was already a bone of contention in Borrow's day. The innkeeper at Ponterwyd assumed that Borrow must have learned Welsh in order to get some advantage over the true Welsh. 'Oh Sir', he concludes, 'you have come to look out for a farm, I see, and to outbid us poor Welshmen; it is on that account you have studied Welsh'. Further north he encountered the kind of English incomer who does not like the Welsh and does not wish to know about their culture and prefers to live in Wales as if it were the same as living in England. This man, the proprietor of Pengwern Hall, therefore remained entirely unaware that one of his tenant farmers was the grandson of the famous Jonathan Hughes, and a learned man in literature and history (from the Welsh perspective and in the Welsh language). One of his beloved books on Illustrious Welshmen was brought down for Borrow to read out to the family in the flagged farmhouse kitchen.

Borrow's knowledge of the language enabled him to get beyond the scenery where the average English tourist was content to linger. He found that the ordinary folk had considerable knowledge of their literary heritage, whatever their situation in life. A dusty millerman was able to identify lines by Taliesin. A drunken militia man boasted of his ability to repeat more of the songs of 'the Eos' Huw Morris, the Nightingale of Ceiriog, than Sir Watkin Williams Wyn (the greatest landowner in north Wales, whose initials WWW still adorn many a boundary stone on the moorlands and hills). And he backed up his boast by reciting the death bed verses. 'What a difference', says Borrow to his wife, 'between a Welshman and an Englishman of the lower class. What would a Suffolk miller's swain have said if I had repeated to him verses out of Beowulf or Chaucer?' He is charmed to find a print of Twm o'r Nant, 'the Welsh Shakespeare' in humble cottages with the couplet:

> Llun Gwr yw llawn gwir Awen;
> Y Byd a lanwodd o'i Ben.

(Picture of a man full of the true inspiration; The world was enriched by his imagination)

There *were* occasions when Borrow encountered hostile responses from the Welsh, and he is honest enough to admit it, rather than pretending it never exists. The serving woman in Tafarn Tywarch was *cenfigennus*, jealous, of an Englishman understanding the language, because 'What right have the English to come here speaking Welsh which belongs to the Welsh alone, who in fact are the only people to understand it'. Borrow had a regrettable lapse into tourist colonialism— he overwhelmed the poor woman with his superior knowledge of her cultural history.

In a number of pubs in country districts silence fell when the English-looking traveller came in, and they tried to find out just how much of their language he understood, being suspicious of strangers and inclined to relieve their unease by making fun of them in Welsh with their mates. It was believed (with some justification) that English tongues are not long enough to get round Welsh pronounciation, with its mutations and its 'll' sound and its mysterious vowels. George Borrow, they discovered, had more than the usual tourist smattering of Welsh, and this was viewed with deep suspicion among those not of a literary turn of mind. He was regarded much as a modern sociologist might be regarded, joining a street gang more for his own research purposes than for the good of the gang. He must be after 'the discourse of poor men, that he may learn poor men's little ways and infirmities, and mark them down in one small little book to serve for fun to Lord Palmerston and the other gentlefolks in London'. A new hazard for the tourist with an enquiring mind!

Some of Borrow's encounters with local folk illustrate another problem, which is not unknown today among learners of the Welsh language. You can learn a language but you may not speak it the same way, or tell the sort of stories that a natural speaker does. Borrow got on alright in chatting to literary minded folk with an interest in their own history, but floundered in meetings with your ordinary fellows, who found his Welsh too pedantic and perfect for everyday use, and had not the slightest interest in his ability to reel off fifteenth-century bardic poetry. 'Really, Sir', the Ponterwyd barman said to him, 'I don't know how to reply to you, for the greater part of your discourse is unintelligible to me'. There are, too, incompatable interests between local and tourist topics of conversation. Borrow soon found that hill farmers had no time for chatting about eagles or wildlife in general, nor could they understand the tourist enthusiasm for walking over rough country or admiring views from summits. So the farm boy he met in the hills above Llanuwchllyn had nothing to say in response to hill-walking, but could talk his head off on pig-keeping. To be a natural Welsh speaker is to be rooted in the everyday activities and stories of the place where you live, and the way the language is used grows out of this identity of place. Most outsiders can never acquire this, but it helps to know that it happens.

In Borrow's time, however, to be an English speaker living in Wales, and have no understanding of Welsh, was fraught with practical and emotional problems. There was a young couple from Shropshire who had taken a small farm near Cemaes, and found themselves totally cut off from the local society through their lack of the language. Nor could they learn it, for when the husband went to the pub hoping to pick up a bit of conversation, the landlord accused him of driving away his customers, so loath were they to have any contact with an English stranger and incomer. So there they were, 'poor lost creatures in a strange land, without a soul to speak to except each other. Every day of our lives we wish we had never left Shropshire'.

There were, on the other hand, a small but growing proportion of Welsh in the mid nineteenth century who were anxious to learn English

258

for getting on in the world. 'I think I like English best', said a young woman of Anglesey who had been born in the Liverpool Welsh-speaking community. 'It is the most useful'. 'Not on Anglesey, surely?', Borrow asked her. 'Well, it is the most genteel', she insisted. 'Gentility will be the ruin of the Welsh', retorted Borrow. Then there was the collier in Rhiwabon who boasted of his ability to speak English as well as Welsh, and despised Borrow for 'a low illiterate fellow', because he presumably did not have enough English to speak it regularly, or he would not have lapsed into Welsh.

So English at this time was gaining ground in certain contexts. Those with aspirations to gentility used it, even within the family. It was used in the tourist trade, when 'the gentry come to see the Pistyll'. Talking to strangers was in any case better done in English, since it was an uneasy business anyway, and English was an uneasy language, which therefore kept things more at a distance from the everyday homely things which were in Welsh. English was also, curiously enough, used for swearing at horses. At least some carters believed that Welsh oaths had not sufficient violence for stubborn animals to be moved.

Although Borrow's approach to tourism was centred on dialogue with the inhabitants, and could even be called 'investigative tourism', he was sufficiently influenced by mainstream tourism not to ignore the beauties of nature, the Picturesque, and indulges in a fine purple patch after clambering down the preciptious slopes into the alpine reaches of the Rheidol below the Hafod Arms Hotel (Devil's Bridge):

The fall, which is split in two, is thundering beside you; foam, foam, foam is flying all about you; the basin or cauldron is boiling frightfully below you; hirsute rocks are frowning terribly above you, and above them forest trees, dank and wet with spray and mist, are distilling drops in showers from their boughs. [6]

His conclusion is that the sensitive tourist should be haunted for life by recollections of this aweful and mysterious place. If not, 'they must be very unpoetical people indeed'. But, true to form, he also reveals the more sceptical local approach to scenery: 'A great many English go to see the Devil's Bridge and the scenery near it, though I don't really know why, for there is nothing so very particular about either'. But that was a Ponterwyd innkeeper talking, and he may have been influenced by local rivalries in the matter of loyalty to place.

Twentieth century tourism in Cwmrheidol

In 1902 the picturesque Vale of Rheidol Railway opened, but its main purpose was to carry ore from the lead mines down to the sea port of Aberystwyth. Its terminus was the Devil's Bridge, that scenic tourist spot described so fulsomely by Borrow. This was fortunate indeed, for when the *Lein Fach* opened the lead mines were already in terminal decline, but over the years the narrow-gauge railway bit by bit turned into a tourist attraction rather than a prop to local economic activity, and so was able to survive. The line winds through twelve miles of pasture land and steep wooded hillsides on the south side of the Rheidol Valley, climbing seven hundred feet from sea level at Aberystwyth. It passes on the way the old Rheidol United Mines, where lead ore was loaded in the early days, and further up at Rhiw Fron Halt there is a view of the Cwmrheidol Mine spoil heaps, from where ore was transported to the railway wagons in buckets suspended from an aerial ropeway.

Until the 1930s, when the *Lein Fach* became a summer season only attraction, it was a great convenience to the locals, who would collect their household and farming goods from the halts, and on Mondays would go down to the Aberystwyth market with their eggs and butter and vegetables to sell. There was even an early morning mail train running for a while from 1905, whereas now no mail is delivered to the upper valley before lunchtime. In the same year the evangelist Gipsy Smith came to run revival meetings in Devil's Bridge, and the railway company took advantage of the prevailing revivalist fervour of that time, by providing special trains up the valley.

The tourists were imaginatively catered for in the period between the wars. There were combined rail and charabanc trips to the famous Hafod estate, originally laid out by Thomas Johnes in the 1790s on Picturesque principles, with viewpoints to capture the requisite combinations of water, rocks, wooded slopes and distant craggy peaks. Scenery was still the prime attraction for visitors, so there were attempts to transform the unsightly spoil tips of the old lead mines into something more appealing. The guidebooks speak of 'The Stag', for example, as if it were a natural feature, and not a heap of mine waste accidentally resembling a stag from certain angles: 'the rough outline of a stag, formed by the bare rocks obtruding through the trees on the precipitous slopes'. A couple of hundred yards past the present Cwmrheidol Tea Gardens, in the interwar period, there was The Stag Tea and Pleasure Grounds. The advert in an Aberystwyth tourist brochure read:

To Visitors

Rheidol Falls
The best afternoon drive
or train on the Vale of Rheidol Railway
THE STAG
TEA & PLEASURE GROUNDS
New bungalow   Good catering
Farm teas   Refreshments always
ready at reasonable charges
Large parties catered for

Proprietress:—Mrs Owen

Gwen Morgan, who lives there now, is the granddaughter of Mrs Owen, and can fill in some of the details of valley tourism between the wars. Some visitors came in horse-drawn charabancs, and Gwen's mother's cousin, then a little boy, was paid a penny a bucket for watering the horses. Others arrived at the little railway station and walked down and across the footbridge by the Falls (where the fish ladder now is). The food was all delicious home-made produce, and there was plenty of things for the visitors to do—swings and slides in the gardens, walks by the river and a very sociable atmosphere. In those days a lot of the visitors were local—it was a day out from Aberystwyth into the country, a bit of fun with family or friends. One or two of the lead mines were still working at this period. Gwen Morgan's father worked in the Caegynon mine till the late 1930s and then went to work for Dandrick (the last of the Cwmrheidol Mine captains) in the 1940s. So to the local people the mines meant a living, but to the burgeoning tourist trade they were an eyesore:

> A short run brings the train opposite an unsightly lead mine, now worked only at intervals [Cwmrheidol Mine]. Leaving Rhiw Fron Station the gorges and tortuous windings of the river appear, and a hint of the great beauty of the wooded glens around the Devil's Bridge is obtained.[7]

It was not until the 1970s that industrial archaeology caught the popular imagination and the Cwmrheidol lead mines became a bonus for visitors rather that a mere blot on the landscape.

A spate of technical descriptions of the old mines began to appear, like David Bick's *Old metal mines of mid Wales*,[8], Roger Burt's *Mines of Cardiganshire*,[9] and R. J. Pritchard's *Rheidol United Mines*,[10] soundly based on a mixture of documentary evidence, underground (and very wet) explorations and surface walks to reconstruct mining operations from what it left of the buildings. Pritchard gives a circular walking tour of some of the Rheidol United adits and dressing floors, starting and finishing at the footbridge by the Rheidol Falls, for the benefit of visitors with an interest in industrial archaeology.

A new controversy arose between enthusiasts who want to keep the old mines in their authentic if unsightly state, where the waste and building foundations tell the story of past working, and scenic aesthetes on the other hand, who are in favour of cosmeticizing the sites to restore the beauties of nature that preceded the mining exploitation (the site of the Cwmrheidol Mine was in pre-industrial days known as the Druid's Glen). Public authorities have already smoothed out and grassed over the old Goginan Mine, in the next valley to the north of Cwmrheidol, and the Cwmrheidol Mine is said to be on the waiting list for similar treatment, with assistance from EC funding. But local residents are in favour of leaving it alone. Since it ceased to be a hippy encampment in 1991, there has been a community effort in the upper cwm (with the help of the Countryside Commission) to plant trees by the river and fence off the spoil heaps to keep sheep out and encourage a natural regeneration of scrub birch. The mine is gradually greening over naturally, and the feeling is that upper Cwmrheidol does not need major schemes, whether of tourism or conservation, but small-scale improvements and enterprises to leave things much as they are. It appears that there are a growing number of tourists who want this too, as a refuge from mass consumer tourism and national park honey pots which destroy the original features of appeal.

In Cwmrheidol in the 1980s the tourist thrust was back-to-nature. There are pleasant nature trails through sessile oakwoods, by courtesy of Powergen, who now own the hydro-electric power station, and of Dyfed Wildlife Trust, who bought the woods of Coed Simdde Lwyd. There are bird boxes the size of tea-chests to house barn owls, and rows of tiny boxes for tits and tree creepers to nest in. The ground under the trees is carpeted with dog violets, wood anemones and golden saxifrage, with a variety of ferns and mosses in the damp places.

The Countryside Commission for Wales has bought another stretch of oak and birch woods in the upper valley, and is setting about a plan for natural regeneration, by fencing out the sheep and thinning the long neglected trees, while also providing a woodland walk for locals and visitors to enjoy. After long neglect the valley woods are receiving attention. But it is not all sweetness and light, because there is always a conflict of interests between earning a living from the land, and conserving it for tourism. So when the Forestry Commission in 1991 sold off the mainly conifer plantations in the valley which had been planted in the 1950s, there was concern among locals and visitors and among the Ramblers' Association, whose members often walk the extensive network of woodland paths at the head of the valley. What will happen to the paths when clear felling takes place? Is clear felling the only answer, or is it possible to phase felling so that a large acreage of woodland does not disappear and alter the landscape for the worse at one fell swoop? There are diverse opinions on what should happen to the woods of Coed Penrhiw. To some it's a crop and may provide jobs, but:

'In the long term I would expect felling to be beneficial, but it will need to be controlled in extent, means and route of extraction. With hindsight it is very doubtful if the FC would have seen fit to plant conifers at all in these steeply wooded valleys. Perhaps the new owner will be sympathetic to landscape and other non-commercial uses of the forest?'

'I and my family and friends regard ourselves as very lucky to live near the valley of Cwm Rheidol, where we often walk and enjoy its peace and beauty ... We know it is unreasonable to object to the felling of these plantations, but we appeal for it to be done constructively, to limit the desecration and damage that could be done to paths, tracks and roadside trees ... Cwmrheidol is rare in that it combines outstanding beauty of landscape plus a wealth of wild life, including the red kite, and yet is so accessible and well known to local and holiday visitors. Sensitive management of its natural resources is even more important as all the effects will be visible to all.'

'Timber's a crop like any other, isn't it? It's ready for harvesting, so that's the logical next step. Some people just get up in arms anytime there's a change of any sort on the cards, like we were living in a rustic museum ...'

'It's funny that you can alter landscapes without having to put up a planning application notice like you have to for altering a house ...'

The scenario proposed by the planning authority is that in some parts of Coed Penrhiw clear felling is the only solution, because the woods have never been managed, and suffer from lack of thinning and from windthrow. But they hope for a more diverse age structure in the future management of the woods, and for sensitive replanting with at least a quarter of the new trees being native broadleaves. There will be an attempt to safeguard public footpaths during felling, so that they remain open.

Meanwhile the visitors who come to the valley have their own varied responses to the scenery and to local life. One summer I talked to some of the people who came to picnic and swim by the old Cwmrheidol Mine, or who were doing the local walks, or the long-distance Cambrian Way which crosses the Rheidol by the footbridge or Pombrenplwca. Here are their responses to the valley.

Ways of seeing the scenery in the 1990s

'We came up to visit the Power Station, and after that thought we'd just drive up the narrow road to see where it went. It's nice here, just sitting in the car looking over the river. Very peaceful. You feel you've really got away from it all—that's what holidays are for'.

(Middle-aged couple from the West Midlands staying in self-catering in Aberystwyth and motoring around the countryside)

'It's great scenery you have here, so green and so miniature. I'm from Arizona, and you can't do much walking there, like you can in mid Wales. But I'm amazed how easy it is to get lost in such small country— a real fine network of tracks everywhere, and nothing on the ground looks like it does on the map! I just found myself right down here in the bottom of the valley when I should be up on the plateau there, and now I'm puzzling how to get back to where I left the car at Ysbyty Cynfyn'.

(Young man from the US staying in a B & B in Rhayadr and going on walks every day with the help of locally produced books of guided walks, but without an Ordnance Survey map to show him the bits that the guides leave out—the bits where you take the wrong path)

'Well, what a beautiful spot this is, but how do you stand it in winter? When the clouds came steaming up the valley earlier today it was certainly grand but I thought to myself you could get really depressed in this kind of scenery when the weather closes in'.

(Lone walker from Shropshire)

'We're just driving about really and were looking for somewhere to put up the tent for the night. It's good here by the river, nice and flat and bits of wood around for getting a fire going. Keeps the midges off, they say. It doesn't really but you keep hoping. The scenery? Well, it's just there, isn't it? Kind of background to what you're doing, I suppose. I mean, you couldn't go on staring at it for long, you'd get really fed up'.

(Young couple from Wolverhampton, with ridge tent and mini-van)

'I'm doing some photography, which is my hobby, but I can tell you it's not easy in the valley. The waterfalls are all concealed by the woods, and I nearly broke my neck clambering down the steep bits to get a shot. The scenery is terrific all round, but try to pinpoint one particular feature and it's somehow impossible. It's all atmosphere that disappears when you try to get it on film'.

(Man from the southeast of England, with Volvo and Canon)

'I'm backpacking through on the Cambrian Way route—using the guide book one of the original planners published on his own after all the local authorities and national parks refused to make the Way official. The excuse was they thought walkers would get lost in the desert of mid Wales. I expect the farmers didn't want anybody walking the old paths —they're always blocking them up, even when the local authority puts up public footpath signs—or particularly when the local authority puts up the signs, for that's when they get more walkers. They wouldn't get away with it in Yorkshire, I can tell you. Every time I get to a post office I have to drop in a few postcards complaining to the Forestry Commission and the local authorities about blocked rights of way, and I'm running out of postcards all the time ... Well, I'd better steam ahead to the Youth Hostel and get settled in for the night. I've done my twenty miles today—plus an extra two or three getting around obstacles that aren't shown on the OS 1:50,000'.

(Man in his thirties from Huddersfield, carrying fifty pounds of self-sufficiency:

'Well, I carry a one man tent, bedroll, cooking stove with spare cylinders, survival rations of army biscuits and Kendal mint cake, four season sleeping bag, shell clothing in goretex breathable fabric, plastic water container, Raven freeze-dried meals and spare clothing—in a Karrimor Jaguar rucksack, well-worn.')

266

'I come here to paint—watercolours. I just love spending the whole day like this, getting really lost in what I'm doing. I get *so* absorbed in it, and it carries me along and I don't notice the hours passing—that's real recreation. I've been on painting holidays, but I've decided I'd rather come to places like this by myself. There's nobody to distract you with their kind of painting, and going chatter-chatter all the time. I'd rather be alone with the landscape—ha, ha, you're never alone with a landscape if you know how to look at it properly. Painting is the only way, I think. *And* you can take it home with you . . .'

(Woman from Oxfordshire, with easel and canvas folding stool, painting Pontbrenplwca and the hills beyond)

'Yeah, well, it's a shame, innit? We used to come on the old mine here with our bikes for a bit of scrambling, and now they've gone and fenced it off and spoiled everything doing it up fancy, like. Me and my mates used to come here bank holiday weekend—no harm, just enjoying ourselves, even if a few silly buggers used to moan about the noise. It's a free country, innit? No, we're off now, what's the use, nothing left for us here anymore, bloody improvers!'

(One of a group of bikers in sullen mood)

'It's a good place to come with the children—they like paddling about in the river and going out to the islands. The water's so low at the minute that it's just possible for their tiny legs. I love this place—I am trapped by its beauty. We just keep coming back every year. Why? I can't really explain, something to do with the river, I suppose. I love being by running water. I'm an Aquarian, you see'.

(Englishwoman with young family, picnicking on the banks of the Rheidol)

'The great thing about the head of the valley is that you're not shut in by fields and fences and farms, like lower down. It gives you a sense of freedom. It's good for industrial archaeology too. There's always something interesting to follow up. You can check out the old mine buildings (though they have been disappearing at an alarming rate the last few summers, I've noticed) and the adits, and follow the courses of some of the leats that brought the water supply through to the power wheels. They shouldn't tidy up old mines, like they're beginning to, because it's great to have history there in front of your eyes. People think they're ugly, but they've got a lot of character, and I don't agree with this artificial landscaping lark—takes away the character and makes places all look the same—boring slopes of grass that tell you nothing about what went on in the place before . . .'

(Student from North Staffs)

'We're not visitors—we're from Aberystwyth [indignation at being mistaken for tourists]. We've been driving up Cwmrheidol for twenty years or more and we never get tired of it. It's always the same, so restful —I think because the road ends here and you don't get through traffic. My mother likes somewhere quiet to take a turn, now she's a bit shaky on her feet, and she knows this place so well . . .'

(Middle-aged couple with elderly mother)

A walk with the retired West Midlands couple

'We're from Sutton Coldfield and we're staying near Aberaeron in our touring caravan, and doing walks from these RAC Guides. It's fifteen years since we walked around Cwmrheidol, but it stays in the mind as a place you want to go back to, even when you've walked in the Scottish Highlands and the Peak and the Lake District and Snowdonia.' He stopped to take a photograph of cascades opposite the Cwmrheidol Mine tips, and his wife held the white Highland terrier on an extended lead, because this is sheep country and they were conscientious people. 'What I do is, I take colour photos of the scenery and then I paint watercolours from the photos during the winter. I've got more time now I've retired, and I am going to evening classes on painting, because I always wanted to paint, but never got properly trained. I was going to art school when the war came along and that was the end of that. When I got back to civvies I worked in Dunlops Tyres till the Japanese took it over and the strain became intolerable. They expected you to do what you had done in your twenties. I got angina and had to retire early. Well, now I have the time to walk and to paint as much as I want . . .'

We were walking through the woods and the woman said, 'Is it safe to walk around here? Take our woods in Sutton Coldfield—you daren't go there on your own, or leave your car unattended. We lost £4,000 of stuff out of the last break-in. But I suppose everybody knows everybody else here . . . the country's alright. Where we are, we have to have a homewatch scheme and automatic alarms everywhere. You're always having to worry about things like that with people desperate to get money—not for what they really need, it's drugs are the problem.'

Her husband was delighted with the pattern of small fields and old farms on the top around Ystumtuen, interspread with old lead mines. 'What I like in country like this, is imagining the way they used to live. We went to a slate museum place in Snowdonia, and learnt a bit about the life. Around here it was the lead mines, but it was equally hard, I suppose, with the men living in barracks during the week and walking huge distances to see the family at the weekend. Their health was destroyed, but there was another side to it. It wasn't only material values, was it? They had the satisfaction of being proper neighbours to each other, and mates in the mine, keeping each other going with a bit of a laugh when things were tough. And I can picture the whole family busy making things. You didn't pop down the road to B & Q. They made their dressers from local oak and knitted their own wool. Nothing was wasted like today. Even the scraps would make rag rugs, and the old woollies unpicked for reknitting. I like that.'

When the ruined farmhouse across the river was put up for sale during the great property boom of 1988, the holiday makers showed considerable interest, even though it is only accessible by four wheel drive across a deep ford, or by footbridge a hundred yards to the east of the house.

'Only £25,000? You could pay that for a small building plot where we come from. It's cheap enough. Just look at that site—standing all on its own overlooking the river. Great place for a holiday cottage. The scenery around here is just as good as north Wales, and it's not nearly so crowded. Where's the owner live?'

(Middle-aged couple from West Midlands, taking a short stroll from their car, and discovering possible paradise)

Later, when the ruin had been sold (for permanent residence, not for a holiday cottage) the visitors were still not to be discouraged from their rural idyll:

'It's been sold has it? Well, who's the agent? You never know, he might still be open to offers. Is there anything else on the market around here? This valley is really what they call unspoilt—nice old ruins still waiting to be done up. It's heaven'.

(Family in their thirties, south-east accents, expensively dressed little kids and Range Rover—an advertising agency's dream customers for upmarket products)

Tracing your roots

There's another kind of visitor to Cwmrheidol who comes to find lost connections with the valley. It is a special place haunted by ghosts of their own past, or of their family's pasts. It might just be able to offer them a richer sense of who they are, root them in some continuing tradition. For these visitors the scenery is not just scenery. It is peopled by ancestors who struggled for a living in this land, and when it was too much for them had to leave and go south for work.

'My grandfather was born here in the old farm of Plwca about 1872. He was one of four brothers, and they all left the valley about the end of the century. They couldn't scrape a living any more. The mines were closed down half the time and people had to leave. They couldn't earn a living from the few acres they had. Everybody was going south, for they said there was plenty of work in the coal mines. The four brothers just set out from Plwca and walked the whole way down to the Rhondda to get jobs. One couldn't stand it and came back, but it wasn't any good, it was an empty land. He went off to Patagonia, where, they said, there was good farming and enough people from Ceredigion to keep up the old language. He was well out of it, for two of the three brothers who

270

stayed in south Wales were killed in the terrible pit explosions of Senghennydd and Tylerstown. There was only one left, and that was my grandfather. He lived till 1946, and when we were children he told us about Plwca and Cwmrheidol. I've always wanted to come and see for myself, and so here I am at last. But I have very mixed feelings about coming, because what if you find the house gone or taken over so that the past isn't there any more, and the people in it don't know or don't care about any of it? No, I haven't the language any more, but I need my own past'.

Wartime evacuees

The Second World War brought an influx of outsiders into the valley, evacuees from Merseyside who were sent to the local schools and soon picked up Welsh by living in families where it was the first language, the language of the hearth. One woman holidaying in mid Wales in the summer of 1988 was driving up Cwmrheidol and the gates of memory opened on a forgotten past. She had been here before, a wartime evacuee, just old enough to be sent to the school in Devil's Bridge.

'The lady I was sent to was very kind, though some of the other evacuees were unhappy and made to do a lot of hard work. I can only remember a few isolated feelings now. When I came back from school (a long slanting walk through the woods over there the other side of the river, and across the footbridge) she would always be standing at the garden gate, waving to me. The valley seemed nothing special to look at—it was just the place where you lived. Now I'm on holiday I can see it's beautiful, but that didn't matter when I came here as a child. It was just different from the city streets I was used to, kind of too quiet and empty, like it had never been filled up properly with all the people it could hold. But you just accepted things like that, you never thought to question anything.

'I picked up the language because that was how you spoke here, but I have lost it all now of course. When I was here I took it as natural that everybody spoke this different language and lived the way they did, surrounded by all the wet greenery and sheep. It was new to me you could make a living out of sheep—I was used to people going out and working in a factory for eight hours a day, not wandering round the fields with a dog and shepherd's crook, just looking. But I accepted everything. Being here again after all the years is exciting, it stirs things up, and I realise all these bits of your past are part of who you are. I'm glad my daughter is with me too, so she can know more about me when I was a girl . . .

'The family I stayed with was very religious and Sundays were completely different in those days. Everybody would be going to services and Sunday school and you felt guilty if you weren't doing the same. Well, it's Sunday today and you wouldn't know it, would you, except there's a host of people driving up and down the valley wondering how to pass the time, once they've looked at the waterfalls and done the Power Station tour. You see them peering into the houses (I do it too) as they drive past, as if they hoped to discover something but don't know how, because they're not part of the real life going on when they're not here. You can be as curious as you like about a place, but if you're only a visitor you're kept out, aren't you? Unless you can find a way through the barrier . . . even if it's only a tiny niche in the past as a Merseyside evacuee . . .' She laughed heartily.

Holiday home owners 1

'The valley is unique with the mature river, and the dead end for traffic cutting it off from the rest of the world, and the steep wooded hillsides. You can't get scenery like this anywhere else. It makes a great base for walking, and there's the added interest of the little railway steaming along twice a day. Right at the back of the house you can just walk off into silver birch and oak woods, so it's very peaceful. When you walk around this valley there is always a shift in the scenery around each corner, whereas walking in the Chilterns, say, you can see for miles but it stays much the same'.

'The feeling of community here is stronger than in Bucks, though we live in a large "village", with a population of about 7,000. People here have more time and wave or nod. They acknowledge you as an individual, and will stop and speak to you, whereas where we live the nod would be very superficial, if there at all. You get more of a sense of belonging here, even if you're only on holiday. Everyone seems to know who we are now, because it is all so small scale and there's the one-way road, and every single house is known about—who owns it and who stays there and when they're there or not, and if there's anybody there who shouldn't be. I get frightened if I feel cut off, but it could never happen to you here'.

'It's good because you're not closed in by fences everywhere. It's open country and you can go anywhere and not worry about being on farming land. I'm specially interested in the old leats and tramways and where the water wheels were when the lead mines were working. I've surveyed all the mines in the valley for a school project, from the Cwmrheidol Mine down to Tŷ Llwyd, about fifteen in all. It was interesting to understand how the people in the valley had worked, and it'll be a shame if they start ''improving'' the old mine sites, because you won't be able to work it out any more'.

'I'm losing the battle with the sheep in the garden-cum-quarry, though it's a great pleasure to me working out there. I'm trying to fill the area in front with shrubs, and plant the walls of the old ruin with rockery plants. I'm happy just pottering about here, or going for just short walks down to the Rheidol Falls, or up to the old mines. It's very peaceful'.

'The valley never loses interest, because it has four or five quite different characteristics, and can be just as exhilarating in winter as in summer. There's the wildlife element—we've seen red kites quite often, as well as the ubiquitous buzzards in large numbers, a great variety of tits around the house here, and sometimes pied flycatchers. There's a heron, too, lives somewhere a bit further down the river and flies over every morning on the lookout for his breakfast fish, I suppose. Up in the woods behind, you get jays and wood pigeon, and we've heard a woodpecker but not seen him yet. Endless magpies, of course, and jackdaws in the old ruins . . .

'Another interest is the railway. I've looked at Green's book which came out a year or two ago. It's good, with a lot of information and excellent old photographs. It gives you a fair idea of what the railway used to be like when it was as much a local service as a tourist attraction. In the very early days they even transported lead ore from our neighbouring mine down to Aberystwyth. That must have been quite a sight, the ore swinging in buckets on the ropeway across the river and up the hill to Rhiwfron Station.

'I like engaging in pseudo industrial archaeology, too, working out how the old mines operated—from what's left on the ground. I don't think they should reclaim them, as they call it. It's vandalistic to remove bits of history. Of course at the present time the hippies have turned up and parked their vans on the mine. I don't exactly welcome them, but it's live and let live, provided they don't do disruptive things or turn the area into a scruffy and unhygienic place. We met some of them while we were out walking, on the path to Devil's Bridge, and chose to say hullo rather than ignore them. I would be concerned not to alienate them, as I don't live here permanently and they just might do damage . . .

'There's no comparison between Cwmrheidol and other valleys in the area—terrific variety here. It's so steep-sided, with a plateau on the top either side. The variety comes from the mixture of land use—farming and forestry and wild land which is just left alone, being too rough and inaccessible for anybody to do anything with it (except for the farmer on the far side who generates electricity from one of the steep little side streams). Although there is wild land, it never has the air of true isolation here, because there's always a building of some sort in sight, so it's peaceful somehow without being dull or depressing. Even when it gets heavy and glowering with rain I don't mind, though some members of the family get depressed and tend to lurk indoors. But I'd be quite happy in Blaenau Ffestiniog in November . . .

'The place names interest me too—that's about as far as I've got understanding Welsh, I'm afraid, though I did get hold of a *Teach yourself Welsh* cassette last winter. Troedrhiwsebon is a wonderful one, I think. "At the foot of the soapy slope"—slippery slope, I suppose it must mean.

'It's a good holiday place for me, because there is a slower pace of life here. People are not in a tearing hurry, running around in circles trying to get too many things done in too limited a time. It encourages me to stop and look, pause and think. That's peace—till I have to hare off again to some unavoidable business meeting. I did once buy a train ticket to Euston from Rhiwfron Halt up the hill there on the Rheidol Line, and did the whole journey from the cottage here by rail. That's the sort of contrast I'm talking about'.

Holiday home owners, 2

'We bought this old cottage in the 1960s and have been coming here every summer since then. We haven't changed any of the basic layout. You can see the inglenook just as it's always been, except the potcrane belonged to Llain and we acquired it when they did up Llain. The present ladder up to the half-loft was remembered by a lady who lived here in the 1920s. I took a sample from the surface of the inglenook wall and analysed it. I found seventy five layers of paint—pink and blue and white and yellow colour washes—they must have painted it very regularly. I suppose it got smoky when the fire was going all the time.

'We love it, but the problem is how to keep intact its history as a house, but make it more habitable. At the moment as you can see we're using candles and lamps and burning wood. We carry buckets of drinking water up from the spring in the woods, and collect washing water in the barrel under the eaves. There are absolutely no modern conveniences. It's just as it was at the beginning of the century. But eventually we'll come and live here—that is our intention, so we have to find a way of putting in modern conveniences—some ingenious way which will not make it lose its tremendous character . . .'

The future of tourism in Cwmrheidol: hard or soft tourism?

There is an instinct in the valley for what the professionals call 'soft tourism', rather than the 'hard tourism' which brings large-scale

275

developments like chalet parks or heritage centres. Soft tourism brings visitors more into contact with the life of the locality, through small scale local services, like the Cwmrheidol Cafe, the farm camping and B & B, the riding activity holidays. It takes account of the way of life of the locals and tries to find ways of fitting tourist activities into the existing work patterns of farming and part-time work outside the valley, rather than ghettoising the tourists in large-scale leisure centres which are not used by locals and often introduce an alien element into landscape and local life, without employing many locals. It also tries to avoid the other extreme, where the locals become ghettoised in a diminishing community, because of the sheer pressure of tourist numbers and the loss of local housing to infrequently used holiday homes.

Powergen's Visitors' Centre is the major tourist operation in the valley, offering guided tours, a video presentation on the hydro-electric scheme, and nature trails, which attract many thousands of visitors annually from all over the European Community and beyond. It has won accolades from the Prince of Wales Committee, the Wales Tourist Board and Wales in Bloom, for its success as a major tourist attraction in the Aberystwyth area. More than that, the CEGB (still in control before the 1990 privatisation) celebrated twenty five years of the Centre's existence in the following terms:

> ... the Centre provides a focus of community life for a hundred or more local indigenous and immigrant residents. Full social integration and social harmony, crossing age, class and language barriers, is realised in Cwmrheidol ... the CEGB displaying itself as a socially aware and environmentally friendly organisation ... the CEGB has not only generated electricity but a community spirit and pride, cherished by all ... [11]

Visitors might be forgiven for thinking that the people of Cwmrheidol have managed to solve all the problems endemic in Welsh rural life—the dilution of the language, the decline of active participation in community culture (the chapels and local entertainments), the impact of incomers, tourists (and hippy travellers, too) on what was a Welsh-speaking close-knit farming community suffering from rural depopulation as the young people left. I would argue for a more open and inclusive presentation of the local culture in the Power Station Visitors' Centre, so that visitors might learn not just about the technical aspects of the hydro-electric scheme, but about the way of life in the valley as a microcosm of rural Wales. Soft tourism makes connections with local life, rather than excluding it, and many visitors have a curiosity about Cwmrheidol life, which is frustrated by lack of local initiative or a failure by locals to imagine that their way of living could be interesting to outsiders.

The majority of Power Station visitors express satisfaction with their visit: 'You learn a lot—it's one of the best places we've been'. 'The family can do things together, like bird spotting and doing the nature trail.' 'It's beautiful here—great scenery and a good place to get out of the rain'. 'They've planned it well. The buildings are in keeping with the place. I like that new stone and timber dormers building—like a big swiss cottage'. 'Well, I like it here because you can go around and find out something about hydro-electric systems. I mean, I find scenery dead boring, so if I have to drive around the countryside with the wife and kids, I'm on the lookout for places like this, where they've done something useful with the scenery'.

So far so good, but some visitors feel they have discovered little about local Welsh culture on their visit to the Power Station, while appreciating the award-winning landscaping and the good technical presentation.

'I'd like to hear more from some of the locals who work here—like the man who runs the fish farm for stocking the reservoirs with trout. I'd like to find out a bit about local life—you come for the differences'.

'The nature trail is great, but I wish they'd organise a farm trail or a mining history trail, or something to do with the people and the way they earn a living—now or in the past. Why just wildlife? Why not human life as well?'

'I feel a wee bit brain-washed by CEGB power policies—they really sock it to you about what a terrific job they're doing. I suppose I would like Friends of the Earth or somebody like that to have an exhibition here as well, putting a different point of view; or maybe recordings of local people talking about what the scheme meant for them'.

'I've heard they speak Welsh round here—a completely different language, not just some English dialect like I thought. But how do you get to hear it? I've spent a whole afternoon here, in the Visitors' Centre and the nature trail and the Cafe, and I haven't heard a word of Welsh. Now that's a big disappointment to me . . . My folks came from Wales to the US of A over a hundred years ago, and they told me I'd still hear Welsh spoken in the back country. It's easier to see red kites, and they're a threatened species too, I've been told . . .'

'Well, it's lovely for the family to picnic here in the grounds—nice flowering shrubs, great display of colour, but I'm raring to drive up that one track road past here and get to the real scenery, not this manicured stuff. The reservoir is alright for bird-watching, but all this is a man-made landscape, like they've taken a number of ingredients and packaged them up—smoothy grass with picnic tables, waterworks railings, stretch of water with ducks etc, and woodland walk . . . What you could call improving on nature, only I'd rather have nature unimproved, or naturally improved by the people who live and work on it, and build dry stone walls or barns because they need them, and grow trees for shelter and fuel and making things . . .'

Cwmrheidol: a future scenario for tourism

A lot of residents would argue for doing nothing and letting well enough alone. There have in the past been successful protests against a luxury hotel at the head of the cwm, and a holiday chalet complex lower down. But every year the number of visitors to the valley increases and there are surprisingly few locals making part or all of their income out of providing tourist services. There may be more development as the farming crisis deepens and people are forced to consider alternative sources of income—diversification. Whatever happens it is important to think ahead to a version of tourist development which follows the principles of soft tourism. The landscape should not deteriorate into empty scenery, which locals have had to leave to find work elsewhere. The valley should remain a living place where tourist activities are interwoven with the rest of life, and indeed may grow out of everyday activities, for more and more tourists are looking for activity holidays, or holidays which connect them with the real countryside, rather than some packaged version of a place which mass tourism has virtually destroyed.

What does that mean in practice? Well in other parts of the European community, in the French Pyrenees for example, there are local communities shaping the future of tourism in their own locale, by assisting the residents to find training in crafts and catering so that they can complement their traditional farming activities; by forming a local cooperative to buy up and renovate old buildings in order to provide holiday accommodation which remains under the control of the community and is a source of local income; and by providing marketing outlets for local goods and crafts through the tourist visitors' centre, which also has video presentations and exhibitions on the local culture.

In Cwmrheidol already in the 1990s a coarse fishing centre has opened at Tai'r Llyn, and a trekking centre is being built up in Aberffrwd. Bird watchers are motored in at present from an activity holiday centre near Devil's Bridge. There is no reason why Cwmrheidol should not develop its own wildlife activity holidays, for which there is a growing demand. Craft workshops where visitors can talk to the workers as well as buying their products are well-established in the Outer Hebrides, even, so why not around here? And what about valley guides to conduct small groups of visitors on a lead-mining trail, or a small-holding trail? The valley is rich in history on the ground as well as rich in revealing current life in rural Wales. On the continent in the remoter upland areas even quite small communities are proud enough of their history and culture to set up and run quite sophisticated local museums, with blownup old photos, videos and recordings of oral history. Would this be a use for the Bethel Chapel in the valley that closed in the 1970s and is now going to ruin with every passing winter?

Soft tourism is about emphasising the differences rather than selling a monotone mass tourism, the lowest common denominator, and it is about making a virtue out of preserving local identity—for that increases the place's interest to outside visitors, while helping the inhabitants to keep their own unique identity. The Valley Cafe already offers some traditional local treats, like *cacen gneifio*, shearing cake, and *teisen fêl*, honey cake, and *pice maen*, Welsh cakes. Why not a full-scale menu of Welsh country fare—and a bilingual menu? Isn't an essential part of the authentic tourist experience the enjoyment of a different sense of place rather than the blight of uniformity—whether we are talking about food or craftsmanship of larger matters of language and culture?

[1] The traveller H. P. Wyndham, quoted by W. M. Condry in *The Snowdonia National Park*, London, Collins, 1966, p. 11.

[2] Dorothy Wordsworth, *Journals*, London, OUP, 1987, p. 88.

[3] W. M. Condry (as in 1 above), p. 9.

[4] William Gilpin, *Observations, relative chiefly to Picturesque Beauty made in 1772 . . .* 2 vols, London, 1876.

[5] George Borrow, *Wild Wales*, London Dent, 1907.

[6] George Borrow, (as above).

[7] National Union of Teachers, *Aberystwyth and District Guide prepared for the NUT conference in Aberystwyth in 1911*, Aberystwyth, 1911.

[8] David Bick, *The old metal mines of mid Wales, part 3, Cardiganshire*. Gloucester, Pound House, 1976.

[9] Roger Burt, *The mines of Cardiganshire*, Exeter, Exeter University, 1985.

[10] R. J. Pritchard, *The Rheidol United Mines*, Sheffield, Northern Mine Research Society, 1985.

CHAPTER 12

Houses as the landscape of history

When you move into an old house in the Welsh countryside, you are taking on more than a nice place to live, in a beautiful landscape. The siting of the houses, the materials used to build them, and the people who lived there in the past, are all part of the continuing story of a locality, and a new owner has a responsibility to acknowledge this. One way is to try to understand the way of life, past and present, in these old houses, and their relationship with the broader sweep of history—farming ups and downs, the rise and fall of rural industries and crafts, rural depopulation or repopulation by incomers and visitors. Older people born and bred in rural Wales have an abiding interest in local history, and are an unfailing source of information on every house in their own locality. The houses themselves, whether in ruins or a jumble of extensions, have their own story to tell. The Census Reports reveal the people who lived there in the last century, and many of those people were buried in the Chapel graveyards, where their headstones still stand. From these sources I have tried to build this picture of upper Cwmrheidol houses as the landscape of history.

Before the twentieth century the cottages in Cwmrheidol were built from local materials by local craftsmen. They had an organic life of growth and decay in response to the size of families and the state of farming and lead mining, from which the vast majority of inhabitants earned their living. Sites were chosen to take account of the climate, so homes were tucked into hollows or backed into the hillside to give protection from westerly gales. They were built along spring lines to ensure a good water supply, and they were protected by a clump of trees to break the force of the winter winds, but not too many, for that would make the house dark and damp by keeping out the sun.

Windows were kept small to conserve warmth, and, until Victorian sash windows came in during the rebuilding at the end of the century, they were often sealed shut. There were plenty of draughts already, seeping under the doors and coming down the enormous open chimneys. The fireplace was literally the focus of the life of the house, a great inglenook taking up almost the whole gable end, with room in it for an oak settle close to the warmth (where elderly relatives or favoured guests were invited to sit), and where all the cooking and baking were done.

There are a few old cottages with mud walls lower down in Cwmrheidol and in Aberffrwd, but in the upper cwm the walls are made of stone—not the great boulders found further north in Snowdonia, but the kind that splits and breaks down into irregular brick-sized pieces. Most have now been rendered with pebble dash or cement, colour-washed, but the buildings on Caegynon Mine are a good example of the original bare stone. The two feet thick walls remain, but the roofs have all been replaced with dressed slates, either modern or from the turn of the century. Before that roofs were either of thatch or of thick slate slabs, and the supporting beams were cut from the local oak woods and roughly trimmed, retaining their knotted 'branchiness'. There were wooden partitions to divide the living space, or to keep animals separate from people in the old long houses, made out of a thin single layer of wooden planks. It was said of some of the old cottages that when the horses were restless the crockery on the oak dresser would tinkle and reverberate to the champing and stamping on the other side of the boards.

The traditional Cwmrheidol house is nearly symmetrical, with a central door, a window on each side of the door, and three windows above, like a child's drawing of a house. One view is that such 'little stone boxes with gable chimneys and vertically-proportioned sash windows evenly spaced about a central doorway . . . are the fag end of the Renaissance concept'.[1] They are seen as the final percolation of the grand tradition of the gentry's hall houses down to the cottages of smallholders and lead miners. This might explain the classic near symmetry of the fronts which are said to be spoiled by modern extensions.

But there have always been extensions and improvements, a dairy or back kitchen, piggeries, or a one-up, one-down addition at the gable. These suggest that traditional cottage buildings owe more to medieval than to Renaissance thinking. The 'culture lag' theory hardly seems justifiable, when one sees the evidence still on the ground of how houses evolved from earlier primitive cabins to the standard two-up, two down Cwmrheidol cottage, with lean-to extensions.

An 1802 visitor to Wales described the *tyddynnwr*, cottager, as living in a single room cottage with a chimney in the gable, a small hole to let in light, and a blanket across the doorway instead of a door:

> The dark mud walls, rocky floor and a few brown rushes, the family bed, suggested the idea of a den; the parents and their numerous progeny were assembled round a small fire of peat.[2]

From there it was an obvious step to divide the ground floor into two by putting up a boarded partition, to give a separate sleeping room, or a working kitchen/dairy/pantry—with the family sleeping in box beds in the warmer living room. The doorway would then be slightly off-centre, because there was no hall and it led straight into the living room, which needed to be larger than the subsidiary room. The Cwmrheidol house always has the door off-centre like this. The next stage was the addition of lofts for storage and extra sleeping accommodation. The *bwthyn croglofft* or half-loft cottage had a sleeping loft only over the smaller downstairs room, with a moveable ladder up to it, and sometimes a skylight in the roof, but more often a small square window in the gable end. Later cottages had full lofts, often partitioned with planks to give two low bedrooms with the roof slanting down to the floor, so that standing up was only possible in the central area. The next step was to construct a permanent stairway in place of the ladder, and this usually goes up from the living room corner, to the right of the inglenook fireplace.

The oldest houses left standing in upper Cwmrheidol provide examples of the half-loft with ladder access (Pantyddwyriw), and the full loft reached by corner staircase (Troedrhiwsebon). Troedrhiwsebon also has a loft over the old stable, with outside steps, where probably farm servants slept in the old days. There are several examples of houses rebuilt at the end of the nineteenth century, where a central hall and stairway have been added to the basic design, and the roof has been raised to give two proper bedrooms, divided by wooden plank partitions, which were usually wallpapered over, and with full-size sash windows in each bedroom.

Various additions were made to the basic house. A byre and twin pigsties were the usual necessities for smallholders, and they were usually built on to the west gable. A cold pantry or *bwtri* for dairying is found either at the rear of the house (by extending the roof downwards, as in Gellifach) or as a lean-to extension usually to the east gable. Some of the houses are dug so deeply into the hillside at the back that there would be no room for a *bwtri* there, but where there was room this was the best place for cold storage, since the houses in the upper cwm are nearly all south-facing and only one room thick, so the back is the cold sunless part.

Depopulation and repopulation in upper Cwmrheidol

There is a 1744 map made by Lewis Morris,[3] the Royal Surveyor of Mines, which shows each little farm with its few acres of land, and the name of the landlord, before the lead-mining boom of the following century changed the landscape and doubled the population. The houses on the map are Dolpelyd, Pantyddwyriw, Plwca Budr, Tyn y Fron, Troedrhiwsebon, Caegynon, Gellifach and Tŷ Poeth. The Powells of Nanteos and the Pryses of Gogerddan were the dominant landlords, owning alternate smallholdings in the upper cwm from then until they sold them off towards the end of the nineteenth century.

Dolpelyd is now a heap of stones in the high meadow, surrounded by conifer plantations planted in the 1950s and due for felling. But a new dirt track has recently been driven through the meadow by the purchasers of a plot of land by the ruin, and while they work on their plans for bringing life back to the old place, they have in the van for inspiration an old framed photo of the house at Dôl which was still occupied between the wars by a relative of Marilyn Morgan, one of the new owners. She has been looking for a place in the valley for years, because of the family connection, and hopes to come back and renew her beginnings, after years of living and having a professional career in Suffolk.

Pantyddwyriw has changed hardly at all, because it is only in occasional use as a holiday house since the 1960s. But it too is facing a revival, for the owners have decided to come and live in it permanently, and have begun renovations which they hope will preserve the essential features of the house while bringing in water and electricity and installing a modern kitchen and bathroom.

Plwca has continued to be lived in, except for a period in the 1970s when it fell into decay, and was used only on occasional summer visits by a London cake manufacturer and his employees. It has been drastically modernised and extended in the last fifty years, so that it no longer bears any resemblance to the original simple two-up, two-down cottage with byre (later stable) extension. But inside there are visible remnants of its former state, the western end having rough-hewn oak beams, two foot thick walls and plank partitions dividing the loft bedrooms.

Tyn y Fron was a roofless stone shell until 1991, when it was bought from the Forestry Commission with twelve acres of land. The new owner is living in a caravan next to the old house, which has been reroofed for use as a barn, until such times as she can get planning permission to rebuild. But that requires agricultural justification, and the plan is to make a commercial success of growing Christmas trees on the two southfacing fields below the house. The first crop was planted in the Spring of 1992.

Troedrhiwsebon has remained in local occupation as a working farm. Even during the lead mining days the family at Troedrhiwsebon stuck to farming rather than working in the mines, having an above average acreage (they rented between 50 and 100 acres in the mid-nineteenth century). Its 70 acres are farmed by Byron Jones, an elderly bachelor born and bred in Ystumtuen, who remembers the old days, when they grew corn and barley and oats, and plenty of potatoes and swedes, and their own hay. But nowadays hay is £110 a ton to buy in, and all you get for a sheep is £12 where it was up to £40 at one time. But his Charolais cattle are doing alright still.

Caegynon Farm has undergone a number of radical changes since the eighteenth century. Lead ore was discovered up behind the house and a cluster of mine buildings grew up there in the nineteenth century, with water wheels to power the machinery. But the farm remained, its occupants dividing their time between mine work and their small-holding. The mine was still giving some work in the 1930s, and Caegynon Farm remained in occupation by an elderly bachelor till the 1960s. It then lay empty for twenty years, and gradually the roof fell in and the stonework sagged as a giant crack opened down the front wall. It came on the market during the property boom of 1988 and was bought by a young English couple, who have rebuilt it themselves, and are now bringing up their two young children in it. The old byre and piggeries have been demolished to make room for the kitchen and bathroom extension, and he is painstakingly facing the concrete blocks with valley stone, so that the new block will be indistinguishable from the rest of the house.

Gellifach was falling into disuse and disrepair when it was bought in the early 1980s by Peter Lord, an art designer and art historian. He restored the house, keeping the room layout, the wooden partition walls and the beamed ceilings, and the slate floor, and making a modern bathroom out of the old lean-to-dairy at the back.

Tŷ Poeth has been in continuous occupation by local valley people, and continues to be a working small holding, the home of Dai Charles and Nancy Evans. Until he took early retirement Dai Charles ran the fish farm at the Cwmrheidol Power Station, where they breed the fish for stocking Dinas Lake, and salmon fries for the National River Authority. Part of the job was acting as water bailiff to keep anglers to the conservation guidelines, and cut down out of season fishing or over-fishing. He and Nancy run their own smallholding with occasional help at busy times with the sheep. They have updated the old house for modern comfort.

The fate of the eight houses shown on Lewis Morris's 1744 map of upper Cwmrheidol is a revealing miniature of Welsh rural history. Three had fallen into ruin by the 1980s, as a result of rural depopulation, but 2 of the 3 are back in permanent use (by English incomers) and the third may be brought back to life by an incomer with valley connections, in the near future. Two are the dwellings of Welsh-speaking local people still. One continues the old way of life farming the land, but now there is no arable—he has cattle and sheep. The other breeds sheep, but has needed to combine this with an outside job on the Power Station fish farm, and his wife has worked as a part-time guide in the Power Station's Visitors' Centre. Two more were only intermittently used and beginning to fall into dereliction in the 1970s, but were brought into permanent occupation again in the 1980s—one by an Irish/English (of remote Welsh ancestry) couple of Joneses, and the other by a Welsh-speaking artist who has become a Welshman by choice. The remaining house is a holiday home currently being modernised for a permanent home by English incomers.

Portraits of upper Cwmrheidol houses

Tyn y Fron

The old farmhouse of Tyn y Fron stands high above the river on a sunny south-facing balcony halfway up the slope of the valley side. From its blind windows there are magical views of the upper cwm and the distant foothills of Pumlumon, where the Rheidol has its source (alongside the sources of the Severn and the Wye). Its high site means that it keeps the sun all winter, when the houses nearer the valley floor are left in the icy shadow of Tyn y Castell, the eight-hundred foot hill that walls in the valley from the south.

The site may seem remote now, because its green lane with overarching hedges of hazel and hawthorn no longer is a passing thoroughfare. But in the days of horse and foot traffic it had its share of passing interest, for this was a strategic track from Cwm Rheidol north into the next valley, and the area was at one time thickly dotted with the lead miners' cottages. There was plenty of industrial activity going on here too, for Tyn y Fron adit lies in the gully below the farmhouse, and a tramway runs for half a mile from there to the Cwmrheidol Mine in the valley bottom, where at the beginning of this century the ore was dressed and dispatched on the Rheidol Railway down to the port of Aberystwyth.

Now only the occasional pony trekker or group of walkers passes in the short summer season, pausing to take the view from the picturesquely sited pig sties, which stand twenty yards to the east of the house on their own little balcony; they have now been converted to a felt-roofed shelter for ornamental ducks who paddle contentedly in the stream between sties and house.

The house is the middle section of a long range of buildings, which probably once served as byre and barn and stable, but it is difficult to tell, for the roof had collapsed and the walls were collapsing before the new owner began to rebuild them a year ago. In front are the remnants of an old orchard of extremely gnarled and twisted and lichened plum trees, still struggling to live. Such orchards were common in the old Cwmrheidol houses, providing fruit for tarts and preserves—though an equally important source was the hedgerows along the green lanes, which were (and still are) a rich source of damsons and blackberries and crab apples and hazelnuts.

Tyn y Fron is a good example of the old Cwmrheidol house, with its slightly off-centre doorway, windows on either side of the door, a big kitchen with inglenook fireplace, and a parlour off it. The dairy is built on at the back, off the kitchen. The inglenook fireplace is still there, though in a state of ruin, and with a later brick fireplace inserted. The worm-gnawed oak beam supporting it still has the date 1738 incised in it. A bakehouse with ovens was added at some point, to the east end.

It seems that at one period in the nineteenth century there was a little country school held in Tyn y Fron, which was attended by Isaac Jenkins who later became a well-known minister and notable writer among the Wesleyans. [4] Small classes held in farmhouses for local children were held before the coming of the government schools in the 1870s. In mid century there were many big families in this part of the valley, since the

288

people could at that time get work in the lead mines, and the population reached its zenith in the 1860s and 1870s. In the 1860s there were three families living in Tyn y Fron, and the fathers all worked in lead mining. There were six children in Tyn y Fron, and big families in the neighbouring houses of Pencnwch, Troedrhiwsebon and Plwca. At this time the average family in Ceredigion had five children, and often they might also be looking after the child of a relative suffering hard times and unable to bring up a child for a time, or a *plentyn siawns*, a love child of a daughter of the family. There was then a large child population to attend the school in Tyn y Fron, but most children in the mining families only attended school for a term, since they had to work from an early age to contribute towards the family income. The future Wesleyan minister Isaac Jenkins, however, progressed well enough to go on to a school in Aberffrwd, where he was taught Latin by William Lewis.

The practice in these little country schools was to get the children to read aloud and to have each say his or her lesson in turn. A central aim was to teach the children to read the Scriptures and memorise verses. Writing was learnt by copying letters and simple words, sometimes in copybooks, but more often (since it was cheaper) by getting the children to copy from the blackboard on to their individual slates.

The lead mining boom which began in Cwmrheidol in the 1840s is reflected in the life of the families who lived in Tyn y Fron from then till the 1880s when it all collapsed and the population went into decline. At the beginning of the forties David and Eliza James and their five children lived there and got their living from farming. They had a baby one month old, not yet given a name in the Census Report, a two year old called David, and three girls—Margaret (7), Eliza (8) and Mary (10). Fifteen year old David Lloyd also lived with them, probably a relative who helped on the farm, for it was common practice in Ceredigion for one or two children of big families to go and board as farm servants, preferably with their own kith and kin.

Ten years later everything had changed. The general increase in population is reflected in the two families now sharing the house. A widow of seventy, Elizabeth Jenkins, and her twenty two year old son

Edward had come to live there, attracted by the possibility of work for Edward in the nearby mines. In addition there is a second family of Stephenses in the house consisting of the father John (63), the mother Eliza (58), a daughter Eliza (15) and a lodger Margaret Davies (16). John Stephen was farming twenty acres, and his wife did the usual woman's work of milking the cows and making the butter and cheese, seeing to the pigs and the poultry, and feeding the family almost entirely from their own produce. The three young people from the house have all got jobs in the lead mines. Edward Jenkins is a fully-fledged miner and Eliza Stephen and the lodger Margaret have labouring jobs in the mines.

After another ten years had elapsed, in 1861, there were three quite different families crowded in Tyn y Fron, and farming has become a side line to be carried out in any spare time left over from working at the mines. The three grown up men, Evan Hughes, Thomas Davies and Richard Richards, are lead miners, and their wives all have young children to look after. The Hughes have a little boy of six, the Richards have three children under eight, and the Davies have two grown up daughters (one of whom has had a child of her own, three year old Sophia) and a ten year old girl called Mary. There are fourteen people crowded into the house.

During the 1860s the comings and goings continue, showing how very unsettled life was in the mining districts of those days. By 1871 the Richards family have moved on, Evan Hughes has died at the age of 36 (the fate of many miners) and Mary Davies has died while still in her fifties. Thomas Davies is still working as a miner at the age of 66, showing that some of the miners did have a hearty constitution to survive the unhealthy working conditions and the damp houses which often led to ravages by tuberculosis. The widowed Mr Davies is looked after by his unmarried daughter Ann (39), and her child Sophia is still with them, now 13 and already an invalid. There is another child in the house, David Lewis (8), a son of one of the daughters who has left home, showing again how common it was for children to be shared around the extended family, either to relieve the mother of a big family, or to provide another pair of hands in the hosting family.

During the 1870s the Davies family went through a bad time, for only Ann was left by 1881. Her father had died, her invalid daughter had died, and her nephew David had grown up and gone away, leaving her with no money and no support. She was forced to turn to the Poor Law Guardians for help, and thus ended her hard life as a pauper. This individual family's misfortunes reflect the wider sweep of economics, for it was during the seventies that the number of jobs in the Cwmrheidol mines dropped from 313 to 189. There was no more work for the people in Tyn y Fron, so they either left or turned back to subsistence farming. Lewis and Catherine Powell were struggling to bring up their own five children here in 1881, along with two other children (perhaps Catherine's sister's children), on the precarious proceeds of their small farm, no longer supplemented by any income from mining work.

The last family to farm Tyn y Fron were the Merediths, who continued there between the two world wars, according to local memory. They belonged to the local Wesleyan community, and lie buried in the graveyard of Ystumtuen Chapel under an impressive headstone which reads: 'The Meredith Family, 1860-1938, William Meredith, Tyn y fron, *Gwyn eu byd*, Blessed their world'. Tyn y Fron began to decay. The two steep fields where it stands were part of a lot bought by the Forestry Commission after the war, and the house was apparently abandoned, though it may have been one of those small holdings the Forestry Commission hoped would find tenants among their employees, so that they could combine forestry work with farming, and occupy themselves during the slack times in managing the conifer plantations. That seems likely, because the two big fields in front of the house were never planted with trees. But whatever the intention, the 1950s were a bad time for rural depopulation, and forestry workers preferred to live a more sociable life in villages than be on their own in an isolated smallholding. Tyn y Fron became a wind-gnawed stone shell until, in the late 1980s, the Forestry Commission privatised their Cwmrheidol plantations and the Tyn y Fron ruins and pasture of 12 acres came on the market: 'Offers invited around £20,000 for the remains of a traditional Welsh cottage in a delightful position overlooking the valley—in total seclusion'. A new lease of life began for the old farm.

Troedrhiwsebon

Miss Ellen Stephens of Troedrhiwsebon died on the 12 September 1962, and was buried in the graveyard of Bethel, fifty yards from the house where she was born and lived her life till the last few years when she retired from the farm and went down the road to Tŷ Melyn. It was the end of an era, for the Stephens family had farmed Troedrhiwsebon for over a hundred years and had taken a significant part in the local Wesleyan Methodist community. They were substantial enough farmers to be above sending their sons and daughters to work in the mines as the poorer Cwmrheidol families had to do. In the nineteenth century they farmed at times as much as one hundred acres, and among them were examples of the finer aspects of the *gwerinwr*, the farmer of the 'little tradition', who

> spoke Welsh fluently and habitually, took a prominent part in the affairs of the chapel where he was deacon. He was a local leader . . . but he remained a *gwerinwr*, widely read, able to participate in 'the little tradition' and to be a link between it and the maintenance of the national culture. [5]

There was Edward Stephens, for instance, who was born in Troedrhiwsebon in 1839 and was influential in the Wesleyan cause in Ystumtuen, the little village on the plateau where the people of upper Cwmrheidol went to school and chapel, and where many of them lie buried. The early Wesleyans met in farmhouses visited by itinerant preachers from Aberystwyth, who would cover great distances on horseback every Sunday—Melin-y-Graig at nine, Tŷ Hir at eleven, Pandy at two, Pontrhydygroes at six . . . But in 1823 the first Salem was built in Ystumtuen. The cause flourished and the Chapel had to be rebuilt in 1838, and again in 1858, when the present Ebeneser was built. By now in 1990 the congregation has dwindled to a score, with many of the members over sixty, but the graveyard has much to tell of the lead-mining days when the Chapel was in its prime. Here lie Davieses of Pant-yddwyriw, Jenkins of Troedrhiwfawr, Joneses of Llain and Pencnwch, Daniels of Plwca, Benjamins of Troedrhiwfron, and Merediths of Tyn y Fron. The slate headstones are locally crafted, and the prevalence of lead is visible in the way the letters on the inscriptions are individually picked out in lead.

By 1872 there were enough Wesleyan Methodists living in Cwmrheidol to justify a new chapel in the valley itself. Bethel opened in 1872. It was built by the local people on land given by the Stephens family of Troedrhiwsebon. People parked their ponies and traps in the farmyard during the services, and the ministers were given their dinners in Troedrhiwsebon kitchen after the services. Every Whitsun there were special services with an invited preacher, and in preparation for these Miss Stephens would have the house whitewashed and would do a thorough spring clean—curtains washed and table clothes bleached. Bethel closed down in 1985, after numbers dwindled away till there were only two deacons forming the congregation—Byron Jones of Troedrhiwsebon and Aneurin Morgan of The Bungalow. Aneurin explains that the Chapel had lost the young people. In the old days they relied on the Chapel for their socials and entertainments, but now they are more mobile and seek their entertainment in the towns. There was talk of a Farewell Service when it was closed, but Aneurin said, 'Well, if they couldn't come to the services enough to keep it open, what is the point of coming when it is closing down?'

Troedrhiwsebon farmhouse like Tyn y Fron was built in 1738, and its basic design has not changed a great deal since. It still has its slate slab floors, inglenook, and slate-shelved dairy. Since Miss Stephens left, the bachelor Jones brothers have farmed there, and have not bothered to do much updating to the house. Byron Jones had come to the farm as Miss Stephens *gwas fferm*, farmhand, and took over from her with the help of his brothers Jack and Moc, now dead. Electricity has been installed, but otherwise there is not much evidence of modern conveniences, and the farm is a visible memorial to Cwmrheidol farming history. The house stands on the single track road, part of a long range which also housed the pony and trap and stable. The rest of the farm buildings are round the rear yard. The public road functions as the farmyard, as was the practice in quiet country districts before the coming of the motor car. It is the pecking ground for the chickens and the patrolling area for the sheep-dogs. Past the house the road is lined with decrepit wooden doghouses and rough shelters where sickly ewes and lambs can be housed during the lambing season. On the other side grew the remains of an old orchard till recently but they have been grubbed up and the cattle have turned the ground into a morass of mud with their stamping and tramping, for this is where feed is put out for them in the winter. Troedrhiwsebon is a good example of the Welsh long-house, with two-roomed living accommodation (and lofts above) at one end, and animal housing at the other end. Its original layout was quite similar to Tŷ'r celyn, Llandeilo, illustrated in Iorwerth Peate's *The Welsh house*[6] (except that the dairy in Troedrhiwsebon is in the house, between the living-room and parlour, rather than built on at the back).

The earliest form of the long house had an upper end, *pen uchaf* for the family, and a doorway through into the lower end, *pen isaf*, for the cattle, often with a feeding walk between the two halves. At first the upper end would be one large room, with box beds to make some kind of division between living and sleeping space. But then a partition of planks was added to make two ground-floor rooms, and lofts added above for more sleeping space. At first a moveable ladder gave access to the lofts, but this was replaced by a corner stairway to the right of the inglenook fireplace. At some point in this evolution the door between upper and lower ends, between animals and people, would be blocked off. A dairy was needed, too, and this was usually added at the back of the house. Troedrhiwsebon has reached something like this stage, never having had the roof raised to provide full height bedrooms, or a modern bathroom or kitchen extension added on, as has happened with most of the traditional longhouses this century.

In the 1841 Census Report we learn that the young Stephens couple who then lived in Troedrhiwsebon were John (25) and Jane (25). They had two babies Edward (2) and Mary (7 months). They employed three

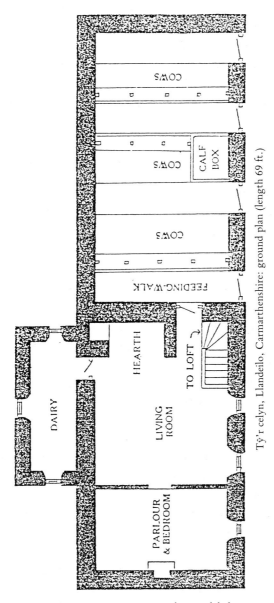

Tŷ'r celyn, Llandeilo, Carmarthenshire: ground plan (length 69 ft.)

(From Iorwerth Peate, *The Welsh house*)

farm servants—Elias Jenkins (15), Jane Evans (20) and David Davies (13). They prospered and took on more land till by 1861 they were working 100 acres. There were then five children in the family between the ages of ten and twenty two—Edward and John the eldest and youngest, and three girls between them, called Mary, Margaret and Eliza. The eldest girl Mary was a dressmaker, one of the few livings open to women, since they could do it at home in between their household tasks. Also living in Troedrhiwsebon at this time were three lodgers from Shropshire who had come to the valley to get work, for this was the height of the lead-mining boom.

When another ten years had passed the Stephens parents were in their mid fifties and had only one grown-up son and one daughter left at home to help with house and farm work, and they had reduced their acreage from the hundred they had farmed in their prime to forty nine. The household was now down to five, compared with the ten who had been somehow packed in earlier. The ageing Stephens were now bringing up their four year old granddaughter Anna Maria Powell, the child of one of their daughters who had left home by this time. Once again this indicates how often children were brought up by near kin, not their parents, as has been noted in other parts of Ceredigion in the 1860s. David Jenkins speaking of Troedyraur in the south of the county says that one household in seven included children being brought up by near relatives, for kinship meant:

a body of people who gave help at times of need and hardship, and who sustained each other in the ordinary events of daily life and in the face of its demands. Those so connected constituted a body of people to whom a man turned, and to whom his first loyalties belonged. The sentiments of kinship pervaded social life in one way or another; they 'informed' man's relations with his fellows.[7]

The 1880s was the time of suffering for the Stephens parents in their turn. John Stephens died and with the departure of the grown-up children John and Margaret, the mother was left running a much reduced farm of twenty seven acres, with the help of her granddaughter

Anna (14) whom she had raised, and one farm servant, Abraham Wright. This was a bad time for farming, because cheap imports of grain and beef were pouring into Britain from the United States, thanks to the opening up of the prairie grasslands and the invention of refrigerated meat ships. Many Cwmrheidol people left the valley as a result of the twin depressions in mining and farming, but the Stephens family stayed on. When the widow died her son John came back home to take over the family farm. It was his daughter Ellen, born in 1894, who lived her whole life there until her final years, and was buried in Bethel in 1962.

The farmhouse at Plwca

Pombrenplwca, the wooden bridge at Plwca, dates back to the middle ages, when it would have been a single plank bridge spanning the River Rheidol at its narrowest point a little up river from the old farm of Plwca, where the river enters a rocky chasm. It lay on a medieval pilgrims' route from the north down to the Abbey at Strata Florida, a Cistercian house which flourished from 1164 till Henry VIII dissolved the monasteries in the 1530s, and which was responsible for many farming developments in its far flung estates and outlying farms. Today Pombrenplwca is a solid metal footbridge mainly used by walkers. It has to be crossed on a popular circular walk between Ysbyty Cynfyn, Devil's Bridge, Cwmrheidol, Ystumtuen and back to Ysbyty Cynfyn by Parson's Bridge. It also lies on the Cambrian Way, a recently plotted long distance route which crosses Wales from north to south, which attracts walkers so dedicated that one wonders if this is a secular equivalent of the medieval pilgrimage.

The farmhouse at Plwca is named in the Nanteos Estate papers of 1690, where it is included in one of the Powell family's marriage settlements. It is mentioned again in 1744, when it is shown on Lewis Morris' map of the locality. Then nothing more is heard of it until the 1841 Census Report. At that point the Daniel family appear on the scene, and remain till the end of the century through the various vicissitudes of lead mining, until driven away by the collapse of their livelihood.

In the middle of the century the Daniel parents Griffith and Margaret were in their fifties, and lived in Plwca with their sons Griffith (15) and James (12). Father and elder son worked as miners, but the family also ran a smallholding to augment their miserable mine wages. When the parents died twenty years later, having lived to a ripe old age in those unhealthy times (both were in their seventies), the older son Griffith took over the farm, which at that time was twelve acres. The younger brother James was unmarried and still living at home. Griffith and his wife Mary (who was ten years older than her husband) had 3 children at home—Rowland, Emma and Frances (13, 5 and 3 years old in 1871). Uncle James worked as a miner, and so did a nephew, Lewis Daniel, who was living with them, making a total of seven in the simple old cottage which had on the ground floor a kitchen and small cramped bedroom, and on the upper floor a low loft divided in two by a wooden partition.

By 1881 the father has taken a job in the mine, but the son Rowland has launched out on a completely new course, as an itinerant tea dealer. The two girls Emma and Frances are living at home in Plwca, helping on the smallholding, rather than working as ore-dressers, as they would have done while the mines are still flourishing. From then till the end of the century the Daniel family fortunes went steadily downhill, reflecting the impact of the wider economic depression in lead mining and farming on individual lives. Mary and Griffith Daniel died in their early sixties and were buried in the Wesleyan Chapel in Ystumtuen. Buried in the same family grave is their granddaughter Emma Ann (daughter of Frances and John Jenkins) who died when two months old. There is no further evidence of the Daniel family of Plwca in the Ystumtuen graveyard, but the rest of the story was told by a descendant, John Daniel of Pontypridd, when he called at Plwca in the summer of 1991. Rowland Daniel had four sons who grew up without hope of work in the valley, and so they set out to walk to the Rhondda to get jobs in the coal mines. Going south was the only solution, and the number of inhabited houses in this part of Ceredigion dropped by half, till the population at the time of the 1914-18 war as low as it had been before the lead-mining boom began in the 1840s.

The farmhouse at Plwca, however, underwent an unexpected revival of fortune in the 1930s, thanks largely to the arrival of Joseph Dandrick from Mittel Europa, in flight from Nazi anti-semitism. Dandrick is still remembered in the valley (and further afield in Ceredigion) as a near-mythical figure whose grandiose schemes were more the product of an overheated imagination and overweening ambition than of sound common sense. He changed the name of the house to Harvest Hall, as if wishful thinking were sufficient to revive the mining bonanza and make him a fortune. For he was the last of the mine captains in the valley, determined to reopen the old Cwmrheidol Mine, and when that failed, to plonk down a luxury hotel on the green apron of land overlooking the river next to the mine. That too failed, because planning permission was conditional on him widening the single track road, which would have eaten up a larger fortune than he ever succeeded in accumulating, in spite of his entrepreneurial instints.

Undeterred by setbacks, he is said to have expanded his land holdings in the age-old manner of his adopted country, by taking advantage of missing or imperfect title deeds, and simply swearing affidavits that he owned 'most of the valley', and the fishing rights on the Rheidol the whole way from Harvest Hall to Cardigan Bay. So when the Central Electricity Generating Board and the Forestry Commission were planning their hydro-electric power station and their conifer plantations in the valley in the 1950s, they had to enter into protracted negotiations with Dandrick over land and river and mining rights which he swore were his. And his land-greed was difficult to gainsay, for land registration is only being finally sorted out in the 1990s, with compulsory regis-tration at a central record office in Swansea. Till then, ancient title deeds in rural Wales were a fascinating but frequently incomprehensible jumble of old plans and affidavits referring to boundaries which are neither clear on the ground (due to the old habit of moving boundaries noted as far back as the twelfth century by Giraldus Cambrensis) nor even on the plans. 'The area coloured brown' or 'the area enclosed by a purple line' turn out to be irretrievable since the colours have faded or have never been added during the copying of deeds in lackadaisical solicitors' offices.

Under Dandrick the farmhouse at Plwca, or Harvest Hall, underwent a rustic gentrification programme which, while it broke any connection with local building styles, at least provided a good deal of employment for local men. He doubled the size of the nineteenth-century cottage by knocking a way through into the cobbled stable and creating there a bay windowed living room with bedroom and bathroom over it. Then he added another third to the house with a further bedroom over a large new kitchen. What had once been a simple cottage exterior with small windows was transformed into a formidable facade with a run of five large 'bauhaus' steel-framed windows along the first floor, and two square bays on the ground floor opening out onto a terrace of concrete (mixed with mine waste), where the second Mrs Dandrick is remembered to have sunbathed—in a leopard skin swimming costume, some say. Elaborate rustic brick fireplaces of Byzantine complexity were installed in the downstairs living rooms. They contain so many niches of various sizes that even an indefatigable collector of *objects d'art* would be hard put to fill them. There are the remnants still of the locally carpentered pigeon holes in which he filed the records of his ambitious schemes. And when the present owners bought the house in the early 1980s they found around the grounds and in the shed the final artefacts of the mining era—a giant bellows of wood and leather, and a low iron-wheeled bogey which had once conveyed lead ore.

Harvest Hall is once again called Plwca, and after the turbulent Dandrick era, it seems to have regained that tranquility which once inspired the Methodist minister Isaac Jenkins to compose a well-known hymn in the garden. Aneurin Morgan still has the diary kept by his great grandfather's brother in the 1870s, which records the occasion. The words of the hymn (still in the Methodist Hymnal—No. 267) are:

Arglwydd grasol, dyro d'Ysbryd,	Gracious Lord, give of your Spirit,
Dysg im llefain, Abba, Dad,	Teach me to cry Abba, Father,
Rho dystiolaeth o'm mabwysiad,	Testify to my adoption,
Gad im brofi o'th gariad rhad;	Let me taste your gracious love;

Dyro wir fodlonrwydd imi	Satisfy me truly
Fod fy enaid yn dy hedd,	That my soul is in your peace,
Llanw f'ysbryd â thangnefedd	Fill my spirit with serenity
Cyn im fynd i lawr i'r bedd.	Before I go down to the grave.
Rho dy hoff gymdeithas imi	Give me your loving fellowship
Tra fwyf yn yr anial fyd,	While I am in the desolate world,
Tywys f'enaid tua'r bywyd,	Lead my spirit towards the life,
A bydd imi'n noddfa glyd;	Which will be for me a warm shelter;
Gad im wledda gyda'th deulu,	Let me feast with your family,
Gwledda ar dy gariad rhad;	Feast on your generous love;
Yn y diwedd dwg fi'n dawel	In the end steal me quietly away
Draw i ddedwydd dŷ fy Nhad.	To my Father's blessed house.

Gellifach

The present stone and slated house of Gellifach is a well-preserved late nineteenth-century Cwmrheidol house, with a parlour to the left of the central hallway, the kitchen to the right, and two bedrooms upstairs. There was a dairy at the back off the kitchen. It stands facing south, with its windowless back against the steep hillside of oak and birch woods which are now conserved by the Dyfed Wildlife Trust as heritage landscape. The surrounding plot has a stone outbuilding, probably once the cowhouse, and a corrugated-iron pig sty. There is an ancient yew tree in the front garden which may well have been there in the eighteenth century when an earlier Gellifach was recorded on Lewis Morris' map. At that time Gellifach was a smallholding on the Powells' Nanteos estate. Such smallholders suffered greatly towards the close of the eighteenth century as a result of a series of bad harvests:

> Wheat rose to famine prices, upland sheepwalks were ploughed up, wastes and commons were enclosed and brought under cultivation with marvellous rapidity ... rents doubled and trebled.[8]

Small tenants did not benefit from agricultural improvements introduced by the big landlords, but continued with their subsistence farming, in an endless effort to pay their rent and taxes and feed the family. There was endemic lack of trust between landlord and tenant farmer which did not encourage improvements, because it was feared they might only lead to increased rent. For a while, during the Napoleonic Wars, prices were good, but the slump that followed led to renewed impoverishment among smallholders. Often they had to sell their livestock to meet immediate needs of rent or feeding their large families, while tithes and taxes steadily increased, leading eventually to the Rebecca riots in south Ceredigion and Carmarthenshire in the 1840s.

In Cwmrheidol the Aberffrwd Baptismal Register which runs from 1814 to the present day, shows the preponderance of farming and self-sufficient craftwork in the early decades of the nineteenth century. From 1814 till 1840 the majority worked at farming and labouring, and there were very few miners. There were millers at Felinfawr and Felin Newydd, two weavers and two shoemakers. The minister of Aberffrwd Chapel lived in Abernant (Rev Evan Evans), and there was a schoolmaster in the valley, though in the 1820s and 1830s about half the people signing the baptismal register used an X, including the schoolmaster's wife Elizabeth Williams! The schoolmaster was John Thomas and, if he did not consider women's literacy important, he nevertheless saw to it that his sons got a good chance in life through education. The family were living in Tŷ Poeth when the son Mesac was born in 1816, and the boy went on to Oswestry Grammar School and Shrewsbury School, and then to Cambridge. He had a distinguished church career, ending up as the first bishop of New South Wales, where, 'as he increased the number of his clergy he provided spiritual comfort for isolated settlers and many diggers on the Araluen and Lambing Flat goldfields . . . stressing that the needs of their own countrymen were greater than those of the heathen'.[9]

Meanwhile, back in Cwmrheidol, the landowners took a rather jaundiced view of the influence of mining on a hitherto quiescent rural tenantry. Colonel Powell of Nanteos said to the Education Commissioners in the 1840s that 'they are less disposed to respect the old families of the county than they used to be, and are less honest than they formerly were'.[10] His land agent added that 'The people are destitute of general information, but the miners have improved this by introducing the English language'. [11]

The families who lived in Gellifach in the mining boom of the 1840s to the 1870s were Colonel Powell's tenants, and their changing occupations reflect the ability to earn money from mining and be less dependent on their smallholding, which no doubt contributed to the attitudes that Colonel Powell deplored. In 1841 John Jones (52) and Anne Jones (50) lived in Gellifach with their two daughters Catharina (3) and Averina (2). (There are other examples in the census reports of women bearing children into their late forties and early fifties). They had a farm servant called Thomas Mazen (Mason) aged 30, and an 'independent' widow of 55, Margaret Edwards, lived with them. Their sole occupation is their smallholding. Ten years later the situation has changed drastically. Anne Jones is now a widow, described as a 'farmer have been', so presumably unable to go on after her husband had died. Her daughter Averina is a labourer in the mine. An older daughter Anne (24) has come home with her husband John Williams (28) and their three children (4, 2 and one month), to live with the widowed mother and because there is now work in the mines, for John Williams is described as a miner.

There were by the 1860s several mines close to Gellifach. The Rheidol United across the river employed at that time twenty young women, girls and boys, on the dressing floors (which were in that mine roofed in from the weather). Caegynon Mine was a hundred yards up the road from the house, and the Gelli Mine was up the hillside to the west (its waste tips form 'The Stag'). John and Anne Williams by that time had six children, and Anne's widowed mother was still living with them, now classified as a 'pauper', on poor relief like so many of the women left without a means of livelihood. John Williams is working in the mines, and their twelve year old daughter Anne is an ore-dresser. The eldest daughter is helping in the house, and the family are farming twelve acres.

By 1871 the parents are approaching fifty years old, and the family is very typical of the economic and family conditions of that time in the valley. They earn their living from their twelve-acre smallholding, augmented by wages from working in the mines. The father and the oldest son William (18) are lead miners. Two of the daughters, Catherine (20) and Averina (16) are ore-dressers. The oldest girl Mary stays at home to help her mother with the housework and the women's work on the smallholding—the poultry and the dairying and the pig. The two youngest children John (14) and Ebenezer (8) are presumably at school, though there is a blank in the Census Report opposite their occupations. Surprisingly the older daughter Ann (22) who ten years earlier had been working as an ore-dresser, is now described as attending school—perhaps as a pupil teacher. The youngest child Ebenezer was born when his mother was in her forties, just as her own mother had gone on bearing children till her late forties.

By 1881 there is evidence of the declining prospects in lead mining, which so greatly reduced the valley population towards the end of the century. The family in Gellifach is down to the parents, two grownup daughters (both helping in the house and smallholding) and the youngest son Ebenezer, now sixteen (according to the Census, but eighteen according to the 1871 Census). Ebenezer and his father are still working as lead miners, but the rest of the big family have gone to seek their fortunes elsewhere.

Sometime towards the end of the century the house at Gellifach was rebuilt, for the present house, though it keeps its old two foot thick stone walls, has a roof of regular cut slates, dressed beams and Victorian sash windows. There are a number of old Cwmrheidol cottages of the same type which seem to have been rebuilt at a time when one would not expect there to be money available for modernising houses. What seems to have happened is that the poorer people left for the coal mines of the south, and the few who remained were the more prosperous ones who could afford to rebuild. It was in the 1881 Census that the first postman and the first policeman are recorded as living in the valley, and the Aberffrwd Baptismal Register reflects the diversication of employment. Although there are few miners, there are carpenters, a plasterer and a stone mason, indicating the amount of building work going on. Whereas in the 1860s there were seventy children baptised in Aberffrwd

Chapel, there were only twenty in the 1880s, and the nadir was reached in the decade of the 1914-18 war, when fewer than half a dozen were baptised. It was only in the 1980s that the population of the upper cwm once more began to climb, as the old ruins were bought for rebuilding by incomers. But there are still only thirty of us living along the single track road beyond the Power Station, whereas in the height of the lead-mining days there were one hundred and fifty.

[1] Peter Smith, *Houses of the Welsh countryside*, London, HMSO, 1988, p. 321.

[2] Rev. Thomas Rees, *A topographical and historical description of the counties of South Wales*, London, Sherwood, Neely and Jones, 1815, p. 101.

[3] Sir Lewis Morris, *Plan of the Manor of Pervedd done by order of the Surveyor General of His Majesty's land revenues, 1744.* (In the Maps and Prints Department of the National Library).

[4] J. Henry Griffiths, *Bro annwyl y bryniau*, Aberystwyth, Cymdeithas Lyfrau Ceredigion, 1988, p. 57.

[5] David Jenkins, *The agricultural community in south-west Wales at the turn of the twentieth century*, Cardiff, University of Wales Press, 1971, p. 35.

[6] Iorwerth Peate, *The Welsh house*, London, Honourable Society of Cymmrodorion, 1940, p. 73.

[7] David Jenkins (as above), p. 178.

[8] Royal Commission on land in Wales and Monmouthshire, *Report*, London, 1896, p. 47.

[9] Typescript lent to me by Mrs Nancy Evans, Tŷ Poeth, Cwmrheidol.

[10] Royal Commission on Education in Wales, *Report*, London, 1847, p. 326.

[11] Royal Commission on Education in Wales (as above).

CHAPTER 13

The old magic and the new magic

The pagan Celts believed in the presence of supernatural spirits all around them, in trees and streams and hills, in caves and mines, thunder and lightning. Spirits concentrated particularly at crossing places— where roads met or where someone had died, for there the borderline between life and death was thin and the veil between different layers of consciousness might more easily be twitched aside for a moment. The result for the passerby could be illumination or madness, for the spirits are essentially ambiguous. For this reason they have to be placated or 'good-mouthed', just as in Greek mythology the Furies or Fates who spin our lives are called the Eumenides, the Well-disposed goddesses, in the hope of warding off their darker gifts.

In the Cwmrheidol district, as in many other parts of rural Wales, the fairies were similarly good-mouthed, up to the early part of this century. They were called the *tylwyth teg*, the fair tribe, and their blessing was the *bendith y mamau*, the mothers' blessing, a continued expression of the pagan belief in mother goddesses, who had strong connections with the earth, with rivers and wells, with groves and sacred trees like the protecting rowan. How did Christians square their continuing pagan customs with their religious practices? One way was to accept that human knowledge here below is partial and limited. 'The light of eternity will shew myriads and myriads of the things which we cannot know here, nor are fit to know; and which we shall there certainly and infallibly know, without error, as they are, and no otherwise',[1] explained Edmund Jones, vicar of a rural parish in south east Wales in the eighteenth century. The Christian churches in the end had to absorb elements of the pagan culture if they were to keep their converts, so they put holy wells and sacred stones under the protection of Christian saints rather than pagan powers. The church of Ysbyty Cynfyn on the top of

306

the Rheidol gorge near Devil's Bridge is built on an old pagan site, and the ancient standing stones can still be seen, built into the churchyard wall.

Old superstitions, *hen ofergoelion*, linger on tenaciously in country districts, even if today people make a joke about them. Friends from Capel Seion walked down through the wood of Cwmseiri in recent years to visit John in Cwmrheidol, and were anxious to get back while there was enough light for them to pick out the path. John laughed and teased them about it. 'Yes', he said, 'you'd better get through the wood before nightfall, or the ghost will get you, that's for sure'. Their route lay through the replanted wood of Cwmseiri where, according to Capel Seion minister and local historian D. J. Evans, there was an old tradition that someone had met a violent death; but there was an even older tradition that *Y Ladi Wen*, the White Lady had appeared there till her ancient oak woods had been cut down.[2]

Christian clergy have shown an admirable zeal in collecting the pagan folkways of their communities. A mile to the north east of the head of Cwmrheidol lies the village of Ystumtuen, where the inhabitants of the upper cwm went to school and chapel in the old days before motor cars. Here the Reverend Henry Griffiths collected the local lore[3] and concluded that his people had been more superstitious in the old days than any other community he had heard of. They warned their children not to step inside fairy circles, those darker green patches on the pasture made smooth by the dancing of fairy feet. One young farm lad whose parents were keen for him to go into the ministry, but who showed more inclination for hunting and fishing and open air sport of every kind, disobeyed these injunctions and was carried off by the fairies for two years. When he turned up again, convinced he had only been away for a day or two, he had many a story to tell of blissful days in the company of the little people who carried him off to a magic bower in the middle of a great wood. There is a Christian twist to the story however, which is unusual in tales of enchantment. He was able to speak in tongues and was now converted to the idea of the ministry. He achieved his parents' ambition, and became a curate in a local church. The more usual end to dancing with the fairies is to lose one's Christian soul and return exhausted and prematurely aged, to find one's nearest and dearest long dead, and a changed community with no place in it for the alienated self.

But fairies could be benign as well as ill-disposed to humans, just as in Celtic mythology the spirits are essentially ambivalent. Celtic mother goddesses are nurturing and all-providing, but have a reverse side which is all-devouring and destructive—the good is not all good, nor the bad all bad. So the leadminers of Cwmrheidol and Goginan believed strongly in benevolent spirits who led the lucky miners to rich deposits of ore, by imitating the sounds of hammering and drilling in their subterranean habitat. Even the much-travelled Sir Lewis Morris, Crown Surveyor of Mines in the 1750s, took the side of the fairies against rational sceptics. The little people, he wrote, worked hard day and night, and were heard by an abundance of honest sober people. The miners looked on 'the Knockers' as members of their own tribe and profession, a harmless people who meant well to them. The Knockers had been a boon to him in opening up the Esgair y Mwyn workings, no matter whether they were 'aerial beings called spirits, or whether they are people made of matter not to be felt by our gross bodies, as air and fire the like'. In his opinion the miners who could *not* hear the Knockers were the ones to worry about, for in his experience they had no proper notion of mining either.

To live close to nature is to be more aware of the cyclic nature of things, of the signs that tell of changing seasons and weather, of the waxing and waning of human and animal life, the greening and withering of crops and vegetation. So a pervasive element in folk lore is the belief that there is a right time and a wrong time to undertake projects, or set out on journeys, or to meet significant people. These beliefs are found too among the pastoral peoples of the Old Testament:

> There is a time for everything, a time for every occupation
> under heaven:
> a time for dying
> a time for planting
> a time for uprooting what has been planted.

A time for killing
a time for healing
a time for knocking down
a time for building.
A time for tear
a time for laughter
a time for mourning
a time for dancing.
A time for throwing stones away
a time for gathering them up
a time for embracing
a time to refrain from embracing.
A time for searching
a time for losing; a time for keeping
a time for throwing away.
A time for tearing, a time for sewing
a time for keeping silent, a time for speaking
a time for loving, a time for hating
a time for war, a time for peace. (Ecclesiastes 3: 1-8)

According to the Capel Seion minister whose flock included Cwmrheidol people early this century, the people had a wide range of tell-tale signs for good and bad omens.[4] They did not start anything important if they had a glimpse of the new moon through glass, or heard a cock crow in the night, or someone had opened an umbrella in the house, or brought in a branch of ill-omened thorn blossom. They did not start a journey if they could avoid it, when a single crow or magpie flew ahead of them, and they took care to plant crops and put eggs to hatch when the moon was waxing and not waning, to make sure that the energies were going with them. A New Age traveller who recently passed through Cwmrheidol subscribed to much the same set of beliefs but he called himself a Taoist, explaining that you have to go with the Tao, the flow of energy, and not use your will against the tides of the fundamental energies.

One idea behind good and bad omens is that significant events throw their shadow before them, and we can have insight into past and future events if we do not shut ourselves up in a linear view of space and time. Death was a far more visible event in the old days when people died in

309

their own homes rather than in hospital, and a whole body of lore grew up around dying. The Reverend Evans remembered an old woman in this district who had seen many *canhwyllau cyrff*, corpse candles, which shine their ghost light outside the houses of those about to die. Many told, too, of seeing the *deryn corff*, the bird of death, tapping at the window of the room where the dying lay. There are people who still feel uneasy when a bird taps at the window after dark, or gets into the house, and a few will not even have photographs of birds hanging on the walls, perhaps because of these unlucky associations.

Belief in the *teulu (teulu Gwyn ap Nudd)* was a common thing. There was heard the sound of passing feet and horses' hooves and wheels churning past on their way to the cemetery, and anyone who happened to be in the way of the ghostly funeral procession was in danger of being crushed to death. These pagan beliefs coexisted alongside Christian practice, as if people had to explain their own daily struggles with nature and the capriciousness of fortune (sickness, lost harvests, death of children) in some ancient way that made more sense than the official Christian message of the Good and Just God, which they heard from the chapel pulpits.

Parry-Jones in his reminiscences of rural Pembrokeshire, tells of the recurrent dilemmas of farmers torn between their Christian duty, their pagan heritage and their economic necessities. An old farmer who decided to get his hay in on a Sunday during a very wet summer, brought down the wrath of Heaven in the form of a violent thunderstorm. At first he laughed and shouted to his helpers that he was not superstitious, and to get on with the job, but in the end he had to give in to their fears, as the thunder and lightning grew worse. '*Rhown y gore iddi, fechgyn. Mae Hi wedi'n gweld ni*'—'Give it up, boys. She has seen us'.[5] Although God is always He, according to conservative Welshmen, it seems that in a few rural parts there remain reminders of the pagan Celtic goddesses who once presided over fertility and harvesting, and these have been absorbed into the Christian idea of the Deity.

There are traces again of old pagan Celtic beliefs in the meaning of the gift in traditional rural communities, and this still operates in many places. The gift sets in motion a cycle of obligations which includes an instinct for reciprocity which is neither too mean or too generous, but matched to one's material circumstances. It connects and sustains members of tribe or community.

The gift can take many forms in Celtic tradition. Banquets were perhaps the ultimate in generosity, setting up a widespread network of mutual obligations between host and guests. Thus it was the height of treachery to kill or injure anyone who sat down to table with you and shared your food and drink. Hospitality remained a sacred obligation as long as the traditional communities lasted. A traveller could not be turned away without a meal and a rest, but the obligation on him or her was to tell news and stories from other places, as a return gift. Elements of this remain amid cultural tensions.

Fostering children was another form of the gift. It you gave a child to be brought up among kin or allies, you were extending your network of kith and kin beyond the immediate household and strengthening the community connections, since foster children formed strong bonds with their 'out' families, as well as providing an extra pair of hands. A diluted form of fostering the children of kin seems to have gone on in Cwmrheidol till the end of the last century. Many families brought up the child of a sister or a daughter or a cousin, although they had plenty of their own children. It seems that there were financial reasons, where the blood parents were in difficulty and could not keep the child, or the fostering parents needed more help to run their little farms, if the father was working in the mines. But even so, the frequency of sending children to kin for bringing up does suggest echoes of tribal child gift, with all its advantages for knitting together extended communities, through a net of obligations.

There is another practice which irresistibly reminds us of the ancient significance of the hoard in Celtic custom. Why do old farmers still hoard money about the place, when inflation is constantly eroding its value and they could be earning good interest in bank or building society? Well, it is an ancient practice to bury treasure for safekeeping, and valuable pre-historic hoards of coins and torques and weapons have been excavated. But caches of treasure were also buried on the boundaries of fields to ensure fertile fields and healthy herds and children. The idea of a fortune meant until recently much more than money. It meant a providential prosperity, bringing health and good returns on you land and good alliances. The hoard was a magical investment, not just a safekeeping. It went too with the idea of sacrificing present riches for future benefit, and perhaps that struck a chord with ideas of Christian sacrifice as well.

Water divining

In our valley the public water supply stops a mile beyond the power station, and the dozen houses in the upper cwm all have their own private supplies. These old wells and springs occasionally give signs of changing their course, or drying up in droughts, or losing themselves through archaic collecting tanks which leak away half the water. If that happens you call George who lives lower down the valley. George is not only an engineer who designs water filters in his converted parlour-workship, but a gifted water diviner as well. It is as if he manages to combine the old wisdom with the new technology, which is a rare combination these days. I asked him could he explain these things, and he laughed and said:

'Nobody can explain these things exactly, in proper engineering jargon, can they? I saw this programme on the telly recently about water divining. There was a fellow who found water underground and could even say how deep they would have to dig and approximately what the flow would be. The BBC went back to check it out, and found he was dead accurate. I do my bit in these parts to find water for folks like yourselves and the young ones rebuilding Caegynon, and I'm thinking of going off the mains myself and using my own spring . . . but I can't explain it either. That worries me, for I've been an engineer all my life and my job is to analyse how things work and find good logical answers to practical problems. That's OK most of the time, whether I'm designing a water filter in my workshop, or doing something silly—like the time the train driver on the Rheidol line going past my house had his glasses whipped off by an overhanging branch. I sat down and worked out where they would have landed according to the speed the train was going at, the wind force and the likely angle of trajectory . . . Yes, I was lucky, he found them just where I said . . .

'But I'll tell you a strange thing that happened to me recently. I was helping someone with a problem she had designing a moving water sculpture which had to be self-perpetuating. I sat at the table for a while, not getting the answer, so I was fed-up and went to bed at around midnight. The next morning I woke with a splitting headache, and I'd scribbled a note with some calculations on it in my sleep. I had the answer. All I had to do was go to my workshop and it was dead easy to make—a seesaw with a point of rest kind of thing, basically a metal tube with a central stopper, no problem, because I just *knew* how it should go, without knowing how I knew. What I'm saying is, there are times when you have to be able to tap into some deeper energy that's been around since the world began. Sometimes the harder you try the worse you do, because you're all will-power. Reason is not enough, and if that sounds cranky, well, so was Archimedes when he got his inspiration. You can't pin down butterflies without killing them.'

There is a Welsh saying which expresses much the same truths: '*Mae'r tegell yn dal i ferwi, ond does dim llawer yn gallu ei glywed yn canu*',[6] the kettle goes on boiling, but few can hear it singing. Perhaps too many are trapped in the Bacon-Cartesian paradigm: 'I think, therefore I am', and 'I know more and more about less and less, for I have done the research according to the scientific method'.

Revivals in alternative healing

If you go into the wholefood shop in Aberystwyth you will find there is a large noticeboard covered with PR for alternative therapies being practised in the area. It indicates the growing surge of interest in holistic treatment for physical and psychological ills.

'Headaches? Try my lavender sleep pillow.'

'Holistic healing—Energy balancing—Intuitive Massage. Works on the whole person at different levels. Helps to balance a person's energy, gives a feeling of well-being. Releases tension, brings relaxation, improves circulation and helps to contact the healing process going on within you.'

'Aromatherapy at Body Natural. Relaxing theraputic massage with essential oils, for the relief of minor body ailments and the treatment of stress. Oils are chosen carefully to suit a person's own personality and individual needs.'

'Shiatsu is used to rejuvenate the mind and body by stimulating points along the meridian—to rebalance the body's energies.'

'Body Natural. Dietary consultations and Way of Life suggestions based on oriental medicine.'

Most of those offering holistic treatments are English incomers, though there is a growing Welsh indigenous presence in this field, albeit a small one as yet in Mid-Wales. But down in Gwent Francis P. Xavier runs a healing centre called 'Iachaol', based on 'the revived ancient Celtic healing art of Iachaol which uses the natural healing power of the body to heal itself; physically, mentally and emotionally'.[7] His logo is the Celtic cross from early Christianity, the wheel cross, which many argue represents not just the crucifixion but the pre-Christian solar wheel adapted to represent the divine light of the Trinity. This makes it acceptable to the post-Christian New Age healers who dislike the emphasis of sin and suffering in mainstream Christianity.

In Ceredigion today it is still possible to come across healers in the indigenous Welsh tradition, the *dyn hysbys* or shaman, who continue the old ways. There is such a healer in one of the villages to the north of Aberystwyth, who practises the ancient healing art of 'measuring the woollen threads', as a means of alleviating depression and stress. The woollen thread is stretched from elbow to middle finger. The principle is that it shortens according to the seriousness of the illness, and only when it has stretched out to its original length is the patient fully cured, thanks to the concentrated attentions of the *dyn hysbys*, who channels the individual sufferer's own healing energies in the right path.

In upper Cwmrheidol in the last century there lived a wise woman called Elinor Mason (1840-1924) who collected and grew her own herbal remedies. Her home was in the remote upper meadow in either Dôl or Dolpelyd, which lie in ruins today, and her grave is in Ystumtuen churchyard. According to the tradition that has been handed down in her family (her great granddaughter has recently come back to the valley and has bought the site of the old house in the meadow) she was a herbalist, midwife, and layer-out of bodies. Her healing fame was such that local people who had emigrated to America still wrote to her to ask her advice and remedies for the treatment of various diseases. Her healing remedies were derived from the classic herbalists, like Culpeper, translated into Welsh. Her great granddaughter Mari Morgan still possesses a copy of her book of remedies.

Further south near Llandovery were the most famous early healers in the Welsh herbal tradition. The physicians of Myddfai were said to have got their healing lore from the Lady of Llyn y Fan. This Otherworld woman fell in love with a human and bore sons, but eventually left him after he had given her the three undeserved blows which offended against the Otherworld truth of paradox. She burst into tears at a merry wedding; she laughed out loud at a gloom-stricken funeral; and she refused, finally, to fetch his horse from the field for him, after he in courteous duty had fetched her gloves from the house for her. The Lady disappeared back into the lake, only appearing once again to hand on to her son Rhiwallen a bag of medical remedies to relieve the ills of mankind—a nice reversal of the Pandora's box myth. She showed him the healing plants growing in a nearby dingle, and left for ever. The foundation for holistic healing in Wales was this combination of natural remedies combined with the concept of the medieval temperaments (the 'sanguineous', choleric, phlegmatic and melancholic) which took account of individual differences in patients.

To the modern sufferer accustomed to neat chemical pills, many of the remedies of the Physicians of Myddfai seem to make excessive use of mucky poultices and human urine concoctions. Yet on fairer inspection there emerge a number of parallels with modern holistic treatment. There is the idea of preventive medicine—you drank a potion of rue and mead during dangerous epidemics. There is a recipe for 'strengthening

315

the brain' which sounds remarkably like some New Age approaches to reducing modern stress, with its undertones of aromatherapy and relaxation techniques and the right musical rhythms:

> Smelling musk and camomile, drinking wine moderately, eating the leaves of sage frequently, keeping the head warm, washing the hands often, walking moderately, listening frequently to a little music and singing, smelling red roses, washing the eyebrows with rose water, drinking water in going to sleep, reading a little before sleeping, and light diet. [8]

There are similarities between old and new, too, in the assumption that you need to develop insights into your own constitution, because the right remedy has to be linked with the individual characteristics. The qualities of the healer would not come amiss today in training either orthodox or alternative physicians. The Physicians of Myddfai insisted that he or she must be skilled in herbal lore and plant recognition, of course, but it was equally vital to be a virtuous person who cultivates a wide range of learning and spiritual excellence, so that no native or foreigner, friend or foe, will have any hesitation in asking for their help. Like the new wave of alternative healers in rural Wales today, the traditional healers had some access to eastern approaches, with their concern to balance the yin and the yang, and to restore a patient's inner energies to balance and harmony. He or she was expected to be 'cunning' in the ways of past masters, whether written in the *Cymraeg*, the Latin or the Arabic.

Today in this part of rural Wales, the increasing numbers of alternative holistic healers draw on the Welsh indigenous tradition, the native American tradition, and the more modern principles of homeopathy. Here is the story of one of these modern healers, who practices in Aberystwyth and lives in Capel Bangor.

Hilaire Wood, homeopathic healer

I come from a medical family—father and grandfather were doctors, and mother and grandmother were nurses—so I never questioned orthodox medicine while I was growing up. But I'd had polio when I was two, and in the mid 1970s when I was living in London I began to have problems with my knee, and went though a horrible experience in the Royal Free Hospital. They exhibited me as a case in front of a lot of medical students, and told me ''Your knee's just going to wear out. Prepare for a wheelchair and in the meantime here are some painkillers.'' I felt it was a purely physical approach, and took no account of my own will or energy. So the strong criticism I have of orthodox medicine is that it encourages you to give up, accept the drugs and mechnical aids, whatever the quality of your life. There is no tapping into people's own healing resources.

'I went to an osteopath who made a lot more sense. My body had got out of balance and so my knee joint was playing up. He gave me exercises and said I should do as much as possible (by contrast with the straight treatment of doing as little as possible, having splints and taking painkillers). The osteopath's optimism was important as well, and the treatment was an integrating experience which allowed me to go on and live my life—and that was specially important then because I was moving to Wales.

'Fifteen years on, I have had a good run, and it was the beginning therefore of trust that there was another way of healing. It had been important for my son Jamie as well, because when he was a baby he had earaches and I didn't like him having antibiotics all the time. I met someone who treated his child with herbal remedies (rosemary for fever) and I learned there was another way.

'I came to Wales to do a Postgraduate Library Diploma, and it was quite by chance that one day in the Quarry Shop Cafe in Machynlleth I saw a notice about weekend courses in homeopathy in the Happy Valley near Tywyn. I went along and everything fell into place, because it was a farmhouse and I was able to bring Jamie along to be with the other children there. I was hooked by the philosophy and have never looked back. One of the main things was looking beyond the specific and the material symptoms, so that if you have what allopaths diagnose as liver infection, you see the liver as a part of your whole self, physical, spiritual and mental. That is true holism. It all came together for me, and a spiritual dimension really came into my life through homeopathy.

'Homeopathy is a dynamic energy medicine. In a physical sense, after a low dosage, there is no trace of the substance left, so it is considered ridiculous by straight medicine. Yet healing results, so to me healing happens in a world beyond the merely physical, and it involves healer and patient. When I'm working it's almost as though I and my problems take a back place, and I see things on a different plane. You're there to understand their problem, but you get insights into yourself too.

'From that first course I went on to take a full course in the first College of Homeopathy to be set up (in London). Strangely there is no College yet in Wales, though hundreds have been set up since the 1970s. Yet homeopathy resonates with a lot of people in Wales, because there is a strong indigenous tradition of going to a wisewoman or a healer in the community. But it is as if the two ends are not quite meeting yet—the Welsh tradition and the new tradition, because there are very few Welsh-speaking practitioners as yet, though quite a few patients.

'In homeopathy illness does not arise on the medical plane, but on the dynamic plane, so the stimulus is to correct the imbalance. It's an oriental approach to work on correcting the balance, bringing the sufferer back into harmony, and bringing into play the healing energies of the patient and of the healer. The catalyst is the homeopathic remedy. In healing the catalyst is the healer's energy. I get a cross section of illnesses from eczema to depression, and I take a psychological approach (some homeopathic healers go more for physical symptoms). I get a lot of children and babies, which is good, for children's energies are fresher and sounder than grown-ups' and they respond very well. Whereas people of 50, say, can be ingrained in their ways and it takes longer to correct the imbalance. Healing work has its own time and its own organic growth, so it may take a long time to reactivate the energies and organise someone back into a healthy pattern. You get people who can't get any help from the orthodox medical system because they've been given up. Or people who don't like the system and can now come out with their dissatisfaction, or know there are alternatives, whereas ten years ago the atmosphere was less encouraging and people hesitated. Indeed homeopathy is getting to be widely used now by a number of vets as well, because of the work of George McLeod and Christopher Day. There is someone over Newtown way who treats animals with homeopathy, and also someone over Carmarthen way. A TV programme called QED a couple of years back was very positive about homeopathic treatment for animals. It included satisfied farmers who had homeopathic remedies put in their cattle's drinking water to prevent mastitis, and that was saving them a lot of money—but it was controversial in homeopathic circles, because if you treat the part and not the whole, it can suppress the illness but that may be a short term gain because symptoms are a safety valve and the body may find other ways of expressing its problems.

'If you have a mother with mastitis and you clear up the breast inflammation the mother might develop other symptoms like depression, because it's possible her mastitis might be a protection against further draining of her energies through breast feeding. So you have to treat the mother as a whole person and consider her situation. A lot of patients have taught me about how illness—even cancer—can force people to re-evaluate their lives, and give them a chance to improve the quality of their life, which can itself be a healing thing. Cancer for instance has a lot to do with life not being lived—the cancer cells are cells in a state of anarchy which is sometimes rebellion at life not being lived. It has happened that a business man who only lives for his business gets cancer and is forced to give up work to spend his last six months doing something he always longed to do—and finds himself cured.

'Everyone practising homeopathy pursues their own pathway. Some people have quite a clinical, intellectual approach, and others use a more psychological approach. Over the last two years I have reacted against my earlier intellectual approach, which had gone too far in that direction, and so wasn't earthed for me. There is an intellectual strand (as done by Samuel Hahneman one of the influential founders) but the beginnings were empirical. *Cinchona*, the bark of an Andean tree, gave him malarial symptoms, but he discovered it was also the basis for the

319

quinine cure for malaria. He tested this on family and followers and observed the results in order to develop homeopathic principles.

'I have done some work recently with native American Medicine Wheel in the Tregaron area, where an American woman of half Native American ancestry runs workshops every summer on the native American approaches to healing. My experience of this has been very powerful, very earthy and very grounding—in the natural world of rocks and trees and animals. The sweat lodge in this tradition is associated with cleansing and healing, and it is like going into the womb for another birthing. There is too the idea that everything has its own vibrations, so you can use drumming in healing—if someone's rhythms go out of balance you can use drumming rhythms to bring them back into balance. Sound therefore is another dimension to use.

'I found the native American tradition of healing very reviving and full of wisdom, but they are not my traditions, so at the beginning of 1992 I joined a Druid order. A lot of druidical healing work has been handed down from fragments in the Celtic tradition. So I'm currently doing a three year course (partly by post, partly by going on workshops) which is taking me through the Bardic Grade (first year, focussing on creative expression); the Ovate Grade (second year, focussing on healing and divination); and the Druid Grade (third year, on philosophy and counselling). It is my attempt to find a balance, and it has been nice because I am reading and writing poetry again as I once did, until my creativity all went into homeopathy, and the balance is being restored . . .

'There are problems and new beginnings. Druidry seems to have been rather patriarchal up till now, but Philip and Stephanie are redressing the balance and bringing the female element back in. On the creativity side, I want to grow my own plants and be able to recognise healing plants for myself. Up till now I have been getting my homeopathic supplies from the chemist, but it would be more satisfying to grow them . . . The latest development is that six of us in the alternative healing tradition have just set up a new Centre in Baker Street Aberystwyth, which is offering psychotheraphy, healing massage, osteopathy and homeopathy. Ten years ago some of us tried to develop a healing centre in the Barn

Centre, but the time was not ripe. Now I think people are more receptive and open to alternative healing approaches . . .'

The old magic in the modern cult of horror

The latest use of the old magic is to be found in two recent novels set in rural Wales, which focus on community tensions between English incomers and local Welsh-speaking communities, but develop their plots by taking the more sinister elements of folklore 'over the top', to appeal to modern devotees of the horror cult. One is by the Welsh-language novelist Islwyn Ffowc Elis, and the other by an English-incomer journalist, Phil Rickman.

In *Y gromlech yn yr haidd, The cromlech in the barley*, Ffowc Elis presents us with Henderson, an English-incomer farmer determined to get rid of the prehistoric standing stones which impede the efficiency of his mechanised hay harvesting. His old Welsh neighbour warns him against such sacrilege, recalling that a previous owner who used a bit of the stones for a gate post was punished by sudden death. 'A heart attack', shrugs Henderson, deriding the old customs with the retort that 'Stone is stone. That's all. Only stone . . . Keep your primitive taboos to yourself, man.' But to the Welsh locals Henderson is '*yn beiriant o ddyn sy'n tynnu hanes i fyny o'r gwraidd*', a machine man who pulls history up by the roots, and deserves the punishment coming to him. As the first of the three 3,500 year old standing stones is dragged from its resting place, his wife slips in the dairy and has a miscarriage, so Henderson loses the son he was hoping for, to help on the farm. The local ancients are not surprised, for they do not subscribe to scholarly attempts to explain away the supernatural as an illusion caused by individuals' ignorance or madness. Benni Rees indeed concludes that it is the rationalists who are ignorant of true ways of seeing:

Y peth hawsa'n y byd ydy lapio tipyn o wybodaeth newydd mewn parsel a tharo label arno a dweud, 'Dyna fo ichi, bobol: y gwir, yr holl wir a dim ond y gwir . . .' Pe cawn i'r cyfle mi ddweudwn i wrth bob gwyddonydd a seicolegydd smyg, 'There are more things in heaven and earth, Horatio, than are dreamt of in your philosophy.'[10]

321

The easiest thing in the world is to wrap up a bit of new knowledge in a parcel and stick a label on it and say, 'There you are, people: the truth, the whole truth and nothing but the truth . . .' If I had the chance I would say to every smug scientist and psychologist, 'There are more things in heaven and earth, Horatio, than are dreamt of in your philosophy'.

But English-incomer Henderson is clearly not a devotee of his national bard, and, having been a sapper in the British army, persists in blowing up the two remaining prehistoric stones himself, after the local JCB contractors have had cold feet and refused to go on. With the demolition of the second stone, his cattle get foot and mouth disease, and after the third, he loses his reason and is possessed by the spirit of an Iron Age being, whose burial place he has disturbed. It is all over with rational man, and *Hendre* is once again on the market, to be reclaimed for the *Cymry Cymraeg*, or to fall into the hands of another English incomer? 'Someone with a bit more respect for its past', it is hoped.

The final say goes to Benni Rees: 'He was lucky to escape with his life. The cromlech was very merciful'.

In Phil Rickman's *Candlenight*[11] affluent English incomers who dilute the fragile Welsh-language culture in the close-knit rural community of Y Groes die horrible deaths one after another. First they see the cold blue flame of the *cannwyll gorff*, the corpse candle, dancing weirdly before their eyes. They smell the stench of decay and hear the ghastly bird of death tapping at their window pane, or glimpse the *toili*, the ghostly funeral procession that crushes whoever encounters it. Finally they are destroyed by the fierce forces of the *hen ofergoelion*, the old dark forces, for 'What else in Wales is truly powerful these days, other than our traditions?', as one of the community spokespersons asks.

There are concessions to rationalism in that many of the victims die of conventional diseases, leukaemia or heart attacks or tumours or accidents, but these result from defence mechanisms destroyed by the dark forces around them, and they succumb to the irresistible power of the 'old things', the old Welsh things which are threatened by the mass influx of English into rural Wales. Y Groes is, after all, the final resting

322

place of Owain Glyndŵr, in this novel, and the local community leaders are the direct descendants of the four medieval stalwarts who brought his body back here and have been under his psychic protection ever since the fourteenth century. Even the local vicar, Elias ap Siencyn, is no ordinary Christian cleric, but a *dyn hysbys*, a shaman with supernatural powers, whose rectory lies thickly embowered in a druidical oak wood, and who presides over the *Gorsedd Ddu*, the Dark Magicians who are the timeless servants of Owain Glyndŵr, and guard the old traditions.

As in *Y gromlech yn yr haidd*, there are characters voicing the social tensions underlying the community conflict. To some English the locals are 'these tiresome people with their impenetrable language', and the local 'witch' Bronwen Dafis, is 'a withered crone who dispensed herbal remedies and told fortunes', and brings up her grandchild in those *hen ofergoelion*, old ways, which are the community's last defences against invasion and extinction of their culture, but seen by outsiders as 'legends. Folklore. Country bullshit, right?'

One difference between the two novels is that *Candlenight*, though at first sight more melodramatic and painted on a truly vivid supernatural canvas, does have one or two characters who try to bridge the stereotypes of local and incomer fanatics. The Welsh school teacher Bethan who has been away and come back again to her Welsh-speaking culture, says in protest against her *Gorsedd Ddu* co-teacher's methods: 'I don't believe that little children should see the woods not as the home of squirrels and somewhere to collect nuts and acorns, but as the place where the *Gorsedd Ddu* hold their rituals. I don't believe that when they hear the thunder they should think it's the sound of Owain Glyndŵr rolling around in his grave . . . or the hounds of Annwn gathering for the hunt . . .' Bethan puts the case for rationalism, but only so far and no further, as when she realises that she has been impregnated by the *tylwyth teg*, the local fairies who ensure that the dark defensive forces are transmitted to future generations, and decides to have an abortion in South Wales!

Neither novel holds out much hope for a resolution of community conflict between incomers and locals, since they make powerful cases for the irrational emotional forces that underlie the would-be rational attitudes of both sides in the conflict. The last word however should be about the conciliatory act of Owain Glyndŵr's ghost towards the end of *Candlenight*. Having been ousted from his tomb in the church of Y Groes, he appears as a benign hooded figure and performs a humane miracle, by bringing back to life the beautiful English visitor Miranda, who has been having a brief affair with the local Plaid Cymru candidate Guto! Perhaps there is hope after all, if the old magic can be made new in the cause of modest reconciliations.

[1] Edmund Jones, *A geographical, historical and religious account of the parish of Aberstrwyth in the County of Monmouth*, Trevecka, 1779.

[2] D. J. Evans, *Hanes Capel Seion*, Aberystwyth, Cambrian News, [1935], p. 133.

[3] J. Henry Griffiths, *Bro annwyl y bryniau*, Aberystwyth, Cymdeithas Lyfrau Ceredigion, 1988.

[4] D. J. Evans (as above).

[5] D. Parry-Jones, *Welsh country characters*, London, Batsford, 1952, p. 174.

[6] Ifan Gruffydd, *Gŵr o Baradwys*, Dinbych, Gwasg Gee, 1963.

[7] *Directory of New Age services, Chalice* 3, Spring/Summer 1992.

[8] Physicians of Myddfai, *Herbal remedies*, Felinfach, Dyfed, Llanerch, 1988, p. 63.

[9] Physicians of Myddfai (as above).

[10] Islwyn Ffowc Elis, *Y gromlech yn yr haidd*, Llandysul, Gomer, 1970, p. 53.

[11] Phil Rickman, *Candlenight*, London, Duckworth, 1991.

CHAPTER 14

Bridges between Them and Us: voices of the future

'It's a shock to find that even when the Welsh and the English speak the same language, we do not mean the same things.'

'It's a shock to find that though you are not leaving your culture, your culture is leaving you.'

The discovery of a different language and culture can be a traumatic experience for English incomers to rural Wales, and their responses are often emotional beneath a surface rationality. The problem for Welsh-speaking Wales is equally traumatic, as they see their fragile cultural heartlands overwhelmed by such a flow of incomers that absorption becomes impossible and Englishness dominates, whether the newcomers join existing local activities or practice a kind of cultural apartheid. How then do you build bridges between Them and Us, so that the different communities who share the same locality can stop stereotyping one another and begin a dialogue about sharing a common future? At one extreme that would defuse Meibion Glyndŵr's arson attacks on English owned houses and businesses. At another extreme it would de-ghettoise the many incomers who never get to know any Welsh people beyond the formal courtesies of daily greetings. Between these two extremes are the many ordinary people who have a more important role to play in their communities than perhaps they realise, for bridge building has to be interwoven with everyday lives at a grass roots level, rather than left to political parties or public bodies.

At the level of political party policy Plaid Cymru, the Party of Wales, sees itself as hospitable to people who come and settle in Wales, provided they are aware of the different culture and community which they are joining. The former party leader Dafydd Elis Thomas made it clear that the party welcomes 'refugees from Thatcherism ... who come with skills to offer and a contribution to make to the community'. But he added that 'some people think they are still in the South East of England and want to bring it with them. It is important that people who do come here really want this part of the world to make a go of it'. But some incomers as well as some Welsh people continue to associate Plaid Cymru with an outdated nationalism which excludes rather than includes, is divisive rather than unifying of the different peoples who live in the same place and want to make a contribution to the economic and cultural diversity of that place. And Plaid Cymru can be carelessly associated in the popular mind with nationalists like the Covenanters who insists on 'Wales for the Welsh', and sound perilously close to the 'ethnic cleansing' policies which can escalate into racial hatred of the kind that is tearing Yugoslavia apart. This continues, even though the party has moved in recent years towards a Greener, more inclusive community stance.

Thatcherite and Majorite conservatism proposes its own form of *English* nationalism, in which the sense of identity rests on a monolithic identity, a British way of life, whose validity is determined at the English core, and excludes the peripheries of Scotland, Wales and Northern Ireland when these countries try to express their own distinctiveness. In this attitude British Conservatism is out of line with other EC nation states who have seen no difficulty in devolving democracy to regional governments within their states. However the Tories have given Wales, via the Welsh Office, a national curriculum in its schools which recognises the significance of the Welsh language and Welsh history for the children of Wales. And yet, as Ioan Bowen Rees points out, 'However heroically they may hide the fact from their patients, clients and pupils, the professionals in most of the Welsh public services today feel frustrated to the point of demoralisation by the sheer ignorance and impatience which has characterised so much government policy-making' under the Tories.[1] It is Welsh community values that are threatened under this regime, for it is undermining 'our deep attachment to state education, health and social services, and to genuine

326

democracy'. What is going to happen to the family business or the family farm, rural transport and the environment under the relentless rule of the market? These are as much the components of rural communities as the much-quoted linguistic and cultural factors of Welsh 'nationalism'.

The Labour Party is desperately seeking a new role for itself during its long years in the political wilderness, and could have challenged the Tories' monolithic view of British nationalism, by giving a voice to communities of place and a healthy cultural diversity. But they too fear archaic views of 'nationalism' or simply see peripheral national identities as a threat to their own power bases in Scotland and Wales, so they are likely to continue down the road of a very muted neo-Liberalism that pays lip service to cultural diversity and democratic devolution, but keeps postponing the action needed for an authentic communitarianism.

At the general election of 1992, the constituency of Ceredigion and North Pembrokeshire returned a Plaid Cymru/Green Party MP, Cynog Dafis, and made political history by ending an era of Liberalism rooted in Welshness which had a long and proud tradition in rural Wales, and by giving Britain its first Green MP. This was the beginning of a new kind of bridge building, because it united Green incomers and a progressive nationalism in the hope of linking local issues with global concerns, and fostering a cultural diversity rooted in the common ground of community and a sense of place—this distinctive place of rural west Wales.

Voices of the Future 1,—Cynog Dafis MP

At the opening meeting of the 1992 general election campaign, the Plaid Cymru/Green candidate Cynog Dafis shared a platform with Jonathon Porritt, and explained how he personally had come to be convinced of the compatibility between the two parties:

'I have been a member of Plaid Cymru since I was 16 years old. I was brought up to value and assert Welshness, and became increasingly fascinated by the endless variety and richness of the Welsh cultural tradition (using cultural in its broadest sense), and inspired by the idea of

327

this finding expression in a self-governing Wales taking its place in the modern world. Having said that, being involved in the Welsh national movement throughout the sixties gave me an overwhelming sense of swimming against the tide of history (in spite of the flowering of protest and the first great political breakthrough of those years). Wasn't the modern world all about centralisation, transnational companies, ever larger units of economic production and political organisations, and cultural homogenisation . . .?

'Then from the early 70s, and only if you listened to the right voices, the whole picture began to change. First Frank Fraser Darling's remarkable Reith Lectures, then *Blueprint for Survival*, the Club of Rome report, Barbara Ward's *Only One World*, the Ecologist magazine and the founding of the Ecology Party—they were all saying that the economic-industrial machine, the triumph of the modern world, was unsustainable. The profligate consumption of the earth's resources, the accompanying pollution of land, sea and air, the assumption that material improvement must be based on constant and unending growth in production and consumption, and that somehow the natural environment had the capacity endlessly both to provide and to absorb— these, it was now being said, could not but lead to social and environmental crisis, or at the very least to making the world an infinitely less hospitable place for our children and grandchildren. And what kind of parents are they who steal from their own children!

'Significant to me, and right at the heart of the changes that must be brought about to avert that crisis, was the need for radical decentralisation—social, political and economic—alongside overall global coordination of key policy areas . . .

'Apart from being totally convinced by the analysis presented by the Ecologists (later renamed the Greens), it struck me that here was a broad context within which Plaid Cymru's ideas about small nations run on democratic decentralist lines within a framework of international cooperation and peace, made complete sense. And as soon as one saw that, one could also dare to say that it was only within such a context—a

Green world—that there was room for such small nations and minority cultures to survive and flourish . . .

'What this cooperation is enabling us to do is to campaign energetically (the Greens and Plaid Cymru) on the needs of Wales without neglecting the enormous world-wide questions which are being pushed to the fringes in this campaign . . . the Earth Summit on the Environment and Development, which has named 50 major causes of concern in the "serious degradation of life-sustaining systems in the world" . . . We are emphasising that they be solved in a way which enables the poorer countries of the world to enjoy sustainable development, freedom from poverty and fairness in their relations with the developed world . . .

'There is no conflict between what I have just said and the need to campaign for a democratic Wales, an elected senate, and direct access to the institutions of the European Community . . . The lack of a Welsh assembly means that our farmers are poorly represented in Brussels, that we have had to suffer the poll tax, that local government is undermined, and there is chaos in our education system, and a weakened health service. Of course decentralisation is not just about a parliament for Wales. The Plaid Cymru/Green campaign is committed to democratic empowerment through revitalised local councils, including community councils. But we do see it as playing a key role, not just as an expression of Welsh nationality, but as a means of enabling us to implement the development policies we need in Wales. And here again the Welsh and Green perspectives come together. Perhaps the most thrilling thing about the cooperation here in Ceredigion has been the way it has generated ideas and policies, and resulted in campaign documents—on Young Farmers, Small businesses, Alternative Energy, Coastal pollution, Woodland development—and Housing in the pipeline. . . The combination of ideas enables us to create a voting coalition capable of creating *change* . . . a coalition of people with differing but compatible priorities.

'Generally speaking three cultural-linguistic groups make up the electorate, Welsh-speaking Welsh people, non Welsh-speaking Welsh people, people who have moved into Wales, mainly but by no means entirely English. But wait a minute, there's a fourth—immigrants to Wales, mainly English, who have learnt Welsh. A new Wales, a meaningful Wales, must be constructed from these different elements, and their coming together must be a creative process, though it may not always be easy . . .'

At another speech in Felinfach, Dyfed, Cynog Dafis defined the kind of community which the Plaid/Green campaign was aiming at—it should be a society that is sustainable culturally, economically and ecologically; be just and egalitarian on the basis of mutual responsibility and obligation; and have a strong but tolerant sense of identity shaped by its own citizens . . .

'The search for common ground between the Green Party and Plaid Cymru is a hopeful new beginning in building bridges between the Welsh culture and incomers, but it is not without problems. On the Welsh side there is a suspicion that the Greens are more concerned with the conservation of scenery and wildlife than with the equally threatened Welsh-speaking culture. Earth-friendly economic policies are dubiously regarded by the traditional farming community who have survived with the help of subsidies and chemical fertilisers, both of which are now under attack, leaving them in crisis. Ceredigion Greens are supportive of the local culture and many of them make an effort to learn the language, but they often live their lives in incomer circles and are active in environmental groups like Friends of the Earth which have not as yet attracted the local Welsh in significant numbers. Nonetheless a dialogue of a hopeful new kind has begun which could suggest new ways forward for rural Wales beyond the tramline thinking of multinational economic development.

'The other half of the "incomer problem" is the exodus of native Welsh from rural communities in the search for jobs. But conventional economics has not fully solved the problem by setting up advance factories and trying to attract high technology businesses from outside, for these often provide more jobs for highly trained incomers than for locals, and so dilute communities even more. There is also a disproportionately small number of local people on enterprise training schemes, or taking up enterprise grants. This is being taken up by *Menter a Busnes*, founded in the late 1980s to encourage more Welsh speakers to take business initiatives and wean them from the dependence mentality which subsidy farming has incidentally caused. As early as the middle ages Giraldus Cambrensis observed in his usual caustic way that the Welsh were more noted for their creative imaginings and *hiraeth* or romantic longings, than for their executive abilities. But perhaps a Schumacherian small-is-beautiful locally-based business ethos would prove more acceptable to them, and that is one of the ongoing projects of the Ceredigion Plaid Cymru/Green programme—to develop small businesses which use local products, employ local people, and find local (as well as external) markets for value-added farm or forestry products, for example. There are already successful models for this approach, like Rachel's Dairy Produce at Borth, where the Rowlands family has developed a profitable organic dairy produce business on their family farm; or *Pren* wood products developed by incomer Rob Osborne at Bronant, which uses ecological woodland management to provide a whole range of forest products like garden furniture of Welsh oak, and native oak shelving for Rhiannon's craft shop in Tregaron (itself a successful community business where Rhiannon designs exquisite Celtic jewellery in silver and gold for the local trade and for world-wide export). Such small businesses have a vital role in community bridge building, for they encourage enterprise in rural communities; are connecting links between their employees and between themselves and their customers; and build informal communications networks which keep adding new links to the chain of producers/processors/customers.

'On the housing front there is a serious need for better understanding too, for, though poverty and homelessness are not nearly so visible in rural areas as they are in cities, they are there and growing steadily worse, as first time buyers cannot afford even the cheapest property to come on the market, and there is no longer enough council housing left to provide for other than urgent priorities like one parent families. The housing associations under the umbrella of *Tai Cymru* struggle on to fill the gap, but their resources are always inadequate, and many poor people

331

are thrown on the mercy of the private landlords, who have the advantage that the Aberystwyth area is a university town and then a holiday resort when the students have gone down, so the market dictates surprisingly high rents. The responses to these problems have included the launching of the '*Nid yw Cymru ar werth*', Wales is not for Sale, campaign in the 1980s, and more recently demands for a *Deddf Eiddo Nawr*, a Property Act Now, which would somehow ensure first time local buyers a toe-hold in the property market, or establish a quota for the proportion of holiday homes in a particular community. It is not very clear how a Property Act would ever be feasible, however, when one gets down to the practical details. There are one or two awful stories told by Welsh-speaking Welsh about how, on principle, they sold houses to locals rather than incomers, but had to accept a lower price, and a few years later found the purchasers selling on the same house to incomers and making a packet. In any case few locals can afford such philanthropy, now that house prices are again falling. You take the highest bid, full stop.

'The problem was much aggravated by the property boom in the south-east of England in the late 1980s, which spread westwards inexorably till it hit west Wales in 1989. Until then you could sell a modest terrace house in the home counties and buy a detached Welsh country cottage with a bit of land, and still have money to live on for the first year or two, or to invest for unearned income. So local estate agents for a time were aiming their publicity at well-off incomers, and one or two even took their blurbs and photos of desirable Welsh country cottages to English cities like Chester—until *Meibion Glyndŵr* carried out arson attacks on their offices. Right thinking Welsh people condemned Meibion Glyndŵr for their violent tactics, but remained resentful of wealthy English buying up local farms, smallholdings, pubs and village stores. A letter to the *Cambrian News* in December 1988 put it like this:

> I do not believe that any good ever comes from an act of violence against property or person. Violence begets violence as surely as peace, understanding and justice beget their like ... [But] the smouldering resentment among ordinary Welshmen is growing into a hearty dislike of English

immigrants in general, and is fuelled by any actions or attitudes that are seen to be unfriendly, patronising, uncaring or ignorant.

The letter ended with a plea to all English incomers to take an interest in, and be sensitive to the Welsh culture in which they found themselves. In seeking a spirit of reconciliation the writer also begged Welsh men and women to do their bit, by guiding their new neighbours towards an understanding of Welsh history and life, and encouraging them to learn and to speak Welsh. For a start they could learn to pronounce their new address properly!'

Commonsense suggestions like these may sound obvious but are in fact rare and valuable because they bring bridgebuilding down to neighbourly level, and propose that locals and incomers each have initiatives to take in their own community's everyday life. This is a healthy antidote to the ideological racist cries which one sometimes comes across on both sides. Like Cith ap Henri (National Freedom Group) who insists on restoring Welshness by sweeping away (or at least denigrating) all forms of Englishness, including the English language. On the other side are the angry English parishioners of St Cadfan's Church, Tywyn, who tried to censure their vicar for racism when he gave his report on the state of the church roof and quipped, 'It's not the Welsh slate that's at fault—it's the English nails'. They claimed that 95% of the congregation were of English origin, and the roof was being repaired with mainly English money, so they called a special meeting of the church council to make the vicar apologise for his anti-English joke!

In 1988 a new movement, *PONT* (the Welsh for bridge), came into being with the specific purpose of building bridges between locals and incomers in all parts of Wales. It was the brain child of Dr Gwynfor Evans, who envisages it as a forum for incomers to understand and support 'the cultural, historical and linguistic heritage of the communities in which they have come to live'; and for indigenous Welsh people to explain their culture to newcomers and welcome them to become part of the local community rather then remaining uncomprehending or antagonistic. Both aims are important, for while many Welsh-speaking people agonise about their disappearing culture in Ceredigion, say, many newcomers suffer alienation and isolation which may end in flight or even suicide attempts, as the Samaritans or other counselling services know only too well.

PONT is a nationwide movement, with local branches which develop individual programmes according to the needs of their own areas. *PONT* Gwynedd produced a bilingual booklet for newcomers, *Getting to know Gwynedd*, which explains in outline the language situation, education policies, and the community heritage, and directs readers to useful sources for further information. *PONT* Gogledd Ceredigion runs monthly meetings on a whole range of themes, from 'Living with two languages', to Welsh poetry in English (with Gillian Clarke reading her own poems, many of which are rooted in her Welsh rural experiences). The meetings are held alternately in Welsh (with translating facilities) and English, and include convivial theatre trips to Welsh-medium drama and Christmas dinners in *Yr Hen Efail* (another fine example of a local enterprise which has bilingual menus, special Welsh dishes and a beautifully designed restaurant in a converted smithy at Furnace). Other *PONT* branches have emphasised family outings—walks and coach trips and carol singing to bring incomers and locals' whole families together. And there has been considerable cooperation in the Aberystwyth area with the University's Extramural Department, where Gerald Morgan has run winter courses on Welsh history and literature, and organised summer trips to go around historical places of interest like the Dysynni Valley. The Reverend Enid Morgan works in her own parish of Llanafan at similar bridge building work, by offering winter courses for church members who want to learn Welsh for use in her bilingual services. She approaches the problem from the other side too by working on translations from English into Welsh of inclusive language hymns and prayers, so that the Welsh-speaking culture is in touch with modern feminist theology.

There are clearly problems for any bridge building movements, whether church or secular. Mutuality has to be the keynote, so that incomers can make their distinctive contribution as well as finding out about the existing cultural situation; and locals can explain and convey their culture to incomers, without falling into anti-English clichés or clinging to a fixed rather than a dynamic definition of culture. It is a delicate tightrope to tread for both sides, but worth it, because each has something to offer that the other lacks. Incomers lack the local network of kith and kin, friends and neighbours rooted in a place, which locals can help them to overcome by offering a welcome in the community, and introducing them to local events. Incomers in turn who are seeking the benefits of a small community life style, may be able to offer energies and ideas which can be fed into building sustainable and supportive small communities. But is there room in traditional rural communities for an open dialogue about ecology, or community schools, or interfaith religion, which are just some of the issues incomers bring with them to their new homes? There are often problems of English incomers seeming to take over meetings with their confident fluency, and locals responding by retreating to secret cliques to try and keep things the same as they have always been. Them and Us stereotypes get a new lease of life, and people on both sides undoubtedly get a great deal of fun out of sticking labels on the alien Other, but none of that is going to save the culture or give rural Ceredigion a better future. And always the question of the language hovers uneasily over community meetings—if there are incomers who have not learned Welsh the whole meeting has to change to English and the language is threatened once again with decline and death. Neither Welsh Greens nor Plaid Cymru are likely to follow the example of Estonian Green Nationalists who in 1992 recommended that 'every applicant for Estonian citizenship (including the thousands of Russians resident there for decades) should be able to recite any 200 verse extract from the 19,000 verse national epic *Kalevipoeg*, a 13th century saga of the Viking era and the fight against the invasion of German crusaders'.[2] So the following extract about a 21st century Welsh Republic is only a Utopian fantasy by the writer Jan Morris. Her proposed Welsh immigration laws have entry quotas which take

335

account of profession, ethnic origin and age, and citizenship is dependent on a commitment to learn the Welsh language:

> The legislation called *Dewis Mawr*, the Great Choice, was promulgated at the time of independence, and decrees that those who declare themselves Welsh, and who are prepared to honour the Welsh language and culture, *are* Welsh. It has not, however, made for mass immigration. The language proviso is so demandingly enforced, by repeated examination, and the standard of living in Wales is relatively so simple, that the flow of settlers has long since dried up. [3]

Ultimately, however, in the communities of rural Wales, political parties and local societies and church groups can only be as effective as their individual members are at building bridges between neighbours and colleagues at work or in leisure. So what is it at the grass roots level that facilitates bridge building? Here are some local and incomer voices which may suggest models to follow, for each of them has genuinely listened to the Other and not evaded the issues of community tensions by retreating to his or her own ghetto's comfortable platitudes.

Voices of the Future, 2—'Jane Brown'

'I'm a community doctor in rural Wales, but I'm from North Staffs originally. When I first came here I had no idea I would settle down. It just happened to be the place where I got my first fully-fledged appointment in a family practice. I soon became aware that some of the people I was seeing expressed themselves a bit awkwardly in English, and I learned that Welsh was their first language. Well, I have always held very strong views about community medicine and the need for the doctor to fit in with the local community and be part of the local networks. So I felt I had to start learning Welsh, even though my time was limited. I didn't get very far with formal classes, but then one of my patients, a retired teacher who goes to the same church as me, offered to help. I can honestly say it changed my life. It wasn't just the language, it was the way she interwove it (and me) with the whole cultural thing and way of life and so on round here. I saw the world with different eyes, because I knew the significance of the history of the locality and the famous figures of the area, past and present, whom you would never hear of in the English-speaking world that occupies the same geographical space but is so very far removed . . .

'It's thanks to that retired teacher, now my friend, that I can stay on here and feel satisfied with my work. It's so important to me that a medical practice looks at the community context of the people's health. Communities as well as individuals can be sick or well, and I believe that there are connections between the two. I used to feel quite uneasy the first year I was here, without being able to put a finger on the problem. Now I can see it wasn't just my personal problem, feeling as if I wasn't fully part of what was going on—it was the community problem as well, the kind of splits you get when a little place with a homogeneous identity has to cope with a big influx of outsiders, a lot of them going on behaving as if they were still in the West Midlands or Manchester . . . or, alternatively, suffering from paranoia because every time they hear the Welsh language they think somebody must be saying something nasty about them . . .

'Now I understand a lot more about cultural health and community sickness than I ever did before I came to live here, and I tend to analyse it in a medical kind of way. It's no problem observing the symptoms and diagnosing the disease as a mild (but occasionally subject to severe outbursts) endemic form of cultural schizophrenia. The problem is finding ways of alleviating the symptoms since total cure is impossible given the circumstances. All I can suggest is that it's down to individuals in their own work and living to do the kind of things my retired teacher did for me—introducing newcomers into the culture—or what I try to do in my own community practice, where you have to have your patients' total trust if you're ever going to help them with the social context of their medical problems, like domestic violence, drunkenness and so on . . . You can only expect to win their total trust if they see you as part of their own community network . . . '

Voices of the Future, 3—Mrs M.G.

'We *need* incomers who have something to offer to the Welsh culture. They bring in fresh ideas and shake people out of their old-fashioned ways. There are some people in Ceredigion who never want anything to change. They think that you preserve things by putting them in a glass case to keep them safe from nasty outside influences. But there have always been outsiders coming into Wales and giving the *Cymry Cymraeg* a bit of a jolt forward. Or else people of Welsh family, like Saunders Lewis, who got a good grasp of European politics and literature before coming back and working for his own country . . .

'I'll help anybody who has something to give and is prepared to work hard. I have my young mothers practising Welsh so that they can use it with their children. I have read plays with a little group of learners before going to see them live on stage, and I like to help poor young teachers who are struggling with this new national curriculum, and some of them with only enough Welsh to keep one step ahead of their own class. Some learners do give up too easily, but others just don't get enough help from the *Cymry Cymraeg*. It's easy for the Welsh to go on about saving the language, but they soon get worried when they actually have to do anything with real live learners. They don't know what to talk to learners about, so they are embarrassed at being asked to help them practice the language. The learners don't know the ins and outs of a locality, or the ancient history of all the gossip, so they're handicapped in everyday conversation, and I've heard women in *Merched y Wawr* say, "Well, what can we talk to them about?"

'If you want to save the language it's no use retreating into your burrow and criticising everybody else for not doing anything about it. I'm very unpopular with some people, because I've always been going around saying what I really think, but I don't mind being unpopular one bit. I must have been born with enough feeling of security to last me a lifetime, for it doesn't matter to me when people don't like what I do. I always ask for a Welsh speaker in shops or when I ring up the bank or Manweb. Sometimes it's a learner and then it's no use going on fifteen to the dozen at my usual speed (as some *Cymry Cymraeg* do, and expect the poor learner to understand the message). You'll destroy their confidence for ever that way, and it's all a question of confidence in the end.

'I sometimes say to young Welsh people who start talking to me in English, "You've got a language of your own. Why aren't you using it?" And they just stare at me as if I was mad. They don't realise that if you don't value your language and use it, it will soon disappear and it won't just be the fault of English incomers. Sometimes we Welsh are our own worst enemies. Look at Dr Alan Williams and that Blodwen Griffiths—the Education First people who are attacking Dyfed's bilingual schools. The majority of the English incomer parents are in favour of their children learning Welsh and being a part of the community they are growing up in, but there are the Welsh themselves trying to do down their own language and culture, and some of them don't bother to read Welsh stories to their children even, like some of my incomer learners do with theirs . . .

'Of course there are incomers who have no idea that they're coming to a different culture with its own history and language. They just think they're retiring to another picturesque bit of Britain where they've spent some pleasant holidays. Or they come to work here with a company, or set up their own factory because of the financial incentives, but they might as well still be living in Surrey or wherever it was they were living before. It's a terrible shock to people like that when they hear employees speaking Welsh, or their children come home from school speaking a language the parents cannot understand, or never thought existed. Because a lot of English think Welsh is some kind of English dialect. They don't realise it is the oldest language in Europe with its own literature going back to about the year 800—about the time the English King Alfred was burning the cakes. If they've heard of the Welsh Princes like Owain Glyndwr at all, it's only as rebels against England, or because they are mentioned by their own national bard Shakespeare . . .'

Voices of the Future, 4—Patrick Thomas, Vicar of Brechfa

Patrick Thomas has been building bridges between the different sub-cultures in the Brechfa district (and further afield) for the past eight years, by running his own free classes in the Welsh language for incomers, by producing a bilingual community newspaper for his parishes, and by evolving church activities which seek to revive that sense of community based on place and everyday things that goes back to the early Celtic church in Wales, when the *llannau* were the focus for people of every walk of life and background in scattered rural communities. He has contributed his ideas to *The Church in the Welsh Countryside*, the 1992 report of the Church's Rural Commission:

'One of the key problems of such a fragmented community is that the members of one sub-culture or group become effectively invisible to the members of another group (except where conflict breaks out between them). When a local councillor in one parish remarked that "*Dim ond tri theulu sydd ar ôl ar y mynydd erbyn hyn*", "*Only three families are left on the mountain now*", he meant only three Welsh families—the dozen or more English families didn't count. A similar attitude is apparent among the hippy sub-culture who talk about "people" (meaning people like themselves)—those who are not people are of no importance. Such attitudes naturally reinforce the divisions and suspicions within the community, fuelling misunderstanding and prejudice. Individuals are no longer valued for themselves, but are defined (and accepted or written off) in terms of the group or sub-culture to which they belong . . . the language of worship can become a bone of contention among a congregation, turning the Church from a place of healing into a place of hurt, exacerbating divisions rather than breaking them down . . .

'Where Churches have been actively involved in building bridges between the different sub-cultures, much of what has been achieved has been as a result of the actions and attitudes of a very small number of people . . . who have the imagination and empathy which enables them to span the different groups . . . these "bridge people" are essential to the harmony of any rural community as complex as many in rural Wales have become. Their approach and attitude reflects the basic Christian

340

truths that all men and women are made in the image of God, and that in Christ all barriers of culture, race and background are broken down ... Within this pattern the clergy continue to have an essential role in rural areas. Their traditional function as mediators becomes even more important in a very fragmented society. Because of the unique nature of their office (whether it be regarded with *"parch"* [respect] or with gentle amusement) they can build bridges and create understanding between individuals from different groups and help and encourage others to do the same.'

Patrick Thomas believes the traditional values of rural Wales— of belongingness, of being at home in your own locality, of a mutual and personal interchange between members of a community—have much to offer today, when the urban way of life has so often failed to give people security or significance in society. In his booklet *The opened door*[4] he reminds us that the early Celtic churches were based on a community network which eventually lost out to the centralised hierarchical approach of Augustine of Canterbury. But we can still revive the core tradition, for 'the spirit of the Celtic Church persisted and is still discernible in some of the rural communities of West Wales'. In this revival the influx of newcomers as well as the direct inheritors, could play their part, for 'Many who have come to our area are seeking to fill a spiritual vacuum in their lives: the product of dissatisfaction with the barren materalism and arrogant self-centredness of a dominant culture which sometimes seems to threaten the very existence of our world'. This Celtic spirituality is rooted in a continuing sense of community as being more than a collection of individuals, and in a sense of inter- dependence between people, and between people and the natural world.

But there are problems with some kinds of Green theology which seem keen to save the environment of God's creation at the expense of the people working in it who are equally part of God's creation:

'There is no point in the type of environmental or "green" theology which tries to drive a wedge between an environment and the community that has always lived in it ... Listening to people and then starting from where they are, rather than attempting to impose often inappropriate ideas and ideals on them from outside, is essential in responding to the complex mixture of social, pastoral, environmental, economic and spiritual problems which exist in rural Wales'. Bridge-building individuals prepared to enter into real conversation with the Others, that is what is needed, rather than ideologies of whatever kind—whether Green Theology or Environmentalism—which do not connect with the everyday lives being lived in a community.

Voices of the Future, 5—Bob Shaw, teacher of countryside skills

Bob Shaw has worked in rural Wales for over twenty years, first as a shepherd and then in reviving traditional skills like drystone walling and wood bodging. He works to revive old ways of managing woodland, which are also new ways of growing woods ecologically and channelling the timber products to local users, including craftspeople. He practices what he preaches, by using wood from sustainable woodland for his practical workshops. In the summer of 1992 members of his one day courses went to Coed Tamsin, a typical Welsh wood not far from the Aberystwyth Arts Centre, to learn the practicalities of the wood bodger's traditional skills and techniques—used for making chairs, spoons and household utensils as well as farm tools like hay rakes and hurdles. The skills of putting together a Windsor chair were skilfully set out, using the traditional techniques of cleaving, shaving and pole lathe turning, adzing elm for the seats and turning green ash for the backs and legs. Bob Shaw is an active member of Friends of the Earth, and helps organise Green Fairs every year in Aberystwyth to bring together people concerned with a more ecologically sustainable approach to farming and forestry and energy, and to try to get these new ideas across to the public (of all ages, origins and backgrounds). He has his own views about how to get over the current farming crisis, and is a strong advocate of more diverse farming and forestry.

'The sowing of green manure crops instead of the current Set Aside would be of greater benefit. Now is the time to bring back into use the many intelligent systems of agriculture which have operated in the past, but have been lost and are now ripe for rediscovery. Bringing our woodlands back into traditional management, for instance, would do a whole lot of things at one go. It would help provide firewood, fencing materials, cover for game birds, wildlife protection etc. And in the long term you would also get a valuable timber crop, but in the short term you would use thinning and selective cutting to give you an interim crop. As these systems develop there would be a need for a greater workforce, and that would mean housing. I like to think it would be possible to use timber from our own conifer plantations to build sensitively placed (and sensibly priced) homes and cabins, etc . . .

'As more and more conifer plantations are clear felled, they could be mostly replaced with birch or other fast-growing broadleaves suitable for pulp, carcassing, veneers etc, while lessening the damage done by acidification . . .

'There are many ways which follow from these new/old approaches to managing woodland, that would enrich rural life here, and would benefit more local people, and not just the handful who cream off all the profit at the expense of others. We now have a huge environmental problem which affects everybody on earth, and none of us can avoid asking ourselves, ''Are we to go on headlong with our consumerism, just like sheep running faster and faster just to keep up with the rest, without giving a thought to the results of our actions?'' Think about it, the sheep question here in Wales. There are eleven million of the woolly maggots consuming virtually everything in sight without a thought for sustainability. It wasn't like that in the old days—they had diversity in farming. Anyway the question for every one of us is, ''Do we now begin to use our faculty of far-reaching insight and start on the job of acting more responsibly in our own locale, remembering that by doing that we are also going to benefit the global complexities as well?''

'Our individual actions, however small, have far-reaching consequences, so e.g. refusing to buy unnecessary packaging in the supermarkets, taking your recyclable materials along to the paper skip or bottle banks in Gateways car park or at the Coop, putting pressure on your local council to do more rubbish recycling and to make it possible for you to do more yourself—all those things are small things but they cumulate,

343

they matter, and it gets you into a more conscious habit of thinking about these problems, too. Then you can find out about specific problems in your own community, join environmental organisations, *do* something whenever you can.

'If we personally don't take action, there is a danger of rural Wales becoming a wasteland, with nothing but national parks, national nature reserves and cultural heritage centres to show tourists not how the countryside is—sustainable farming and forestry which give people a living—but only how it was . . . Hill farming communities are already breaking up as former cottages belonging to agricultural workers are sold to incomers who do not understand anything about the countryside beyond the nice views. And then there's this rash of bungalow development for retiring farmers raging across the country without much regard for planning laws or architectural harmony with the old housing. It's time for each and every one of us to wake up and do something about it, and not just wait for somebody else to act . . . '

Voices of the Future, 6—Ken Jones, Ceredigion Green Party

'My scenario for the future of rural Wales is encapsulated in a fable for the next century. Whether it remains a utopian fable or gets translated into reality depends on us all in rural Wales and how far we are prepared to be a bit more green than just using bottle banks and ecological Daz.'

Pentre Gwyrdd, a village in rural Wales in the year 2050

'I was surprised at the size of the village—evidence of the rural repopulation by young people from the towns. There were old people who could still recall the village as a ghost of a place, with prettified cottages empty most of the year, and surrounded by nothing but sheep walks and conifer plantations. It is now a busy, thriving place, with new dwellings spreading out into clearings in the beautiful varied woods.

'Mair explained that much of the woodland is communally owned, just like the traditional common grazings which it shelters and fertilises. There are also privately owned holdings, but their size is limited by law.

Agroforestry is a family way of life for the small farmers, not an agribusiness for making external profits. Just looking at the varied pattern of the community's landscape showed how livestock, forestry, organic arable, and the several little timber and food-processing businesses all supported one another. ''What we take from nature we put back'', said Mair. Everything possible is recycled. We believe in keeping our wealth in the community. It's now difficult to imagine those crazy times when human manure was mixed with toxic industrial wastes and, at great expense, was pumped into Cardigan Bay!

'From Mair's garden we could see the biggest group of buildings in the village—the community timber yard. The village retains most of its timber for household and community fuel, and for the use of the small businesses which make timber-frame buildings and household utensils and fittings. Looking around the kitchen garden was a reminder of how much the global warmup had encouraged people to grow their own produce, though a lot was sold or bartered at the local weekly market, or through the village shop. Now that the heavier energy taxes make it expensive to bring in long-haul foodstuffs there's a bigger incentive towards local and regional self-reliance—and the control that it gives to communities.

'Mair's house was lined with pine, real wood, not laminated chipboard—warm, insulating and beautiful. As is now the fashion again, household goods are enough but simple. Cheaper, long-lasting furniture mingled with attractive hand-crafted things. Since the house is near the centre of the village it benefits from the community owned heat and power system, based on a wood chip generator back of the timber yard. Outlying houses have their own high-tech woodburners, supplemented by cheap electricity from the community generator (which also sells into the grid). I was reminded that by now 20% of Welsh energy needs are met by both large and small coppicing of willow, poplar and other energy plantations.

'Mair introduced me to the facilitators of the different enterprise groups through which the community council runs much of the local economy as well as the social services. Just about everyone is in the

345

network somewhere, because this community tries to live up to the three watchords on its headed notepaper:

Cydweithio — Antur — Digonoldeb
(Cooperation — Enterprise — Sufficiency)

Of course Ceredigion like other Welsh District Councils is very much a power in the land. Modelled on the Swiss cantons, they say, these days. It uses this to empower and to enable willing community councils to manage and even to create their own local services. Typical is Pentre Gwyrdd Citizen Committee (which has a majority of older people on it) which provides care and support for the elderly, with the backup of specialist help and advice from the District—not that many people really ''retire'' in a place like Pentre Gwyrdd. But here as everywhere of course there are a number of elderly chronically sick folk to care for, not just the result of people living longer, but because of the steep rise in cancers and nervous and degenerative illness arising from the multiple chemical effects of local and global pollution.

'Of the community leaders many were now women and all were bilingual. After all it was the women who really pushed through the Green Revolution, and added that great pool of specially *female* talents which the community now uses and doesn't ignore or waste as in the old days. As to the Welsh language, we have got beyond the business of schooling everyone in it and then letting it go. There is so much going on in the community that you just feel you have to learn it, if you're not a natural speaker. It's amazing we used to make such heavy weather of the ''language problem''. They recognise across the European Community that ''small languages'' are not just a literary heritage but an integral part of our way of life, and nowadays every educated person here, as in the Basque country, Switzerland and Belgium, is bilingual or trilingual. People have discovered at last that being brought up bilingual makes it easier not harder to add other languages later.

'The village school has a secure future, thanks to rural repopulation, even though it is considered very unfashionable now to have more than one, or at most two children, to leave future space for others' children without overconsuming our resources. The teenagers are so involved in community life that some of them have not yet used their first overseas air travel coupon. Public transport is now cheaper and easier for them to use and there is plenty going on in the countryside and not just in the towns. Besides, computer networking is all the rage at the moment.

'If it all sounds a bit utopian, I have to say that there was plenty of disagreement and conflict arising from time to time. Even around here you still find selfish people who are still obsessed with making their own pile and setting off the growth-mania all over again, though it is harder now with the changes in wealth and income tax. However there are more and more people around who put the emphasis on behaviour that is cooperative, mediating and conflict resolving, rather than on the old virtues of acquisitive and competitive traits.

'Mair said that one element in this was the revival of a Celtic spirituality that is Green and meditative, in the churches and chapels and beyond. The scatter of Buddhist and other low profile groups concerned with "right-mindedness" and "right livelihood" has also been an influence. It is now very much the thing to "do your own inner work" alone or in a small network, your spiritual family, as it were. The spiritual revival, which is not quite the same as a religious revival, has common ground with the early Celtic churches in Wales before they were finally brought under the control of Canterbury and Rome. It is a Green spirituality not just from its concern with *all* of creation, but because it is small-scale, person-to-person, inner and outer work in the world at the same time. Maybe that is one reason people are less driven, more relaxed in their energies. The old people say our generation is more contented, has more time for things . . .

'How did it all happen? Eventually enough people in rural Wales realised that things had to change if we were to have a future, and that we couldn't wait for the politicians to do it all for us. And a different kind of person began to go into politics. It has been easier for us in the rural areas, because there were models to follow in our own past and elsewhere—like in Scandinavia they had been practising agro-forestry for more than a century. Anyway they say Wales is a community of communities. Perhaps that is why the Great U Turn has been easier here than elsewhere.'

Is this only an utopian fable, or are there signs that rural Ceredigion has a role in showing the way ahead by remoulding the best of its community traditions to modern needs? Well, when *The Archers* decided it was time to bring organic farming before its mass audience, the BBC sent their production team to a farm in the Aberystwyth area which has been practising organic farming for half a century. The Rowlands family near Borth initially produced their organic cheeses and yoghurts in a small way, but expanded and promoted their approaches so that educational trips and interested visitors could go round their farm trail, and eventually they reached the crucial decision that faces all small businesses—shall we expand or is it better to stay as we are, in spite of increasing demand for the products? Rachel's Dairy took the risk of expanding and now have a contract with Sainsbury's and a processing plant on the Aberystwyth Industrial estate, which means local jobs in an area that desperately needs them. So the 'small—or local—is beautiful' philosophy has to be tempered with a business enterprise mentality. Here is therefore another voice of the future, Ian Jones, who is in fact a cousin of Rachel Rowlands and himself a prime example of the enterprise culture.

Voices of the Future, 7—Ian Jones, Cwmrheidol

'Here in west Wales we need a fairly major diversification out of farming, but that will require a change of psyche—into the enterprise frame of mind. In Ardwyn, when I was at school, to contemplate a career in industry or commerce was tantamount to heresy. That was why I went on to do physics at university, and when I became clearer about myself had to change to my real interest in civil engineering. The young people who leave the area have great pressure on them to get their A levels and a nice professional job—doctor or accountant or solicitor. But there's a very limited demand for those jobs in an area of small population like this. What nobody says to them is, "Why not start your own business? Develop a service or a process and get out there and sell it. You don't have to go down the professional road''.

'I remember when we were little and looked after the chickens or other bits of work for my father, it was on a joint venture basis, not payment by the hour. We got a percentage of the profit on the eggs or whatever it was. There is an idea around that you're a victim of your circumstances—that's very prevalent. When I left this area in the 1970s the farmers were universally hard working and though not as wealthy as they are now, they were more attuned to the market. Now the Bateman Report says that because farming is going down the jobs are going down too. *But* you can in fact put more work into farming and increase the labour side, by cutting the heavy input costs (of fertilisers, chemical sprays and expensive machinery). You can also go direct to the market with your products, as Rachel's Dairy does. What our farming leaders are telling us is that we're victims of the CAP, so all you can do is wring your hands and wait for someone to rescue you. Instead of asking, 'What are *they* going to do about it?' people should be asking themselves, ''What are *we* going to do about it?''

'Our problems here are that we have no manufacturing base and no effective communications with markets, so we cannot be another Newtown. It is whistling in the wind if we think we're going to have a manufacturing economy here in west Wales, with the Cambrian Mountains between us and our markets. So the strategies are, if we want to create jobs, to replace outside businesses with local firms (developers, construction, etc). I think we will have cracked it when we don't feel we have to go outside the area to get the expertise to solve the problems we have in rural Wales. At present the Council seems to think always in terms of bringing in an expert consultant—always from at least a hundred miles down the road. We will have a proper integrated economy when we no longer have to go looking for these outside experts, because we have expert people available in the area. The problem is that experts—a structural engineer, say, in Aberystwyth— would need outside work as well as local work to keep going, but that is getting easier with fax.

'Another big problem is in tourism. Every time anybody proposes to enhance tourism, people say no, we don't want to destroy this environment as it is now. But this environment is only sustained by exporting young people year after year, so I would call that an unbalanced environment. Anyway, if I am developing tourism, it's not in my interests to detract from the beauty of the valley, because that is what you're selling to the tourists. You can't put things in aspic ... and you have to aim for a critical mass in tourism. What we haven't done in this area (though they did it in Aberystwyth at the turn of the century) is to achieve this critical mass. (Cornwall has achieved it—there's lots for tourists to do there and no boredom whatever the weather, because of all the activities). The season is short, but a lot of the schemes that would lengthen the season are opposed because they don't fit in with what people deem the environment demands. This is a beautiful valley, but it was a mining valley too. If you wanted to develop tourism here you would have to have an integrated package to offer people a wide choice and achieve the critical mass. You could have linked bridleways for trekking holidays, walking linked with the nature trails, and you could take advantage of existing local attractions like the golf course at Capel Bangor, to offer a good variety (run by different people but linked up for marketing). You need bad weather activities as well, but you already have the Visitors Centre. Then you could bring a lot more income into the valley and keep more of the young people here, developing their enterprise schemes. At present I'm doing my three year stint on the Development Board for Rural Wales, and that's what we're working at —trying to find ways of keeping the best of the young people in rural Wales.

'You have to remember that there are far more remote and inhospitable places than rural Wales which have successfully grown economies like Israel (marketing problems with hostile neighbouring countries on every frontier) and Japan, which has no raw materials, no large markets on its doorstep, and started with a lousy infrastructure, but is now a world wide success. That's because Japan has an extremely powerful enterprise culture. So I think what we should be aiming for in our schools and in our communities is the enterprise way of thinking.'

And where does all this talk about livelihood leave the arts in the countryside? Here are people talking about the changing attitudes to art in the landscape that have been evolving since the late 1970s.

New meanings for art in rural Wales

Shelagh Hourahane, Chair of *Cywaith Cymru*, Art Works Wales, has drawn attention to the changing attitudes to art in the landscape since the 1970s. The emphasis is now on issues of place, community and conservation, rather than on simply placing studio objects in an outdoor setting in the hope of attracting a wider audience.[5] A more ecological approach means that even the redundant mines and quarries of Wales may occasionally be taken over for land sculpture projects, rather than becoming land-fill sites for Britain's rubbish, or grassed over so that their history is no longer visible on the ground. At the Wales Garden Festival in Ebbw Vale in 1992, for example, Mike Petts created his 'Mother Earth', using eighty metres of real soil and *growing* materials, to signify renewal in a place scarred by derelict steelworks. He also used fast growing willows to make a giant bird's nest and a willow tunnel for children to play in, thus getting away from the traditional view that works of art must not be touched or used by the public. Along the Pembrokeshire Coastal Path are Alain Ayers' 'Eyes of the Sea' sculptures which use sandstone and limestone natural materials, and shapes derived from the local occupations of fishing and lime kilns, that once flourished in this area. David Nash, who lives and works in Blaenau Ffestiniog, aims at an 'organic naturalism', which is an increasing trend across Europe, from rural Wales across to the (former) Yugoslavian national park of wood sculptures. In an effort to design works well-suited to their surroundings, these sculptors use materials from the locality (slate or stone or wood) that are biodegradable, and will eventually decay through natural processes of erosion by weather or in some cases wildlife (deer consumed David Nash's first 'Willow Ladder' in the Grizedale Forest Sculpture trail in the Lake District National Park). This acceptance of natural cycles of growth and decay can sometimes successfully echo the history of rural communities, which have themselves been eroded by changing economic and cultural events. But some of these sculptures remain alien to their locality, or are rejected by the public, in spite of their ecological underpinning. In the Forestry Commission's Visitors' Centre at Bwlch yr Arian near Goginan, a geometrical arrangement of Douglas Fir planks called 'Side Step', was cut down in 1991 to make way for a children's play site. There had been much adverse comment from visitors, although the artist conceived its stark angularities as echoing the zig-zig silhouettes of the surrounding hills and conifers.

Voices of the Future, 8—Peter Lord

How then can you ensure that art in Wales resonates with a sense of place, past and present, that is accessible to local people as well as to visitors or other artists? Peter Lord, who lives in Cwmrheidol and is designer of the Hywel Dda Memorial in Whitland, Dyfed, and the Glynllifon Park *Gwerin y Graith* sculpture in Gwynedd (which commemorates the literature of Kate Roberts, Caradog Prichard and T. Rowland Hughes) talks about the problems and his personal approaches:

'I have been involved with the Glynllifon project since 1986, first developing the concepts and then having to carry them into practice in my own project. "Site-specific art" is the trendy thing now, but I see it as fundamental to all my art, and always have done. You have to respond to the physical location, but not as your primary object. In Glynllifon the sites are subject-centred and that subject is not the place but the literature of Gwynedd. Nothing in the site is specific to Kate Roberts, for example, but there is a symbolic connection, because you can see her slate quarry village Rhosgadfan on the horizon on a clear day. I am primarily concerned with NOW, and what I am talking about is Kate Roberts' and Caradog Prichard's literature NOW. That is why the sculpture is about the meaning of tradition—a metaphor for the condition of Wales … So the central symbols are the fallen and smashed jugs which continue to flow (with water, milk or blood, who can tell?), because they are symbols of the things in the literature that are gone or broken. But that literature is still real and works—the vessel may be broken but the flow goes on. There are wider references, too, because the jugs are linked with classical symbols of the well-spring or healing source. It is linked to Celtic symbolism—the Queen of Llyn Du (the Black Lake) and the Queen of Wyddfa (Snowdon) who appear in Caradog Prichard's work are the light and the dark side of the Celtic goddesses, and are there in my design . . .

'I feel very passionate about the subject, and I identify very strongly with Caradog Prichard's *Un nos ola leuad* (One time when the moon was full). The site was chosen because of the visual association with Rhosgadfan, but then I had to respond to the site and its particular qualities, which are the waterfall, the heavy growth of trees and laurels, the small lake . . . As you climb up the site through the heavy over-growth you get to the top of the waterfall (where I am putting the ruin) and there is open space to a huge sky. I am trying to revitalise a ruined drama, to reinterpret tradition for now, so as you climb up by the waterfall you come to the ruin at the top, through which a stream flows from the lake behind, and inside the ruin two trees go on growing—they are part of the natural growth on the site. The slate quarrymen's strike of 1900-1903 is shown on a mural around the outside of the ruin (that's from T. Rowland Hughes' novel *Chwalfa*, the *Dispersal*). But inside the ruin are pure white walls and a slate floor, and over the fireplace a portrait of Kate Roberts' uncle who died in a quarry accident when he was twelve. From the window you see the Queen of the Black Lake (from Caradog Prichard) and the memorial column from where you can see Rhosgadfan. At the bottom of the column is a table laid for tea, because so many of Kate Roberts' stories are about the women as the backbone of the communities (rather than the quarry work), and the home support that keeps the people going whatever their hardships. So I see inside the ruin as about order and cleanliness and domestic strength and comfort, while the outside is a jagged ruined silhouette—the masculine by contrast with the feminine of the inside. On the spot where you can see Rhosgadfan the column stands with three jugs on the top of it, pouring blood down the side of the column . . .

'Who is this design for? Not for artists but for everybody. But especially for the kind of audience who have this year (1992) been responding to the Eisteddfod Exhibition—where I arranged the historical bit. I was talking about it on the telly during Eisteddfod week, and for the first time people here in the valley have responded to what I am doing as an artist—they have actually spoken to me about my work, and that is wonderful, because what I do is normally outside people's experiences here and though they might be curious they don't ask me about it. And yet all the things I am trying to do, or to write about, are trying to make the connections between art and people's real experiences in Wales, past and present. I always regret bitterly that art is so often kept apart from life, or seen so often as irrelevant to real lives, when in fact I am trying to give expression to those lives, not through talk or music, but through visual means, that's the only difference. So what I am doing in Glynllifon is primarily for the people of Gwynedd, because it is about their past and their present—but also about the past and present of the Welsh culture, and its tragic *chwalfa*, or dispersal. I'm not an insider to the Welsh-speaking culture of Gwynedd, but a certain distance actually gives you an edge, because it creates a tension . . .

'As for the rage for ecological art, the trendy 'site-specific' art that is in fashion, I am deeply suspicious of the whole Green thing with which it is associated. It is not that I don't acknowledge the seriousness of the problem, but I am suspicious of the Green movement which has arisen to respond to the problem. I see much of it as the contemporary response to the need for apocalypse (just like in the nineteenth century there was religious mania in expectation of the second coming of Christ). The Green movement in art of course produces some very nice things (as in Grizedale Forest), but the humanity of a general kind which the Green artists aspire to is not for me. That to my mind can make art obvious and superficial, and I am first and foremost concerned with art as explanation of the condition of a specific culture in a specific place, which for me is

354

Welsh-speaking culture and the nation of Wales. That is what my sculpture in Glynllifon is about.'

The big question then about the future of rural Wales seems to be how to build bridges between the different standpoints represented by these 'voices of the future'. The traditional Welsh-speaking culture cannot build a future on its own, for it continues to be diluted by the influx of incomers, and needs to play a bigger part in enterprise culture if it is to stem the departure of its younger generation. The enterprise culture cannot build a future on its own without a greener face and a rooted concern for life in rural communities, for otherwise the profits are exported and the skills imported with little advantage to the people who live here. And the Green culture cannot build a future on its own, but has to translate its generalised ideals into practical strategies that are seen to be concerned with local livelihood and local cultures. This is where, to my mind, individuals in their own communities have a part to play, whatever their political allegiance or cultural origins, so long as they want to contribute to building a common future. And here I would like to return to the words of Mary Robinson, the first woman President of Ireland, to emphasise the symbol of the 'Fifth Province' as an attitude of mind that is hospitable to growing and convivial to other people in the best old Celtic tradition:

> The fifth province is not anywhere here or there, north or south, east or west. It is a place within each of us—that place which is open to the other, that swinging door which allows us to venture out and others to venture in . . . tradition has it that the fifth province acted as a second centre, a necessary balance.

It's preferable to take part in change than to ignore it and hope it will go away. Consider Machynlleth, the small town where in 1404 Owain Glyndŵr came near to uniting the Welsh nation, and established a Parliament House for Wales. It has since the 1980s become in a modest way a Green trendsetter, with the Centre for Alternative Technology attracting hundreds of thousands of visitors every year from all over the world. Its model wind generators are an indication of how west Wales might be a leader in alternative energy, for small companies have taken root there, like Dulas Engineering, which are acting as consultants not only to farmers in mid Wales who are looking to wind farms in their efforts to diversify, but to third world countries as well who need to use solar power to keep their hospitals functioning in a sustainable way.

Consider, too, the Welsh Tourist Board, which in the 1990s is trying to work out a new philosophy, combining the need for increased income from tourists with a celebration of the indigenous culture. In 1991 they joined with Ireland and Brittany to develop a programme which included workshops on Celtic myth and magic, courses on Celtic Christian spirituality run by the OFFRWM retreat centre at Pennal, Machynlleth, and activities in the National Museum Cardiff to highlight the language, arts and culture of Wales, past and continuing. In Aberystwyth there was an Age of Saints pageant, in which St Padarn once again landed on the beach (with the help of the RNLI, as the day proved stormy) from Ireland to found his monastic dynasty at Llanbadarn Fawr. And local schools and churches played their part in music and dance to turn a theatrical tourist event into a more organic community event linking past and present.

So the river runs on. You can't step in the same dream twice, but there is the ever-renewing message of *Finnegan's Wake*, where the end literally becomes the beginning again:

In the name of Annah the Allmaziful, the Everliving, the Bringer of Plurabilities, haloed be her ever, her singtime sung, her rill be run, unhemmed as it is uneven . . .

Welcome to the plurabilities.

[1] Ioan Bowen Rees, 'Devolution: Wales cannot wait', *Planet* 94, 1992, p. 3.

[2] News item in *Green Line*, August 1992.

[3] Jan Morris, 'The Republic of Wales', *The Independent Magazine*, 1 August 1992, p. 32.

[4] Patrick Thomas, *The opened door: a Celtic spirituality*, Brechfa, Silyn Publications, 1990. (Final page of an unnumbered pamphlet).

[5] Shelagh Hourihane, 'Sculpture in the landscape', *Planet* 86, 1991, p. 43-53.